Education Policy and Administration on Higher Education

Education Policy and Administration on Higher Education

Editors

Dr Kandi Kamala
&
Dr Kalvapalle Padmavathi

KALPAZ

ISBN: 978-93-5324-974-8 (HB)

First Published, 2023

Published by

Kalpaz Publications
C-30, Satyawati Nagar,
Delhi – 110052
Ph.: 011-47034999, 9811692060
www.kalpazpublications.com
E-mail: kalpaz@hotmail.com

Printed at: Gyan Press, Delhi.

Contents

Navin Mittal, IAS
Commissioner

Prof. Jayashankar Vidyabhavan,
Nampally, Hyderabad -500 001.
off: +91-40-2474 5021
+91-40-2461 5669
commissioner.cete.ts@gmail.com

Collegiate Education & Technical Education Department

MESSAGE

Dated:10.11.2022

I am happy to know that the Department of Political Science, Government Degree College for Women, Begumpet, Hyderabad is bringing out the proceedings of the International Conference on "New Dimensions in Higher Education in the Post Covid-19: Global Perspective" in the form of an ISBN book.

A glance at the book shows that the volume focuses on the transformation of the Indian Higher Educational Institutions (HEIs) in meeting the emerging challenges in the post Covid-19 scenario and converting the challenges in to opportunities in multiple ways in the form of collaborations and partnerships across boundaries, merging and clustering of institutions to achieve the desired results. It also provides an in-depth analysis of the critical dimensions of higher education in India by covering growth, expansion of private sector and the National Education Policy (NEP) 2020 and their implications for the society at large. It also examines internationalization of higher education and global ranking of the Indian HEIs.

Further, the volume takes up the issues such as programs, skill formation, employability, pedagogic practices, standards in curriculum, research & development and the wider externalities in terms of promoting India's soft power at global level. The work is useful to students, academicians and policy makers for future planning and implementation of education policies.

On this occasion, I congratulate the editors of the book, Dr K. Kamala and Dr K. Padmavathi, who is also the Principal of the college, and the contributors of the papers on their academic achievement.

(Navin Mittal)

Foreword

The last several decades have seen dramatic changes to education. Our fundamental accounts of learning have broadened from purely behavioral explanations to include cognitive, social, constructivist, and connectivity perspectives. However, higher education today is facing umpteen challenges. While the student numbers and also the number of institutions are rapidly increasing, the quality of higher education is becoming a major concern, with poor quality of graduates resulting in rising graduate unemployment – open and hidden, and poor quality and quantum of research output. Not even one among the existing one thousand Indian universities figures in the top one hundred universities in the global rankings. There are several reasons for the dismal state of affairs. The entire system of higher education – from under graduate colleges to central universities, including institutions like the Indian Institutes of Technology, suffers from a severe shortage of quality teachers. Not only in quality, but also in terms of number of teachers, almost all institutions are facing a high degree of shortage. Second, a large number of institutions of higher education have very poor quality infrastructure – classrooms, lecture halls, libraries, laboratories, playgrounds, and facilities for accommodation of students and teachers, and all are working in impoverished conditions. High technology based laboratories, smart classrooms etc are severely limited in number. Third, we do have a small number of high quality institutions like the Indian Institutes of Technology, Indian Institutes of Management, Indian Institutes of Information Technology, central universities, central laboratories, etc., but all, working in isolation, have very little effect on the vast system, having no horizontal or vertical linkages. Fourth, the curriculum and the pedagogic methods that are currently in practice are found to be no more relevant for the country's transformation into a vibrant knowledge society of the 21st century associated with a new industrial revolution (industry 4.0), artificial intelligence, and an altogether new knowledge society. Fifth, the inefficient structures and mechanisms of governance that we have, have their own adverse effects on the overall environment, which result in demotivated teaching faculty, dissuaded student community and lacklustre research output. The severe shortfall of funds that almost every institution faces is perhaps one of the most important reasons for the crisis in higher education.

While the small number of central institutions tend to focus on quality and standards, the large number of state level institutions of higher education aim at expansion of higher education, rather massification. The state level institutions, in their task, heavily depend upon private sector. As a result, today we have one of the largest private systems of higher education in the world, which depends exclusively on student fees. In fact, growth in private universities, private colleges and other institutions of private higher education which are based on pecuniary motives, has been alarming, unregulated and somewhat chaotic, producing devastating effects on the quality of and equitable access to higher education and on the values that education imparts among the youth.

While the union government and some states have taken important policy initiatives in the recent past towards reforming higher education, they are found to be not sufficient. Quality enhancement programmes are being launched on a large scale. The absence of a long term policy for the development of higher education is being addressed with the most recent efforts to make a new National Policy on Education. The *Policy* promises development of 'a new architecture for higher education, with large, well-resourced, vibrant multidisciplinary institutions of higher education.' Aiming at excellence in higher education as the most important goal, the *Policy* promises integration of higher education of all levels and types – under graduate, post graduate and research; professional, technical, and general; and liberal, classical and modern, in such a way that an organically closely linked higher education system is evolved that will contribute to the national transformation in diverse ways in the years to come.

It is in this overall background, this book edited by Dr Kandi Kamala & Dr Kalvapalle Padmavathi, consisting of more than 42 articles contributed by a galaxy of young and experienced scholars, deserves a mention. These papers were intensively discussed in a seminar organised by the Government Degree College for Women (A+ Autonomous), Begumpet, Hyderabad. Addressing a wide variety of issues relating to higher education in India, I am sure, it will attract the wide attention of all those who are engaged in higher education development in the country.

Jandhyala B G Tilak

Former Vice Chancellor, NUEPA

Currently ICSSR National Fellow & Distinguished Professor

Council for Social Development, New Delhi

Preface

The recent pandemic Covid-19 disrupted multiple sectors including education. Students were confined to their homes for almost two academic years. Imparting education during this period shifted from face to face to online mode. Many innovative digital tools emerged during the pandemic phase. Government of India has formulated National Educational Policy (NEP-2020) which has five pillars affordability, accessibility, equity, quality and accountability to achieve these objectives major changes are sought to be introduced in the education process particularly teaching-learning, research and regulatory system.

In the present knowledge era, high quality education is the backbone for empowering the individual and for the development of the nation. Providing quality education to the marginalized sections is a serious challenge. The present education system has many limitations in contributing to the holistic development of students. Knowledge acquisition needs to be blended with inculcation of values and capacity building. While accepting the best global practices in imparting education in the Indian context efforts should be made to integrate the wisdom of national civilizational ethos and the requisites of Sustainable Development Goal – 4 (Education). This book deals with multiple dimensions pertaining to higher education scenario in the present context. Educational process of teaching learning and research are discussed. The need for integrating technology into the pedagogical process is elaborated. The need for greater academic flexibility and autonomy are described. Challenges in providing quality education to the economically backward sections are addressed. Quality teachers and adequate infrastructure facilities are essential for promoting excellence in education. Above all sufficient financial resources and efficient regulatory system is required for imparting quality education at all levels.

I appreciate Government Degree College for Women and the Department of Political Science for conducting international conference in which many papers presented covering wide range of areas covering in the field of education. This book is a good addition to the existing literature in the concerned areas.

Prof. T.Tirupati Rao (Retd.)
Chancellor - Manipur University

Acknowledgement

The Department of Political Science, Government Degree College for Women, Begumpet, Hyderabad has organized an International conference on "**New Dimensions in Higher Education in the Post Covid-19: Global Perspective**" on 24th & 25th March 2022 in Collaboration with ICSSR, New Delhi, TSCHE & NAAC. The conference was inaugurated by Dr. K. Padmavathi Principal, Government Degree College for Women, Begumpet. The Chief Guest of the conference Shri. Navin Mittal, IAS, Commissioner of Collegiate Education. Prof. D. Ravinder, Vice Chancellor, Osmania University, Hyderabad, Prof. R. Limbadri, Chairman, Telangana State Council of Higher Education (TSCHE), Prof T. Tirupati Rao, Chancellor of Manipur Central University. The conference has received 122 full papers and selected papers has been published in UGC Care listed journal in two volume 1 & 2 August 2022 ISSN No. 2347-7180 and remaining articles will be published ISBN Publication. I am very thankful to International speakers of USA, Singapore, Hong Kong & China and Academicians, scholars who have participated from nearly 15 states. I express my special thanks to Prof. Jandhyala B.G Tilak, Former Vice Chancellor, National Institute of Educational Planning and Administration, New Delhi who has delivered a keynote address. I feel highly honored and greatly indebted to Prof JLN Rao who has been a constant source of inspiration and for sparing his valuable time to guide this work and motivation which enhanced me to complete the conference proceedings in the form of Gyan Publication edited book. Eminent Professor Hara Gopal discussed on NAAC upgradation and quality enhancement, Prof. Kancha Ilaiah, Prof. T. Mrunalini, Ajay Gudavarthy, Associate Professor and Shri. Chiranjeevulu, IAS, participated in the conference. I am very much thankful to our beloved Principal, Dr. K. Padmavathi for support & continuous encouragement without which I would not able to conduct the conference and thanks to Vice Principal, Dr. M. Vasudha, IQAC Coordinator, Annie Sharon, Dr. M. Ramachary and teaching and non-teaching staff for **timely supporting and for their suggestions** and these efforts are going to be fruitful in the form book and thanks a lot to everyone for their love and support and I hope this will be continued and finally I am very thankful to my family who have given immense strength and support.

Dr. Kandi Kamala
Asst.Professor
Dept. of Political Science

List of Contributors

Murli Krishna, Lecture Of Dept. of Economics, Hyderabad, Telangana, India

N Vijayalakshmi Assistant Professor of Political Science, Hyderabad, Telangana, India

J. Naga Ratnam Dept of Political Science, Sangareddy, Telangana, India

Dr. Nagaratna S, Guest Faculty, Karnataka, India

Ms S Nirmala, Asst. Professor of Statistics, Vgdc, Vidyanagar, Hyderabad, Telangana, India

Ms M Anusha, Lecturer in Statistics, Gdc (A), Begumpet, Hyderabad, Telangana, India

Pothula Likhitha, Research Scholar, Department of Commerce & Business Management, Warangal, Telangana, India

Dr. P. Prameela Margaret, Associate Professor, Department Of Political Science & Public Administration, Kadapa, Andhra Pradesh, India

Ms. Priyanka Sharma, Research Scholar, Department of Educational Studies, Jammu, India.

Dr. Aman, Assistant Professor, Department of Educational Studies, Jammu, India

Prof Dr. Rakesh Kumar Yogi (Dean & Faculty), Department of Media Studies, Gurugram, Haryana, India,

Dr. Deepika Faculty, Department of Media Studies, Gurugram, Haryana, India

Dr. Shweta Chaudhary Faculty, Department of Media Studies, Gurugram, Haryana, India

Prof. K. Srinivas, Head lecturer, New Delhi, India

Kajal Yadav, Research Scholar, New Delhi, India

M. Rajender Assistant Professor, Hyderabad, Telangana, India

Dr. A.N.P.P. Anantha Lakshmi, Assistant Professor, Hyderabad, Telangana, India

Dr. P. Rajyalakshmi, Associate Professor,HOD, Department of English, Hyderabad, Telangana, India

Mrs. V. Shanthi, Assistant Professor, Department of Commerce, Hyderabad, Telangana, India

Ramshankar Varma, Research Scholar, Dept. of Education, Haryana, India

R. Rasheeda Begum, Research Scholar, Department of Education, Madhya Pradesh, India

Dr G Kamalakar Researcher, Dept. of Political Science, Hyderabad, Telangana, India

Dr. M. Samatha, Waranga L Telamgana, India

Dr. M.T. Jyotsna, Ananatapur, Andhra Pradesh, India

Sameera Nazneen, Assistant Professor of Political Science, Medak Telangana, India

M. Samuel Praveen Kumar, Asst. Professor of Political Science, Karimnagar, Telangana, India

Dr. Md. Shafiq Ahmed, Lecturerin Public. Admn, Narayanapet, Telangana, India

Shaveta Thakur, Punjab, India

Vishali Mahajan, Punjab, India

Sapna Chadha, Punjab, India

Dr. G. Sreenivasulu, Lecturer in Political Science, Kadapa, Andhra Pradesh, India

M. Srilatha, Research Scholar, Centre for English Language Studies, Hyderabad, Telangana, India

Dr. Shree Deepa, Associate Professor, Centre for English Language Studies, Hyderabad, Telangana, India

B. Suchetha, Assistant Professorof Commerce, Hyderabad, Telangana, India

Dr. M. Sudhakar Reddy, Principal, Piller, Andhra Pradesh, India

Dr. T. Vinila, Assistant Professor,Chittoor, Andhra Pradesh, India

Sukka Kiran Kumar, Research Scholar, Warangal, Telangana, India

Dr Susmita Banerjee, Ex Associate Professor, West Bengal, India

Saikat Majumder, Data Manager, Department of Health & Family Welfare,West Bengal, India

Thota Suresh, Phd Economics, Kakatiya University, Waranga L Telamgana, India

Dr. K.V. Vijayaveni, Guest Faculty, Dept. of Music & Dance, Vishakhapatnam, Andhra Pradesh, India

Yedavelly Srinivas Reddy, Associate Professor, Department of English, Hyderabad, Telangana, India

Bolleddu Amruth Kumar, PhD, English and Foreign Languages, Hyderabad, Telangana, India

K. Ennuyir Kannapiran, Ph.D. Research Scholar, Department of Political Science & Public Administration, Annamalai, Tamil Nadu, India

Dr. P. Saravanakumar, Assistant Professor, Department of Political Science & Public Administration, Annamalai, Tamil Nadu, India

Dr Gopal, Asst Professor, Department of History, Hyderabad, Telangana, India

Dr. Thallapelli Sanjeev, Assistant Professor, Department of Political Science, Kakatiya University, WarangaLTelamgana, India

Dr M. Ramana, Assistant professor, Department of Political Science, Hyderabad, Telangana, India

Nandavaram Mridula, Assistant Professor, Telugu Department, Hyderabad, Telangana, India

Dr. I. Sandhya Jyotsna Assistant Professor, Department of History Government Degree College for Women, Begumpet (A) Hyderabad

Dr. Enapa Upender Rao, Assistant Professor (Contract) Dept. of English University College for Women, Koti Osmania University Hyderabad India

M Krishna Kumar, Associate Professor & HOD Dept. of Political Science, Nizam College, Hyderabad, Telangana, India

V. Radhika, Assistant Professor R.G. Kedia College, Esamia Bazar Chaderghat, Hyderabad Telangana

Dr. K. Aruna Bai, Asst. Professor, Dept. of Telugu Government Degree College Shantinagar Telangana India

Dr. M. Vigneshwar Reddy, Asst. Professor Dept. of Geography Govt Degree College for Women Begumpet, Hyderabad Telangana India

1

Higher Education Reform in India

Murli Krishna

Abstract

India, one of the world's largest economies, has made enormous strides in its economic and social development during the past two decades, but India can do much more to leverage its strengths in today's knowledge-based global economy. According to the National Knowledge Commission (NKC) 2006, the country needs a massive expansion of opportunities for higher education, with 1500 Universities. Nationwide. The higher education scene in the country is set to experience a dramatic change but the ability of the state universities to cope with this change is extremely doubtful. The success of the new central universities and the proposed national universities will come about at the cost of the state universities, which cater to the majority of students in the country. This article proposes that postgraduate teaching and research in state universities will have to be taken over by the central government to ensure the survival of this important part of the higher education system. Liberalisation of higher education services in India should not be viewed from the point of view of generating revenues but as a strategy to promote the quality of its own higher education system. Further, attracting students from outside for postgraduate study and research opportunities in India will be able to fuel innovation and enterprise in the higher education system. Of the three factors involved in production - land, labour and capital, it is labour and more particularly the quality of labour that is the key determinant for a country's competitiveness. It is, therefore, not surprising that there is a strong correlation between endowment of skilled labour and the gross domestic product (GDP) per worker across countries. Higher education enhances a country's capacity for participation in an increasingly knowledge based world economy and has the potential to enhance economic growth and reduce poverty.

Key words: liberalisation, policy reform, India, Economic, GATS, trade in services.

Introduction

The National Education Policy 2020 (NEP 2020), launched on 29 July 2020, outlines the vision of India's new education system. NEP

2020 focuses on five pillars: Affordability, Accessibility, Quality, Equity, and Accountability - to ensure continual learning. It has been crafted consistent with the needs of the citizens as a demand for knowledge in society and economy called for a need to acquire new skills on a regular basis. Thus, providing quality education and creating lifelong learning opportunities for all, leading to full and productive employment and decent work as enlisted in United Nations Sustainable Development Goals 2030, forms the thrust of NEP 2020. The new policy replaces the previous National Policy on Education, 1986 and forms a comprehensive framework to transform both elementary and higher education in India by 2040.

The NEP 2020 calls for key reforms in both school and higher education that prepare the next generation to thrive and compete in the new digital age. Thus, there is much emphasis upon multidisciplinarity, digital literacy, written communication, problem-solving, logical reasoning, and vocational exposure in the document.

Higher Education in NEP 2020

The NEP 2020 was conceived to raise the Gross Enrolment Ratio (GER) from the current 26 percent to 50 percent by 2030 in the higher education space. It aims at building the overall personality of students by strengthening infrastructure for open and distance learning, online education and increasing the use of technology in education.

Moreover, the National Research Foundation (NRF) will be set up to boost research work in the country. A National Accreditation Council (NAC) envisaged as a single regulator for higher education institutions across the country will be established. The Higher Education Council of India (HECI) will have multiple verticals to fulfill various roles. Efforts will be undertaken to set up a National Recruitment Agency for all government recruitment exams, and a Common Eligibility Test (CET) for various recruitment exams of the same level.

Moreover, the courses and programme in subjects, such as Indology, Indian languages, AYUSH systems of medicine, yoga, arts, music, history, culture, and modern India, internationally relevant curricula in the sciences, social sciences, and beyond, meaningful opportunities for social engagement, quality residential facilities and on-campus support, etc. will be fostered to attain this goal of global quality standards.

Accreditation in Higher Education

Regulatory mechanisms of higher education would have "accreditation" conducted by an independent body amongst other key functions. Institutions will have the option to run Open Distance Learning (ODL) and online programme, provided they are accredited to do so, to enhance their offerings, improve access, increase GER, and provide opportunities for lifelong learning.

The accreditation scheme for improving credibility of Learning Service Provider (LSP) has been developed by National Accreditation Board for Education and Training (NABET), Quality Council of India (QCI) under Department of Industrial Promotion and Internal Trade (DPIIT), Ministry of Commerce and Industries, Government of India. Accreditation ensures Quality Assurance of Trainer/Faculty, Infrastructure; Programme Design (Development and Delivery); Training Management System (3 Dimensions: Hardware, Software, Humanware / Skinware).

Education and Skilling in Cyber Security

As per the Global Risk Report 2021 of the World Economic Forum (WEF) 2021, 'Cyber Security Failure' ranks fourth most critical threat to the world. As education and learning have already moved to cyberspace due to the ongoing pandemic, it has become utmost important to protect the privacy and security of each individual. Thus, as adoption of digitisation takes centre stage, it is extremely important to make our networks and cyberspace secure. In this current scenario, it becomes pertinent that capacity building for 'Cyber Security Resilience' is given prime importance and is included in higher education curriculum irrespective of stream of learning.

Research and Innovation in Higher Education

One of the key thrust areas of NEP 2020 is to encourage high RandD investments from government and private sectors. This will encourage innovation and innovative mindsets. To facilitate the same, there is a need for a strong industry commitment and close intervention with academia for industry led skilling / upskilling/ reskilling.

Further, it becomes pertinent to inculcate the skill sets for driving knowledge about "Intellectual Property Rights (IPR)" and its protection for delivering benefits from it.

The National Education Technology Forum (NETF)

The NETF envisaged to be established under NEP 2020 is a step in the right direction. The hosting of Quality Ed-Tech tools in all the dimensions of teaching-learning delivery would enable institutions of learning to adapt quickly. The emphasis needs to be towards hosting indigenous Ed-Tech tools on "open-source development platforms" with built-in cyber security resilience to ensure 'privacy and security' besides adherence to cyber security standards, adoption of firewalls and Intrusion Detection System (IDS) from external threats and vulnerabilities. This will secure the 'personal privacy of individual students'.

Reforms in the Higher Education System

While early childhood to semi-adult stage, K-12 segment is the founding pillar of holistic child development, higher education system equips a student for a professional life. With the increasing need for creative, multidisciplinary, and highly skilled workforce for employment, Indian higher education system needs to be re-adjusted and revamped to meet the emerging requirements. Some of the key reforms introduced vide NEP 2020 in the Indian higher education system include:

1. Quality Universities and Colleges: Recognising the problems which are currently prevailing in the higher education system in India, which inter alia include poor employability of educated workforce, severely fragmented higher educational ecosystem, poor learning outcome and development of cognitive skills of students, rigid separation of disciplines with too much early specialisation and streaming of students into narrow areas, NEP 2020 intends to completely overhaul and re-energise the higher education system in India. NEP 2020 envisions to introduce certain key changes to the higher education system, which inter alia include:

(a) moving towards a higher educational system consisting of large, multi-disciplinary universities and colleges, with at least one in or near every district;
(b) moving towards a more multidisciplinary undergraduate education;
(c) moving towards faculty and institutional autonomy;
(d) re-vamping curriculum, pedagogy, assessment and student support for enhanced student experiences;
(e) establishment of a National Research Foundation to fund outstanding peer-reviewed research and to actively seed research in universities and colleges;
(f) governance of higher education institutions by highly qualified independent boards having academic and administrative autonomy; and
(g) increased access, equity, and inclusion through a range of measures, including open schooling, online education and Open Distance Learning, keeping in view the needs of learners with

disabilities and substantial increases in scholarships at private/ philanthropic universities for disadvantaged and underprivileged students.

2. Institutional Restructuring and Consolidation: NEP 2020 intends to end the fragmentation of higher education by transforming higher education institutions into large multidisciplinary universities and colleges, each of which will aim to have 3,000 or more students. The idea is to build vibrant communities of scholars and peers, break down harmful silos, enable students to become well-rounded across disciplines (including artistic, creative and analytic subjects as well as sports), develop active research communities across disciplines (including cross-disciplinary approach) and increase resource efficiency, both material and human across higher education.

The higher education system is thus proposed to have multidisciplinary institutions of higher learning that offer undergraduate and graduate programme, with high quality teaching, research, and community engagement. All higher education institutions will move towards becoming large multidisciplinary institutions with programme across disciplines and fields, offered either in their institutions or through higher education institutions clusters. The vision is to have all higher education institutions (existing as well as new) to evolve into research-intensive universities, teaching universities and autonomous degree granting colleges. In addition to teaching and research, all higher education institutions shall also have other crucial responsibilities which they will discharge through appropriate resourcing and structures. These include supporting other higher education institutes in their development, community engagement and service, contribution to various fields of practice, faculty development for the higher education system and support to school education system.

3. Shift Towards Holistic Education with less Rote Learning: NEP 2020 advocates for promotion of holistic arts education to ensure well rounded development of students. It is thus proposed that multidisciplinary universities and colleges will facilitate the move towards high-quality arts education with flexibility in curriculum and engaging course options being developed and offered to the students. Pedagogy for these courses will strive for significantly less rote learning and an increased emphasis on communication, discussion, debate, research, and opportunities for cross-disciplinary and interdisciplinary thinking. Departments in Languages, Literature, Music, Philosophy, Indology, Art, Dance, Theatre, Education, Mathematics, Statistics, Pure and Applied Sciences, Sociology, Economics, Sports and other such subjects needed for a multidisciplinary,

stimulating Indian education and environment will be established and strengthened at higher education institutions across the country. Furthermore, to ensure that students actively engage with the practical side of their learning and improve their employability options, as part of holistic education, students will also be provided with opportunities for internships with local industry, businesses, artists, crafts persons, villages and local communities, etc., as well as research internships with faculty and researchers at their own or other higher education institutions or research-institutions.

4. Internationalisation: NEP 2020 focuses on promoting India as a global study destination providing premium education at affordable costs. It is thus intended that high performing Indian universities will be encouraged to set up campuses in other countries and similarly select universities will be permitted to operate in India. A legislative framework shall be formulated and introduced facilitating the entry of foreign universities in India, and such universities will be given special dispensation regarding regulatory, governance and content norms on par with other autonomous institutions within India. Additionally, research collaboration and students exchange programme between the Indian institutions and global institutions will be promoted and the credits acquired in foreign universities will also be permitted to be counted for award of degree.

5. Teacher Education: Recognising the importance of creating a team of teachers that will shape the next generation, NEP 2020 lays equal emphasis on revamping teacher education as well. To reach the levels of integrity and credibility required to restore the prestige of teaching profession, the regulatory system is empowered to phase out substandard and dysfunctional teacher education institutions that do not meet basic educational criteria. The teacher education needs to be conducted within composite multidisciplinary institutions having departments of psychology, philosophy, sociology, neuroscience, Indian languages, arts, history, and literature as well as various other specialised subjects such as science, mathematics, etc.

Furthermore, by 2030, the four-year integrated B.Ed offered by multi-disciplinary higher education institutions is proposed to be made as the minimal degree qualification for school teachers. The said four-year integrated B.Ed. will be a dual major holistic Bachelor's degree, in education as well as a specialised subject (such as a language, history, music, mathematics, computer science, chemistry, economics, etc.). For the purposes of maintaining uniform acceptable standards of education, the admission to pre-service teacher programme shall be through a single nation-wide entrance examination to be conducted by the National Testing Agency, which test may contain both subject and aptitude tests.

6. Professional Education: NEP 2020 envisages that professional education will become an integral part of the overall higher education and thus it must also significantly involve critical and interdisciplinary thinking and research. Thus, the practice of setting up stand-alone technical universities, health science universities, legal and agricultural universities or institutions in these fields shall be discouraged and all existing stand-alone professional education institutions will have to become multi-disciplinary institutions by 2030, either by opening new departments or by operating in clusters. The professional education standards, viz. technical, health and legal education are also proposed to be restructured to ensure that the education standards are globally competitive and adapt to the challenges evolving with time.

7. Promoting High Quality Research: Recognising the importance of knowledge creation and research in growing and sustaining a large and vibrant economy and uplifting the society, NEP 2020 focuses on a comprehensive approach for transforming the quality and quantity of research in India. Thus, to focus on research and promote research culture in all higher education institutions in an interrelated and coordinated fashion, NEP 2020 provides for setting up of a National Research Foundation (NRF) which would bring a quantum jump in funding and support for research. The overarching goal of NRF shall be to enable a culture of research to permeate through universities and higher education institutions across India. In this regard, NRF shall inter alia provide a reliable base of merit-based peer-reviewed research funding, helping to develop a culture of research in the country through suitable incentives for and recognition of outstanding research. NRF shall also competitively fund research in all disciplines across the academic landscape viz. science, technology, social sciences, arts, and humanities.

8. Transforming Regulatory System of Higher Education: Presently, the mechanistic and disempowering nature of the regulatory system has been rife with very basic problems, such as heavy concentrations of power within a few bodies, conflicts of interest among these bodies and a resulting lack of accountability. Furthermore, India also has some of the toughest requirements in the world for setting up higher education institutions, which requirements are largely input-centric, focusing on land and space norms, endowment funds and their sources, etc.

To address the currently prevailing issues in the higher education system within India, NEP 2020 mandates for setting-up of a common regulatory regime for the entire educations sector, eliminating duplication and disjunction of regulatory efforts. A single regulator, the National Higher Education Regulatory Authority (NHERA) will be set up to regulate in a 'light but tight' and facilitative manner. Few importance matters viz. financial probity, good governance and full online and offline public disclosure of all finances, procedures, faculty/staff, courses, educational outcomes will be very effectively regulated.

Separately, a new General Education Council (GEC) shall also be set up to frame expected learning outcomes for higher education programme, also referred to a 'graduate attributes'. A National Higher Education Qualification Framework (NHEQF) will be formulated by the GEC and it shall be in sync with the National Skills Qualifications Framework.

Higher Education Grants Commission (HEGC) will be created which will take care of funding and financing of higher education based on transparent criteria including the IDPs prepared by the institutions and the progress made in the implementation of the IDPs. HEGC will be entrusted with disbursement of scholarships and on developmental funds for starting new focus areas and expanding quality programme offerings in HEIs across disciplines and fields.

In terms of NEP 2020, the fundamental design principles of an effective regulatory system will thus be:

(a) a clear separation of functions to enable adequate focus on each essential role while eliminating conflicts of interest;

(b) a single, empowered, responsive, but minimalistic regulatory authority to ensure basic regulatory requirements, such as financial probity and full public disclosure of finances, procedures, course and programme offerings, and educational outcomes, while otherwise empowering institutions to make their own decisions for the pursuit of excellence;

(c) accreditation through the establishment of independent high-quality accrediting bodies, overseen by a meta-accreditor, as the basis of regulation; and

(d) each body in the regulatory system run by Independent Boards consisting of persons having high expertise in the relevant areas along with integrity, commitment, and a demonstrated track record of public service.

Comments and Observations

Reforms in the Indian higher education system were also long overdue, and NEP 2020 marks a significant shift in the long-standing and established rote and herd learning education practice followed in India. The main focus of NEP 2020 is not only on improving the quality of education, but NEP 2020 also focuses on formulating an effective regulatory regime for higher education institutions across India.

With an aim of improving the operative environment for higher education institutions across India, NEP 2020 clearly prescribes the intent of the government to curb commercialisation of higher education in India. NEP 2020 clearly prescribes that all educational institutions will be audited as per standards of audit for section 8 company (not-for-profit company) and the Institute of Chartered Accountants of India may also refine the norms for educational institutions, including for ensuring that related party transactions, services or charges by any other names are not used to profit from the institution by the promoters/sponsor/management. Any surpluses will compulsorily need to be reinvested within the institution. These standards are possibility being introduced to curb the rampant profiteering engaged by educational institutions by adopting related party services arrangements and structures.

One of the long-standing demands of the industry has been to allow entry of foreign universities in India. Draft rules and entry of foreign university bills have been previously proposed but the legislation for entry of foreign university did not see the light of the day. The earlier bill had received lukewarm responses from foreign universities owing to its stringent capitalisation and mandatory reserve fund norms, which was further compounded by the 'not for profit' structures. NEP, 2020 has acknowledged the need to allow entry of foreign universities in India and has proposed formulation of a legislative framework, with the suggestion to give such universities special dispensation regarding regulatory and governance norms on par with other autonomous institutions within India. Only time will tell if the Government is able to bring out a legislation which balances the interest of students and the concerns of foreign universities.

Conclusion

Furthermore, to promote India as a global destination for higher education, NEP 2020 encourages the use and integration of technology to improve multiple aspects of education, provided the interventions are rigorously and transparently evaluated in relevant contexts before they are scaled up. An autonomous body, the National Educational Alliance for Technology is also proposed to be created to provide a platform for use of technology to enhance learning, assessment, planning, administration, etc.

Thus, while the introduction of NEP 2020 and the proposed reforms in the regulatory regime for higher education institutions is a positive step for revamping and streamlining the higher education segment within India, the actual results and changes will depend on ground level implementation of the proposed reforms.

References

Berger and Kostal (2002). Financial Resource, Regulation and Enrollment in US public higher education, Economics of Education Review.21 (2002) pp.101-110.

Bhushan, Sudhanshu (2005). Knowledge Economy and Higher Education, Indian Journal of Labour Economics (IJLE) Vol. 48 (4), Oct-Dec, pp.869-880.

Bishop, John (1978). The Effect of Public Policies on the Demand for Higher Education. The Journal of Human Resource, 12 1978, 285-307.

Blaug, M. (1966). An Economic Interpretation of the Private Demand for Education, Economica, 33(1) 166-182, 1966.

Blaug, M. (1976). The Empirical Status of Human Capital Theory: A Slightly Jaundiced Survey, Journal of Economic Literature, 14 (3) 1976, 827-855.

Chang and Hsing (1996). A study of Demand for Higher Education at Private Institutions in the US: A Dynamic and General Specification, Education Economics, 4(3), 267-278.

Campbell, and Siegel (1967). The demand for Higher Education in the United States, 1919-1964, American Economic Review, (June) 1967, 57, 482-494.

Canton and Jong (2005). The Demand for Higher in the Netherlands, 1950-1999, Economics of Education Review, 24 (2005) 651-663.

Cohn, Elhanan, (1978). Higher Education Enrollment Projections, Review of Higher Education (Winter 1978): 18-30.

Charles, T. Clofelter and Michael Rothschild (1993). Studies of Supply and Demand in Higher Education, University of Chicago Press.

Duchesne, I. and W. Nonneman, (1998). The demand for higher Education in Belgium, Economics of Education Review 17, no. 2:211-218.

Feldman, P. and Hoenack, S. A. (1969). Private demand for Higher Education in the United States. In The Economics and Financing of Higher Education in the United States. Washington, D.C.: The Joint Economic Committee, 1969.

Arnold, R. D., and Wade, J. P. (2017). A Complete Set of Systems Thinking Skills. Insight, 20(3), 9-17. https://doi.org/10.1002/inst.12159

Barth, M., and Rieckmann, M. (2012). Academic staff development as a catalyst for curriculum change towards education for sustainable development: An output perspective. Journal of Cleaner Production, 26(December), 28-36. https://doi.org/10.1016/j.jclepro.2011.12.011

Bianchi, G. (2020). Sustainability Competences - A Systematic Literature Review. December 2020, 1-6. https://doi.org/10.1145/3452144.3452277

Blok, V., Gremmen, B., and Wesselink, R. (2016). Dealing with the Wicked Problem of Sustainability in advance. Business and Professional Ethics Journal. https://doi.org/10.5840/bpej201621737

Brauksa, I. (2013). New Challenges of Economic and Business Development. June, 88-95.

Chiong, K. S., Mohamad, Z. F., and Abdul Aziz, A. R. (2016). Factors encouraging sustainability integration into institutions of higher education. International Journal of Environmental Science and Technology 2016 14:4, 14(4), 911-922. https://doi.org/10.1007/S13762-016-1164-3

Diesendorf, M. (2000). Sustainability and Sustainable Development. Topic-Driven Environmental Rhetoric, January 2000, 213-233. https://doi.org/10.4324/9781315442044-11

Dlouhá, J., Heras, R., Mulà, I., Salgado, F. P., and Henderson, L. (2019). Competences to address SDGs in higher education-a reflection on the equilibrium between systemic and personal approaches to achieve transformative action. Sustainability (Switzerland), 11(13). https://doi.org/10.3390/su11133664

Dzhengiz, T., and Niesten, E. (2020). Competences for Environmental Sustainability: A Systematic Review on the Impact of Absorptive Capacity and Capabilities. Journal of Business Ethics, 162(4), 881-906. https://doi.org/10.1007/s10551-019-04360-z

Eizaguirre, A., García-Feijoo, M., and Laka, J. P. (2019). Defining sustainability core competencies in business and management studies based on multinational stakeholders' Perceptions. Sustainability (Switzerland), 11(8). https://doi.org/10.3390/su11082303

Evans, T. L. (2019). Competencies and pedagogies for sustainability education: A roadmap for sustainability studies programme development in colleges and universities. Sustainability (Switzerland), 11(19). https://doi.org/10.3390/su11195526

Fingar, P. (2004). Systems Thinking?: The " Core " Core Competency For. September, 20-21.

Geden, M., Smith, A., Campbell, J., Spain, R., Amos-Binks, A., Mott, B., Feng, J., and Lester, J. (2019). Construction and Validation of an Anticipatory Thinking Assessment. Frontiers in Psychology, 10(December), 1-10. https://doi.org/10.3389/fpsyg.2019.02749

Giangrande, N., White, R. M., East, M., Jackson, R., Clarke, T., Coste, M. S., and Penha-Lopes, G. (2019). A competency framework to assess and activate education for sustainable development: Addressing the UN sustainable development goals 4.7 challenge. Sustainability (Switzerland), 11(10), 1-16. https://doi.org/10.3390/su11102832

Glasser, H., and Hirsh, J. (2016). Engaging Change-Makers: A Profile of the Leadership for Sustainability Education Graduate programme. Sustainability (United States), 9(4), 178-184. https://doi.org/10.1089/SUS.2016.29054

Gray, R. (2010). Is accounting for sustainability actually accounting for sustainability...and how would we know? An exploration of narratives of organisations and the planet. Accounting, Organisations and Society, 35(1), 47-62. https://doi.org/10.1016/j.aos.2009.04.006

Hopper, M., and Stave, K. (2008). Assessing the effectiveness of systems thinking interventions in the classroom. Proceedings of the 26th International Conference of the System Dynamics Society, January, 1-26. http://www.systemdynamics.org/conferences/2008/proceed/papers/STAVE390.pdf

Jelenc, L., and Swiercz, P. M. (2004). Strategic Thinking Capability. ResearchGate, 1-25.

Kamangar, F., Rohani, R., Salavati, A., and Karimi, M. S. (2013). Developing strategic thinking. Journal of Basic and Applied Scientific Research, 19(3), 546-552. https://doi.org/10.1016/0024-6301(86)90201-3

Klien, G., and Snowden, D. (2011). Anticipatory Thinking. Informed by Knowledge Expert Performance in Complex Situations, January 2011, 1-418. https://doi.org/10.4324/9780203847985

Komasinski, A., and Ishimura, G. (2017). Critical Thinking and Normative Competencies for Sustainability Science Education サステイナビリティ学教育に対するクリティカル・シンキング的と規範的コンピテンシー J. Higher Education and Lifelong Learning, 24.

Kordova, S. K., Frank, M., and Miller, A. N. (2018). Systems thinking education-seeing the forest through the trees. Systems, 6(3), 1-14. https://doi.org/10.3390/systems6030029

Lans, T., Blok, V., and Wesselink, R. (2014). Learning apart and together: Towards an integrated competence framework for sustainable entrepreneurship in higher education. Journal of Cleaner Production. https://doi.org/10.1016/j.jclepro.2013.03.036

Leicht, A., Heiss, J., and Byun, W. J. (2018). Issues and trends in Education for Sustainable Development. http://www.unesco.org/open-access/terms-use-ccbysa-en

Lozano, R., Merrill, M. Y., Sammalisto, K., Ceulemans, K., and Lozano, F. J. (2017). Connecting competences and pedagogical approaches for sustainable development in higher education: A literature review and framework proposal. Sustainability (Switzerland), 9(10), 1-15. https://doi.org/10.3390/su9101889

Mensah, J. (2019). Sustainable development: Meaning, history, principles, pillars, and implications for human action: Literature review. Cogent Social Sciences, 5(1). https://doi.org/10.1080/23311886.2019.1653531

Perez Salgado, F., Abbott, D., and Wilson, G. (2018). Dimensions of professional competences for interventions towards sustainability. Sustainability Science, 13(1), 163-177. https://doi.org/10.1007/s11625-017-0439-z

Pisapia, J. (2011). Strategic Thinking Skills: Validation and Confirmation of Constructs. November, 1-10. http://www.academia.edu/755209/Strategic_Thinking_Skills_Validation_and_Confirmation_of_Constructs

Pisapia, J., Pang, N. S.-K., Hee, T. F., Lin, Y., and Morris, J. D. (2009). A Comparison of the Use of Strategic Thinking Skills of Aspiring School Leaders in Hong Kong, Malaysia, Shanghai, and the United States: An Exploratory Study. International Education Studies, 2(2). https://doi.org/10.5539/ies.v2n2p46

Rausch, A., Seifried, J., Wuttke, E., Kögler, K., and Brandt, S. (2016). Reliability and validity of a computer-based assessment of cognitive and non-cognitive facets of problem-solving competence in the business domain. Empirical Research in Vocational Education and Training, 8(1). https://doi.org/10.1186/S40461-016-0035-Y

Schweighart, C. (2011). E Nvironment , S Ystems T Hinking and T Eaching . 1-12.

Taimur, S., and Sattar, H. (2019). Education for Sustainable Development and Argumentation. January, 55-88. https://doi.org/10.1007/978-981-13-2369-0_3

Thibodeau, P. H., Frantz, C. M. P., and Stroink, M. L. (2016). Situating a Measure of Systems Thinking in a Landscape of Psychological Constructs. Systems Research and Behavioral Science, 33(6), 753-769. https://doi.org/10.1002/sres.2388

Timuroglu, M. K., Kula, M. E., and Naktiyok, A. (2016). Strategic Thought and Learning Orientation. ResearchGate, April 2018, 5-30.

Torbjörnsson, T., Molin, L., and Karlberg, M. (2011). Measuring attitudes towards three values that underlie sustainable development. Utbildning and Demokrati - Tidskrift För Didaktik Och Utbildningspolitk, 20(1), 97-121. https://doi.org/10.48059/uod.v20i1.945

UNESCO. (2017). (PDF) Education for Sustainable Development Goals: Learning Objectives.

Vare, P., Arro, G., de Hamer, A., Gobbo, G. Del, de Vries, G., Farioli, F., Kadji-Beltran, C., Kangur, M., Mayer, M., Millican, R., Nijdam, C., Réti, M., and Zachariou, A. (2019). Devising a competence-based training programme for educators of sustainable development: Lessons learned. Sustainability (Switzerland), 11(7), 1-21. https://doi.org/10.3390/su11071890

Wiek, A., Withycombe, L., and Redman, C. L. (2011). Key competencies in sustainability: A reference framework for academic programme development. In Sustainability Science (Vol. 6, Issue 2, pp. 203-218). https://doi.org/10.1007/s11625-011-0132-6

Withycombe, L. K. (2010). Anticipatory Competence as a Key Competence in Sustainability Education. In Arizona State University: Vol. MA Thesis (Issue August).

Zsiga, P. L. (2007). Self-directed Learning Readiness, Strategic Thinking and Leader Effectiveness in Directors of a National Non-profit Organisation.

2

Equity and Inclusion in Higher Education in India

N Vijayalakshmi

Abstract

Higher Education in India has seen massive expansion since Independence. India has over 700 universities and thousands of colleges which include central, state, private and deemed universities and institutions like IIT's and IIM's and other institutions of national importance. Higher Education contributes to the national development through dissemination of specialised knowledge and skills among the young students. In this twenty first century the students who get degrees must be able to face the competitive world. Education the GER is only 25.2 percent which is very less compared to the countries like US and China. There is no equity and inclusion of marginalised sections of the society. The basis of exclusion are caste, religion, gender region and poverty. The Constitution provided reservation to the scheduled castes and scheduled tribes to improve their educational and socio-economic-conditions. It is the responsibility of the state to provide quality education to all students. There are challenges before the Government and the educationists to solve the problems so that everyone gets a fair chance to get education. This paper focusses on the issues of equity and inclusion in the field of Higher Education.

Key words: Knowledge, Underprivileged, Opportunity, Exclusion.

Introduction

In India Higher Education system has grown extensively and enrollment of young students has increased which is needed for the national development. The Constitution of India gaurantees the Right to Education to all children upto 14 years of age. Education is the tool by which an individual enriches his or her personality and also contributes to nation building. Education equips with knowledge skills and values to the youth and the capacity to contribute to the nation. Educated youth is the asset of the nation. India is one of the largest growing and vibrant economies in the world and Higher Education sector is expanding to cater to the needs of the millions of students who are entering colleges and universities.

The developed countries like USA, Australia, UK and Germany are knowledge economies and attract a large number of international students.The developed countries are knowledge driven and utilise the human capital to produce resources. Our country has to develop its human resources to grow in all areas and particularly the scientific and Research Institutions have the responsibility to render services to the benefit the society and the world at large. Fostering global citizenship is the goal of our new education policy which promotes mutual respect for all the people of the world and caring for our environment wherever we live.

Equity is just and fair inclusion and when there is equity in education each and every individual must be able to reach full potential. It takes individual circumstances into consideration. Equity is often referred to as levelling the playing field in the classroom. The students may be different in their abilities but they need resources to suit their needs for learning and achieve their goals. The UNESCO views that "Inclusion is the process which is concerned with the identification and removal of barriers of education and ensures the presence, participation and achievement of all students and their diversities." The principle of Inclusive Education was adopted at the world conference on Special Needs Education Access and Quality Salamanca Statement, Spain 1994. The member countries adopted a new Framework for Action the guiding principle of which is that the ordinary schools should accommodate all children, regardless of their physical, intellectual, social, emotional, linguistic or other conditions. The children who have been traditionally excluded should have the real learning opportunity to get education and no one should be left behind.

Constitutional Provisions

The Constitution of India guarantees the Right to Education under Article 21A from six years upto the age of 14 years which is a fundamental right. Under the Directive principles of state policy Article 45 says that the state shall provide compulsory and free universal education upto the age of 14 years. The Ministry of Social Justice and Empowerment provides Prematric and Post matric Scholarships. National fellowships and Free Coaching for SC's ST's and OBC's. The persons with disabilities (Equal opportunities Protection of Rights and Full Participation Act 1995) was enacted to protect the rights of the persons with Disabilities.

According to the Kothari commission one of the important objectives of education is to equalise opportunity enabling the backward or under priviledged classes and individuals to use education as a tool for improvement of their social and economic condition. However, in Higher Education there is no equity and Inclusion in the Gross Enrollment Ratio. There are disparities in enrollment for men and women, forward and socially disadvantaged and underpriviledged classes, urban and rural areas and religious and ethnic communities and also abled and disabled students. According to the report of All India Survey on Higher Education 2019-20 GER is 27.1 percent GER for male is 26.9 percent and for female it is 27.3 percent For Scheduled Castes it is 23.4 percent and for Scheduled Tribes it is 18 percent,

The National Education Policy 2020 is highly aspirational policy with a target to reach 50 percent Gross Enrollment Ratio in Higher Education by the year 2030. The main pillars of NEP 2020 are Access, Equity, Quality,Affordability and Accountability which has brought a paradigm shift in Higher Education in India. With the sub-continental size of our country and a huge diverse population within the age group of 18- 23 it is a big challenge before our policy-makers and educationists to provide education and unless the socially deprived groups enter the education system social integration is not possible. It is the responsibility of the state to deliver quality educational services to these students and equip them with twenty first century skills to face the global society. The socially and educationally disadvantaged groups such as the tribes who live in remote areas should be declared as Special Education Zones which will facilitate speedy implementation of Government schemes and policies. The NEP 2020 advocates inclusion of all social and economically disadvantaged groups at the three levels of access, participation and learning outcomes. All types of barriers such as social stratification and bias must be removed to bring these groups into the mainstream so that an equitable society is established.

The Government run colleges cater to the socially and economically backward sections of the society but they suffer from lack of permanent faculty, poor infrastructure and political interference. The private institutions attract the richer classes. The majority cannot afford the education in private institutions due to the cost. Most of the students of these socio-economically poor background join the traditonal courses and their representation in Science Technology Engineering and Management courses is lower when compared to forward castes students.

The socially disadvantaged groups such as the SC's ST's BC's Women Minorities and persons with disabilities, transgenders suffer from discrimination and harassment due to the prejudices towards them. The SC and ST students are the first generation literates where the medium of instruction is the regional language till their school education and when they enter the colleges they cannot compete with the other students who can afford English medium education in private institutions. During the Covid-19 Pandemic the rural students had no access to online classes due to lack of devices and internet facilities. These students have lagged behind in their education which has created the digital divide between the urban and rural areas.

Steps to be taken by the government

The Government has to ensure that rule of Reservation is followed in private colleges and universities. Scholarships must be provided incentives such as free textbooks, uniforms, must be provided.

Training and coaching centres should be set up for the students. Vocational Education should be given. Hostel facilities should be made available to the rural students.

Equal Opportunity Cells must be constituted. All institutions must have facilities for disabled like ramp for wheel chairs and braille textbooks, Audio and Video materials.

Public transport for rural students must be improved. More funding for the development of colleges in rural areas.

Life skills and human values like tolerance, respect for Indian culture, patriotism, environmental protection and gender sensitisation must be thaught. There should be Zero Tolerance towards discrimination and harassment on the basis of gender, caste etc.

Bilingual method of teaching will help the students and Learning resources like must be improvised.

The Government in partnership with the local NGO's can improve enrollment and reduce dropouts. Akshaya Patra Foundation is feeding nutritious mid day meal in Government schools and colleges across the country.

Conclusion

The policy makers and educationists and Non Governmental Organisations need to look at these issues of diversity and implement programme for inclusive education. We have to provide safe learning environment to each and every individual. Technology based online learning, conducting brigde courses, remedial classes for slow learners and also by mentoring and counselling the students will help them to cope up with their studies. All the stakeholders have a responsibility to make our Education system more equitable and inclusive.

References

1. Higher Education in India Issues, Concerns and New Directions Recommendations of UGC 2003.
2. Higher Education in India Issues Related to Expansion Inclusiveness Quality and Finance UGC 2008.
3. National Education Policy Ministry of HRD, GOI Report.
4. Educational status of Socially Disadvantaged Groups in India -Sunita Bhatla SRJIS Online ISSN 2278-8808 copyright @2017
5. Hindustan Times .com NEP 2020 Increasing GER in Higher Education How To Make Vision A Reality.
6. Inclusivity vis-a-vis National Education Policy 2020 published by National Law University Delhi, 2021.

3

Modern Technology in Classrooms

J. Naga Ratnam

Abstract

The most recent technology has found a place in our daily lives. Mobile phones, smart phones, laptops, tablets, and other electronic devices are all available. When it comes to education, technology plays a significant role. Students and teachers have been able to stay linked through e-classrooms, especially since the emergence of Covid-19. Today, technology is used in more than just computer laboratories; it may also be accessed directly in the classroom. Students are attracted to smart classrooms because they may learn new topics in a pleasant and engaging way.

Students can use technology to maintain their interest in studies. With the use of technology, students can better absorb and retain information by using pictorial representations of teachings.

Now students can experience one on one education. Even when they are sitting in classroom with other classmate with the introduction of E-books it becomes easier for students to get access to numerous books over the internet with just a click there is much scope to go beyond the syllabus and learn in depth about any subject.

Students can also connect to several platforms to gain knowledge and share their experiences with similar interest groups. This increases their visibility and interest in developing their knowledge. However, technology can be equally harmful as its benefits. Parental control and guidance are a must to make the best use of technology. There are various E-learning platforms and e-learning apps available to students to study. Be it a primary grade student or a postgraduate student, technology is equally important for both.

The pandemic has taught how technology can provide us a virtual learning space for students and teachers. Facility human life but it cannot replace human afforts. Finding creative ways to use technology in the classrooms can both make your life easier as a teacher and boost students excitement levels and enjoyment with lessons. From helping with communication among teachers and students (as well as peer-peer) to organising.

Literature Review

Sumakul, *et al.* (2022) in their study reveals that, AI is a relatively new technology, but it is changing the world. Particularly, in the field of language teaching and learning, there have been some developments affecting how teachers teach and how students learn. This study has revealed some of the issues regarding this matter. To have a better understanding on this issue, however, more data involving more teachers with different contexts are needed. It would also be more complete if this could be seen from the point of view of the students and other stakeholders of education in general or in the context of language teaching and learning in particular.

Lisenbee, P. (2016) in his study, in the twenty first century, technology has become a pervasive presence for teachers and students in and out of the classroom causing a generation gap between the two cohorts in their expectations for using technology in classrooms. Teachers are encouraged in standards to engage students with technology to actively explore, participate in collaborative groups, interact with others and make connections to real world experiences. Additionally, teachers are encouraged to embrace and embed technology as another instructional method in classrooms so students can learn to use technology independently to construct knowledge. The EMSCI Model offers a process for both students and teachers to work towards independent use of technology in a collaborative manner. Changes brought about by teachers reimagining their classrooms and reshaping their pedagogy will fade the shadows of a generation gap duc to the shining success of teachers and students independently using technology in classrooms.

Baylor, A. L., and Ritchie, D. (2002). In their research, the level of technology leadership and support for professional development. It appears that administrators who promote the use of technology, not only in words but also in action, lend credence to a technology culture. Our interview was designed to look beyond administrators who superficially endorse technology, and identify those who actively use, model, and reward teachers who infuse technology into their classroom. The bottom line appears to be that administrators who wish to nurture a technology culture need to figuratively "roll up their sleeves and join in" rather than sitting by the side. Although we found that administrators contribute to the positive interactions of technology in a school, of greater importance were teacher attributes. Long-range planning for software developers and schools of education should include a vision that nurtures decision-making and development by teachers, rather than implementing systems solely from the level of policymakers. Currently many technology initiatives rely upon policymakers to communicate the value of technology to teachers, instead of involving teachers from the start. By helping teachers find ways to actively infuse technology, investments in time and money will pay off in greater content acquisition and higher-order thinking skills for students and greater teacher competence and morale.

Teachers' Perceptions

Teachers' perception is related to how teachers view a certain concept or practice in their teaching and learning processes, and is an important aspect in the success of their students' learning. Synthesising from a number of previous studies, Cope and Ward, (2002) came up with a diagram showing why teachers' perception matters (see Figure 1).

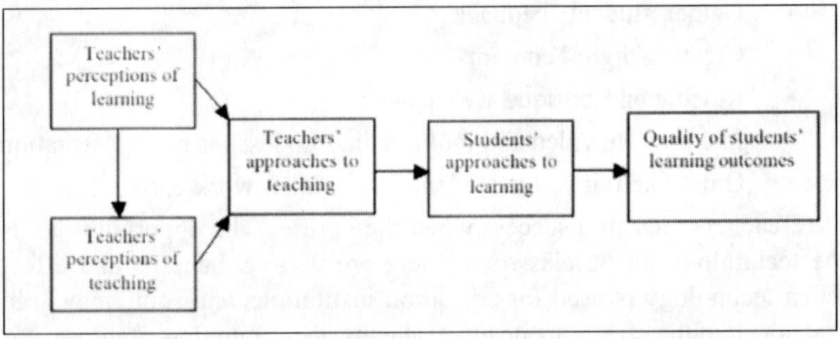

Figure 1 : Teacher-student Perception and the Quality of Students Learning Outcomes (Cope and Ward, 2002, p. 68).

Teachers' ideas of learning and teaching, as shown in the figure, influence how they approach teaching and how students approach learning. All of these factors would eventually have an impact on the pupils' ability to learn. Teachers' perceptions may not have a direct impact on students' learning, but they are an important component of students' learning success.

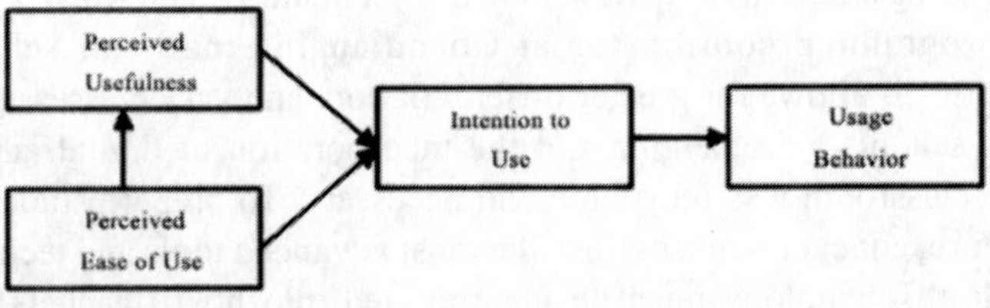

Figure 2 : Technology Acceptance Model (Davis, 1989).

The interplay of some aspects impacting technology use is depicted in the diagram. Along with perceived ease of use, perceived utility influences intent to use, which influences use behaviour, or how a person uses technology. In other words, as shown in Figure 1, how instructors view technology integration will influence their desire to utilise it and, eventually, how they use it in the classroom. Teachers, in general, are the ones who decide whether or not to utilise technology, how pupils should use it, how often they should use it, and for what reason. This could be one of the reasons why instructors' perspectives on technology use are important to investigate.

Enhance learning, some examples

- Digital field trips
- Integrate social media
- Gather student feedback
- Creating digital content
- Review and critique web pages
- In corporate video and multimedia into lessons and presentations
- Online activities for students who finish work early.

Teacher often find success when they present the opportunity to use the technology in the classroom there are various benefits and effects when technology is used for education institutions and some may argue that not all of the effects are positive. Having an infinite flow of information and entertainment available at any given time could be seen as a distraction but it technology is integrated into the classrooms.

The use of technology during whole class instruction can foster student engages for audio and visual learners. Integrating simple technologies power point, games, internet homework, assignments, or online grading systems can be different makers in student growth in the classrooms.

Technology is a driving force in education, opening up many doors and preparing students for what lies ahead, not behind", said Kelly, Primacy years programme coordinator at Conadian International school in Singapore. "it allows for greater differentiation, and varied assessments". Today's schools are changing and the incorporation of digital advances into the classroom was inevitable and necessary. To prepare students for their future, education must utilise the most advanced tools and techniques available. "Technology must be incorporated into how [teachers] teach and assess students." Kelly added in a phone interview with Global Citizen. "There must be a shift in mindset, for teachers, parents and students." "students inhabit a twenty first century world for 18 hours a day", Jim Tracy, headmaster at Cushing Academy in Ashburnha, Massachusetts told US News and world report. "and, all too often, educators put them in a nineteenth century classroom for six hours of that day, and the students feel a tremendous disconnect." Education institution form kindergarten to postgraduate programme are incorporating new technology at a rapid pace. Some classroom are starting to look more like the move Minority report than the classrooms most adults today remember. Here is a tour of the technology shaping today's classrooms.

Creative spaces

"Stuffing school with high tech tools isn't the answer to offering dynamic learning experiences," said Danish Kurani and Zoe Balaconis in an article for EdSurge, a website about the intersection between technology and education. Kurani is an architect and designer and her colleague Balaconis is the co-founder of Misadventures, a women's outdoor adventure magazine. The two led a pilot programme testing classroom designs with a public school in Columbine, Colorado. The driving concept of the programme was "new learning needs new environments." Their pilot programme redesigned a classroom to utilise technology and new teaching techniques to make education more "personalised, adoptive and real-world" focused. The new classroom had a "Skype mountain," a tiered sitting area where "students can sit, congregate, and connect with the world." The classroom also included small discussion areas, individual, pupil directed, learning zones, and large learning galleries that can be updated to fit whatever topic is being taught.

Objective of the Study

1. Students the learn more information through e-classroom
2. To identify the interest of students
3. Smart classroom can attract to the student interest
4. To the students to learn new things in a fun and interesting way
5. Classroom attendance and attention of the students also increase
6. The effective use of digital learning tools in classroom can increase student engagement
7. To help teachers improve their lesson plans and facilitate personalised learning
8. It also helps students build essential twenty first century skills

Way to use technology in classrooms

- Learning management system
- quiz are game based learning platforms
- QR code
- connected classroom forums
- blogging

Educational apps and games etc suggestions classrooms in the future will need new investment of both creativity and finance the technology in entering the industry but of course finance is will be a barrier to building these new classrooms "at the same time Technology can replace some cost of traditional resources it can also save administration cost and time" not every educational institution will be able to install smart boards are Skype mountains in the next few years instead they can look at updating lessons structures to fully utilise and available Technology. Resource sharing among students and Rethinking their educational spaces within their budgets.

Conclusion

Students across the planet need the best most uptodate education to prepare themselves for the future and the old leads the best prepaid students to have a better future. Technology has become a pervasive presence for instructors and students in and out of the classroom in the twenty-first century, resulting in a generation gap in their expectations for using technology in the classroom. Teachers are encouraged to actively engage students with technology to actively explore, collaborate in groups, interact with others, and create connections to real-world experiences, as outlined in the standards. Teachers are also encouraged to embrace and integrate technology as another educational approach in the classroom so that students can learn to develop knowledge using technology on their own.

More data from more teachers in diverse circumstances is needed to gain a deeper grasp of this issue. It would also be more complete if this could be perceived through the eyes of students and other education stakeholders in general, as well as in the context of teaching and learning in particular.

References

1. Eristi, S. D., Kurt, A. A., and Dindar, M. (2012). Teachers' Views about Effective Use of Technology in Classrooms. Online Submission, 3(2), 30-41.
2. Hoffmann, M. M., and Ramirez, A. Y. (2018). Students' Attitudes toward Teacher Use of Technology in Classrooms. Multicultural education, 25(2), 51-56.

3. Lisenbee, P. (2016). Generation gap between students' needs and teachers' use of technology in classrooms.
4. Baylor, A. L., and Ritchie, D. (2002). What factors facilitate teacher skill, teacher morale, and perceived student learning in technology-using classrooms?. Computers and education, 39(4), 395-414.
5. Daniel, M. C., and Cowan, J. E. (2012). Exploring Teachers' Use of Technology in Classrooms of Bilingual Students. GIST Education and Learning Research Journal, 6, 97-110.
6. Cope, C., and Ward, P. (2002). Integrating learning technology into classrooms: The importance of teachers' perceptions. Journal of Educational Technology and Society, 5(1), 67-74.
7. Ritzhaupt, A. D., Dawson, K., and Cavanaugh, C. (2012). An investigation of factors influencing student use of technology in K-12 classrooms using path analysis. Journal of Educational Computing Research, 46(3), 229-254.
8. Dwyer, D. C., Ringstaff, C., and Sandholtz, J. H. (1991). Changes in teachers' beliefs and practices in technology-rich classrooms. Educational leadership, 48(8), 45-52.
9. Debele, M., and Plevyak, L. (2012). Conditions for successful use of technology in social studies classrooms. Computers in the Schools, 29(3), 285-299.
10. Sumakul, D. T. Y., Hamied, F. A., and Sukyadi, D. (2022). Artificial Intelligence in EFL Classrooms: Friend or Foe?. LEARN Journal: Language Education and Acquisition Research Network, 15(1), 232-256.

4

Among Covid-19 Pandemic: Achievement Motivation of Undergraduate Students from Aided Degree College in Kalaburagi

Dr Nagaratna S

Abstract

The influence of Covid-19 on the Achievement motivation has been recently researched by several investigators. Achievement motivation was considered to be an important element for student achievement, particularly at the degree level. The aim of this study is to find out the achievement motivation of undergraduate students from aided institution in Kalaburagi. To conduct the study 115 students (Second and third year students enrolled in 202-2021) were selected through convenience sampling technique. The collected data were analyzed with percentage analysis and the same were interpreted. The results revealed that the undergraduate students have responded positively. There achievement motivation level is high and they want to improve themselves in this pandemic situation.

Key words: Pandemic, achievement motivation, Undergraduate students.

Introduction

The outbreak of the Covid-19 pandemic, many governments worldwide introduced a lockdown to contain it. This entailed closing most non-essential businesses and venues, and ordering people to stay at home. In most countries this included educational institutions (e.g., Hirsch, 2020; Crawford et al., 2020). Even Universities and Schools elsewhere were abruptly forced to close their doors. Students and faculty personnel were ordered to stay at home, which meant moving the lectures and other academic activities from physical classrooms to an online environment using videoconferencing. Students had to adapt in a short amount of time to a drastically changed situation. They could not attend physical lectures or study and interact on campus. However, this transformation may link to different types of challenges at this point (Crawford et al., 2020). Due to this, all teachers and lecturers delivered the lesson through online learning classrooms such as Google Meet, Zoom Application and so on. They also urged to use work from home period to enhance their knowledge with the implementation of virtual classes and online assessment. Lecturers upload instructional materials such as videos on social media. The new generation students, who are highly exposed to technology, are well accepted and capable of learning through online learning platform such as E-learning, Google Classrooms, and innovative classroom and so on.

The influence of Covid-19 on the Achievement motivation has been recently researched by several investigators (D'Alise 2020, Masaali, 2007, Pasion et al., 2020, Zaccoletti et al., 2020). Achievement motivation was considered to be an important element for student achievement, particularly at the degree level (Orsini et al., 2015). Beck (2004) defined achievement motivation as the rationales for students' attending to, commitments, and attempts concerning learning and accomplishing at school setting, which focused solely on the reasons why individuals decided and continue university education (Muza and Muhammad, 2020, Schunk et al., 2008). Achievement motivation involves the desire to do something well in a particular area (Masaali, 2007). Besides, attitudes and behaviours pertaining to achievemnt motivation involve maintaining difficult assignments, working intensely to learn to new things, and selecting effort requiring tasks.

Motivation is an essential element in academic performance. High levels of motivation are associated with good academic performance (Kusurkar, Ten Cate, Vos, Westers and Croiset, 2013). Highly motivated students tend to expend more effort in learning, leading to better results (e.g., Gottfried, Marcoulidis, Gottfried and Oliver, 2013).

The aim of this study is to find out the achievement motivation of undergraduate students from aided institution in Kalaburagi.

Review Literature

Shartini Devi Krishnana, Norlizah C. Hassanb (2021): Study entitled "Online Peer Learning amid Covid-19 Pandemic in Malaysian Higher Learning Institution". This study aims to determine the relationships between online peer learning and academic achievements, and the differences between genders in academic achievements. The study was based on the quantitative method in nature with correlation design using questionnaires. Cluster sampling techniques applied and a total of 225 responses were collected. Result indicated highly perceived mean score on engagement of undergraduates' use the social media for learning purposes. There is a positive correlation between online peer learning and undergraduates' academic achievement. The T-Test analysis revealed that there is a significant different between gender in academic achievement and female undergraduates had the highest mean score. The findings illustrate undergraduates' emotional engagement appears as an essential aspect in their learning process.

H. Deniz Günaydin (2021): The title of the study is "The impact of social problem skills on academic motivation by means of Covid-19 fear". In this study, it was aimed to a construct structural equation model by which the impacts of social problem-solving skills on academic motivation by means of Covid-19 fear were studied. Therefore, 513 university students participated in the study and completed Social Problem-Solving Inventory-Short Form, the Fear of Covid-19 Scale, and Academic Motivation Scale. The SEM model analysis indicated that rational problem solving, negative orientation to problem, impulsive/careless style and avoidant style predicted 15 percent of the Covid-19 fear. Altogether rational problem solving, negative orientation to problem, impulsive/careless style, avoidant style, positive orientation to problem and Covid-19 fear explained 32 percent of the academic motivation.

Micaiah Andrea Lopez, et.al. (2021): The study entitled "Amidst Covid-19 pandemic: the self-efficacy and academic motivation of the college students from the private higher education institutions in the Philippines". This study investigates the relationship between the self-efficacy and academic motivation of the 304 freshmen college students from private higher education institutions in the Philippines. Based on the data gathered, the participants' level of self-efficacy ($\bar{x}$= 3.27) and academic motivation ($\bar{x}$= 5.93) is high. Further, the statistical analysis concluded a relationship between self-efficacy and academic motivation (r=.002, at 0.05 level) among the graduating college students. Implications of the study were discussed, and recommendations for future research were suggested.

Methodology: The study find out the achievement motivation of undergraduate students from aided Degree College in Kalaburagi. The researcher utilises a quantitative method. The researcher chose the questionnaire as the source data-gathering tool to find out the achievement motivation of the students.

Participants: The participants of this study were second year and final year students from aided degree college in Kalaburagi that are enrolled during the pandemic, the year 2020-2021. Thus, the study utilises the convenience sampling method with a total number of 115 students or participants.

Instrument: To find out achievement motivation of undergraduate student, the researcher used general achievement motivation questionnaire. This questionnaire consists of 10 questions regarding achievement motivation.

Procedure of the study: To acquire the necessary data of the study in determining the achievement motivation of the students, the researcher prepared some questions to acquire data on achievement motivation. The data were obtained with the help of Google form. It's quite easy and effective to analyse data. Thus, the researcher could complete the current study with the positive and good response from the students.

Statistical Technique: Percentage analysis was used.

Data interpretation:

The obtained data is interpreted with the help of pie graph.

1. I have satisfied gaining knowledge of new things during pandemic.

The pie graph shows that 55.6 percent students are agree, 12 percent students are strongly agree, 23.9 percent students are neutral, 7.7 percent students are disagree. Thus, we can say that students satisfied to gain knowledge of new things during pandemic.

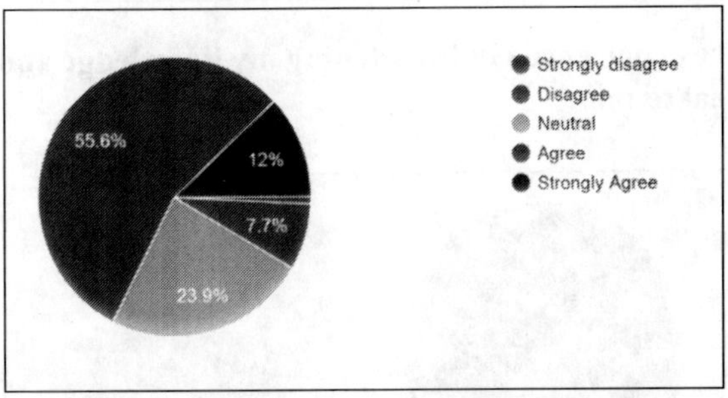

2. I am willing to share my own ideas and experience with my friends.

The pie diagram reveals that 55.6 percent students agree, 19.7 percent students are strongly agree, 21.4 percent of students are neutral. Therefore, we can say that the students willing to share their ideas and experience with their friends.

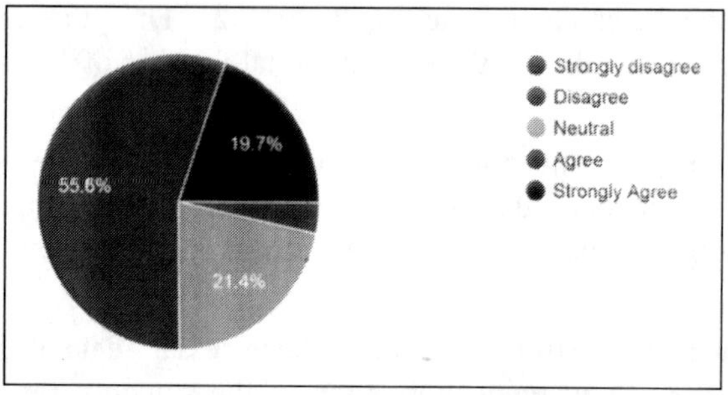

3. I have felt satisfaction when I am in the process of accomplishing difficult academic activities.

The diagram shows that 53.8 percent students agree, 9.4 percent students strongly agree, 23.9 percent students are neutral. This shows that the students felt satisfaction when they accomplishing difficult academic activities.

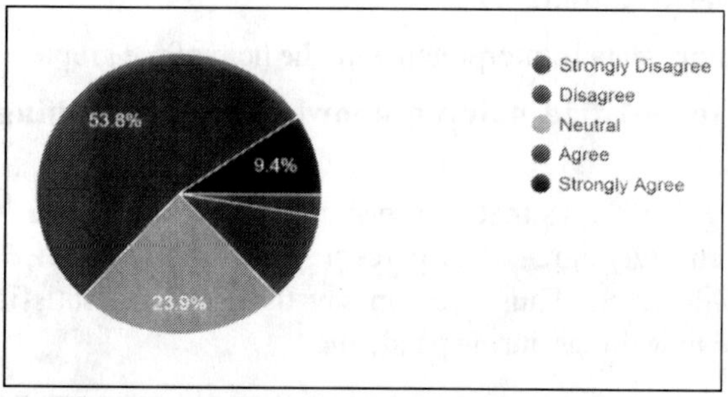

4. I have experienced in broadening my knowledge about subjects which appeal to me.

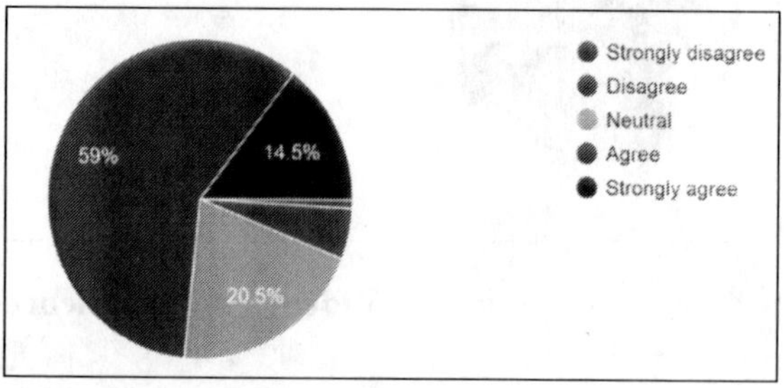

The pie diagram clearly reveals that 59 percent of students are agree, 14.5 percent students strongly agree and 20.5 percent of students are neutral. Thus we can say that the students are broadening their knowledge.

5. I think that college education will help me better prepare for the career I have chosen.

The diagram shows that the 42.7 percent students agree, 39.3 percent students were strongly agree and 12.8 percent students says neutral. Therefore, we conclude that students are strongly agreed that college education will help them better preparation for their career.

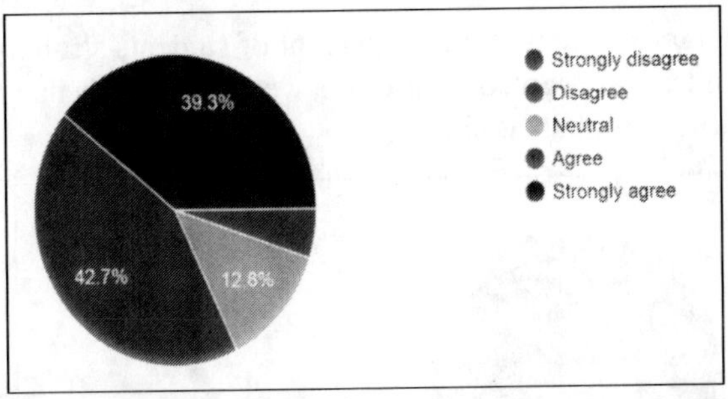

6. I want to improve my competency during online class education.

The diagram shows that the 54.7 percent students agree, 10.3 percent students are strongly agree, and 14.5 percent students disagree, 18.8 percent of students are neutral. Therefore, we can say that students want to improve their competency during online education.

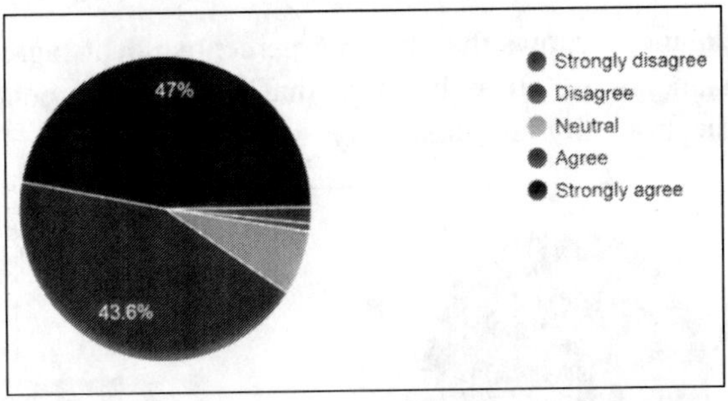

7. I want to show myself that I can succeed in my studies.

The pie diagram reveals that 47 percent of students strongly agree and 43.6 percent of students are agreed. Hence we can say that the students shows themselves succeed in their studies.

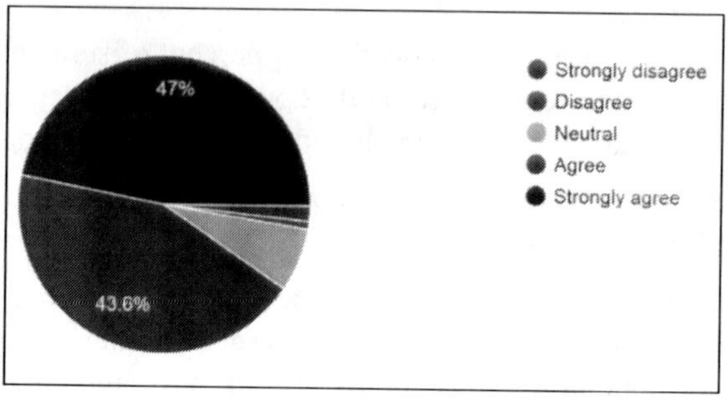

8. I want to confident with my aims.

The diagram shows that the 53 percent of students strongly agree, 41 percent of students are agreed. Therefore, we can conclude that most of the students confident with their aim.

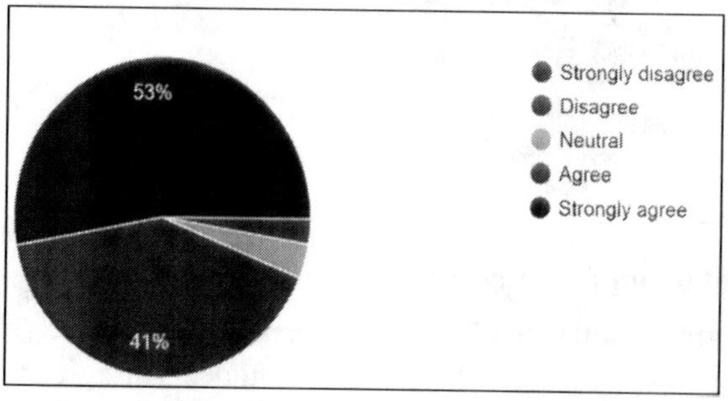

9. I want to do assignment or other works given by teachers enthusiastically and creatively.

The pie diagram shows that the 55.6 percent students agree and 32.5 percent of students are strongly agree that to do assignment given by teachers enthusiastically and creatively.

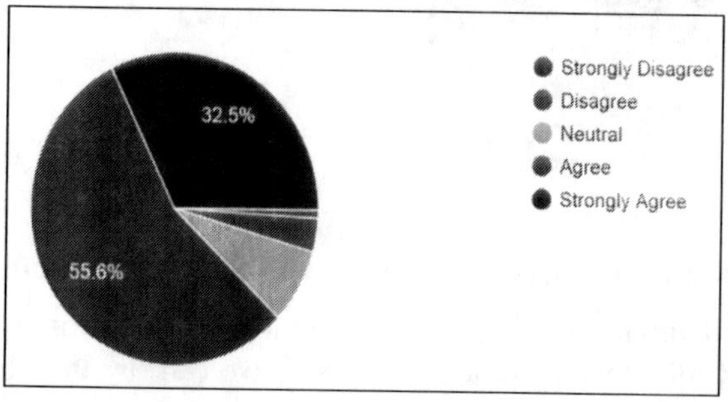

10. I want to avoid doing worse than other students.

The diagram shows that 58.1 percent of students agree, 19.7 percent of students are strongly agreed and 15.4 percent of students are neutral. Hence, we can say that the students don't do worse activity.

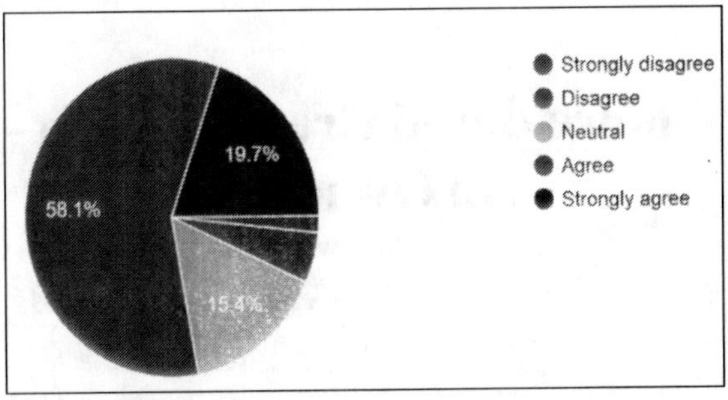

Discussion and conclusion

The results revealed that the undergraduate students have responded positively. There achievement motivation level is high and they want to improve themselves in this pandemic situation. To conclude, I can tell that it was an attempt to know achievement motivation level of undergraduate students, I wish their achievement motivation will be continues till completing their education.

References

1. Shartini Devi Krishnana , Norlizah C. Hassanb (Vol.12 No.14 (2021), 1010 - 1019). Turkish Journal of Computer and Mathematics Education. Retrieved from 10382-Article percent20Text-18495-1-10-20210808.pdf
2. https://link.springer.com/content/pdf/10.1007/s12144-021-01665-z.pdf
3. Micaiah Andrea Lopez et.al. (2021). Amidst covid-19 pandemic: the self efficacy and academic motivation of the college students from the private higher education institutions in the Philippines. Vol-7 Issue-3 2021 IJARIIE-ISSN(O)-2395-4396.
4. Javaeed, A. et al. (2019). Assessment of Academic Motivation Level of Undergraduate Medical Students of Azad Kashmir, Pakistan. Cureuss 11(3): e4296. DOI 10.7759/cureus.4296.
5. https://www.frontiersin.org/articles/10.3389/fvets.2020.594261/full

5

Choice Based Credit System - An Overview

Ms S Nirmala and Ms M Anusha

Abstract

India was partitioned and given independence in 1947. After which there was remarkable improvement in scientific and technological education and research, illiteracy however remain high. Education continued to be the prime responsibility of State governments and Central government continued to assume responsibility for the co-ordination of educational facilities and the maintenance of appropriate standards in higher education and research.

In 1947, the government of India appointed three important commissions for suggesting educational reforms.

(i) AICTE - 1945: All India Council of Technical Education

(ii) UGC - 1953: The University Grants Commission

(iii) NCERT - 1961: The National Council of Educational Research and Training

The first body advised the government on technical education and maintain standards for the developments of technical education. The second body promoted and coordinated university education and maintained standards of teaching, examinations and research in the Universities. Also it allocates grants to the universities.

The annual systems refers to a University education system where the exams are held after one academic year. It is the traditional system. Mr. Mani Sundaran who was member of the University of Madras in the mid 1960's,when the Vice Chancellor Prof. A.L.Mudhaliar introduced the semester system only for engineering programme as pioneering project.The semester system has been introduced by the government to improve the quality of education during 1970's in higher education. In semester system each school year is split into equal parts of about six months each during which teaching work is conducted and assessment is completed.

"CBCS - Choice based system which provides a chance for the scholars to settle on courses from the prescribed courses comprising core, elective /

minor or skill based courses. The courses can be evaluated following the grading system which is considered better than the conventional marks system". In CBCS continuous and comprehensive evaluation (CCE) refers to a student evaluation system which covers all aspects of activities related to student development. Education aims at making student capable of becoming responsible, productive and useful members of society.

Key Words: CBCS, CCE, SGPA, CGPA, AECC, SEC, GE, Grading, Grade Letter, Grade Point, Semester, UGC, AICTE.

Introduction

Choice based credit system (CBCS) is an approach in which students can chose the courses of their choice, learn at their own phase, undertake additional courses, acquire more than the required credit, adopt an inter disciplinary approach to learning and also it provide greater flexibility with multiple exits and pathways, vertical mobility. In short the CBCS is

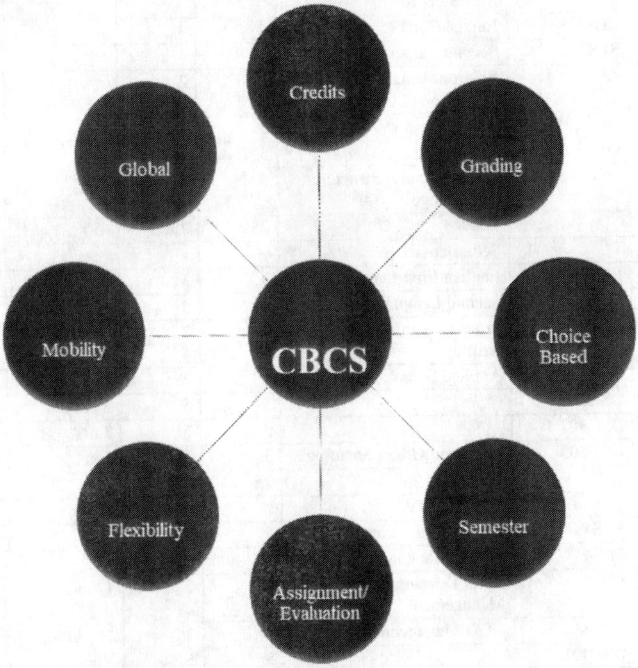

1. Credit: Credit earned as basic measuring unit for course work. It determines the no. of hours of instructions required per week. On credit is equivalent to one hour of teaching or two hours of practical work per week. Credits are calculated keeping in mind the following three components.

(i) Lecture

(ii) Tutorials

(iii) Practicals

Faculty of Social Sciences, Osmania University

BA

CBCS COURSE STRUCTURE

w.e.f 2019-20

SI.No.	Code	Course Title	HPW	Credits	Exam Hrs	Marks
1	ELS1	English(First Language)	4	4		
2	SLS1	Second Language	4	4		
3	AEC1	Environmental Science/ Basic Computer Skills	2	2		
4	DSC101		5	5	3 hrs	80U+20I
5	DSC102		5	5	3 hrs	80U+20I
6	DSC103	Fundamentals of Sociology	5	5	3 hrs	80U+20I
		Total	25	25		
		Semester- II				
7	ELS2	English(First Language)	4	4		
8	SLS2	Second Language	4	4		
9	AEC2	Environmental Science/ Basic Computer Skills	2	2		
10	DSC201		5	5	3 hrs	80U+20I
11	DSC202		5	5	3 hrs	80U+20I
12	DSC203	Indian Society: Structure and Change	5	5	3 hrs	80U+20I
		Total	25	25		
		Semester- III				
13	ELS3	English(First Language)	3	3		
14	SLS3	Second Language	3	3		
15	SEC1	Project Planning and report writing	2	2	1 ½ hrs	40U+10I
16	SEC2	Applied Sociology	2	2	1 ½ hrs	40U+10I
17	DSC301		5	5	3 hrs	80U+20I
18	DSC302		5	5	3 hrs	80U+20I
19	DSC303	Rural and Urban Sociology	5	5	3 hrs	80U+20I
		Total	25	25		
		Semester- IV				
20	ELS4	English (First Language)	3	3		
21	SLS4	Second Language	3	3		
22	SEC3	Rural Development and Management	2	2	1 ½ hrs	40U+10I
23	SEC4	NGO Management	2	2	1 ½ hrs	40U+10I
24	DSC401		5	5	3 hrs	80U+20I
25	DSC402		5	5	3 hrs	80U+20I
26	DSC403	Research Methodology	5	5	3 hrs	80U+20I
		Total	25	25		
		Semester- V				
27	ELS5	English (First Language)	3	3		
28	SLS5	Second Language	3	3		
29	GE	Social Issues, Policies and Development	4	4	3 hrs	80U+20I

30	DSC501 A B C		5	5	3 hrs	80U+20I
31	DSC502 A B C		3T+4P/5	5	3 hrs	50T+35P +15I 80U+20I
32	DSC503 A B C	Sociology of Development Social Stratification and Social Mobility Social Anthropology	5	5	3 hrs	80U+20I
		Total	27/25	25		
		Semester-VI				
33	ELS6	English (First Language)	3	3		
34	SLS6	Second Language	3	3		
35	PR	Project Report (or) Gender and Society	4T 2T+4R	4 4	3 hrs 1 ½ hrs	80U+20I 40U+10I 35R+15V
36	DSC601 A B C		5	5	3 hrs	80U+20I
37	DSC502 A B C		3T+4P/5	5	3 hrs	50T+35P +15I 80U+20I
38	DSC503 A B C	Industrial Sociology Political Sociology Medical Sociology	5	5	3 hrs	80U+20I
		Total	**29/27**	**25**		
		Grand Total	**156/152**	**150**		

SUMMARY OF CREDITS

S.No.	Course Category	No. of Courses	Credits Per Course	Credits
1	English Language	6	4/3	20
2	Modern Language	6	4/3	20
3	AEC	2	2	4
4	SEC	4	2	8
5	GE	1	4	4
6	Project Report	1	4	4
7	DSC	12	5	60
8	DSE	6	5	30
	TOTAL	**38**		**150**

2. Grading

(a) Grade Letter: It is an index to indicate the performance of a student in a particular course (Paper). It is the continuous evaluation of actual marks secured by a student during a course/ paper. It is indicated by a Grade Letter F, E, D, C, B, A. There is a variety of marks for every Grade Letter. In case the scholar is absent for any exam, Ab is indicated within the memo in situ of the Grade Letter.

(b) Grade Point: It is weightage allotted to each grade letter depending on the marks awarded in a course/ paper

Award of Grades

Secured percent of Marks given Grade Letter and Grade Point

? 85 to 100 O 10

? 70 to < 85 A 9

? 60 to < 70 B 8

? 55 to < 60 C 7

? 50 to < 55 D 6

? 40 to < 50 E 5

< 40 F 0

Absent Ab -

(c) Semester Grade Point Average (SGPA)

Credit Points for the paper= No. of Credits assigned for the paper x mark secured for that course/ paper

SGPA indicated the performance of a student in a given Semester. SGPA is predicated on the entire credit points earned by the scholar altogether the courses and therefore the total number of credits assigned to the courses/ papers in Semester.

SGPA=? (Letter Grade Points) X (Credits)/ ?(Credits)

CGPA= ?(SGPA) X (Credits)/?(Total Credits)

3. Choice Based : In Choice Based System a curriculum is well planned and carefully designed by educational institutions of the government. Focusing on the general learning experience provided by a course, it emphasizes essentially on the mental and physical development of the scholars. Undergraduate education aims at making students capable of becoming responsible, productive and useful members of society, knowledge skills and attitudes are limit through learning experiences and opportunities created for learners in Higher Education.

4. Semester : In CBCSsystem a academic year is divided into two equal parts of about 6 months each i.e. 1 semester= 6 months; i.e in a academic year there will be two semesters in which 15 weeks= 90 days are for teaching also in Continuous and Comprehensive Evaluation (CCE) after 45 days there will be first internal assessment is conducted and one assignment has to be submitted for 15+5= 20 marks. Similarly after second 45 days of teaching again an internal assessment is conducted and one assignment has to be submitted for 15+5= 20 marks. The average of marks is taken from both the internal assessment and 20 marks are awarded.

After 90 days there will be end semester examinations which are conducted for 80 marks. In semester system the pass chance is 40 i.e. is for 80 marks external examination the pupil should get 32 marks and over, and overall pass would be addition of (internal external) marks = 40. According to the marks secured by the pupil O, A, B, C, D, E, and F grades are given and SGPA is calculated on 10 point scale. In under scale we've 6 semesters, taking 6 SGPA's normal, CGPA is given and degree is awarded for 150/120 credits.

5. Assessment: Within the semester system the observers assess the scholars continuously. Thus from the side of the scholars the semester system is better for pupil attention and literacy. It facilitates better understanding of the subject further emphasis is laid on lot. CCE refers to pupil evaluation system, which covers all aspects of conditioning related to pupil development.

Evaluation in the CBCS system non-stop evaluation of the scholars in all the consecutive semesters till end is done through Internal Assessment, semester end examinations and assignments etc. Course contents of each UG programme are designed to meet the ever changing conditions of the assiduity/ job request/ need of society. Each subject paper/ Course is assigned a specific number of credits and the marks secured by a pupil are converted into grade points and credit points. The performance of a pupil in a semester is expressed as SGPA and the combined performance of a pupil in all the 6 semesters of the UG programme is expressed as CGPA. UG courses in the CBCS are offered within the semester pattern. There shall be five orders of courses/ papers in the UG programme

(i) AECC (Capability Improvement Mandatory Course)

(ii) DSC (Discipline Specific Course)

(iii) DSE (Discipline Specific Elective)

(iv) SEC (Skill Enhancement Course)

(v) GE (Generic Elective)

The AEC is mandatory and its end is to enhance the social and leader boat skill that are pivotal for scholars to succeed in their professional and particular life. And it's of two kinds (a) AECC and (b) SEC

(a) AECC Capability Improvement Mandatory Courses are the courses grounded upon the content that leads to knowledge improvement (i) EVS (ii) Communicative English etc.

(b) SEC "SEC" courses are value- grounded and/ or skill grounded are aimed at furnishing chops, capabilities etc.

DSC (Discipline Specific Course) The course which is offered by the main discipline/ subject of study

DSE (Discipline Specific Elective) The optional which is offered by the main discipline/ subject of study.

GE (Generic Elective) An optional course chosen generally from an unconnected discipline/ subject

Evaluation System for AECC, SEC and GE

(i) Semester end examination of AECC/ SEC and GE shall be conducted by the University and their marks become a part of SGPA and CGPA.

(ii) AECC/ SEC and GE has two credits and will be estimated for 50 marks 10 marks assessment (10 MCQs and 10 Fill in the blanks of half mark all); 40 marks for semester end test (Section A 10 marks-2 short answers of 5 marks each, one from each unit; Section B 30 marks-2 long answers of 15 marks each, from all units with internal choice a or b).

6. Inflexibility : The CBCS provides inflexibility in designing class and assigning credits grounded on the course content and hours of tutoring by different Universities/ Institutions.

7. Mobility : CBCS offers compass for pupil to study at different institutions to complete one course credits earned at one institution can be transferred.

References

1. https://www.iitms.co.in
2. https://collegesat.du.ac.in/UGC-credit-Guidelines.pdf.
3. https://www.mapsofindia.com/my-india/education/what-is-cbcs-or-choice-based-credit-system-how-does-it-work,24/06/2015.
4. https://www.du.ac.in/du/upoads/07052019_Generic_Elective_OR.pdf/
5. https://www.britannica.com/education/The_postindependence_period_in_india
6. www.ugc.ac.in
7. www.britannica.com
8. www.ccets.cgg.gov.in
9. www.mguniversity.ac.in
10. www.deshbhagatuniversity.in
11. www.mzuir.inflibnet.ac.in:8080

6

Tribal Educational Development in Telangana - A Perspective

Pothula Likhitha

Abstract

Social and economic justice, equality of status and opportunities, assurance of the individual's dignity are insured by the Constitution of India for all the citizens among other things. The constitution of India is enriched with several provisions for scheduled castes and scheduled tribes to safeguard and promote their cultural, social, educational, and economic interests in order to bring them in the mainstream of the nation. However, traditional tribal societies are undergoing a rapid change with the mainstreaming policy of the Indian government. For the tribal communities the process of becoming a part of the mainstream has meant a declining control on their resources and erosion of their cultural heritage. The major issue affecting the tribals in India is displacement: not merely displacement by large projects but resource displacement, thus violating the basic survival rights of tribal communities. Tribal areas reveal a high degree of land alienation. Non-tribals have invaded tribal protected areas. Deforestation, mainly due to exploitation of forests for industrial purposes, is another manifestation of resource displacement. This has resulted in decreasing access to forest resources by tribal communities. This paper to be discussed Tribal Education Development in Telangana.

Keywords: Social and Economic Status, Scheduled Tribes, A.P. Government, Visakhapatnam, Education Development.

Introduction

The total number of tribal communities recognised by the government as Scheduled Tribes is 572 in number. Scheduled Tribes are those tribal communities who have been listed so by the President of India in keeping with Articles 341 and 342 of the Constitution. These tribal communities mainly live in Scheduled Areas, or those outlying areas, which during the British times did not come under the direct purview of civil, criminal and revenue administration.

However, traditional tribal societies are undergoing a rapid change with the mainstreaming policy of the Indian government. For the tribal communities the process of becoming a part of the mainstream has meant a declining control on their resources and erosion of their cultural heritage. The major issue affecting the tribals in India is displacement: not merely displacement by large projects but resource displacement, thus violating the basic survival rights of tribal communities. Tribal areas reveal a high degree of land alienation. Non-tribals have invaded tribal *protected areas*. Deforestation, mainly due to exploitation of forests for industrial purposes, is another manifestation of resource displacement. This has resulted in decreasing access to forest resources by tribal communities. With increasing globalisation and privatisation, the land rights of tribal areas is under even greater threat since these are regions, which have a high natural resource base and has tremendous potential to meet multiple market demands. Added to resource displacement is project displacement where development projects have threatened the livelihood needs of tribal communities. More than 40 percent of displaced persons of all large development projects are tribals.

More importantly displacement has been accompanied by erosion of the identity of tribal communities, which is being subsumed within the dominant culture. There is a breakdown in their own community institutions, which hitherto safeguarded their resources, traditional practices and values. In the process the richness and wealth of their knowledge systems, identity and survival with integrity is being destroyed.

Although there are protective laws governing tribal areas these laws are being circumvented or not implemented in spirit. For example, the Fifth Schedule of the Constitution of India which is a protective legal framework for tribal areas is under threat of being amended due to the mining lobby in India which is keen to exploit the minerals from the habitats of tribal people. The forest laws and land acquisition laws also run counter to the land rights of tribal communities. The government programme especially earmarked for tribal areas do not reach the people for whom they are meant due to ineffective implementation systems.

The Education in the Tribal Areas of Telangana

The population of tribal people in Telangana is 4,199,481 (6.3 per cent) of the State's population. The literacy rate for total population of the State as per the 1991 Census was 44 percent (male 55 percent and female 33 percent) and these figures have gone up to 61 percent (male 71 percent and female 51 percent) in the 2001 Census, apparently due to the intensive literacy drives initiated by the State government. The corresponding literacy rate among the tribal population was 17 percent (male 25 percent and female 9 percent) as per the 2011 Census and 22 percent in the 2015 Census. This reveals the gap between the general population and the tribal communities.

Although the statistics show a vast change in literacy levels, the issue of literacy depends on how it is defined and the extent to which it is enabling in qualitative terms. While there are special programme initiated for adult education, the implementation process is far from effective. Fifty-four years after Independence on November 28, 2001 the Government enacted the 93rd Amendment to the Constitution making the Right to Education a Fundamental Right. It puts the onus of sending children to school on parents rather than the State. It is not enough to talk of fundamental rights and fundamental duties of the citizens. It is equally necessary to dwell on the fundamental duties of the government. The extent to which this enactment will be increasingly backed by resource allocation will be the test of the seriousness of purpose of the government to implement the law.

It is pertinent to look at the education scenario of Telangana in this context. As far as elementary education is concerned, the government has undertaken several measures to reach out to tribal communities, such as the Girijana Vidya Vikas Kendras (GWKs) with standards I and II in areas where 'primitive tribal communities' reside; mandal (sub-district) level elementary schools; special residential schools called Ashram Schools mainly in tribal areas; the 'Alternative Schools' etc., and monitoring systems such as the School Complex System. There have also been some special programme such as bridge courses and back to school initiatives for dropouts. For adult literacy, the State has launched a special programme known as 'Akshara Sankranthi' which is for 'adults' above 15 years of age.

All these attempts fall far short of the specific educational needs in tribal areas. Apart from access to education is the issue of quality of the education process. Many of the existing schools do not have adequate number of teachers. The quality of teaching leaves much to be desired let alone the content, which does not take into account the tribal reality situation.

Defining 'Education' in the Tribal Context

For us 'education' is an integral part of the empowerment process. Empowerment of the tribal community means capacitating tribal communities to secure access and control of their land, forest and water resources as well as sustain and promote viable alternatives for security of their livelihoods. Empowerment thus is an interactive process whereby tribal communities are enabled to participate actively in local governance (decision-making that affects their own life situation).

It is in this context that we need to define the role of adult education. For us, educating tribal communities in a more concrete sense means to facilitate processes, which will enable tribal representatives to:

1. develop an analytical capacity for assessing their external and internal environment impacting on their own communities;
2. develop confidence and capacity to articulate their interests and perspective thereby participating in decision-making processes leading to better governance;
3. develop skills to initiate local relevant alternatives to improve livelihoods and challenge external pressures;
4. value self and community history with a critical appreciation of traditional knowledge systems.

We do recognize that adult literacy constitutes an important part of adult education and we have made some attempts in this direction. From 1992-1997 we facilitated tribal youth to take up night schools as a part of the government drive for adult literacy. Several of the trainers were absorbed into the State-run literacy programme initiated in 1998.

However, our major involvement has been with young adults who have been dropouts of the school system. School dropouts have very little opportunities for further education. The percentage of enrolment in schools is 79 percent (89 percent for male and 68 percent for female). But the dropout rate among the tribals is as much as 71 percent while for the general population it is only 65 percent. The ambitious ones tend to be frustrated with an alienating education experience and some of them often land up joining extremist groups in the area.

Mainstream educational institutions do not 'educate' because the curriculum does not give due consideration to the rich traditional knowledge and value systems prevalent within tribal societies. These institutions do not create an opportunity to develop and learn skills which are relevant to the needs, lifestyle and aspirations of tribal communities. We believe that it is important to invest in the youth because it is they who are going to steer the future of tribal societies. Hence we have been focusing on 'alternative education' mainly with tribal youth.

Yuva Parichay was a one-year process initiated in 1991 and discon-tinued in 1998 after the training programme was decentralised. The trainees were drawn from tribal areas of seven districts in North Telangana Each batch ranged from 30 - 40 trainees in the age group between 18-25 years. The minimum educational qualification was basic reading and writing skills or those who had dropped out after completing Standard V.

The need for initiating an educational process with youth emerged in 1989 when the land rights of tribal communities were under tremendous threat because the State was seeking to repeal a land regulation in favour of tribal communities. During this time a campaign against the repeal of the law was initiated all over the state by several concerned organisations. An analysis however of the campaign revealed that local tribal youth although involved in the campaign, did not demonstrate an understanding of a broader vision of tribal rights.

The thrust of the training was to facilitate a relevant response and a meaningful educational process, which took into consideration the problem situation, the tribal learner and the principles of learning. Over a period of time the programme content underwent several changes. In time equal emphasis was paid to learning skills on micro alternatives and on exploring values.

Advocacy in tribal areas today

- Decreasing access and control over natural resources on which the survival of the tribal communities depend
- Lack of access to basic services, health, education and infrastructure
- Violation of their identity rights leading to cultural erosion
- Encroachment of their right to self-governance

From our experience it is clear that we need to recognize that major learning in the tribal context takes place through struggles on issues focusing on human rights of tribal communities. The development of general awareness of multiple stakeholders is crucial for perspective building on tribal reality. More specifically, structured, systematic training initiatives for developing change agents add lasting value on internalising learning processes. Also, education on alternatives, which challenge the existing processes of development, is crucial from the perspective of sustainable livelihood.

Hence as stated before, it is imperative that indigenous 'education' must be an integral part of the empowerment process. For a lasting impact, youth must be the centre of development activity. Therefore, the need to invest in the education of young men and women in tribal areas. Governance functions in the future will be played by today's youth so the direction of development of tribal areas depends on them.

Adult Education Processes

1. human rights education especially in the current context where there is an increasing threat to access and control of natural resources by indigenous communities;
2. development of skills to initiate and sustain relevant micro alternatives that address livelihood issues from a long term perspective; and
3. value based education with critical appreciation of traditional knowledge systems and relevant responses to the changing external environment.

Strategies for empowerment

Need to create special opportunities to respond to the educational needs' of women. Consequences of the development processes are not neutral. They militate more against women than men and hence tend to result in greater negative effects on women. Loss of access and control of resources in tribal areas tend to push women out of productive activities. This also affects adversely their status in their family and community as their participation in the economy decreases. Lack of basic services, particularly related to health and education makes women especially vulnerable. Moreover, atrocities on women are on the increase, as tribal areas become accessible to outsiders and commercially oriented activities. The major strategy to address this issue is to educate the 'panchayat' representatives to safeguard the position of women. In the areas under their jurisdiction.

Need to develop an informed cadre of tribal citizens in law related processes is vital. A critical understanding of the customary laws and the legal provisions in the tribal context is necessary to achieve social justice. The legal machinery in the current circumstances is either insensitive or manipulative in character.

In order to safeguard human rights and ensure enlightened governance there is a need for a special focus on educating elected leaders on relevant laws, their role and functions. In the light of the specific application of the 73rd Amendment of the Indian Constitution to tribal areas, a pertinent law known as the Panchayat (Extension to Schedule Areas Act) was enacted in 1996. This Act facilitates the participation of the 'gram sabha' and the panchayat leaders in playing a role in governance issues at the grassroots level. Several NGOs all over the country have taken this up as a challenge. However, the point remains that respective State governments are slow to act. For example, in Telangana even the rules and regulations pertaining to the Act are not framed as yet!

What Need to be done?

Tribal institutions of secondary education are irrelevant and do not 'educate'. The main reason for this is that the content of education does not take into account their traditional knowledge systems, an understanding of their own environment which is rich in natural resources, relevant skills to provide access and control of their environment and a recognition of their own identity as tribal communities. Also where relevant, a major concern is the need for providing primary education in their mother tongue in order to create an opportunity for them to enhance their learning capacities. Mainstream educational institutions tend to create an alienated group of youngsters with few opportunities to use their capacities. There is a need to review the relevance of curriculum and methodologies of education currently in the tribal context. More specifically we need to campaign for a policy, which takes into consideration the learning needs of tribal youth dropouts at the school and pre-university levels.

Summing up

Need to strengthen literacy levels by promoting opportunities for reading at the grassroots level. Even daily newspapers hardly reach remote villages. Decentralised libraries run by literate youth could be one initiative. Any educational process has to be sustained through creating conditions for being updated on current events and how they impact local communities. This means that processes of creative literacy must be accompanied by follow up measures whereby avenues for deliberation and some reading material is made available on a continuous basis.

References

1. Chauduri, Buddadeb (1992). Socio Economic and Ecological Development, Inter-India Publishers, New Delhi, India.
2. Das, Rajat Kanti (1988). Tribal Social Structure: A study of the Maring society of Manipur, Inter-India Publishers, New Delhi, India.
3. Keller, Stephen (2019). Uprooting and Social change- Refugees, Manohar Book Services, Delhi, India.
4. Khare, P. K. (1991). Social Change of Indian Tribes: Impact of planning and economic development, Deep and Deep Publications, New Delhi, India.

5. Pandey, G. D. and Tiwari, R. S. (2003). "A study of socio cultural factors affecting reproductive health among the primitive tribes of Madhya Pradesh" in Adak, eds, "Demography and Health profile of the tribes", Anmol Publications, New Delhi, India.
6. Raja, Ratnam, B. (2021). "Impact of institutional credit on socioeconomic development of tribal: A study of Khammam district in Telangana", Journal of Rural Development, Vol. 23, No. 2.
7. Sachidanand (1978). "Social structure, status and Morbidity patterns: The case of tribal women" Man in India, Vol. 58, No.1, Jan-March.
8. Singh, Ajit Kumar (1998). Forest and Tribals in India, Classical Publishing House, New Delhi, India.
9. Singh, K. P. (1988). Tribal Development in India: Problems and Implications, Uppal Publishing House, New Delhi, India.
10. Singh, R. S. (1986). Challenges occupational Structure of Scheduled Tribe, One India Publications, New York.
11. Sunder Raj, D. and Venkata, Ravi (2005). "Tribal Development in India : A Panoramic View" in Vasudeva Rao, B.S, eds, "Tribal Developmental Studies", Associated Publishers, Ambala, India.
12. Valentina, G. (2005). "Impact of road improvement in the Tribal economy of Orissa" in Vasudeva Rao, B.S, eds, "Tribal Developmental Studies", Associated Publishers, Ambala, India.

Related Websites

1. http://www.frontline.in/static/html/fl2704/stories/20100226270403300.htm
2. http://www.indiankanoon.org/doc/1186468/
3. http://www.indiankanoon.org/doc/25951781/

7

Emerging Trends in Higher Education in India

Dr P. Prameela Margaret

Abstract

Education has the basic development process of India or for that matter of all countries. It is central to their scientific and technological and socio- economic growth as well as the upward mobility of the individuals. The significance of the production and dissemination of knowledge is universally recognised for progress and well being in society. Education thus a potential instrument for human empowerment it provides an opportunity for co-operating and being willing participants in the dynamic of social reform and reconstruction. The government has to take positive steps to protect and strengthen the democratic rights of all participation in education including students, teachers and parent's management society at large, and ensure at the same time that they also contribute their share towards the building up of the social enterprises of education on collaborative rather than a competitive platform. Each society has its own particular challenges to meet with when promoting and maintain a state education system, particularly challenges to meet with when promoting and maintaining a state education system particularly one of high quality.

Introduction

Education is one of the main factors in socio-economic development although the causality is by no means fully clear. A country which gives its citizens an extensive education is there by creating a potential for development but it doesn't guarantee the latter. On the hand an education which is only geared to economic development maybe less possible even harmful, if the preconditions for economic development rapidly improving.

Higher education has a vital role in the social and economic development of all countries. The sector however faces a significant number of critical issues to be addressed, major challenges to be met and significant opportunities to be grasped and higher education institutions are now expected operate, manage, complete be creative and innovative and provide intellectual leadership in a world characterised by increasingly rapid pervasive and fundamental change. The other major function of education is social equality. It is believed that the cause of inequality is mainly is that people are prevented from realising their full potential due to unequal chances. If education were provided equally for all we would occupy their lower positions while those with the most abilities would occupy the higher positions but would be the best for every day at least better than other ways for distributing positions in society.

Impact of Covid-19 Pandemic on learning methods

In this digital era, a lot of students are slowly but steadily shifting towards online digital courses in almost every field including business, arts, engineering as well as programmeming languages and technical tools. In each and every field, there are numerous courses available digitally across the world and the learners are eagerly filling up the seats. Digital learning is an advanced technological medium providing learners with a great deal of flexibility, allowing them to study at any time from any place at their own convenient speed without worrying about timetables and schedules. It allows students to pursue what they want to learn and what they don't. Digital education is providing both teachers and students new opportunities to teach, learn, and grow thereby improving the overall learning process.

The expansion of technological advancements is bringing new changes in the way education is being imparted and perceived. The outreach of educational programme is becoming better with every passing day with the digitalisation of education The pandemic has made it clear that virtual learning is here to stay. In the West, the big question is whether it will dilute the quality of the college experience and education. Student reach and engagement is higher as it combines various instructional styles. It gives each student the exposure to world-class education, something that was not available in a chalk and talk approach. It is a very flexible way for studying sitting in the comfort of one's own room. In India, which grapples with digital divide, the question remains whether this will reach most people at all. The role of teachers is changing. They can now access the entire classroom through digital screens.

Conclusion, we can say that there are three key factors that created learning challenges for students: lack of access to technology and the internet, a gap in learning resources (such as instructor feedback, structured course materials and opportunities for collaboration), and limited prior experience with online learning.

References

Emerging trends in higher education in India concepts and practices. K.N Panikar and M. Bhaskaran Nair.

Higher education recent trends emerging issues and chellenges. Larry Robert Smith.

8

Enhancing Understanding of Abstract Concepts through O LABS: A pathway towards Quality Experimentation in Science

Ms Priyanka Sharma and Dr Aman

Abstract

Modern technology provides a variety of digital tools that allow teachers to teach experimentation with a viewpoint to work smarter, not harder thereby improving quality of learning and achieving better learning outcomes. With the rise of digital learning, many higher education institutions are now substituting traditional learning resources with educational technologies in an attempt to keep up with their digital learning population. Experimentation is one of the key aspect in science stream as it helps in gaining laboratory experiences and development of critical thinking and problem solving attitude. The present paper is thus an attempt made to study the role of O Labs on transforming the elements of educational space by providing the basic understanding of how this technology has been designed to assist the process of teaching-learning in science by providing real life experiences and how it can be implemented to the fullest. The shift in learning from traditional to digital has lead many teachers scrambling to find effective ways to deliver instructions, thereby allowing students to collaborate. The idea behind O Labs is that lab experiments can also be demonstrated and performed in less expensive manner using the Internet. A real world lab environment is created making use of simulation. These labs are a boon to students who have no access to physical labs or where equipments are not available due to high cost or scarcity. This helps the students to compete with schools with better lab facilities, thus reducing the digital divide and overcoming geographical distances. Another advantage is experiments can be accessed anytime anywhere, overcoming the constraints of time.

Keywords:- Digital tools, Experimentation, Classroom setup, Learning Outcomes, Quality Education.

Introduction

Technological advancements in the field of Education have bought drastic changes in how we perceive education .Technology has provided us with a variety of tools and technologies that have brought a shift from the traditional ways and methods of teaching and learning to online methodology of teaching. From origin of eighteenth century till date, researchers and scientists have studied the importance of laboratory experiences of theory and their importance in the field of Science. Science education is concerned with understanding how and why things work. Science is founded on observational method of gaining knowledge. Experimentation is an important activity in Science for learning how to convey new knowledge and clarify concepts which students usually find difficult to grasp. Experimentation in particular, allows a group to learn collectively and quickly and allow students to build new ideas quickly and collaboratively. To clarify the role of experimentation in the discipline of scientific fields Roberts wrote : "Students achieve a deeper level of understanding by finding things out for themselves and by experimenting with techniques and methods that have enabled the secrets of our bodies, our environment, and the whole universe - to be discovered.". (Okam and Zakari, (2017) noted that practical activity supports the development of positive attitude in students and hence increasing motivation for effective science learning. As a result, positive attitude towards practical work has a significant impact on student's science achievement (Hinneh, 2017). Furthermore, practical work helps in encouraging and inculcating students' likelihood towards science and fosters engagement. For example, when students perform chemistry experiments in a laboratory setup, they discover that the field of chemistry is applied and not merely rules and theoretical principles as stated in their textbooks. The importance of practical learning in science education cannot be overstated (Hofstein and Lunetta, 1982; Hofstein and Mamlok-Naaman, 2007). Laboratories can be utilised in the educational process to generate scientific notations and models that can be used for check ideas. Lab work also help in comprehending the distinction among data observation and presented data (Lawson, 1995). Laboratory activities also behave as a manner of helping students to study with understanding while also engaging in a process of developing knowledge by getting practical experiences, according to the evidence (Tobin, 1990).

Concept of Online Labs (O LABS)

Since 1985, India's government body, the Ministry of Human Resource Development (MHRD), has been making efforts to improve educational opportunities for Indians. Early in 2009, the Cabinet Committee on Economic Affairs approved the MHRD's National Mission on Education via Information and Communication Technology, approved a comprehensive programme by utilising information and communication technology for education titled, the National Mission on Education through Information and Communication Technology (NME-ICT).

GOALS OF NME-ICT

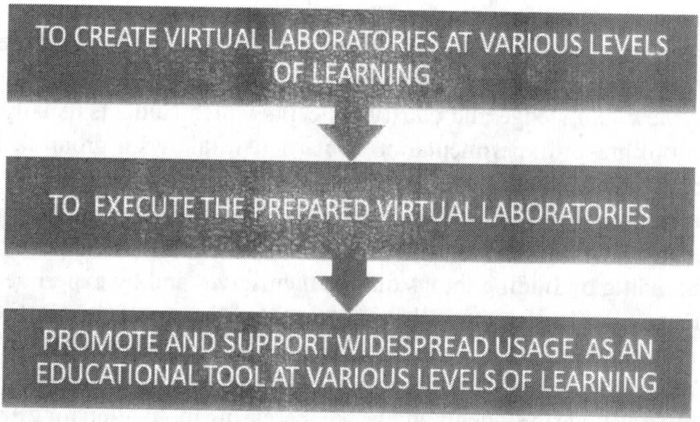

The Sakshat Portal Project established in 2006 is another education portal for inscribing the needs of those connected with the learning process including students, teachers, scholars and those interested in life long learning. The Sakshat Portal is another pillar of the NME-ICT and is attached with the purpose of carrying out a only web portal for providing access to e-learning initiatives introduced by MHRD. With the advancement in the field of communication technology, in the recent years, there is a evolution of a eLearning combined with simulation called online labs. (Achutan, 2011)

The concept of "virtual labs" is one of the most recent advancements in science. Virtual laboratories offer interactive environments and digital replicas of operations typically carried out in physical labs. Virtual labs simulate the tools, equipment, tests, and methods used in chemistry, biochemistry, physics, biology, and other related fields. Virtual labs allow students to do learning according to their own need and foster an eagerness to undertake experiments among them. Virtual Labs also include a comprehensive learning management system that allows students to quickly find extra web materials, video based lectures, demonstration via animations, and tools to evaluate oneself. Students can now perform virtual experiments that imitate the functioning of real life experimentation.

The objectives of this project that focuses on virtual labs, according to Section 3.14.1 of the NME-ICT mission Document, are:

- To crystallise the idea of a Virtual Lab setup, that would mainly consist of a handy visual front end functioning in synchrony with a back end, which may consist of a simulated engine that runs on a server or a real experiment.
- To determine which topics would be most appropriate for visualisation in virtual labs for providing maximum benefit to students.
- To design Virtual labs in such a way that they complement NPTEL, in addition educating students about the fundamental ideas while also stimulating their imaginative ideas and foster curiosity.

In 2009, a board of 12 institutions met with the objective of identifying the academic areas which require the development of virtual labs, to discuss how virtual labs interfaces would look like and feel for virtual labs interfaces, and to decide what institutions would provide what contribution to the development of which particular virtual lab. The educational areas that were chosen for implementation were as following:

- Electronics and Communications
- Computer Science and Engineering
- Electrical Engineering
- Mechanical Engineering
- Chemical Engineering
- Biotechnology Engineering
- Civil Engineering
- Physical Sciences
- Chemical Sciences

The Online Labs is an educational effort that was started by Amrita CREATE, the Amrita Center for Research in Analytics, Technologies and Education at Amrita Vishwa Vidyapeetham in cooperation with CDAC, Mumbai; developed as a result of research grant from the Department of Information Technology, Government of India. Amrita University contributed in development of virtual labs for Biotechnology Engineering students, the field of Physical Sciences, and the field of Sciences. Amrita University's has committed to provide virtual laboratories experiences to students pursuing higher education within India with approach to virtual laboratories, permitting them to experiment, to find out new things, and have learning experiences in similar manner as the students who can avail real laboratory. The lab provides experiments related to Physics, Chemistry and Biology for students in grades 9 through 12, with content prescribed according to NCERT/CBSE curriculum. Recently O Labs have added Mathematics and English lessons. Online Labs access is free for Schools on registration.

There are no constraints such as time and space as each student has plenty of time acessing the virtual lab. This is a economical step as it saves cost of setting big laboratories and purchasing expensive instruments is reduced. Simulated environment has another advantage as it permits more safety and security from dangerous chemical substances. The O Labs is based on the idea that lab experiments can be teached or instructed using the Internet, more efficiently and in a less expensive way. The labs can also be made available to students who are deprieved of facilities of physical labs or where equipment are unavailable due to scarcity or high cost. O labs assist the students by helping them to compete with peers studying in better facilitated schools and reduces the unequity in distribution of digital resources and geographical distances. The experiments are thereby accessible anytime anywhere, thereby reducing the constraints of time and space in comparison to when physical lab settings are available for a shorter duration of time.

The features of O Labs include:

- Content as prescribed according to NCERT/CBSE and State Board Syllabus.
- Physics, Chemistry, Biology Labs from Class 9 to Class 12. English and Maths lessons for Class 9 and 10.
- Interactive simulations, animations and lab videos.
- To clarify concepts and to develop understanding of the experiment through conceptual clarity.
- Helps in developing skills and abilities required to perform, record and learn experiments - anywhere, anytime, and to foster individual practice in all areas of experimentation.
- The 'learning-enabled assessment' through O Labs helps in facilitating the assessment of; developed procedure and manipulation skills of the experiment, the conceptual understanding of the experiment and help in assessing student's reporting skills of a process and interpretation skills.

The development of O Labs involves the use of mathematical techniques to demonstrate the abstract functions in respective divisions of science. The labs make use of recent simulation technology to mimic real world procedures. Real lab scenarios are shown via simulation by live demonstration of the experiment on the Reel, thus recreating and simulating a real.

Recommendations

1. There is a need to recognize similar platforms that bring out best in the learner and bring conceptual clarity with the development of scientific attitudes.

2. Despite the biggest advantages of online laboratories discussed above I feel that students feel bored and monotonous due to constant exposure to screens and this in turn creates learning gaps. Due to unfavourable geographical distribution, internet connectivity also acts as a barrier in learning, Also in competencies related to usage of technologies develop anxiety, inferiority complexes in learning that further distract from the advantages of online learning and focus on its disadvantages. I suggest blended mode of learning over pure online or traditional method of learning.

3. There is need to recognize online laboratories at lower level of hierarchy because marginalised section is still unaware of its optimum usage.

Conclusion

Online labs are a new innovation in the field of education, an initiative by MHRD, with a viewpoint to develop conceptual clarity and promote scientific attitude in the field of experimentation related to various disciplines of education. The present paper focuses on how online labs can be used in the discipline of Science, and how conceptual clarity can be obtained by virtual laboratory settings.

For video for demonstration visit: www.olabs.edu.in

References

1. Hofstein, A., and Lunetta, V.N. (1982). The role of the laboratory in science teaching: Neglected aspects of research. Review of Educational Research, 52(2), 201-217.
2. Tobin, K. (1990). Research on science laboratory activities: In pursuit of better questions and answers to improve learning. School Science and Mathematics, 90(5), 403-418.
3. Lawson, A.E. (1995). Science teaching and the development of thinking. Wadsworth Publishing Company.

4. Krishnashree Achuthan(2011). "The VALUE @ Amrita Virtual Labs Project: Using Web Technology to Provide Virtual Laboratory Access to Students", 2011 IEEE Global Humanitarian Technology Conference, 10/2011.
5. Shahaf, D., Guestrin, C., Horvitz(2012). E.: Trains of thought: Generating information maps. In: Proc. 21st Int. Conf. World Wide Web, pp. 899-908.
6. J.T. (2017). Attitude towards Practical Work and Students' Achievement in Biology: A Case of a Private Senior Secondary School in Gaborone, Botswana. IOSR Journal of Mathematics (IOSR-JM), 13(4).
7. Okam, C.C., and Zakari, I.I. (2017). Impact of Laboratory-Based Teaching Strategy on Students' Attitudes and Mastery of Chemistry in Katsina Metropolis, Katsina State, Nigeria. International Journal of Innovative Research and Development, 6(1), 112.
8. Shana, Z.J., and Abulibdeh, E.S. (2020). Science practical work and its impact on students' science achievement. Journal of Technology and Science Education, 10(2), 199-215.

9

The Future of Digital Universities in India: Teacher-Student Attitude (TSA) Towards Access to Effective Education Through Virtual Mode

Prof Dr Rakesh Kumar Yogi, Dr Deepika and Dr Shweta Chaudhary

Abstract

The digital education model is not a new concept in contemporary India, as in traditional teaching methodology the use of ICT for distance learning is quite common practice followed in past decades. In recent years, Indian education sector has gone through major teaching challenges due to Covid pandemic, that restricted traditional classroom methodologies in both teaching and learning perspectives. To overcome such situations education sector somehow found transformation in form of transition from traditional to virtual model, these shifts opened possibilities for all ages to communicate as well as learn in the age of severe pandemic situations. However, in contemporary time after post-Covid now, when situations are most likely shifting towards normal in such developments government of India has proposed for the modification of higher education with implementations of Digital Universities in India to enhance easy access towards higher education. Within these parameters this paper tries to explore 'The Future of Digital Universities in India'. Leaning toward quantitative methodology based on survey and case study conducted between February 2022 and March 2022 this paper will therefore, discuss the attitude of teacher-student towards the access, scope and benefits of digitalisation of higher education. Finally, it also explores the areas/channels of barriers and limitations, if any.

Keywords: Digital Education, Higher Education, ICT, Digital University, Attitude, Virtual Learning.

Introduction

In recent years, digital platforms are proved to be a powerful tool for academic activity and eases the monitoring process at every level (such as teaching, lecture delivery and administrative). Moreover, the basic aspects of digitalisation of higher education are to provide security, ensure discipline and provide innovative academic services. During pandemic these fundamental aspects of higher education are fulfilled through digital solutions to some extent. The digitalisation brings efficiency, effectiveness and transparency into the overall monitoring process. Specifically, management and administrative activities can be easily monitored along with the date and time of the activity which makes things more explicit (Habib et al. 2021, 522). It is witnessed that during Covid-19 online teaching and professional development appear to be more approachable in a social distancing restriction through virtual mode (Mosteanu et al., 2020). Therefore, digital campus, in its whole concept, can help to have a continuity for the education process in the era of uncertainty (Mo?teanu 2021, 1).

Digital technologies have transformed the way institutions and society interact with each other and also transform value. Therefore, an investment in developing the university campus based on modern technologies consequently benefits the entire economy (Yadav and Pavlou, 2014). Decades back such virtual interaction for instance Hamill and colleagues in their book 'new development in online marketing' defined as new global culture in form of (web 2.0) that has transformed the way people use online platforms; their expectations and experience for such uses (Hamill et al. 2010, 181). The implementation of digitalisation in higher education has been discussed in many international research (Hamill et al., 2010; Hazemi et al., 2012, Yadav and Pavlou, 2014) and also provided its scope of use and implementation (Evdoshin and Pesotskaya, 2019, Mosteanu et al. 2020; Marin, 2021, Mosteanu et al. 2021, Habib et al. 2021, Javorcik and Havlaskova 2021) during the Covid-19 situation.

In previous research on 'academic institutions in the digital era in India' Velmurungan Ch (2012) had discussed that how "E-learning has given a new dimension to the distance education in the world, it is yet to catch up in Indian universities". In India e-learning is a very recent phenomenon and currently restricted to IT sector. However, he detailed that in some of the Indian universities, television broadcasting is commonly used in distance learning and distance education courses are also being conducted through video-conferencing but, they are not catching up as fast as expected (Ch 2012, 98). Over a period of time education sector in India has also gone through many transitions and transformation (Chatwal, 2019); and these emerging technologies have always followed risk routes before these are finally assimilated in a society. (Chaudhary and Sharma, 2019, 2). While, following the technological concept of 'Digital Universities' in recent Budget 2022 government of India has proposed for the start-up of Digital universities in India, while already the first digital university in Kerla has set-up in 2021 by state government and is in progress. These technological advancements and opening are providing scope for research scholars in contemporary academic research practices in the area of 'future of digital universities in India'. Emerging as a recent field of enquiry with limited work done in both quantitative as well as qualitative methodological perspective (Velmurungan Ch 2012; Chaudhary and Sharma, 2019; Chatwal 2019), present paper will look into the scope, benefits and limitations of higher education through virtual mode. As virtual education likely to provide some engagements in learning during the time of pandemic, considering such previous implementation and experiences of online teaching and learning as a piolet study, this paper will therefore detail the teacher-student attitude (TSA) towards future of digitalisation of higher education in India.

Objectives

1. To find out teacher-student preferences on how digital universities will beneficial in promoting meaningful higher education.
2. To find out what teacher-students think on the role of digital universities in promoting quality education.
3. Explore the differing expectations of students as a user of digital platforms and to examine the perceived barriers in adoption of technology as medium or channel of communication (such as its success in higher education among those who are marginalised).

Research Questions

1. To find out how and in what ways Digital universities will benefit students in learning and pursuing higher education?
2. Does complete virtual mode will be beneficial for both teachers and students for learning and self-development in any sense?
3. In what ways it will promote quality education?
4. Does digital platforms will be beneficial in building practical learning environment?
5. What will be the measure of barriers between teacher-student interactions in mode of digital education other than technical noise?
6. How with other barriers (such as income, gender, reach for gadgets, use of gadgets) the digital education will possibly able to provide gateways of learning among the student of marginalised groups?

Methods

The Questionnaire survey is conducted between February and March 2022. 50 students and 20 Assistant Professors are randomly selected from different departments of Gurugram University. A structured electronic questionnaire is used including both open as well as closed questions and in-total 10 questions are asked to gather teacher-student perception and attitudes on the subject of scope and future of digital universities in India. Aside from personal details two separate questionnaires are used where some questions were similar for both the teacher-student participants while few questions are differently formatted. However, to draw suggestion and limitations leaning towards case study method two face-to-face focus groups are conducted in the month of March in university campus (one for teachers and one for students) where primary qualitative data is collected.

Interpretation and Analysis (Student Group)

Among 50 students who participated in survey 84 percent students are of age group between 20-25 and rest 16 percent student belong to the age group of 25-30 (see figure-9.1 in Annexure A). Among them 56 percent are female participants and 44 percent are male (see figure-9.2 in Annexure A). Around 60 percent of students are studying in post-graduation, 36 percent are studying in under-graduate courses and only four percent of student participated who are enrolled in Ph.D (see figure-3 in Annexure A) in various departments of Gurugram University. On asking their opinion on the concept of digital universities

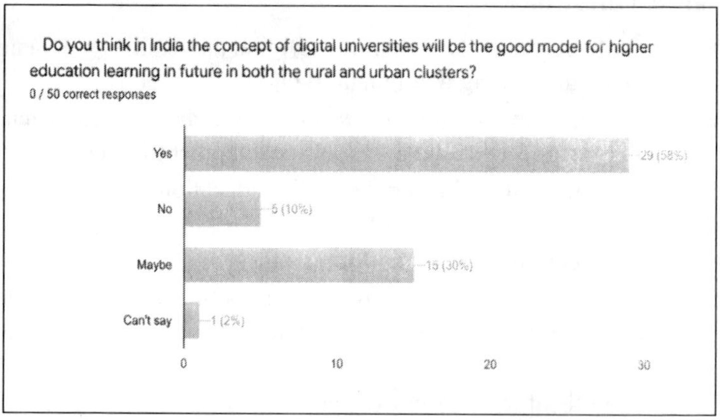

Figure - 9.1: Detailing the student responses for digital universities and their benefit in India.

as a good model of teaching for higher education in both urban and rural clusters around 58 percent of student says yes, 30 percent student says maybe, 10 percent students say no and two percent student opt for can't say (see figure-9.1).

On the question regarding scope of digital platform for online practical work and online assignments submissions about 62 percent student replied yes, 18 percent replied no, 10 percent say maybe and 10 percent say can't say (see figure-9.2).

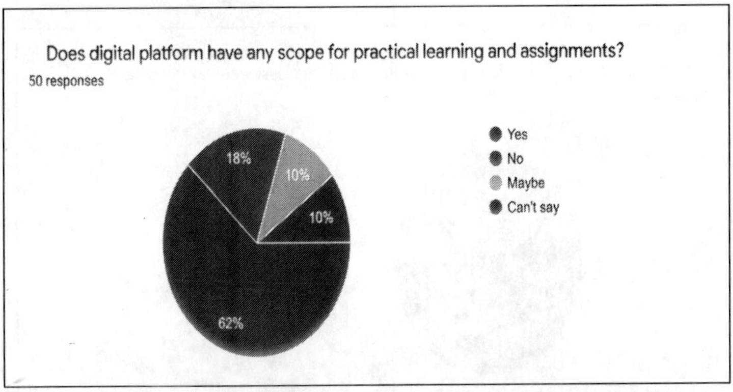

Figure-9.2: Detailing the student responses for scope of digital platform for practical and assignments

On asking their what they think on online classes have any effect on the physical or mental health 60 percent student strictly say yes online classes can affect their physical and mental health as they say overuse of

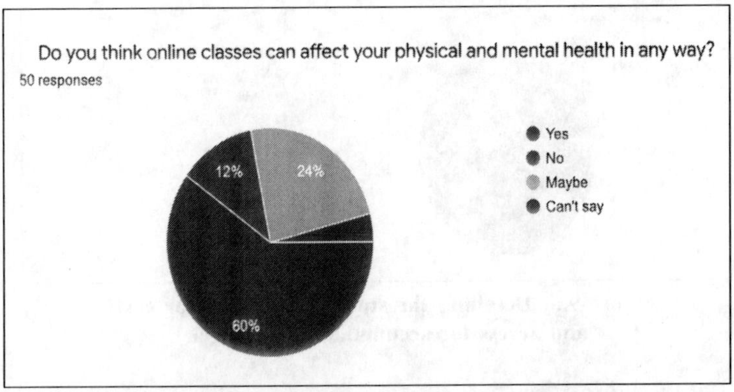

Figure-9.3: Detailing the responses of students for use of digital platform and their effect on health.

technology can have negative effect on their eye sight, while some student referred that it can also turned into addiction of technology. 24 percent student replied maybe, 12 percent student believe that it has no side-effect on their health in any way and rest of four percent opt out for can't say (see figure-9.3).

Remembering the experiences of online classes during Covid-19 around 84 percent students answer yes for facing technical issues, 14 percent says they do not face any technical issues and rest of 2 percent respond for maybe (see figure-9.4).

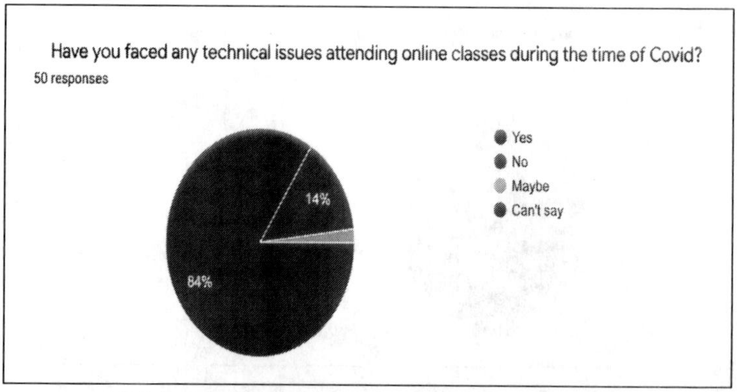

Figure-9.4: Detailing the responses for technical issues that are faced in online classes during Covid-19.

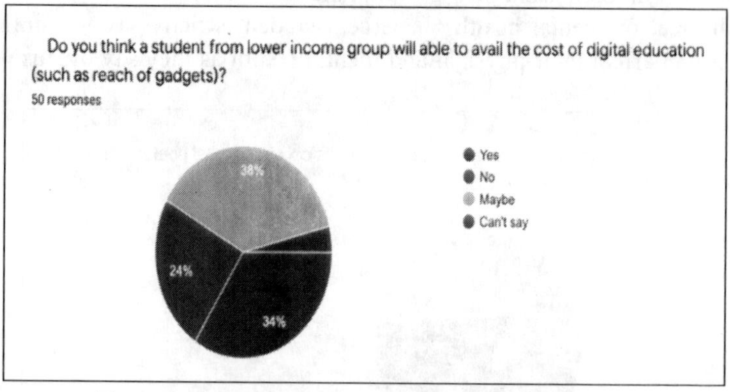

Figure-9.5: Detailing the student responses for cost and access for accumulation of gadget.

On asking their responses for marginalised group students and access to accumulation of gadgets 34 percent students says yes, they will spend for the accumulations of technological gadgets because it is a one-time expense that will cover the cost of admission fee, hostel fees, mess charges, travel expenses', clothing, books stationery and many more; 38 percent student say maybe, 24 percent student opt for no and only four percent opt for can't say (see figure-9.5).

Interpretation and Analysis (Teachers Group)

Figure-9.6 shows that 45 percent of teachers think that the concept of digital university is a good model for higher education, 35 percent say that it may be possible that digital university can get successful in both the rural and urban cluster, 15 percent of our respondents feels that the concept of digital university will not be a well-turned model and 5 percent are not sure about the concept of digital university.

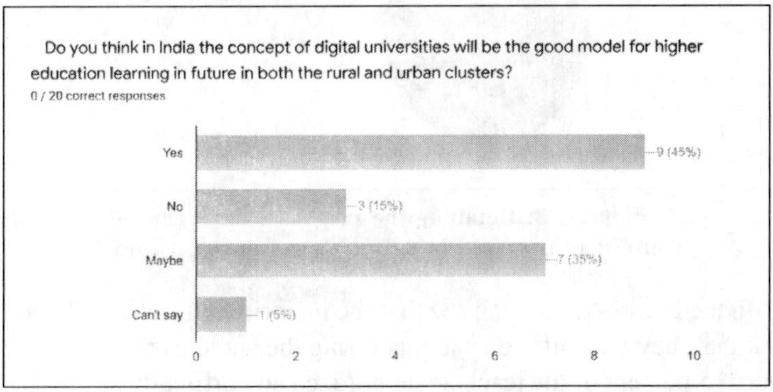

Figure-9.6: Detailing the teacher responses for digital universities and their benefit in India.

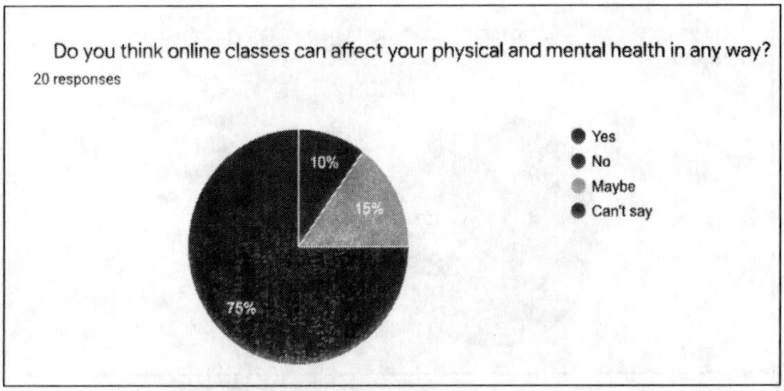

Figure-9.7: Detailing the responses of teacher for use of digital platform and their effect on health.

In figure-9.7 we can see that a large majority of the teachers (75 percent) think that online classes can affect physical and mental health, 15 percent teachers are not sure about this and 10 percent believe that online classes do not affect physical or mental health of the students.

From figure-9.8 it is evident that the majority of the teachers (75 percent) faced technical issues during online classes while 25 percent of the teachers faced no issues taking online classes.

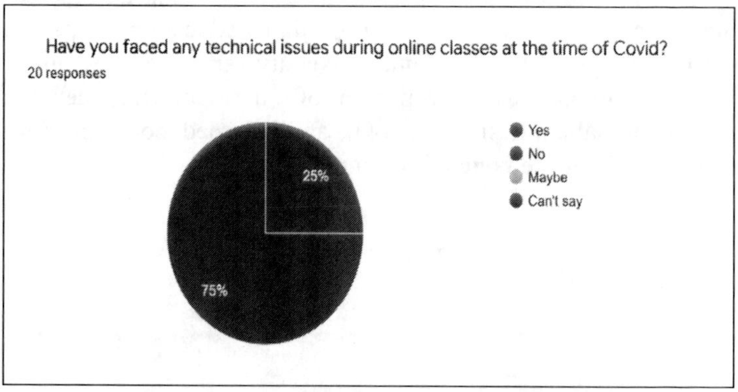

Figure-9.8: Detailing the responses for technical issues that are faced in online classes during Covid-19.

In the Figure-9.9 we can see that the majority of teachers (75 percent) think that they face difficulty in mentoring the students through an online mode, 15 percent of the teachers do not face any difficulty and 10 percent believe that there may be difficulty in mentoring the students via online mode.

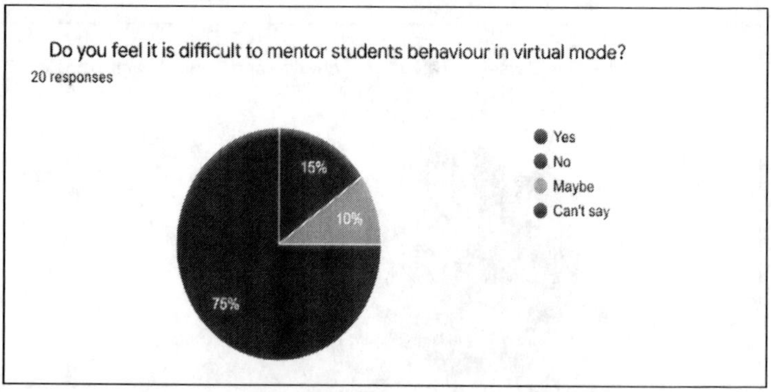

Figure-9.9: Detailing how teacher mentor the student behaviour in virtual mode.

Digital University : Acceptance and Oppositions

Many students believe that yes teaching through digital platform will allow a fair chance for creative learning, some of them says it will make topics creative and thus easy to understand although, are not clearly able to specify the routes for such creativity as for some these were limited with use of (PPT, live projects, sharing of video content and presentations). In resonance with the ideas of Mosteanu and colleague that digital universities will be helping reduction of water, electricity and paper waste, as many activities will be conducted online, and the water and paper supply necessity will be much lower, compared with the necessary one used for a face-to-face campus (Mosteanu 2021, 1) some students discuss that how digital education will approaches for less time consumption, saving water, electricity and paper, thus will cut down the campus infrastructure cost, Sweety Yadav post-graduation student says "Yes, due to flexible timings and locations situations we can any time connects with our teachers"; "if implement in planned way everyday induction and activity would be easily possible without any time barriers" says (Gaurav, M. A media studies).

The meaningful and creative learning aspect stem from the methods and initiatives of teaching, though in student opinions online classes would to hamper the practical learning experience for the students and the overall competitiveness "It helps develop critical thinking and logical reasoning skills in students" says (Arushi, M.A media studies) she adds "Yes, online teaching would approach towards creativity and will give a chance to use technologically". Certainly, it will give fair chance to all and with upcoming implementation of new education policy it would be quite beneficial. In focus group some students clearly give statements such as "It will definitely work for rural youth specially for girls due to safety reasons some time they have to drop out education" in similar context Mosteanu and colleague reported that when comes about uncertainty and safe environment, Digital campus comes to support (Mosteanu 2021, 1). In another study Velmurungan Ch (2012) detailed that the only option for working students is to pursue higher studies, either by leaving their jobs or go on leave-without-pay. It is in this situation that e-learning can play an essential role of a virtual education center, where the student and teacher can interact through various interfaces, from different geographical locations.

Discussing on the issues of presences of barriers or distraction in virtual communication other than technical noises remembering their online classroom experience some student connect it with the issues of available personal space and surroundings. Naina student of M.Com for instance say "the comfort shell that a student makes in their own home during an online class is one of the reasons of distraction from the running class". They say sometime family environment (that might be different for different person), infrastructure facilities and peer groups connections are responsible for such distractions "yes, sometimes we are distracted by the family members or environment too but such distractions can be handled with effective management. I think digital learning is the future of education so it should be brought into practice by a well-planned execution" (Nishant, M.A Political Science).

In opposition with the concept of online education and digital universities however, some students opposed and statement that a physical environment is different from a digital environment where they have much better chances of learning. Making an assignment and participating in face-to-face practical is a process of fun for all when students enjoy their work, they understand it in a better way. With being creative, one can think of multiple solutions to solve a problem. Thus, they demand for digitalisation in traditional classroom where they ask to follow such innovative methodology in for face-to-face teaching.

Findings

1. Digital teaching is found as a significant platform for creative learning, as both student and teachers articulates that online teaching and learning are creative mode of understand topic and concepts.
2. Some student recommends that if the model will be implemented and monitored well then it will significantly helpful for working students and young students in Rural sectors in India and specifically for young girls.
3. Both student as well as teacher believes that digital education will approaches for less time consumption, saving water, electricity and paper, thus will cut down the campus infrastructure cost.
4. In the case of evening courses female students as well as teachers' mention that it is safer for them to induct through virtual class room in late at night and household tasks are also performed because of less time consumption even employment opportunities will also increase because they will able to apply for an evening and late-night options.
5. Similar to the study of Habib and colleague (2021) it is found that it is easiest to control the presence of students in virtual

classroom to avoid distraction as it is not possible in the case of face-to-face classroom teaching.

6. In some cases, it is reasonably found that family environment, infrastructure facilities and peer groups connections are responsible for communication distractions other than technical noises.
7. Access and accumulation of technological gadgets is not found as an issue of expense because some students accounts that it is one-time expense that will cover the cost of admission fee, hostel fees, mess charges, travel expenses', clothing, books stationery.

Limitation

1. Classroom teaching is found as a better solution for practical learning as student suggests that each teacher follows different pedagogy. It depends how much technical savvy they are and also are capable of using such technology to create practical learning possible through digital modes.
2. In some cases, physical environment is observed as a better platform of teaching as some students believe that face-to-face learning is different from a digital environment where they have much better chances to learn.
3. Majority of teacher and student respond that they face technical errors in online classes.
4. In majority of cases, it is found that online classes can affect their physical and mental health as overuse of technology can have negative effect on their eye sight and even in psychological development (such as lack of confidence in public speaking, language skills, logical and reasoning skills).
5. Majority of teachers feel that it is difficult to mentor student behaviour in virtual platforms as they depend on cameras.

Conclusion

It is clear from these responses that there is substantial scope for the implementations of future of Digital universities in India. With the help of planned executions and monitoring system technology will give boost to higher education sector and will increase the demand of online courses. As both teacher and student gave positive insights for acceptance and use of technology in many ways. They find online education as a platform of creativity, flexibility and innovative learning. In addition, they justify it with advantageous such as (less time consumption, can go paperless, spaceless, enhance saving of time, money).

Other then, attributes such as gender, income, time, space, location have significant relation with teacher-student attitude (TSA) choices for adopting and opposing Digital Universities. Although they observed and already experienced the limitation and benefits of online classes during the pandemic, in-spite of the fact they are positively in the favours of implementation of digital universities in India as for them advantageous are more than the disadvantageous.

References

Avdoshin, S., and Pesotskaya, E. (2019). SuperBook Concept for a Digital University. CEUR, 2514, pp. 248-258. Retrieved from CEUR-ws.org

Chatwal, T. (2019). Digitalisation of Higher Education in India: A Boom or A Bane. Research Journal of Humanities and Social Sciences, 10(4), 1083-1088. doi: 10.5958/2321-5828.2019.00178.5

Chaudhary, P., and Sharma, K. K. (2019). Implementation of digital strategy in higher educational institutions in Indiathan. J. Business and Globalisation, 1-25. Retrieved from https://www.researchgate.net/publication/331113539

Habib, M. N., Jamal, W., Khalil, U., and Khan, Z. (2021). Transforming universities in interactive digital platform: case of city university of science and information technology. Education and Information Technologies, 26, 517-541.

Hamill, J., Tagg, S., Stevenson, A., and Vescovi, T. (2010). New developments in online marketing'. Journal of Marketing Management, 26(3-4), 181-186. doi:https://doi.org/10.1080/02672571003640524

Hazemi, R., Hailes, S., and Wilbur, S. (2012). The Digital University: Reinventing the Academy. Springer.

Javorcik, T., and Havlaskova, T. (2021). Future Teachers' Attitude Toward Using Digital Technology in Instruction: Questionnaire Survey Results. 20th European Conference on e-Learning. doi:DOI: 10.34190/EEL.21.047

Marin, L. (2021). On the Possibility of a Digital University Thinking and Mediatic Displacement at the University. Springer.

Mosteanu, N. R. (2021). Digital Campus - a future former investment in education for a sustainable society. E3S Web of Conferences ICIES 2020 (pp. 1-5). EDP Sciences. Retrieved from http://creativecommons.org/licenses/by/4.0/

Mosteanu, N. R., Faccia, A., Cavaliere, L. L., and Bhatia, S. (2020). Digital Technologies Implementation Within Financial and Banking System During Socio Distancing Restriction-Back to the Future. International Journal of Advanced Research in Engineering and Technology (IJARET), 11(6), 307-30=15. Retrieved from athttp:/ /iaeme.com/Home/issue/IJARET?

Velmurugan, C. (2012). Rearch On E-Learning Initiatives With Special References To Academics Institution In The Digital Era In India- An Introduction. International Journal of Library and Information Management, 97-102.

Yadav, M. S., and Pavlou, P. (2014). Marketing in Computer-Mediated Environments: Research Synthesis and New Directions. Journal of Marketing, 78, 20-40.

10

Blended Learning: Teachers' Perceptions in the Changing Dynamics of Teaching-Learning

Prof K Srinivas and Kajal Yadav

Abstract

Blended learning is an innovative strategy that integrates face-to-face teaching with web-based learning. This mode usage is increasing slowly and gradually. As a result, it is necessary to investigate the theoretical foundations of blended learning research as well as how blended learning adoption and implementation in the Indian setting. Western studies done in past proved that improving teaching-learning environment blended learning is an effective technique. But in India, due to lack of awareness, infrastructure, proper access, digital gadgets, etc. is lacking that affect implementation of blended learning. However, in the new normal, it is critical to know and appreciate the value of blended learning in India in order to improve educational quality.

The purpose of this qualitative study is to understand teacher perceptions of blended learning as an instructional methodology for addressing the needs of diverse learners. The researcher explored the perceptions of teachers of higher education institutions. The researcher examined the experiences of teachers as they learned to adapt pedagogical practices to address the learning needs of twenty first century students through blended learning. The researcher sought to gain a better understanding of how teachers perceived that utilising a blended learning methodology impacted pedagogical beliefs, practices, and student learning. The paper also aims to highlight the challenges faced by teachers. In this exploratory study, the researcher used the qualitative research methodology. Based on the research questions guiding this study, data was collected from questionnaires, semi-structured interviews with fifteen educators. The researcher analyzed data using thematic analysis.

Introduction

The use of new technologies in teaching and learning, e.g. e-learning, can assist in both the enhancement of traditional teaching methods and the development of students' technical skills. At present, there are several e-learning technologies available (Garrison, 2011). Many of these address mobility of student learning, which enables students to learn anywhere, anytime, and with various devices (Herrington, 2012). These include learning management systems providing a virtual platform for students to access teaching resources and interact with peers and other students, web-based flexible learning environments, and media to encourage collaborative learning among students. In regard to developing technological skills, a wide range of technologies can be used to assist in training students. These can range from videos for demonstration, recording, and reflective analysis purposes to simulation-based e-learning (SIMBEL) systems.

A recent circular (2021) by the University Grants Commission (UGC) proposes that all higher education institutions (HEI) should teach 40 percent of any course online and the rest 60 percent offline. The concept note circulated by the UGC argues that this blended model of teaching and learning paves the way for increased student engagement in learning, enhanced student-teacher interactions, improved student learning outcomes, and more flexible learning and teaching environments, among other things.

The policy document on education, NEP-2020, highlight the major objective of blended learning is "to make the process of learning not only impactful but also engaging, encouraging, interesting and challenging for the learner". It has also stressed the need for extensive use of technology in teaching to enhance learning in students, to attain the goal of 100 percent literacy. The policy calls for the development of digital infrastructure as well as to empower teachers to create high-quality e-learning resources. Importantly, blended learning will assist in achieving the NEP-2020 objectives of internationalising indigenous knowledge through digitized course content while maintaining traditional learning and teacher roles. Additionally, to improve teaching-learning skills there is an emphasis to increase the use of ICT.

According to the UNESCO World Education Report "Teachers and Teaching in a Changing World" (1998), as new technologies emerge, the teaching profession is shifting from a focus on teacher-centered lecture-based instruction to a focus on student-centered, interactive learning environments (UNESCO, 1998). The use of ICT is widely acknowledged as a key component of educational reform to design and implement educational programme. At the same time, no modern technology can substitute the place of a teacher. Electronic devices, in conjunction with the teacher, can help to enhance learning experiences. Blended Learning "New Models for the New Normal" UNESCO (2020) and World Health Organisation (2020) reported that the Covid pandemic has accelerated the uptake of distance learning approaches across the globe.

On the other hand, traditional teaching is now referred to as a passive teaching approach since it discourages students from practical usage. Only focusing on face-to-face interaction leaves no room for active and collaborative learning, nor does it allow educators to use higher-order thinking skills. Many university students believe that what is taught in class is boring and unrelated to practical critical thinking and analytical reasoning requirements. They don't frequently see the classroom environment as stimulating or encouraging. Students' experience is changing as the way they learn and communicate in and out of class while adapting and implementing technology. As a result, teachers must reorganise the learning process and change their teaching resources. According to Laster, (2005), having a diverse group of students with varying learning preferences, the use of several learning modalities to convey the appropriate content in the appropriate format.

Rationale

Blended learning is important because it breaks down the traditional walls of teaching, one that doesn't work for all students. It is a live interaction between teacher and student that uses technology as well as face-to-face teaching. This type of learning allows flexibility for students and teachers. It offers flexible time frames that can be personalised to each person, offering them the ability to learn at their own pace. It allows students to personalise their learning experiences by using additional tools beyond the classroom. Learners can identify areas that need more attention and personalise their learning schedule that suits their study plan through blended tools. Teachers can also use blended learning methods to enhance their lessons. They can interact with students more efficiently by monitoring their growth and giving instant feedback. This is a modernised way of teaching that can have a positive impact on a student's training experience. This type of learning prepares students to work at digital-based jobs that require technology proficiencies.

This paper is an exploration of the need for a blended learning approach in addressing rapid technology change in higher education to gauge learning and teaching efficiency and evaluate content and use of new technologies in education. The key purpose of this research is to understand the teacher's view on blended learning, what are their perceptions towards it, and the real ground phase of blended learning in higher education. Next, the paper also attempts to know the challenges and barriers of blended learning while implementing and adopting it.

Review of Literature

The reviewed paper results are discussed below:

- Shah (2020) examined ICT competency among teachers and teacher educators. The article offers suggestions from teacher educators to include ICT in the classroom.
- Maheswari and Seth (2019) used Content understanding, student academic achievement, cognitive capability, Maheswari and Seth peer collaboration, in-class involvement, and student inclination with a learning environment to assess the success of flipped classroom settings. Results have proven that flipped classroom is useful for students.
- Nayer and Koul (2019) conducted an experiment with Indian students looking into various learning tools divided into three groups- Doodling, note-taking, doodling, and note-taking; each with 40 participants. Both the doodling and note-taking groups had higher recall efficiency, indicating that blending is the best strategy to produce a beneficial learning outcome.
- Carrim and Dresselhaus (2019) conducted a survey-based study to assess the self-efficacy of Indian female students receiving dialogue education via blended learning. The outcome was determined using a 5-point Likert scale. The authors discovered that a multicultural background has a significant impact on the efficacy of seals among female students in India. They also discovered that blended learning was efficient in boosting self-efficacy.
- Dey and Bandyopadhyay (2018) did a comparative true experimental study on blended learning. Researchers used audio-visual aids and online classes' expert teachers to conduct their research. According to a study, blended learning is quite efficient in giving quality education to underprivileged students. A blended learning environment can boost achievement and improve the well-being of students.

- Lalima and Dangwal (2017) study talked about the various types of computer-assisted learning, including blended learning. They discovered that efficient implementation of the blended learning technique takes a great deal of effort and a good mindset. The study also shows that the utility of implementing blended learning methodologies in the Indian educational system can help with a variety of contemporary educational issues.
- Subramaniyan (2015) published a review paper that comprises a thorough examination of prior papers in order to comprehend the characteristics, methods, and pedagogical perspectives of blended learning strategies in the Indian context. In order to handle the new problems of the twenty-first century, it was determined that blended learning methodologies are extremely beneficial and may be the future of Indian teaching and learning environments.

After discussing papers, it can be said that blended learning improves students' understanding and can be a game-changer in the field of education. But proper implementation and adoption of blended learning is missing in the Indian scenario.

Definitions of Blended Learning

Despite its popularity, blended learning is defined differently by different authors, researchers. There are many definitions of blended learning-

- Bates (2015) suggested that blended learning has many forms:
  (a) Using technology as classroom aids (e.g., PowerPoint slides, clickers);
  (b) Using learning management system to support classroom teaching (e.g., online discussions);
  (c) Using captured lectures for flipped classrooms;
  (d) Keeping short periods of lecture for hands-on experience or training in the campus followed by concentrated study time online;
  (e) Hybrid or flexible learning necessitates the redesign of teaching to enable allow students to do a majority of their learning online and just visit campus for specific in-person sessions (e.g., laboratories).
- Clayton Christensen Institute highlighted an "element of student control over time, pace, place and/or path" as well as the

significance of integrated training across the online and face-to-face modalities (Horn and Staker, 2014).

- Watson (2011) defines blended learning as "a method of personalising learning, allowing thoughtful reflection, and differentiating instruction from student to student across a diverse group of learners by combining the best features of online delivery of educational content with the best features of classroom interaction and live instruction."
- Graham (2006) defined blended learning systems as a combination of face-to-face with computer-mediated instruction.
- Ross and Gage (2006) blended learning enhanced courses that incorporate online supplementary components within traditional courses without reducing face-to-face time rather in-class time is replaced by online course work.
- Laster (2005) defined blended learning as primarily concerned with combining two distinct paradigms: synchronous classroom instruction and asynchronous internet instruction.
- Garrison and Kanuka (2004) explained "blended learning is a thoughtful integration of classroom face-to-face learning experiences with online learning experiences."
- Singh (2003) blended learning is the use of different delivery modes to enhance teaching-learning. Instructors can employ live chats, self-paced learning, instant messaging, social networking, blogs and forums, software, and webinars to incorporate online opportunities into their classes.
- Driscoll (2002) defines blended learning as the intermixing of any instructional forms to attain an educational purpose.

Objectives

The core objectives of the study are:

- To understand the faculty/ teachers' perceptions towards blended learning
- To explore the challenges of blended learning faced by higher educational institutions

Research questions

In order to fulfil the objectives and current scenario of blended learning in higher education, the following research questions have been identified.

- What are teachers' views on blended learning adoption and implementation in higher education?
- How do applications of blended learning influence teaching-learning?
- What are the main issues and problems teachers perceive of using blended mode?

Methodology

The methodology design of every research gives focus to the research and gives direction to the researcher. This helps to attain the objectives set out.

Qualitative research with exploratory research design is planned for this research to understand participants' opinions, their experiences and to gather in-depth insights into the problems.

Under the methodology section, the following would be looked at: the study tools, the locale, the population/ participant of the study, and the sampling strategy.

Research study tools

This research study tool includes a survey questionnaire via Google form and semi-structured interviews via telephonic conversations and G-meet. Questionnaires included both open and closed-ended questions. Interviews contained a set of questions not strictly in a fixed pattern but structured such that the subject matter of the research is not lost.

Locale of the study

The principal objective is to determine the perception towards blended learning in higher educational institutions and the grounded reality of it and for the same Delhi-based universities, colleges, and higher educational institutions were chosen as the locale for this study.

Participants Selection and Sampling

Higher education institutions were taken. Purposive sampling and snowball sampling from non-probability sampling has been used for the research because the sample has been drawn from the smaller population.

Data analyses

The data collected is subject to qualitative analysis. Using thematic analysis, data is analyzed.

Result and Discussion

Based on the responses received from participants in regard to blended learning perceptions, challenges, adoption, and implementations in the Indian scenario the findings are discussed below:

Demographic profile of teachers

As shown in the given below Tables, the educators who participated in this study's personal profile details have been tabulated. The educators' demographic profile is distributed as per designations, gender, and teaching experience using blended mode.

Designations	
Heads	2
Professors	3
Associate Professor	2
Assistant Professor	8

Gender distribution	
Females	5
Males	10

Blended learning experiences

At present teachers at higher education institutions are not using a blended mode of teaching, rather it is either online or offline. Teachers use chalk and board methods in face to face traditional classrooms. During the pandemic they used online platforms like zoom, gmeet, google classroom. However, the teacher highlighted that soon blended mode will be adopted and implemented to make an active learning process.

Teaching experience using the blended mode	
Teaching using the blended mode	0
The initial phase of blended mode	2
No blended mode teaching experience	13

Faculty perceptions and views on Blended Learning

Survey and online interactions were conducted to analyze the perceptions of teachers and to identify common themes among the group of educators. The researcher transcribed each survey and discussion.

The table below identifies the common perceptions of teachers that emerged from interview data that pertained to blended learning as an instructional methodology. Educators had strong perceptions regarding understanding blended learning as an instructional methodology, implementing and managing a blended learning environment, the strategic use of technology to enhance learning, differentiating and importance of instructors with technology-enabled learning, and immediate support and feedback to learners.

Table visually displays the questions bullets asked during the survey and semi-structured, one-to-one discussion and the theme to reveal their perceptions towards the blended learning.

Pointers	Emergent Themes
Understanding of Blended Learning	Instructional Methodology Multiple teaching and learning approaches
NEP & UGC emphasis on blended mode	Uninterrupted teaching and learning Distribution in course
Implementing and Managing a Blended Learning Environment	Not institutionalized yet
Teachers' attitudes and beliefs	Personalized Learning Changed mindset Increase in Workload
Challenges and problems	Training and development Infrastructure, access, internet connectivity Professional Development and technical skills
Strengths and benefits	Active learning & student engagement Improves Quality

The survey is categorised based on the research questions to ensure the survey questions reflected research objectives and topic of challenges faced by teachers' while adopting and implementing blended learning. The themes were keywords, concepts, or words mentioned by each participant.

Challenges faced by teachers

The challenges of offering Blended Learning are:

Attitudinal Barriers and Psycho-social well-being- It was observed that female participants faced dual responsibilities while agreeing to blended mode, they believe that their workload increased after online. They had to manage online classes assigned tasks like pre-preparations and household duties as well. While few respondents mentioned that we need to change the mindset towards online or blended mode. They said that blended mode is so prevalent, we are using just online or either offline mode but towards blended mode, we need to change our thoughts and gradually start initiating it in our teaching.

Teachers believe that the pandemic situation impacted education, students were worried, it is essential that psychological counseling to students is essentially other than classes. In the future such situations do not emerge, we need to set plans. An online method shall be optional, not compulsory. It may overburden teachers. Let them blend it as per their discretion. Such responses are also received while collecting data.

Course Design: Designing a blended learning course that maximizes the potential of both the face-to-face and online components raises questions: How much of each modality should comprise a course? How to design the blended course? Students and faculty should not view the face-to-face aspect of a blended course and the online element as separate components. The instructional design perspective requires a re-evaluation of teaching and learning to blend or harmonize the distinction between the two made even more formidable by the presence of the new learners. Facilities to record videos and devices to support it are also the major difficulties.

Time commitment: There is a lot of time required for designing and delivering a blended learning course as compared to traditional classroom teaching-learning. The increased time commitment involved in a blended course is regarded as the number one challenge by faculty. Initially, it takes time for the teachers to set up with all resources and timing and further students take time to understand this mode of learning.

Instructional Design and Professional Development of teachers-Faculty to teach blended learning courses to need to be well conversant with new emerging technologies in designing such courses and delivering media. To ensure a successful blended learning experience for students there must be faculty support for course redesign and learning new teaching and technology skills. The course redesign support must be provided to faculty. Effective technological skills, training, assistance, support needs must be accomplished. Faculty indicated that they needed to acquire new teaching skills such as how to foster online learning communities, facilitate online discussion forums, and address and manage students' online learning problems. Later updating is important.

Access and technical Challenges: The major technical challenges include digital connectivity, limited digital skills, Internet and network facility at places. Secondly, access to digital gadgets, not all students have electronic devices access. Additionally, technical challenges are not about getting technology to work on networks. Rather, they consist of ensuring the success of the programme by utilising and supporting appropriate technologies and consensus building on students regarding the software and technology that can be used. Ensuring participants can successfully use the technology. rather than resisting the urge to use technology simply because it is available were major issues highlighted by participants.

Other major issues identified by faculty were : It excludes the visually impaired and blind students. No LMS is addressing them at all. They feel challenged teaching such students. Another is to get hold of students. On the pretext of network issues, they try to avoid timely submissions. Teachers wrote that managing and monitoring the progress of students, results, and exams evaluations are challenging in online mode. Cheating has become a common feature. They don't try to learn because they have an open book exam.

Conclusion

To sum up, blended learning is, to a large extent, the solution to the challenges that our educational system faced. Blended learning is becoming one of the most popular pedagogical concepts, and it will continue to grow as technology and learning analytics improve. It can help students become more interested in studying, as well as boost their attitude. If properly planned, it has the potential to become the future of the educational system. Following NEP 2020 and UGC concept note, slowly and gradually the focus will shift to its adoption and implementation. Its execution necessitates the use of a pre-designed learning or learning management system that can be simply implemented in any educational institution.

Most universities provide faculty members with course management systems, such as Blackboard, smart boards, and others as a way to organise and transmit course materials to students. In order to assess the pedagogical value of blended learning at a university-level first, it is necessary to view the environment through a critical lens and adequately train faculty in the need for and use of the features of the blended learning and learning management software (LMS). The researcher investigates the various pedagogical and theoretical issues of incorporating blended learning in higher education, and critically examines the issues involved in implementing the programme.

As technology innovations spread, types of blends will emerge and various technologies will be used in education, but the basic question to be solved will remain the same: "How can we design such learning environments to facilitate learning effectively?" The response is that we should investigate how to include constructivist and collaborative models into blended learning environments, with the goal of educating students in a more creative and imaginative manner.

The integration of face-to-face and online learning environments should be carefully and strategically planned in order to get the most benefits from this strategy. More research and development should be done on how to make a good combination. Seminars, discussion forums, and awareness programme for teachers, students, and parents should be organised to better understand blended learning methodologies and their benefits. It is in our best interests to begin using blended learning as soon as possible.

References

- Allen, E., Seaman, J., Garrett, A. (2013). Changing Course: Ten Years of Tracking Online Education in the United States. Wellesley, MA: Babson College.
- Bates, T. 2015. Synchronous and Asynchronous Tools. Global perspectives, local designs. Pfeiffer.
- Buran, Anna and Evseeva, Arina. (2015). Prospects of Blended Learning Implementation at Technical University. Procedia - Social and Behavioral Sciences. 206. 177-182. http://dx.doi.org/10.1016/j.sbspro.2015.10.049
- Carrim, N. M., and Dresselhaus, F. (2019). Vicarious education, dialogüe education and self-efficacy among Indian female students in a diversity management course. Africa Education Review, 16(5), 29-46.
- Das, B and Das, M. (2021). Are you eager to adopt blended learning outside and inside classroom? Centurion University of Technology and Management. Odisha. Retrieved from https://www.edexlive.com/opinion/2021/jun/02/are-you-eager-to-adopt-blended-learning-in-classrooms-not-so-fast-21294.html
- Driscoll, M. (2002). Psychological foundations of instructional design. Trends and Issues in Instructional Design and Technology, pp. 57- 69.
- Dey, P., and Bandyopadhyay, S. (2019). Blended learning to improve quality of primary education among underprivileged school children in India. Education and Information Technologies, 24(3), 1995- 2016.
- Garrison, D. R., and Kanuka, H. (2004). Blended learning: Uncovering its transformative potential in higher education. The Internet and Higher Education, 7 (2), 95-105.
- Graham, C. R., and Robison, R. (2006). Realizing the Transformational Potential of Blended Learning: Comparing Cases of Transforming Blends and Enhancing Blends in Higher Education. In the Handbook of Blended Learning: Global Research Perspectives, pp. 83-110. San Francisco.
- Herrington, A., Schrape, J. and Singh, K. (Eds) (2012). Engaging students with learning technologies. Perth: Curtin University.
- Horn, M. B., and Staker, H. (2014). Blended: Using disruptive innovation to improve schools. San Francisco, CA: Jossey Bass.
- IANS. (2021). Indian students comfortable with online learning: Survey. New Delhi. Retrieved from https://www.edexlive.com/opinion/2021/jun/02/are-you-eager-to-adopt-blended-learning percent20in-classrooms-not-so-fast-21294.htmlhttps://timesofindia.indiatimes. percent20com/home/education/news/54-of-indian-students-comfortable-with-online-learning%20survey/articleshow/

82179145.cms

- Lalima, D., and Dangwal, K. L. (2017). Blended learning: An innovative approach. Universal Journal of Educational Research, 5(1), 129-136.
- Laster, S., Otte, G., Picciano, A. G., and Sorg, S. (2005). Redefining Blended Learning. Presentation at the 2005 Sloan-C Workshop on Blended Learning, Chicago.
- Maheshwari, P., and Seth, N. (2019). Effectiveness of flipped classrooms. International Journal of Educational Management.
- McCarthy, J. (2010). Blended learning environments: Using social networking sites to enhance the first-year experience. Australasian Journal of Educational Technology, 26, 729-740.
- Ministry of Education. (2020). National Education Policy. NCERT. Retrieved from https://ncert.nic.in/pdf/nep//NEP_2020.pdf
- Nayar, B., and Koul, S. (2020). The journey from recall to knowledge: A study of two factors- structured doodling and note-taking on a student's recall ability. The International Journal of Educational Management, 34(1), 127-138.
- Ross, B., and Gage, K. (2006). Global perspectives on blending learning in higher education, Handbook of blended learning: Global perspectives, pp. 155- 168. San Francisco, CA: Pfeiffer Publishing.
- Rooney, J, (2003). National Educational Technology Trends: 2011. Transforming Education to Ensure All Students Are Successful in the 21st Century. State Educational Technology Directors Association.
- Shah, G J. (2020). Training for 'ICT in Education' Via Blended Learning Mode: Educators' Experiences and Perceptions. i-Manager's Journal of Educational Technology, 16(4), 42.
- Singh, H. (2003). Building Effective Blended Learning Programs. Educational Technology, 43, 51-54.
- Subramonian, G., and Suprabha, K. (2015). Blended Learning Approach for Enhancing Students' Learning Experiences in a Knowledge Society. Journal of Educational Technology, 11(4), 1-7.
- United Nations. (2020). Policy brief: Education during COVID-19 and beyond. United Nations. Retrieved from https://unsdg.un.org/resources/policy-brief-education-during-covid-19-and-beyond
- UGC. (2020). Blended Mode of Teaching and Learning: Concept Note. New Delhi. Retrieved from https://www.ugc.ac.in/pdfnews/6100340_Concept-Note-Blended-Mode-of-Teaching-and Learning.pdf
- UNESCO. (1998). World declaration on higher education for the twenty-first century: Vision and action. World Conference on Higher Education. Retrieved from https://unesdoc.unesco.org/ark:/48223/pf0000141952
- UNESCO. (1998). World education report 1998: teachers and teaching in a changing world, UNESCO, Paris. Retrieved from http://www.iiep.unesco.org/sites/default/files/nl_1998-2_en.pdf
- UNESCO (2020). UNESCO Rallies International Organisations, Civil Society, and Private Sector Partners in a Broad Coalition to Ensure #LearningNeverStops. UNESCO. Retrieved from https://en.unesco.org/news/unesco-rallies-inter-

national-organisations-civil-society-and-private-sector-partners-broad

- Vaughan, N. D. (2007). Perspectives on blended learning in higher education. International Journal on E- Learning, Vol. 6(1), pp. 81-94.
- Wang, M. J. (2010). "Online collaboration and offline interaction between students using asynchronous tools in blended learning". Australasian Journal of Educational Technology, 26(6), 830-846.
- Watson, J. (2012). Blending learning: The convergence of online and face-to-face education. NACOL. America. Retrieved from https://files.eric.ed.gov/fulltext/ED509636.pdf

11

A Study on Use of Technology in Classroom

M. Rajender and Dr A.N.P.P. Ananthà Lakshmi

Abstract

The technology is a 360° Approach to student success by transforming education, changing how, when and where students learn, and empowering them at every stage of their journey. During the Covid-19 pandemic, technology plays an important role in the teaching and learning process. On the path to personalised learning, technology empowers the students by giving them ownership of how they can transform learning methodology and preparing them for digital futures. With the technology, they can also access the resources beyond the classroom walls and students are inspired to become problem-solvers, critical thinkers, collaborators, creators, etc. The effective use of technology in the teaching and learning process can prepare the students for the twenty first century workforce with modern technology skills and competencies. The successful integration of technology in the classroom can also give educators access to real-time feedback through digital formative and summative assessments and data. This paper concentrates on the various strategies of technologies that can be implemented in the digital learning process.

Keywords: Education, Modern technology, teaching.

Introduction

The era of Twenty first Century is often regarded as an era of technology. Technology plays an important role in our day-to-day life. It is seen as a basis of growth of an economy. If any country has the poor technology means they can never grow in the present scenario. This is because technology makes our work easy and within the time. The impact of technology can be felt in every field and one of the field is Education.

Modern technology in education

According to the latest insights, how the students prefer to use of technology in todays and how does their learning methodology is impact by using of technology. All these revealed that the use of modern equipment technology and tools, leads to increase students participation and interaction in Classroom. The transfer of knowledge becomes very easy and convenient, as well as effective by using the technology. What this means is, when our mind assisted with the modern technology then it's tends to work faster and be it in any part of life, but here we talk about education. The reliance and dependence of such innovation, simply makes life an easy, smooth journey and it is completely unavoidable these days even in schools, universities and colleges. Students today can make use of technology in the following ways:

Internet connection and round the clock connectivity

The internet has adult in importance by several folds, over the method of decade. Its importance within the education world will currently never be undermined. Despite the possibilities of fraud and disadvantages, the employment of the web is sort of a blessing for college students. Nowadays, the internet is something that we can use everywhere. From television to gaming things such as I-pads and phones etc. The use of the internet allows the students to find amazing convenience, they can find various kinds of help, tutorials and other kinds of assisting material which could be used to academically improve and enhance their learning methodology.

Using projectors and visuals aids

Using projectors and visuals to aid in learning methodology will create more interest to the students in classrooms. Because the visual images have always a strong appeal as compared to words. The top institutions around the world, currently showing importance to the Power Point, presentations and projections, in order to keep the learning interactive, easy and interesting. The technological tools such as projectors and visuals to aid when we use within the schools and colleges can keep the learning interactive, easy and interesting. Through the technology the learning process becomes efficient.

Digital footprint in the education sector

If we have a tendency to point out digital and education, then the penetration of digital media at intervals the education sector has presently mature. This penetration has resulted in around the clock property with different students in different forums which are available to help them in learning process. As the power of digital is increases that leads more applications that will assist to students in development and learning process.

Online degrees with the use of technology

Nowaday's Online degrees are become a very common phenomenon. People are like to take up the online courses for their learning and certifications through SWAYAM and SWAYAM PRABHA. The top institutions are offering many online programme with the use of various applications and the internet. The online degree courses are offered by the institutions according to the flexibility of the learner.

Importance of technology in education

The role of technology within the field of education is four- fold: it's enclosed as an area of the curriculum, as a tutorial delivery system, as a means of aiding instructions and also as a tool to developing the entire learning process. Because of technology; education has gone from passive and reactive to interactive and aggressive.

Education is crucial in company and educational settings. Within the former, education or coaching is required to the workers to do the things differently before they did. In the latter education is back-geared towards making curiosity in the minds of students. The use of technology can help students to understand the concepts better.

Factors affecting technology in education

Although lecture rooms might have access to technology initiatives, there are many circumstances that have an effect on the correct implementation of technology in lecture rooms such as poor infrastructure, inadequate technology, lack of sufficient technological tools, effective professional development (external factors), and low teacher confidence etc.

Gressard and Loyd (1985) asserted that teacher's attitudes toward computers are a key factor in the successful implementation of ICT in education. They pointed out that teachers do not always have positive attitudes towards computers and their poor attitudes may lead to a failure of the computer-based projects.

Butler and Sellbom (2002) and Chizmar and Williams (2001) is reliability. Reliability included hardware failures, incompatible software between home and school, poor or slow internet connectivity and out of date software which are available mostly at school while the students/ educators are having more up-to-date software at home.

Impact of ICT on education

In educational context, ICT improves the effectiveness of education by facilitating mobile learning and inclusive education. Tinio (2002) asserted that ICT has a tremendous impact on education in terms of acquisition and absorption of knowledge to both teachers and students through the promotion of:

Active learning: ICT tools are help for the measurement and analysis of knowledge obtained by the student for examination and also it helps in preparation of students performance reports through the computers so that all the information is available easily. In difference to memorisation-based or rote learning, ICT promotes learner to participate in the learning activity with their own pace and work on real life situations' problems.

Collaborative and Cooperative learning: ICT encourages interaction and cooperation between the students and teachers. It also helps the students to work with people from different cultures and working together in groups, hence it helps students to enhance their communicative skills as well as their global awareness. Researchers have found that typically the use of ICT leads to more cooperation among learners within and beyond school and colleges and maintain interactive relationship with the teachers. Grégoire et al., 1996 "Collaboration is a philosophy of interaction and personal lifestyle where individuals are responsible for their actions, including learning and respect the abilities and contributions of their peers." (Panitz, 1996).

Creative Learning: ICT can modify the existing information and to make one's own information to produce a tangible product or a given instructional purpose.

Integrative learning: ICT promotes the integrative approach for teaching and learning, by eliminating the synthetic separation between theory and practice unlike in the traditional classroom where emphasis encloses just a particular aspect.

Evaluative learning: Use of ICT for the purpose of learning is student-centered and also provides useful feedback through various interactive features. ICT allows the students to discover and learn through new ways of teaching methodology which are sustained by constructivist theories.

Positive impact:

Enhanced Teaching and Learning methodologies

Technological developments like digital cameras, projectors, mind training software, computers, zoom, and Google meet, Power point presentations, 3D visualisation tools; all these have become great sources for teachers to help students grasp a concept easily in class room.

It has to be understood that visual explanation of concepts makes learning fun and enjoyable for students and easy. They're able to participate more in the classroom and even teachers get a chance to make their classes more interactive and interesting.

Globalisation

When school in different parts of the state and country, students can "meet" their counterparts through video conferencing such as zoom and Google meet without leaving the classroom.

Some sites, such as www.glovico.com are used to help students learn foreign languages online by pairing a group of students interact with the teachers from another country.

No Geographical Limitations

With the introduction of online degree programme there is no need to present physically in the classroom. Even several foreign universities have started online degree courses that student can join as per their flexibility.

Distance learning and online education have become very important as the part of the education system nowaday.

Negative impact:

Decrease the Writing Skills

Due to the excessive usage of online chatting and shortcuts, the writing skills of today's young generation have declined quite tremendously.

These days, children are relying more and more on digital communication that they have totally forgot about improving their writing skills.

They don't know the spelling of different words, how to use grammar properly or how to do cursive writing.

Increase the Incidents of Cheating

Technological developments like graphical calculators, high tech watches, mini cameras and similar equipment have become great sources to cheat in exams.

It is easier for students to write formulas and notes on graphing calculators, with least chances of being caught.

Lack of Focus

SMS or text messaging has become a favourite pastime of many students. Students are seen playing with their cell phone, i-Phones day and night or driving and very often even between lectures.

Being ever-connected to the online world has resulted in lack of focus and concentration in academics and to some extent, even in sports and extracarricular activities.

Advantages

- It makes students more excited and interest to learn.
- It also help students within busy schedules, freedom to work at home on their own flexible time.
- It can train the students' to learn new technology skills that they can use later in the work place.
- Decrease the paper and photocopying costs and promote the concept of "green revolution".

Disadvantages

- Many experts and experienced people say that, due to such technology in education, students, imagination is affected, their thinking ability is reduced.
- Sometime it's also time-consuming process from teacher's point of view.
- It is costly to install such technology in education institutions.
- There can be health issues too when used over limit.

Conclusion

The technology has a positive impact on education system and at the same time may also pose negative impact. Teachers and students should take advantage of this in the good light and eliminate the limitations which are pulling back many of the students as well as schools and colleges from the achieving of excellence. It is the time for every country to introduce a more and more technologically equipped education sectors in the future.

References

Beringer, V. (2009, October 20). For kids, pen's mightier than keyboard. Futurity.org. Retrieved February 25th 2013 from http://www.futurity.org/society-culture/for-kids-pens-mightier-than- keyboard/#more-4909.

Bounds, G. (2010, October 5). How handwriting trains the brain - forming letters is key to learning, memory, idea. wsj.com. Retrieved February 25th 2013 from http://online.wsj.com/article/SB10001424052748704631504575531932754922518.html

Bransford, J., Brown, A., and Cocking, R. (2000). How people learn: Brain, mind, experience, and school. Washington, DC: National Academic Press.

Brill, J. M., and Galloway, C. (2007). Perils and promises: University instructors' integration of technology in classroom-based practices. British Journal of Educational Technology. 38(1), 95-105.

12

Transforming the Regulatory System of Higher Education

Dr P. Rajyalakshmi and Mrs V. Shanthi

Abstract

Taking into account the rapid change in technology, inevitable changes in education sector are going to happen. A lot or research is taking place to understand the pros and cons of online education in comparison to classroom education. In India, there are a lot of challenges and opportunities for online education. With a comprehensive literature review, in this paper, I have identified the key factors which will develop the online education in India. We have identified internet penetration; low cost of online education, ease of doing course, initiative by government, employer's recognition and bridging gap are the key factors the growth of online education. There are certain factors which are creating a hindrance in the growth which include insufficient digital infrastructure, credibility and language used in online education. With the increase in number of internet users in India, the paper also looks into what opportunities are there in future in education sector.

Keywords: Online education; Face-to-face education; Challenges and opportunities; Digital Infrastructure.

Introduction

The growth of technology has brought tremendous change in the almost every sphere of life. Technology has also impacted the process of education. The face-to-face education has experienced a remarkable change in the last decade. Although face-to-face education is still considered the norm, but acceptance of online courses is also increasing in the field of management and engineering. Some of the reasons for the exponential growth of online education is that it is instant, online, anywhere accessible, self-driven and on the go.

The major reason for the phenomenal growth in online education is MOOCs (Massive Open online courses). According to Kaplan, Andreas M.; Haenlein, Michael (2016), MOOCs are online courses which are aimed at unlimited participation and offer open access through the web. MOOCs have gained lot of popularity since the time of its development in 2008. Over 800 universities around the world have launched at least one MOOC till date. According to report by Class Central, there were 83 million students who had registered or MOOCs by December, 2017. The list of top five MOOC provider by registered users include Coursera, edX, XuangX, Udacity and FutureLearn.

The government is supporting online education in India because of its potential to prove education quality and reach through the Digital India initiative. Government of India in Association with Ministry of HRD has initiated a programme named SWAYAM (Study Webs of Active -Learning for Young Aspiring Minds) that is designed to achieve the three fundamental objectives of Education Policy i.e., access, equity and quality. The main objectives of this effort are to take the quality teaching learning resources to all, including those who cannot afford. This programme SWAYAM seeks to provide education to those students who are not yet aware of the digital revolution taking place and are still not able to join the mainstream of the knowledge economy. Nearly 2000 online courses are offered through Swayam and approximately 150 million students across the globe are enrolled in different courses.

Review of Literature

There are many definitions of online learning. Khan (1997) has defined online learning as the delivery of instruction to a remote audience using the web as an intermediary. Elaine Allen, Jeff Seaman (2011) have defined Online courses as those in which minimum 80 percent of the course content is delivered online and Face-to-face instruction are those courses in which less than 30 percent of the content is delivered online.

According to Stack, Steven Dr. (2015), online education has proliferated in the last decade. His research has not found any major difference in the scores of the students taking online course and face-to-face classes.

Another research done by Dr. Fahad N. Al-FAHAD investigates the students' attitudes and perceptions of 186 University Student's from different colleges towards effectiveness of mobile learning in their studies. Their research findings indicate that students perceive Mobile technologies as an effective tool in improving their communication and learning.

According to a report by Google and KPMG, the online education market in India at the end of December, 2016 was $247 million and it will reach $1.96 billion by 2021. Also India's online education market is the second largest market after US. The findings of the report also states that the paid user base for online education services will also grow at least by six times i.e. approximately 9.6 million users by 2021.

Drivers of online education growth in India

Acceptability of online education in India is growing at an exponential rate because of the following factors:

1. **Internet penetration in India:** According to a report by IAMAI and Kantar IMRB, there were 481 million users of internet in India and this is growing at the rate of 11.34 percent. Also internet penetration in urban India was 64.84 percent while in rural India it was 20.26 percent till December, 2017. The main reason for the growth of internet users in India is the increase in number of smart phone users. According to a report by eMarketer, the US-based market research firm, there were nearly 291.6 million smart phone users in India by the December, 2017. They are expecting that this number will grow by 15.6 percent to reach 337 million by the end of 2018. The key factors behind this growth are the upsurge in smart phone usage and availability of more affordable smart phones. Availability of internet at fast speed and at very affordable price is the reason for growth in mobile internet user. Because of internet, world class education becomes easily accessible to urban and rural population.
2. **Online education saves money and time:** As online education is through internet, so it can be easily accessed anywhere, anytime. You can access the content early morning, late evening, at home, in cafeteria, or on the train. As the content is generally preloaded, so you can download the lectures / videos and watch them at your convenience time and again. Also cost of online education is very low in comparison to face-to-face education. Also there is a great savings on hostel and transportation fees. Since all the content is available online, so you need not buy books also.
3. **Ease of doing courses for working professionals:** Online education offers great opportunity for working professionals as they cannot leave their jobs to pursue higher education. Online education offers them a variety of courses to choose from and this can help in finding new career options for them. This is also

supported by the report from Google and KPMG which states that reskilling and online certification is the biggest sector in online education. Another online platform 'upgrad' is offering online courses on Big Data and are also providing jobs in this area.

4. **Initiative by Government of India:** Government of India is also taking initiatives to promote online education. They have started Swayam through which they are offering free education and certification courses to all. Main objective of this initiative is to provide quality education for which they have tied up with IITs, IIMs and NPTEL. They are also tying up with universities by which student can earn credit though online courses. In order to establish digital infrastructure in India, the government has also launched National Optical Fiber Network. The main objective of this initiative is to increase broadband connectivity and create a fast network. Government has started online National Digital Library in which 17 million digital books and journals are available. There are 32 lakhs registered users are accessing NDL free of cost. Government has provided Wi-Fi facility to all the central universities.
5. **Gaining recognition among employers:** Today most of the universities in US are offering at least one online course. In India also many of the prestigious institutions are offering online courses where otherwise admission is very difficult and costly. Online courses done from well respected universities/ institutions are accepted by employers. Employers also understand that online education requires self-discipline, drive and other skills that they are looking for in a candidate. So proper care should be taken in selecting the university from where you are doing course. Also there are hundreds of options to choose from. Right selection from right educational institute can help you make right career growth.
6. **Bridge the gap between education level and industry expectations**: According to a report in The World Employment and Social Outlook - Trends, there were 18.3 million Indians unemployed in 2017 and it is projected to increase by 18.9 million by the year 2019. According to a report, India's working age population is increasing and is expected to reach 64 percent of the population by 2021. Do you think it is because of sufficient job opportunities are not available in India? Nascom says six

million people will be required in cyber security by 2022. According to Tech Mahindra CEO C P Gurnani, 94 percent of IT graduates are not fit for hiring.

According to opinion given by Sanjay Bansal, 58 percent of unemployed graduates and majority of the unemployed post-graduates (62%) states that jobs matching their skill and education are not available and this is the primary reason for their unemployment. So online education is one of the alternatives to bridge the gap between what industries expect and what the educational institutes are delivering. Online education offers an opportunity to enhance skills through advance courses available in different domains.

Challenges in Online education

There are a lot of challenges faced by people in online education in India. Some of these challenges which need to be overcome are:

1. **Insufficient digital infrastructure:** Although Government of India is taking initiative to develop digital infrastructure but a lot need to be done in this direction. High speed internet and stable power supply are the biggest problem. India stands 89th worldwide on internet speed and stability. According to the report of World Economic Forum, only 15 percent of the households have access to the Internet, and mobile broadband remains accessible to very few i.e. only 5.5 subscriptions for every 100 people. Further, currently reach of broadband is just about 600 corridors, largely in and around the top 50 to 100 Indian cities, leaving rural areas with poor connectivity. 5G networks technology is the requirement of today's which will increase the speed of downloading the data.
2. **Limited Social interaction:** Since online education can be accessed at home or any other convenient place, there is very limited direct interaction with the teacher and other people doing the course. According to Dhirendra Kumar (2010), especially those courses which are self paced, there is very less discussion among the peers. Most of the discussion takes place through e-mail, chat room or discussion groups. There isn't any campus atmosphere to improve social interaction. So you are not able to develop any social links which do help in the career growth.
3. **Questionable credibility of degrees:** Although industry has started recognizing online degrees, there are still a lot of fraudulent and non-accredited degrees being offered online. The number of

scam operators is rising who are offering fake certificate which does not have any credentials. These scams not only losses the credibility of the online certificates but also the faith of prospective employer in online programme.

4. **Motivation:** Some students need the push to get to the class. In case of self paced online programme, student may procrastinate. The dropout rate in online education is very high. Self motivation and discipline is required to complete the assignments and upload them timely. If you have difficulty working independently, staying organised and meeting deadlines, you might struggle in an online programme.
5. **Language of the Course:** India is a multi-linguistic country, and a vast majority of the population comes from rural areas. The content offered by most of the online courses is in English. Hence, those students who are not able to speak English struggle with the availability of language content. Hence, it is the duty of computer professionals, educators, administrators, language content creators, and content disseminators, to sit together and give a viable framework and standard solution to the learners knowing only Indian languages.

Opportunities in Online Education

Change in technology is offering many opportunities for all stakeholders in the online education sector which includes entrepreneurs, education providers and learners. Some of the factors offering different opportunities in this domain include:

1. **Mobile Learning:** According to a report in Stastia (2018), in the year 2017 there were 320.57 million people who accessed the internet through their mobile phone. This figure is projected to increase to 462.26 million by the year 2021. The surge in users is credited to availability of 4G internet and smart phones at very low price. Going forward, IAMAI hopes that the National Telecom Policy (NTP) 2018, which is focusing on new technologies like 5G, will promote better quality data services at more affordable prices and help address the digital divides that will promote internet penetration in the rural areas through mobile internet. According to report by Zenith, mobile devices will account for 73 percent of time spent using the internet in 2018. So the vast majority of students in future will have access to e-learning through mobile phones.

2. **Investor's Interest:** A large number of entrepreneurs are venturing into online education as this is expected to see an uptrend in the next five years thanks to the Digital India campaign, the cultural importance given to education and falling mobile data prices. The Chang Zuckerberg Initiative has invested $50 million in Byju's, Bertelsmann India has invested $8.2 million in Eruditus, and Kaizen Management Advisors and DeVry Inc. have put in $10 million in EduPristine. Khan Academy is a non-profit organisation which receives financial support from philanthropic organisations like The Bill and Melinda Gates Foundation, Google and Netflix founder Reed Hastings. Online learning platform Unacademy also raised $11.5 million of funding led by Sequoia India and SAIF Partners; and Eruditus Executive Education, a provider of executive education programme, had raised $8 million funding from Bertelsmann India Investments. So, the online education sector will continue to spark more interest among entrepreneurs, investors and attract more funding.
3. **Blended Model:** There will be convergence of the offline education and online education in future. This concept of blended learning combines online digital media with traditional classroom methods. It requires the physical presence of both teacher and student, but student has some control over time, place, path, or pace. This model will take advantage of both face-to-face classroom practices combined with computer-mediated activities. In future, there will be virtual classrooms where face-to-face offline pedagogy will be aided by digital courses on practical knowledge and soft skills.
4. **New Courses:** Today the most popular courses in online education are related to IT which includes subjects like big data, cloud computing, and digital marketing. But in future demand for different types of courses in unexpected subjects such as culinary management, photography, personality development, forensic science, cyber law, etc. will increase.

Conclusion

Online education can change the whole future scenario in education if it can be implemented in joint collaboration with industry, universities and government. Drastic changes in course curriculum are required to bridge the gap so that students are industry ready after passing out. Education process needs to be changed by making it more practical with the use of technology. Also course should be designed in different languages to increase their reach and more opportunities for youth of rural India. Innovations are required to design ways to increase the social skills of online learners.

References

1. Khan, B. (1997). Web-based training. Englewood Cliffs, NJ: Educational Technology Publications.
2. Kaplan, Andreas M.; Haenlein, Michael (2016). "Higher education and the digital revolution: About MOOCs, SPOCs, social media, and the Cookie Monster". Business Horizons. 59 (4): 441-50. doi:10.1016/j.bushor.2016.03.008
3. Chauhan, Jyoti (2017). International Journal of Computer Trends and Technology (IJCTT) - Volume 49 Issue 2 July 2017.
4. Napaporn, SRICHANYACHON (2014). Turkish Online Journal of Distance Education - TOJDE July 2014 ISSN 1302-6488 Volume: 15 Number: 3 Article 5.
5. Kushwah, Shivpal Singh; Vijayakumar J K. Content creation and E-learning in Indian languages: a model.
6. Stack, Steven Dr. (2015). "Learning Outcomes in an online vs traditional course," International Journal for the Scholarship of Teaching and Learning: Vol. 9: No. 1, Article 5.
7. Fahad N. Al-FAHAD, Dr. (2009). The Turkish Online Journal of Educational Technology - TOJET April 2009 ISSN: 1303-6521 volume 8 Issue 2 Article 10.
8. Herman, T., and Banister, S. (2007). Face-to-face versus online coursework: A comparison of costs and learning outcomes. Contemporary Issues in Technology and Teacher Education, 7(4), 318-326.

Web Links

1. https://www.financialexpress.com/jobs/why-e-learning-has-a-promising-future-in-india/19204/
2. https://www.vccircle.com/the-present-and-future-of-indias-online-education-industry
3. https://economictimes.indiatimes.com/articleshow/63000198.cms?utm_source=contentofi nterestand utm_medium=textandutm_campaign=cppst
4. https://www.researchgate.net/publication/320038196_An_Overview_ of_ MOOC_ in_India
5. https://www.class-central.com/report/mooc-stats-2017/
6. https://www.studyread.com/scope-of-online-education/
7. https://www.encyclopedia.com/finance/finance-and-accounting-magazines/online-education
8. https://swayam.gov.in/about
9. https://timesofindia.indiatimes.com/business/india-business/number-indian-internet-users-will-reach-500-million-by-june-2018-iamai-says/articleshow/62998642.cms

10. https://dazeinfo.com/2018/05/07/smartphone-users-in-india-2018-2022-growth/
11. http://www.indiaeducation.net/online-education/articles/advantages-and-disadvantages-of-distance-learning.html
12. http://onlinelearningsuccess.org/advantages-and-disadvantages-of-online-and-classroom-learning/
13. https://www.theglobeandmail.com/report-on-business/how-employers-view-an-online-education/article36984380/
14. https://www.firstpost.com/india/indias-unemployment-crisis-1-3-million-youth-need-jobs-every-month-eight-million-a-year-says-world-bank-report-4453457.html
15. https://timesofindia.indiatimes.com/business/india-business/94-of-it-grads-not-fit-for-hiring-techm-ceo/articleshow/64442037.cms
16. https://thetechpanda.com/2017/10/28/digital-infrastructure-hospitality/
17. ttps://www.ies.ncsu.edu/wp-content/uploads/sites/15/2015/08/Pros_and_Cons_of_Online_Education_by_Kumar-1.pdf
18. https://www.chartercollege.edu/news-hub/pros-and-cons-online-learning
19. https://core.ac.uk/download/pdf/11879400.pdf
20. https://www.statista.com/statistics/558610/number-of-mobile-internet-user-in-india/
21. https://inc42.com/resources/future-trends-digital-education-india

13

An impact of quality of work life and emotional intelligence on work performance among teaching employees during Covid-19

Ramshankar Varma

Abstract

Emotional Intelligence is a set of qualities and competencies that captures a broad collection of individual skills and dispositions, usually referred to as soft skills or inter and intra personal skills. Work/life balance is defined as a satisfactory level of involvement or fit between the multiple roles in a person's life. In this pandemic, managing the boundary between home and work is becoming more challenging. Organisations need to ensure they not just encourage but mandate a practical and workable work/life balance policy, benefiting and meeting the needs of both the organisation and its employees. The objectives of this study are to study impact of emotional intelligence on performance of employees and to study the relation emotional intelligence and different aspects of work life balance. For the purpose of study, a convenience sample of 100 employees between the age of 35 and 55 years working in corporate office(IT companies) in Nagpur is selected. The data is collected through a questionnaire consisting a 5 point Likert scale. Weighted average will be calculated for all the values on the Likert scales and correlation will be applied to check the impact of emotional intelligence and quality of work life among the employees.

Keywords: Emotional Intelligence, work-life balance, Pandemic, employees, Quality of Work Life.

Introduction

Employment satisfaction may be described as an employee's sentiments about his or her job. Berry et. al., 1997 characterised work fulfillment as "a singular's reaction to their business experience." Job fulfillment alludes to a singular's obligation to their work. Various elements can influence a worker's degree of occupation fulfillment; these variables incorporate compensation scale and remittances, the organisation's advancement framework, social connections, the workplace, the nature of working circumstances, administration, the board style and culture, representative inclusion and independent work gatherings, and the actual work. Numerous writers have hypothesized that emotional intelligence enhances individuals' ability to work successfully in teams and handle job-related stress Salovey and Caruso et. al., 2004. Emotional intelligence may also have an effect on work satisfaction. It is considered that individuals whose jobs need emotional expression are better happy with their work. These individuals are capable of managing their unpleasant emotions and concentrating on good ones. Job satisfaction may be impacted by gender disparities, particularly in occupations that are completely classified as "masculine," such as the military, law enforcement, and heavy manufacturing.

Employment satisfaction refers to an individual's favourable attitude about his or her job Furnham et. al., 1997. Teachers' job happiness is significantly influenced by their work environment Edmonds, Moriarty, Martin and Blatchford et. al., 2001 and in Menon and Christou et. al., 2002. Various analysts distinguished various elements influencing worker work fulfillment, including character attributes, individual qualities, pay, advancement, professional stability, the idea of the work, authoritative construction, initiative and oversight, associations with collaborators, states of being of the gig, and equity.

Emotions are on Intrinsic part of our biological make up and every morning they march into the office with us and influence our behaviour. Emotional intelligence consists off five factors: Knowing one's emotions, managing motions, motivating one, recognizing emotions in others and handling relationship. Emotional intelligences the capacity for recognizing our own feelings and those of others, motivating ourselves, and managing emotions well, in ourselves and in our relationships". From this definition, we can identify that emotional intelligence has two major components:

A. Personal Competence

B. Social Competence.

Personal Competence includes awareness of the self, i.e. understanding one own emotions, feelings etc. and management of the self, i.e. the ability to deal with changing situations. Social competence means social awareness and management of relationships. Social awareness is the ability to understand the feeling of other while management of relationship is the ability to work effectively with other persons.

High EI does not guarantee the development of emotional competencies, it only shows that there is a potential to improve emotional competencies. Therefore, a certain level of emotional intelligence is necessary to learn the emotional competencies. Goleman research demonstrates that emotional intelligence has proven to be twice as important as any other competency in any job role. Quality of work life describes how content an individual is with his or her job. Quality of work life has been defined as a pleasurable emotional state resulting from the appraisal of one's job an affective reaction to ones' job, and an attitude towards one's job. Weiss 2002 has argued that quality of work life is an attitude but points out that researchers should clearly distinguish the objects of cognitive evaluation which are affect emotions, belief and behaviours.

Literature Review

The discoveries of examination on the effect of the capacity to understand people on a profound level on work execution are conflicting. A few explorations demonstrate a positive connection between's ability to understand anyone on a profound level and work achievement. (Caplan and Kelley et al.,1993) found that designers positioned as stars by their partners were more proficient in connecting with others, suggesting that specialists with high capacity to understand people on a profound level showed predominant execution. One more exploration done among Air Force initiates had the same outcomes. The resulting examination showed that individuals who have an undeniable degree of the ability to understand anyone at their core were 2.6 times more compelling than the people who needed it (Caplan and Kelley et al., 1993).

In his exploration, Bar-On et. al., 1997 found a good relationship between work fulfillment and a mix of the attributes of EI, relational connections, intrapersonal connections, self-versatility, stress the executives, and in general inclination. Instructors with a high EI are bound to be happy with their positions (Wong, Peng, Wong et. al., 2010). EI was demonstrated to be related with work fulfillment and hierarchical responsibility in a significant and helpful manner (Asan, Guleryuz, Aydin, and Guney et. al., 2008). Sy, Tram, and O'Hara (2006) found a good relationship between's labourers' ability to understand anyone on a deeper level and work environment joy and execution. Tans (2003) discovered a favourable correlation between emotional intelligence and work satisfaction and contextual performance. Additionally, he discovered that other characteristics such as gender, personal worth, and personality all affect an employee's work happiness and performance.

Omole, et. al., 2010 found that how much ability to understand individuals on a profound level of cops is connected with their degree of fulfillment and execution. In contrasted with cops with poor capacity to understand anyone on a profound level. Also, cops who play male or female parts that require an undeniable degree of the ability to understand anyone on a profound level perform better and are more happy with their positions than officials who assume male or female parts that require a low degree of the capacity to appreciate individuals on a deeper level. Ghadami, Ghoneim, Khouly and Ibrahim et. al., 2011 found that orientation negligibly affects work fulfillment; the ability to understand people on a profound level considerably affects work fulfillment; and the capacity to appreciate anyone at their core and orientation combinedly affect work fulfillment. Farazmehr and Tabatabaei et. al., 2015 additionally found equivalent discoveries.

Tarasi, Yarmohammadi, and Mousavi et. al., 2012 found a significant positive connection between the capacity to appreciate anyone on a deeper level and work fulfillment in an examination of 215 actual training teachers. Also, they found a great relationship between interactive abilities, sympathy, inspiration, and work fulfillment. Just three parts of the ability to appreciate people at their core, specifically inspiration, sympathy, and interactive abilities, were displayed to anticipate educator work fulfillment utilising stepwise relapse investigation. They demonstrated that by expanding an instructor's ability to understand people on a deeper level through preparing, they may support their work satisfaction. Mohammad, Syed, Mohamed, Rohany, and Muhammad et. al., 2012 found a significant positive connection among EI and work fulfillment and observed that gender had no effect on EI or occupation fulfillment.

Going on from the first discussion, the ebb and flow research endeavoured to give replies to the accompanying inquiries: Is there a connection between the capacity to understand individuals on a deeper level and work fulfillment? Does sex separation affect work fulfillment? Is there a connection between the ability to appreciate anyone on a deeper level and gender as far as work fulfillment among grade teachers? Do the five parts of EI mutually and independently foresee work fulfillment?

Objectives

- To study the impact of emotional intelligence on performance of employees.
- To know how to become an Emotionally intelligent organisation.

- To study the impact of emotional intelligence on effectiveness of employees.
- To study the relation emotional intelligence and different aspects of work life balance.

Hypothesis

- There is impact of emotional intelligence and quality of work life among the teachers.
- There is no impact of emotional intelligence and quality of work life among the teachers.

Sample design and Size

The population of study is employees of Shri S K Somaiya Vinay Mandir and Jr. College in Mumbai city. The sample size of 100 employees between the age of 30 and 55 years. This study is based on connivance sampling for which areas are limited to employees of Shri S K Somaiya Vinay Mandir and Jr. College.

Method of Data Collection

To collect primary data as a survey will be conducted on employee's satisfaction through a questionnaire, which will be filled by various teachers of the school. The answers of the respondents are elucidated by asking them to indicate their level of agreement on a given five-point Likert scale with values ranging from 1-strongly disagree to 5-strongly agree. For secondary data, journals, magazines and Internet are referred.

Data analysis and Interpretation: Satisfaction with salary and compensation

Most of the employees are satisfied with salary and compensation provided to them 39 percent of the respondent agrees and 19 percent strongly agree that the with the salary and compensation provided to them whereas 27 percent disagree and 6 percent strongly disagree that they are not satisfied.

Satisfaction with work environment

39 percent respondents are satisfied with their work environment and 17 percent strongly agree that they had a food work environment whereas 15 percent shows an indifferent attitude and 24 percent disagree and 5 percent strongly disagree the statement.

Life Satisfaction

Most of the respondents are satisfied by their life satisfaction as 43 percent of the respondents agree to their life satisfaction and 19 percent strongly agree. Only 12 percent disagree and two percent strongly disagree that they are not at all satisfied with their life satisfaction.

Job Satisfaction

This shows that employees are satisfied with their job to greater extent as 49 percent of the respondents agree and 15 percent strongly agree with the statement, 15 percent of the respondents shows an in different attitude and 21 percent disagree that they are not satisfied.

Correlation value of emotional intelligence and quality of work life is 0.851

Findings

1. There is a strong correlation between EI and quality of work life.
2. Employees are satisfied to greater extent with the intrinsic benefits provided by the company like salary, benefits and frequency of bonuses.
3. Employees are dissatisfied to greater extent with the extrinsic benefits provided by the management.
4. Most of the employees are unhappy with the job and job profile.
5. Employees are dissatisfied with the training and development programme organised by the company.

References

1. Goleman, D. (1998). Working with Emotional Intelligence, Bantam Books, New York.
2. Hay Group (2000). "Transformational leadership as management of emotion: a conceptual review".
3. Abraham Carmeli (2003). "The relationship between emotional intelligence and work attitudes, behavior and outcomes".
4. Lair Kidwell (2011). "The impact of EI in marketing exchange on sales performance and customer relationships".
5. Salovey and Mayer. "Emotional Intelligence and Workplace".

14

Value Oriented Education in India - Changing Global Scenario

Rasheeda Begum

Abstract

Value Oriented education can be studied at micro and macro levels. In the present article this is being studied at the national and state level and even at regional level. There are two ways of understanding Value Oriented Education - either from global to local or from local to global angles - depending upon the canvas against which the issue is being discussed. It has been rightly said that the present form of Indian education system can be traced back to the year 1857 when the first three universities were established at Calcutta, Bombay and Madras and even after that the higher education system has moved from one step to another with changing socio-economic and political scenario. If one goes into the depth of various challenges posed to higher education in general and specially in Indian context, one can visualise the urgency of immediate course of action to bring some fundamental changes in the present educational system.

Keywords: Value Oriented Education, Global Scenarios, Changing Scenarios, Value Oriented Education.

Introduction

While dealing with the problems and challenges in the field of higher education one has to perceive the entire scenario in totality. The socio-cultural, political, economic and technological advancements are to be considered and analysed while viewing the prospects of higher education in our country in the background of a cry for globalisation and over emphasis on the concept of global village. Irrespective of technological and communicative advancement the aim of education remains more or less to be the same and that is to achieve multiple developments and enjoying enlightenment of mind, broadening of vision and character building which can be beneficial to the individual himself and to the society and nation at large. Mental pollution is to be minimized for leading a healthy life because mental pollution lies behind every pollution. The goal of technological advancement may be a creation of robot but without accepting the humanistic approach the educationists, policy makers and the planners would fail to achieve the real underlying goal of human development. The twenty first Century striving for the development of highest technological and informative skills in order to convert the entire world into a global village may fail to produce a real man along with his deep-rooted human values and emotional blending. Hence, the conflict would be between the adoption of a scientific temper and value based education. It would be a difficult task to have a nice blending of these two approaches to our educational system. On the one hand, emphasis is being given to the teaching of vocational, professional and technical courses whereas on the other weightage is still being given to general teaching.

Backdrop of Research Area

During the last decade much deliberation has been made on the challenges of twenty first Century in the field of higher education and a number of seminars, symposia and workshops have been organised on this issue in order to generate attitudinal change and readiness to welcome the fast changing world scenario in the background of technological advancements and information explosion. Now when we have already moved into the twenty first Century every effort is to be made in the direction of meeting the challenges in the field of higher education. The orientation, attitude and vision already developed in the last phase of twentieth century towards the use of advanced educational technologies would give direction to our efforts towards achieving the goal of higher education and utilising our economic and human resources for competing at national and international level.

Higher education must move towards the fulfillment of social needs and man-power requirements and also work towards the attainment of advanced technological skills. With the advancement of educational technologies, computerisation, satellite communication, Internet, teleconferencing and audio-visual aids there can be a shift in setting the preferential goals of education. With the advancement in knowledge and explosion of information technologies there would be a knowledge-based society. Whether general information is imparted or specific scientific, vocational and professional skills are developed, the goal of any educational system is empowerment which is possible only when emphasis is given on Knowledge as power. The individual is to be armed with information and skills but not to act as a robot or a machine but with feelings and sentiments. The human potentialities are to be unfolded and wholesome personality is to be developed. Learning throughout life will be one of the key guides to meeting the challenges of the twenty first century. Four pillars of learning are to be strengthened which are Learning to be, Learning to know, Learning to do and learning to live together. More resources are to be allocated to the development of education if we really believe in the advancement of human knowledge. International cooperation in education with UNESCO as the key player is to be tapped. Universal Basic Education should be given an absolute priority; Secondary education also has a pivotal role to play. Higher education institutions should be diversified so as to take into account their functions and duties as centres of knowledge, professional training and community living. Different nations have to be partners in international cooperation (UNESCO Commission report on Education in twenty first century). The present century dominated by globalisation will bring with it enduring tension to overcome. The main areas of conflict and tension will be between global and the local, long term and short term considerations, competition and equality of opportunities, the unlimited expansion of knowledge and the limited capacity of human beings to assimilate it and finally the conflict between the spiritual and materials. Whatever the diversity of culture and system of social organisations, there is universal challenge of reinventing the democratic ideal to create or maintain social cohesiveness.

Value Oriented Education

While dealing with the application of information technologies and computer networking, adequate policy and action plan are to be made; the preferential position given to education in planning along with raised level of motivation and dedication will be needed. Until and unless the parents, administrators, politicians, reformers, planners and the educationists become fully involved in the development of education ranging from primary level to higher level, simple discussion over the challenges of higher education will not be of any use and would not serve any purpose. Now the time is for implementing the policy and the resolutions taken at various seminars and meetings, failing which there would a wastage of human energy and financial resources. There are various challenges in the field of higher education which are to be met through time-bound action plan. A preferential position to Distance mode of learning over conventional education system may be given for educating the masses in the present century. The fast increasing population and increasing financial burden on the existing conventional education requires some more convenient mode of education and that is distance mode of learning or open learning system which would cater to the needs of thousands of people who want to study but cannot afford to do so through conventional system. The open universities have brought education to door step. This should be of priority that open universities should be fully developed and for which networking at national and international levels is required. If distance mode of learning is not fully developed it would be highly difficult task to education and train our people only through conventional system. Both these systems have to grow side by side as they are supplementary to each other, one system refers to 'university within the wall' and another to 'university without the wall'. With the advanced information technologies and computerisation as well as teleconferencing and Internet, the conventional education system will be in classical mode as the distance education will cater to the needs of millions and formal classes for contact will be required lesser and lesser. Now attempts are being made with TV and digital pictures to bring classroom to every home. This needs a highly developed vision towards distance mode of learning.

Preservation of our own socio-cultural heritage along with acceptance of international exposures and technological advancement constitutes another problem area in the field of education. Emphasis on composite culture is to be given but individual identity is to be preserved. Another issue relates to the relative role of private agencies and government machinery in meeting the financial burden of the universities. The issue thus concerns privatisation vs. State responsibilities. Because of increasing financial constraints the government may not meet the financial demands of the schools and the universities and hence privatisation of education may be a necessary step. The NGO may come as rescue but the quality of education is to be maintained at any cost. A proper planning is needed for incorporating the idea of privatisation and to revitalise the government machineries if we want quality education. Hence, the conflict is between the role of private agencies and the government responsibilities. Within the universities which are financially managed and maintained by the State Government, self financing units, imparting vocational and technical education should be established in order to run themselves on their own. They can come as rescue to the university during financial crisis.

Values and Social Goals

In terms of social goals of Cooperative Learning, Kurt Lewin, known as the founding father of modern social and organisational psychology, who influenced the Group Dynamics Movement, may be mentioned here for his pioneering contributions vis-à-vis group processing, psychological ecology of behaviour settings, cooperative experiential learning experiences, action theory, and resolution of social conflics.

Paulo Freire's (1968) notion of education as a concentrically attuned, democratic, critiquing, and conscientizing experience vis-à-vis the pedagogy of the oppressed and the deprived could be named here as another driving force towards cooperative learning that has consciousness raising-significance. Freire was insistent on defeating the 'banking' concept of education which, as an instrument of oppression, tended to transfer facts into the minds of learners as if 'their minds were passive', and on minimizing 'the teacher-student dichotomy'. He believed in Rousseau's idea of the child as an active learner and Franz Fanon's idea of decolonisation of the mind. Based on 'dialogicity' that promotes bi-directional relationship wherein both the teacher and student learn, his method of learning aims at realizing the essence of education, namely 'freedom in practice'. In his method, no one 'liberates anyone else, nobody liberates himself all alone, and people liberate themselves in fellowship with one another'. Learning is generative, and learning to realize social goals is a social process of learning together by discovering and understanding each one's reality, of acting together by struggling together so as to transform the reality - when it means oppression, and of experiencing fellowship by enjoying freedom in practice. 'No one can create himself in silence, but through dialogue, reflection and action'. This was how Freire espoused the cause of learning, rather cooperative learning by extension.

The impression, that Cooperative Learning for achieve social goals is more suitable to primary or secondary classroom situation than to graduate or postgraduate classroom context, has no scientific basis. Freire's concept of education disproves such an impression. Studies done by McKeachie, Wilbert, Paul Pintrich, Lin Yi-Guang and David Smith (1986), and Whitman, Neal A. (1988), Johnson, David W., and Roger T. Johnson (1989), and others have confirmed that, though cooperative learning is not the easiest way of teaching and it is a tough instructional challenge for the teacher at graduate or postgraduate level, 'the more one works in cooperative learning groups, the more that person learns, the better he understands what he is learning' the easier it is to remember what he learns, and the better he feels about himself, the class, and his classmates'. Kagan Publishing and Professional Development Academy (http://kaganonline.com) has a number of publications and training modules on Cooperative Learning. Cooperative Learning could be a beacon light towards cherishing dreams for a new social order where humanist reasoning and humane development paradigms prevail. From this point of view, reading the writings of Amartya Sen and A.P.J.Abdul Kalam could be a terrific inspiration to teachers at all levels, particularly teachers involved in higher education. Amartya Sen's 'Capability Approach to Education', his concepts of 'development as quest for freedom' and 'quest for development as responsibility' have been discussed worldwide. His comments in his book, *Identity and Violence:* The Illusion of Destiny (2006) on the disastrous effects on young children placed within 'the domain of singular affiliations even before they could start thinking' are a pointer to the need for interactive learning that sustains dialoguing as a core value in any multicultural society.

Great Space Scientist and Former Indian Hon'ble President Late Kalam's discerned understanding of the realities of India, his vision for a new India, his love for teaching with 'peppered anecdotes' and formula for creative leadership, his interactive crash courses elucidating his concepts of PURA (Providing Urban Facilities in Rural Areas) and NPI (National Prosperity Index) and his interactive learning with students as a socially meaningful collaborative venture indicate not only the fact that he is a man of reasonable and realisable dreams but also justify why students as responsible citizens need to cultivate an interdisciplinary approach to learning, adopt and adapt cooperative ways of learning in order to enrich 'knowledge power', build up 'innovative technology', augment 'management stewardship', accommodate multiple intelligences, and promote collective leadership. All these aspects, as he insists, are fuelled by one another. His vision has the prospect of moulding learners as resources for themselves rather than as mere dependents or recipients of received information, and shaping students as 'job-generators' rather than as 'job-seekers', as he himself articulates.

Pursuit of Social Goals

Using communication as a two-way process towards consensus building, Cooperative Learning promotes dynamic stability via disequilibrium. It is a paradox. Creating disequilibrium is one important consequence of Cooperative Learning. It may be construed as a strategy as well. Disequilibrium is not allergic to the ambience and impact of mixed-group abilities. It prevents learners working against each other. When conflicts arise in learning groups, it motivates students to be constructive. When controversies occur, it seeks concurrence. It cautions, educates and motivates high achievers towards appreciating the significance and relevance of peer recognition, acceptance and evaluation.

It accommodates cultural diversity, heterogeneity, differences of perspectives, sustainable levels of mutual challenges, multiple intelligences, manifold wisdom, and individualised attention while magnifying the enjoyable experience of learning together. It subjects, tames and harnesses competitive ethic to the extent that a win-win experience is an indispensable goal so as to build the capacity of learners to appreciate the spirit of interdependence and the need for co-existence. It instills a perception that one's achievement of goals is interdependent with the attainment of others' goals.

In a social set-up where the structures of educational systems are not conducive to cooperative learning and wherein evaluation system is more traditional and extrinsic, many children, particularly competitive children, become blind to cooperative solutions. Mere competitive cultural values ingrained within the traditional modes of evaluation may be beneficial to an already privileged sector of urban children but if they, as Kagan and Associates (1985) point out, 'do not prepare our future generations to behave rationally across the full range of social situations, and work and interact productively', these generations would be out of step with reality, the reality of the workplace and the indispensable need for cooperative strategies and solutions. It is this realisation that should conscientise educational agencies and authorities even at university level about the relevance and importance of Cooperative Learning. Cooperative Learning can be an educational strategy at all levels, from LKG to PG. It can serve both as a temporary strategy and an elongated and enduring one depending on how the groups are formed. It can be extended even beyond formal educational levels and can be applied in manifold life-situations.

Pursuit of excellence is fine but when it happens to be the privilege of a few who outperform, win extra encomiums and receive better teacher approval, and who, in a way, contribute to the elimination of other learners, that too at the cost of national exchequer or limited public resources, it causes disquiet and disparities, and aggravates social tensions. A gifted learner, in all likelihood, is a high achiever by virtue of a sound foundation or innate abilities. A gifted learner's extraordinary academic achievement may give him/ her a personal and individualistic sense of achievement in life. Whether his/her achievements have contributed to eradication of poverty, inequality and societal discrimination, and to the promotion of humane interdependence and solidarity so that occasions for peace are more than occasions for tension, or he/she has become part of the world of cynicism and snobbishness can be a moot point. If seekers and achievers of excellence turn out to be cynics churning out more and more cynics from among the brainy, then it is a sign that our educational systems need comprehensive corrective revamping measures.

The big advantage in Cooperative Learning is that it maximizes group learning not to project individual excellences but to ensure critical thinking and team building. It assumes, as Carolyn Kessler et al (1992) report, that 'learning is NOT necessarily an outcome of teaching' , that 'the quality of understanding is more critical than the quantity of information presented by the teacher', and that learning, a moving process from the concrete to the abstract, connotes kinesthetic experience eliciting feedback. Therefore, as Peterson et al (1992) insist, 'the time is ripe for teachers to work relentlessly to create classroom situations in which students are tempted, cajoled, seduced, provoked and firmly rewarded not for being excellent, but for thinking'. The tendency to include competition, 'healthy competition', as part of Cooperative Learning has been discussed in literatures related to Cooperative Learning methods. The research clearly indicates that cooperation, compared with competitive and individualistic efforts, results in

(a) higher achievement and greater productivity,

(b) more caring, supportive, and committed relationships, and

(c) greater psychological health, social competence, and self-esteem.

Recent research studies have discussed 'the impact of healthy competition' within Cooperative Learning. Staunch advocates of Cooperative Learning have questioned the relevance of healthy competition meaning that it is a myth. Proponents of competitive cooperative learning' have their arguments.

Garnering the Impact of Interdependence

In conclusion, it is time that the era of teacher-fronted lecturing or dispensing information, as if learners were mere recipients, gradually gives way to Cooperative Learning. The nitty-gritty of Cooperative Learning foregrounding the grasp of 'the complexity of the real world', heterogeneity, disequilibrium, multiculturalism, and convergence towards consensus cultivate, harness, and gamer positive interdependence lest civilisations should experience fragmentation and dissolution. It is understandable that gyrations occur in civilisations in ascending and descending order in the sense W.B. Yeats meant. But, no one has the right to wantonly destroy cultures and civilisations as it is happening in Iraq. The sort of hegemony USA has been perpetuating, the sort of xenophobia being practised in different parts of the world in the context of migrations and the presence of emigre diasporas and their progeny, and the ways a small minority of citizenry in every civilisation - India is in no way an exception - appropriates and arrogates opportunities provided by educational policies and systems leaving a pittance or peanut for the rest and marginalising the majority in the name of competitive ethic, are dangerous portents.

It is in the midst of such contextualisations that positive interdependence is projected as a critical value. Children of all cultures are capable of imbibing and nurturing the art of living interdependently. The youth of today are willing to de-learn and relearn so that a win-win environment is provided for the benefit of all, and the other citizenry of the world can be tamed to toe a similar line. John Donne averred long ago: 'No man is island'. We are all part of the entirety of humanity. When a newborn arrives, a part of our humanity is enriched, and when someone dies, a part of our humanity dies. This is the spirit of interconnectivity and Cooperative Learning by extension. The spirit of creativity via inter-connecting organic processing is the spirit of the universe. Constrictions are man-made. Nature has few barriers. I am reminded of Robert Frost. The pine tree in my compound and the apple tree in my neighbour's do meet and embrace each other beneath the dividing compound wall. An ecological view of the world of Nature provides immense scope for reflecting upon concentric, rather than hierarchical, interconnectivity that pervades the whole universe. It is this kind of spirit - spirit of holism - that permeates all the domains of Cooperative Learning, beckoning ceaselessly cooperative learners in all disciplines and at all graded levels to cultivate, harness and harvest interdependence as the most cherished common goal of the human race. In this sense, there is no age bar for anyone to adopt Cooperative Learning as a way of life. I am of the view that Cooperative Learning can have a terrific impact in addressing all major issues and concerns such as racism, casteism, narrow right-wing or left-wing nationalism, and acts of terrorism that haunt both the developed and the developing regions of the world.

Moral Values Global Future Prospect

Either higher education is to be studied in the light of its relevance to social needs and manpower requirement. Education should be given after an assessment of requirement for engineers, doctors, teachers, technicians, unskilled workers, etc. at a given time. This is to be done by skilled planners otherwise unrealistic planning will not meet the demands of the society. The relative significance, attached to the development of primary and secondary education on the one hand and higher education on the other, constitutes another problem area in the field of education. Emphasis on primary education and literacy outcome is greater in developing countries and higher education in developed countries (World Bank Report, 1988). The argument in favour of quality primary and secondary education is that if foundations are properly laid and a child's personality is better shaped during early period for developing competencies towards meeting the challenges of higher education, it would help him in taking advantage of higher education in a more productive manner. On the other hand, some people argue that an effective higher education can produce effective teachers to be engaged at secondary level who can impart quality teaching and thus prepare students at school level to meet the challenges of higher education. Hence, the development of education is to be examined in its totality. Another problem area relates to increased emphasis on girls' education because if we educate a girl child we educate a family. If we talk of various types of empowerment of women it becomes our prime responsibility to educate them at every level. This needs attitudinal change, increased level of motivation and proper planning: Besides men education, another challenge comes out of the realisation that proper educational facilities must be given to socially and economically disadvantaged group as well as handicapped children so that they can unfold their potentialities and prove their worth as member of society and may not suffer from a sense of alienation.

On the whole, if we examine various challenges of higher education it becomes clear that these challenges are to be met by broadening our vision, developing skill and integrating all those aspects which have their direct or indirect bearing on human resource development. Hence, it needs an integrated effort at State, national and international level. Challenges are before us and we have to accept them and try to meet them by effective policy making and time-bound action plan with a practical vision.

Conclusions

Educational vocational value oriented and psychological empowerments are essential for vitalising or revitalising the present system of higher education if we have to move towards total quality control. In spite of rapid development of professional and technical education, the conventional education system is to be strengthened by proper modification and planning. Technical Council of India is also planning to introduce soft courses not covered by the conventional system. Whatever the type of educational system is to be introduced the aim is very clear: the learners have to learn and acquire real knowledge and the teachers in the form of any authority, have to impart real knowledge and make the learners real assets by controlling their limitations. The learners must be made to realise that knowledge is power and they have to make themselves empowered. With this academic weapon only they can take full benefit of the resources available and compete with the fast moving competitive world. Their faith in real acquisition of knowledge and information will provide the internal strength and generate a will to excel. Let all of us move forward towards adopting 'holistic approach' towards acquisition of knowledge in a knowledge-based society in an era of science and technology on which our present system of higher education should be based.

References

1. Altbach, P.G. and Knight, 2013. The Internationalisation of Higher Education: Motivations and Realities.
2. Ausubel, D. P. 1968. Educational Psychology: A Cognitive View. New York: Holt, Rinehart and Winston.
3. Bruer, T. John. 2013. In Search of Brain-Based Education. Phi Delta Kappan (May 1999), 649-57. http:// www.pdkintl.org/kappan/kbru9905.htm
4. Bruner, J. S. 1966. Toward a Theory of Instruction. New York: W. W. Norton.
5. Camoy, M. 2000. Globalisation and Educational Reform What Planners Need to Know, Report No.63, International Institute of Educational Planning, Paris.
6. Cheps 2015. The European higher Education and Research Landscape 2020, Anniversary Edition.
7. Department of Higher Education 2013. Ministry of Human Resource Development retrieved from http:// education.nic.in sector.asp on 2 I $I September 2005
8. Deutsch, M. 1949. A Theory of Cooperation and Competition. Human Relations, 2: 129-52.
9. Development of Education in India (2000-2010). Ministry of Human Resource Development, Annual Report, 2014, Part I.
10. Freire, Paulo. 2015. Pedagogy of the Oppressed. New York: Seabury.
11. Gardner, LHoward. 1993. Frames of Mind: The Theory of Multiple Intelligences. New York: Basic Books.
12. Goodlad, J.I. 2014. A Place Called School: Prospects for the Future. New York: McGraw -Hill.
13. Hahn, K010 In Internationalisation of Higher Education- Foreign Students in Germany, Results of the 17th Social Survey Deutsches Studentenwerk (DSW) conducted by HIS Hochschul-Informations-Systems. Berlin: Federal Ministry of Education and Research (BMBF) Publication and Website Division.
14. Johnson, D.W., and R.T. Johnson. 1989. Cooperation and Competition: Theory and Research. Edina, MN Interaction Book Company.
15. Johnson, D.W., R.T. Johnson, and E.J.Holubec. 1986. Circles of Learning: Cooperation in the Classroom. Edina, MN: Interaction Book Company.

16. Kagan, Spencer. 1994. Cooperative Learning. Edina, MN: Interaction Book Company.
17. Kerr, Clark, "Higher Education Cannot Escape History, Issues for the Twenty-First Century", State University of New York Press, 2014.
18. Kessler, Carolyn. 2015. Cooperative Language Learning. Englewood Cliffs, NJ: Prentice-Hall, INC.

15

New Education Policy (NEP) 2020: A Roadmap for India 2.0

Dr Gedam Kamalakar

Abstract

The National Education Policy 2020 NEP 2020 is formulated to revamp education system and lay down road map for new India. It was approved Indian cabinet on 29th July 2020. This paper is a maiden attempt to highlight NEP 2020 and study India 2.0 vision towards overall transformation education system to meet the challenges of twenty first century. This study is based on secondary data and exploratory in nature. Findings are based on a systematic review of existing literature. It was found that one of the main objectives of NEP 2020 is to increase student's enrolment in all educational institutions such as elementary school, professional and higher education by 2030. To achieve that it has suggested progressive reform in the existing education and governance systems. This study is preliminary review of policy document and it can be taken as base for future research with empirical data to study the impact of NEP after its implementation. NEP 2020 is expected to give big leap to higher education in India. The vision is to create India 2.0 for twenty first century which is bound to take leadership role at global arena. NEP 2020 is largely a very progressive document, with a firm grasp on the current socio-economic landscape and the prospect to meet future challenges. If implemented properly; then it has got everything to make India global hub in education by 2030. Recently adopted the National Education Policy 2020 reaffirmed the commitment of the Government that efforts will be made to reach six percent of the GDP but didn't mention the year by which the government intends to achieve this goal which would have far-reaching implications for the education sector which is still far away in attaining the status of universal school education in the real sense which is also true for the global commitment in attaining sustainable goals in general and education in particular (SDG4 Education). As against the six percent expenditure on education to GDP, the Economic Survey presented in the Parliament on 31st January 2022 indicate that it was

2.8 percent in 2019-20 as against 3.1 percent in 2020-21 (revised) and 3.1 percent in 2021-22. However, the focus of the present note is more on the School Education Department which plays a pivotal role in ensuring that it sends an adequate number of secondary graduates to the higher education without which the goal of 50 percent GER as envisaged in NEP 2020 is not likely to be realised by 2030. Without improving the efficiency of the school education, the higher education sector is not expected to receive an adequate number of secondary graduates because of which the school education department must receive adequate funds to initiate activities as adopted in the NEP 2020.

Keywords: NEP, GER, GDP, SDG, enrolment.

Introduction

The education policy refers to programme and guidelines based on the purpose of the educational administrators, forming a plan on how to conduct learning for students. The National Education Policy (NEP) is a policy prepared by the government to foster education amongst the citizens of India. The policy envelopes elementary education to college in both urban and rural parts of India.

To date, India has had three educational policies. The very first educational policy was implemented in the year 1986, under the guidance of Indira Gandhi and Rajiv Gandhi respectively. The policy was revised in the year 1992 when P.V. Narasimha Rao was the Prime Minister. The third education policy was released on July 29, 2020, under the ministership of Narendra Modi.

The cabinet minister of India approved the National Education Policy 2020, further encouraging the upcoming transformation in the academic reforms in the educational sector of the country. Apart from this, the Ministry of Human Resource and Development will also be renamed as the Ministry of Education. The primary focus of the new education policy is to bring forward major changes in the school and the higher education system. Here's all that you need to know about the upcoming academic reform.

Purpose of NEP

The NEP is a radical framework that assists the overall development of the education system of the country. The policy was introduced earlier in 1964, after Siddheshwar Prasad, former Congress MP reprehended the government for the lack of philosophy in education. The new educational policy is revised every few decades. The latest policy has replaced the 34-year-old NEP implemented in 1986.

Significant Features of NEP 2020

- The government schools will now be offering pre-school education, i.e., nursery, LKG, UKG. The Indian education system, which was previously based on 10+2 structure shifts to a 5+3+3+4 design. The learning structure based on the age of students will be divided into four parts, foundational, preparatory, middle school, and secondary school. Along with that, the new education policy denotes that the students will be taught in their mother tongue till class 5.
- There will be optional subjects for the students of class 10th. This means that the students can choose subjects like art and craft along with the conventional subjects of learning.
- The board exam structure will be redesigned to make it easier for students to perform during the examination. The primary aim of the test will be, to focus upon the core capacity of the student, rather than memorisation. Along with this, the government has introduced the option of two board exams so that the students can check their performance and ponder upon the improvements required.
- The undergraduate programme is now stretched for four years. If the student is pursuing their undergraduate programme with the research they will be further eligible to directly apply for a PhD programme.
- The undergraduate students now have multiple exit options. The students can drop out of their courses at any given point. On completing one year of the course, they will be receiving a certificate, on completing two years they will receive a diploma degree, and on completing three years they will be having a degree in the course itself.
- The higher education system will be multidisciplinary and the single-stream institutes will be fading out by the year 2040.
- Regulators who have been controlling the education system will no longer be in power. Systems like, UGC, AICTE, NCTE will be abolished and replaced by a single regulation.

Implementation Process

The policy will be providing guidelines and the state government is supposed to follow those. As per the policy, it is not a compulsion to follow it, for instance, Tamil Nadu is not following the triple language formula as per the education policy of 1968. Since education is coexistent, both the Center and state governments can have a collaborative approach for implementing the new educational reforms. The changes in the education system will not be immediate, the government has aimed to implement the entire policy by the year 2040.

As per the government, the plan is to set up committees based on various subjects along with the members of appropriate ministries. This committee will work on developing the implementation plan concerning NEP 2020. The overall planning will be followed by the annual review based on the targets achieved. The complete plan comprises a list of actions to be taken by the HRD Ministry, departments of education, schools, NCERT, etc.

Talking about the Difficulties in the Policy

Now apart from having various advantages, the NEP 2020 also has various hurdles to cross before it gets implemented. The policy aims to bring a considerate transformation by the year 2040. Whereas some proposals of this policy will have an immediate implementation, while others will take longer.

The policy is a 100 action plan which requires a steady growth based on time. Implementation of these actions will be done in phases based on regional and institutional development.

The Institutes of Eminence (IoEs) and the Central Universities will be leading the plan of action.

On the lines of legal changes, the draft of the Higher Education Commission of India Bill is still withering in the Ministry for more than a year. The manifesto for the Board of Governors will require changes to be made based on the Central and State University Acts. A note is already passed to the cabinet to form a National Research Foundation, but to make it a completely autonomous body it is necessary to implement an Act.

Another major concern is funding. Free breakfasts can be taken into consideration in the next academic year if the budget allocation covers it. The process of converting the affiliated colleges into an autonomous institution will approximately take 15 years as it requires financial assistance.

The NEP's chief purpose is to reform the education system and bridge the gap between current learning outcomes and those desired. Recognizing the need to keep up with a rapidly changing world and knowledge landscape, the NEP 2020 articulates that "the purpose of the education system is to develop good human beings capable of rational thought and action, possessing compassion and empathy, courage and resilience, scientific temper and creative imagination, with sound ethical moorings and values. It aims at producing engaged, productive, and contributing citizens for building an equitable, inclusive and plural society as envisaged by our constitution."

Such strong emphasis on equity and quality is laudable, as is the effort to broaden the scope of "quality education." The policy proposes a move away from content-heavy curricula in order "to make space for critical thinking, more holistic, inquiry-based, discovery-based, discussion-based and analysis-based learning." Giving equal importance to co-curricular activities (i.e., arts, sports, vocational skills), it mandates a shift toward multidisciplinary education, away from rigid silos of "arts," "science," and "commerce" streams, with renewed focus on twenty first century skills. This is a welcome breath of fresh air, given that the current system is strongly driven by rote learning and content-based examinations, divorced from any real application to life.

The NEP 2020 aims to make India a benchmark in the field of education. The academic year is delayed due to the pandemic and supposed to begin by September-October. The government plans to implement a few policies before the new academic year begins. Experts believe that the new education policy will bring a lot of positive changes in the education system of India shortly. All efforts must be made to improve the quality of public education but there's no reason why for-profit private schools can't coexist. In fact, private schools should be co-opted as partners in the delivering of the educational vision laid out by the NEP. The lessons learnt from 30 years of liberalisation should be now implemented in the education sector, thereby ensuring that India achieves the demographic dividend. The New Education Policy aligns with instrucko's Mission and Vision and with the implication of it within the Indian education system it opens up vast opportunities for bringing quality education home and prepare children to be the leaders of the future.

Conclusion

The new education policy has a laudable vision, but its strength will depend on whether it is able to effectively integrate with the other policy initiatives of government like Digital India, Skill India and the New Industrial Policy to name a few, in order to effect a coherent structural transformation. Hence, policy linkages can ensure that education policy addresses to and learns from Skill India's experience in engaging more dynamically with the corporate sector to shape vocational education curriculum in order to make it a success. There is also a necessity for more evidence-based decision-making, to adapt to rapidly evolving transmutations and disruptions. NEP has reassuringly provisioned for real-time evaluation systems and a consultative monitoring and review framework. This shall empower the education system to constantly reform itself, instead of expecting for a new education policy every decade for a shift in curriculum. This, in itself, will be a remarkable achievement. The NEP 2020 is a defining moment for higher education. Effective and time-bound implementation is what will make it truly path-breaking.

References

Aithal, P. S.; Aithal, Shubhrajyotsna (2019). "Analysis of Higher Education in Indian National Education Policy Proposal 2019 and Its Implementation Challenges". International Journal of Applied Engineering and Management Letters. 3 (2): 1-35. SSRN 3417517

Nandini, ed. (29 July 2020). "New Education Policy 2020 Highlights: School and higher education to see major changes". Hindustan Times.

Jebaraj, Priscilla (2 August 2020). "The Hindu Explains | What has the National Education Policy 2020 proposed?". The Hindu. ISSN 0971-751X

Chopra, Ritika (2 August 2020). "Explained: Reading the new National Education Policy 2020". The Indian Express.

Rohatgi, Anubha, ed. (7 August 2020). "Highlights | NEP will play role in reducing gap between research and education in India: PM Modi". Hindustan Times.

Krishna, Atul (29 July 2020). "NEP 2020 Highlights: School And Higher Education". NDTV.

Naidu, M. Venkaiah (8 August 2020). "The New Education Policy 2020 is set to be a landmark in India's history of education". Times of India Blog.

https://static.pib.gov.in/WriteReadData/userfiles/NEP_Final_English_0.pdf

https://www.orfonline.org/expert-speak/national-education-policy-2020-policy-times/

https://www.highereducationdigest.com/the-impact-of-national-education-policy-2020-on-professional-education/

http://bweducation.businessworld.in/article/NEP-2020-Impact-On-Higher-Education-/07-08-2020-305999/

https://timesofindia.indiatimes.com/readersblog/theaitics/implications-of-the-national-education-policy-2020-on-higher-education-in-india-2-24729/

https://www.hindustantimes.com/india-news/pm-modi-s-address-at-conclave-on-transformational-reforms-in-higher-education-under-national-education-policy-highlights/story-dehOW8q8ZRrONbbFSRjg0H.html

Ajay Kurien: is the Assistant Co-ordinator of Internal Quality Assurance Cell (IQAC), MACFAST. He completed his MBA in Marketing and Finance and his areas of interests are quality assurance, project management and public relations.

Sudeep, B. Chandramana: is an Associate Professor in the Department of Management Studies, MACFAST. He completed his PhD in Consumer Behaviour in Retail Industry. His areas of interests are strategic management, sustainable development and international business.

16

A Comparative Study of Semester System and Annual System

Dr M. Samatha and Dr M.T. Jyotsna

Abstract

Education Universities have distinct strategies to educate the youth. Primarily there are two methods, acquired, in universities - semester system and annual system. In annual system, exams are conducted after one educational year, while in semester system; exams are conducted after five or six months. There are many comparisons in between annual and semester. So, in this paper we are going to describe the pros and cons of semester and annual system. Moreover, this study concentrating on the objectives to discriminate annual and semester systems and to identify the internal value of both systems, regarding students, teachers and Universities perspective.

Keywords: Academic Stress Levels, Annual System, Semester System, Quality Education, University, Syllabus, Evaluation.

Introduction

The basic eligibility for any competitive exam in India is a degree. Even though the eligibility for UPSC exams is also degree. Very few people used to pursue PG after degree in earlier days and secured jobs with degrees. Over time, there were many changes in the educational system and post graduation became common. It is important to note that the standard for the degree education must be strictly concerned as it is the basis for any job. For a student to compete in this competitive world, knowledge is must. There are also many responsibilities on the universities like to care of the standard of the education being provided, conserving the nativity, enhancing the skills of the student, preparing them to secure a job, making them understand the responsibilities of a citizen, and making them a part of national development.

Syllabus designing and conducting exams are two different crucial steps in the educational system. The purpose of education is not getting a certificate but to interpret the knowledge in real life is the purpose of education. Conducting board exams in 10th standard without any prior board examinations in earlier classes makes it difficult for the students to understand the competition outside their schools and colleges. If the examination system of the degree students is concerned, there used to be an Annual exam system till 2016-2017.

Annual system

Exams will be conducted yearly once. Unit tests, quarterly, half-yearly, pre final exams will be conducted respectively in the year. This is a less expensive procedure for universities. Ample of time is given to prepare and print the question papers.

Semester system

During 2016-2017, universities introduced a semester system with CBCS. A year is divided into two parts in a semester system where one semester completes in six months of time. The syllabus is divided into 6 semesters with credits for each paper and grades replaced marks in this system. This procedure is expensive and students find it difficult to cope with this pattern of examination.

Annual vs Semester system

In this comparison, one has to look at the results and the percentage of students will pursue higher education after their degree. The student may neglect their studies if it is a yearly exam pattern thinking of having a lot of time to prepare for the exams. Advantage of this system is it helps students find time to focus on their interests like extracurricular activities. This traditional system made a huge impact on the minds of rural students and their parents. The percentage of students who attend colleges regularly decreased in the Annual system and students find it difficult to secure jobs with traditional degree courses. By hearting the answers and forgetting them after completion of exams left students with nothing. This led to the implementation of a semester system where students study throughout the year and this system succeeded in doing so.The drawbacks of this system is students feel it difficult to learn all the subjects in a Limited period of time and it blocks the students with only education giving them no scope to follow their passions. Teachers along with students have the burden of completing the syllabus, conducting exams and evaluating the students. March used to be the month of exams till Junior College level, but with this system, the period of academic year extended till April in 2021 August .which makes it difficult for the rural students to manage their financial assistance. If a student fails, they have to wait till the next semester to complete their backlogs. Some of the students not interested to continue the studies. Due to Covid-19, all semester exam fees are asked to be paid again by the students which are a great burden on the low income students. Many students drop their education with this semester fee structure as they are economically insufficient.

The main motto of the choice based system is that a student can choose subjects of their interest and seek deep knowledge in those subjects. However, many students are not interested in taking the new courses introduced with the fear of getting a job. Now the semester system has become expensive to the colleges but not to the universities as the colleges is required to print the question papers and conduct the exams. Due to this semester system, many rural area students are dropping out their education. People from urban areas and literate people are continuing their higher education. Another major reason for rural students back stepping for continuing their studies is payment of semester exam fee, failure of the exam, proper credits are not gaining the student is detained these reasons student leave the College. This is not a problem in Annual exams system. During Covid-19 period, many students were promoted without exams whether appeared or not.

On surveying students and teachers for the pros and cons of the two systems of examinations, many of them wished for Annual system of examinations.

Annual

- Lot of time
- Detailed teaching
- Time to prepare for PG Entrance along with their agricultural work
- Fees convenience
- Students start their preparation for exams at the last moment
- Exams are conducted after continuous teaching
- Assessment and evaluation is not burden
- Average learning
- No much interaction
- Better for rural students

Semester

- Short time
- Syllabus completing on time
- Less time to prepare for PG Entrance and other exams

- Syllabus burden
- Students prepare for exams daily-continuous learning
- Assessment and evaluation helps students
- Maximum learning
- More interaction with teachers
- Not better for rural students
- No time for other works

Conclusion

Any examination system, be it Semester or Annual should not become burden to the students. If CBCS system is to continued, then 1,3,5 semesters should be conducted by respective colleges and 2,4,6 semesters should be conducted by universities so that it reduces financial burden on students. Due to Covid-19, changes are made in the pattern of question papers but it would be better if the change comes in the conduct of examinations. Without understanding the system of examination, some rural students feel difficult to face the exams and back steps for the higher education. Students find it difficult to understand the subject due to online classes during the period of Covid-19. Respect for the teachers is not same earlier, online classes made teachers just instructors.

Quality of learning deteriorated, earlier students used to learn the concepts and lessons but now it has become by hearting question and answers that too minimum questions. Open book system is better than by hearting and questions must analyze students thinking skills and should help them present their answers in their own words. The rural student education is affected by the agricultural season like Rabi and Kharif. Because almost every student comes from agriculture families.

References

1. https://pediaa.com/what-is-the-difference-between-semester-and-annual-system/
2. https://pamirtimes.net/2016/07/20/annual-versus-semester-examination/
3. Ancient Education System of India: https://ncert.nic.in/textbook/pdf/heih111.pdf
4. Indian Education: Ancient, Medieval and Modern- Mangesh M. Ghonge, Rohit Bag and Aniket Singh.
5. https://www.collegedekho.com/articles/semester-vs-annual-system-good-move-or-not/
6. www.google.com
7. https://timesofindia.indiatimes.com/topic/semester-system/news
8. Choice-Based Credit System (CBCS) and Semester System in Indian Higher Education- Mn Rajivlochan,Panjab University, Meeta Rajivlochan, RUSA

17

Higher Education for the Women in the Era of Globalisation

Sameera Nazneen

Abstract

The paper revamps education as a tool for enlightenment and knowledge which gives women the confidence they need for success in this era of globalisation. Liberalisation has opened the doors of higher education for students from all walks of life greater access, free flow of information, ideas, and plethora of opportunities across the border, to name of few. However, the result of Globalisation of education has been paradoxical in the Indian scenario, especially in the backdrop of the structural changes struggling with the issue of the equality. No doubt mass education has taken off, yet in practice socio-cultural hegemony exists in the educational institutions. Modernisation and scientific development will increasingly demand competencies and pose challenges requiring more vibrant personnel. Higher education needs to be reoriented to increase women's entry to conventionally male dominated courses and equip them to take up entrepreneurial administration.

Education is undergoing constant changes under the effects of globalisation. Education has been proclaimed an integral part of human Rights. "It must be free and compulsory with regards to basic, elementary teaching. Vocational and technological teaching must be widely available and access to higher education available to all the equally, on the basis of merit." Education is also the driving force behind economic growth and human and cultural development. The application of policies of compulsory basic for all and investment in quality teaching have meant governments and experts have been able to measure the impact on population and the society as a whole. Thus, higher education is a pathway of women empowerment. Institution of higher education should cross their traditional border of teaching only the designed curriculum of traditional courses. National policy for women includes social empowerment, economic empowerment and gender justice. It is the duty of higher education institutions to make provision of training. Employment and income generation activities for women, the path is clear for only strong and positive attitude with assertive efforts on the part of higher education sector and society at large are needed. Then there will be no limit for women except the sky. The paper concludes that women should seize all the avenues open to them to go to Higher education so as to increase their social and political power in the society. It is a strong reason why State governments around should assume the responsibility for providing and financing Higher education especially basic education for women.

Key words: Globalisation, liberalisation, Third World Countries, Education etc.

Introduction

Globalisation and liberalisation has opened the doors of higher education for students from all walks of life greater access, free flow of information, ideas, and plethora of opportunities across the border, to name of few. Women play a key role in the socio-economic progress of any society. They must therefore be equally participant and equal beneficiaries of development programmemes. The United Nations Development Programme (UNDP, 1997) observes that women worldwide constitute half of the population and perform two-thirds of the hours worked, but receive only 10 percent of the world's income and have just one percent of the world' property registered. In last few decades, awareness has mounting worldwide that unless something radical is none to empower women, global progress stands mortgaged. Education at the higher levels has been recognised as "an instrument par excellence for effecting national development" as well as "a dynamic instrument of change". It is the basis for the promotion and improvement of the status of women. It builds 'human capabilities': the essential and individual power to reflect, make choices, seek a voice in society and enjoy a better life.

Globalisation and Education

Globalisation is a process, which has affected many areas of human life. Globalisation is the present worldwide drive towards a globalised economic system dominated by supranational corporate trade and banking institutions that are not accountable to democratic process or national government. In the words of Martin Khor - "Globalisation is what we in the Third World have for several centuries called colonisation". Globalisation, liberalisation, privatisation and mercerisation are synonymous terminologies. If we accept one, it would be presumed that we accept the rest. Few years back education was widely considered to be a public good and free good like air and water. It was unthinkable that on the Indian soil education could be sold for purchased like any other goods. But now it is reality. As air and water have been converted into trade goods, so has been education.

Developing Countries or Third World countries include African, Asian and most of the Latin American countries. One of the greatest problems in third world countries is poverty. Poverty is the condition of having insufficient resources to live a healthy life. The United Nations Development Programme (1996) created three basic minimal essential criteria which are essential for human requirements (to be well nourished, to be able to reproduce and to be educated). The other most pressing problems of the economy of developing countries are unemployment. It is directly related to lack of education, rapid change of technology, recessions, inflation, disability and discrimination in the place of work.

Education is undergoing constant change under effects of globalisation. Education has been proclaimed an integral part of human rights: "it must has free and compulsory with regards to basic, elementary teaching, vocational and technological teaching must be widely available and access to higher education available to all equally, on the basis of merit". Education is also the driving force behind economic growth and human and cultural development. The application of policies of compulsory basic for all and investment in quality teaching have meant governments and experts have been able to measure the impact on population and the society as a whole. That impact can be seen in improvement in health, lowering rate of demographic growth, reduction of child mortality and increases in life expectancy.

Education also means that populations become aware of their rights and obligations a citizen's and are thus able to participate actively in the construction and management of life in their communities. Globalisation is increasingly and everywhere making the education a business. One of the major impacts of globalisation on education is increased pressure to improve the quality of schooling; this is the result of the increased pressure on economies to be more productive in the face of greater competition. The emergence of self-financing education and the withdrawal of state from higher education sector, leads to communalisation in education. Globalisation insists to withdraw government allocation from the service and welfare sector. The major expenditure of the government in the welfare sector is for education. But for getting petty loans from World Bank and IMF as part of economic globalisation these poor countries are now relinquishing its responsibility had handling over the vital section of the greedy private sector.

Growth of Higher Education in India

With the phenomenal growth, higher education system in India emerged as the second largest system in the world after China, producing the second or the third largest stock of scientific and technical manpower. The spectacular growth has also helped the nation in achieving self-reliance in manpower needs and even to export manpower to the advanced countries. The number of graduates produced in the system is so large that the emigration of graduates to other countries is no more regarded as brain drain and as a problem. The massive expansion of higher education has also helped in democratising higher education system to some extent, which has highly elitist and restricted to the high-income groups.

Table 1: Growth of Higher Education in India

Universities	Colleges	Teachers	Enrolment ('000s)	Gross Enrolment	
				(Million)	Ratio(%)
1950-51	28	578	24	0.17	1.5
1960-61	45	1819	62	0.56	4.2
1970-71	93	3277	190	1.96	4.7
1980-81	123	4577	244	2.75	5.9
1990-91	184	6627	271	4.4	8.1
2000-01	254	10152	395	8.94	15.0
2010-11	559	32964	-	-	-
2011-12	700*	35539	933.7	21.7	21.1*

Source: Selected Educational Statistics (Ministry of Human Resource Development. Government of India, New Delhi, various years): Annual Report(s) University Grants Commission, New Delhi, various years); and Twelth Five-Year Plan (New Delhi: Planning Commission 2013).

To about 40 percent of the students in higher education are women and about one-third are from weaker socio-economic strata of the society. The growth in higher education also made a significant contribution to socio-economic and political development of the nation. It's contribution is in strengthening democracy and ensuring political stability is also significant. However, the growth in higher education has not been problem free, nor is it even. Certain aspects of the growth are quite marked. But for the first two decades of development planning in India, the growth rates in higher education have been modest until the beginning of this last decade of the last century. The rate of growth in enrolments was nearly doubled between 1990-91 and 2000-11. In fact much of the growth has taken place between 1995-96 and 2010-11.

According to the gross enrolment ratios estimated based on NSS reports, compared to the 10 percent of the 18-23 age group attending higher education in 1983-84, 23.1 percent attending higher education in 1983-84, 23.1 percent attended in 2009-10; in about 26 years, the ratio increased by three times. In contrast, net enrolment ratio increases at a slower pace; it increased very modestly from 8 percent in 1999-2000 to 10.2 percent by 2004-05 by about 2 point in 5 years (Table-2).

Table 2: Growth in the progress of Higher Education in India. All Population

Gross Enrolment Ratio	
1983-84	7.67
1987-88	8.57
1993-94	8.85
1999-2000	10.08
2004-05	12.59
2009-10	23.05
New Enrollment Ratio	
1999-2000	8.60
2004-10	92.5
Transition Ratio	
2009-10	19.4

The eligible enrolment ratio is a better ratio than gross or net enrolment ratio, as it refer to the students enrolled in higher education as percentage of those who have successfully graduated from schools. On an average according to the available estimates, 53 percent of the high school graduates were found to be entering higher education institutions in 2004-05. Constrained by unavailability of required data, Azam and Blom (2009) have redefined transition rate as total population in the age group 18-23 who either attend or have completed higher education as a proportion of population in the age group 18-23 who have completed higher secondary education. The transition rate thus defined is estimated to be fairly high, higher than eligible enrolment ratio. This ratio was 67.4 percent in 1993-94, which increased to 71 percent by 2004-05 after a marginal decline to 65.2 percent in 1999-2000. These rates suggest that a high proportion like 70 percent of the high school graduates take admission in higher education institutions.

According to the latest All India Survey on Higher Education (AISHE) 2019-20, India's gross enrollment ratio (GER) has increased from 26.3 percent to 27.1 percent in 2019-20.

GER for higher education reflects the percentage of the total population attending college and university - 18 to 23 years of age. Education Minister Ramesh Pokhriyal has released the 'Nishank' survey. "This report provides key performance indicators on the current state of higher education in the country," the Ministry of Education said.In 2019-20, the GER for women will be 27.3 percent and for men it will be 26.9 percent. This means that more qualified women than men are studying in colleges and universities in India. About 49 percent of the total enrolment in 2019-20 will be students.Raising GER is one of the main goals of the new National Education Policy (NEP). The Modi government wants to reach 50 percent GER by 2035 through various reforms included in the NEP.

Women in Higher Education

Women education has its roots in the British Regime. But before independence, education of women was mainly confined to school stage and their access to higher education was limited to the better-off sections only. The literacy rate of women increased from a mere 0.2 percent in 1882 to only six percent in 1947. At the time of independence out of the total enrolment of about 25,000 students (including those pursuing pre-university courses in higher around 23,000 (about 9.2 percent) were women. Nearly 87 percent women pursued general education in Arts, Science, Commerce and Liberal Arts including languages. By way of contrast, during the mid-1950s; British universities and colleges had nearly 25 percent women in the total enrolment (University Grants Commission, 1960). In 1958, the government of India appointed a National Committee for the Education of Women. The Committee submitted it's report in favour of women education. Most of its recommendations were accepted by the government of India..

In 1964-66, the Kothari Commision emphasised explicitly on equal educational opportunities for women. Later the University Education Commission Report pointd out that the education system existing in India is entirely immaterial in women. They also suggestd that the system is a waste and definite disability for the women. Subsequent Five Year Plans and various committees including the National Perspective Plan (1988-2000) stressed the need for greater participation of women in higher education to some extent from 25.78 lakhs in 1993-04 to 42.6 lakhs in 1999-2000 and 56.06 lakh in 2004-05. The corresponding figures for men are 51 lakhs, 69 lakhs. In 1993, the MHRD report also pinpointed this and said that women account only for four third of students at higher education level. So in absolute terms, we can say that women continue to lag behind men.

But the accelerated growth rate in women's enrolement has helped in narrowing the gender gap between men and women. According to figures given by UGC, the proportion of women in higher education stood at a base 10 percent as of 2012-13. While the Mandal Commission tried to equalise caste bias, gender bias hasn't got redressed so far. Public space never been considered as women's area. Hence, in many cases sons are sent to school/college but not daughters. They are sent for miscellaneous short courses that keep them busy until marriage. While total enrolment of students in regular mode in higher education institutes in India is around 241.8 lakhs, 13.47 million are boys and 10.69 million girls of total enrolment (All India Survey on Higher Education, 2013) (Table 3).

Table 3: Men and Women Students - Growth in Higher Education (1950-51 to 1912-13)

Year	Men ('000)	Women ('000)	Total Enrolment	Women a percent of all Students
1950-51	157	17	174	10.00
1955-56	252	43	295	14.60
1960-61	468	89	557	16.00
1965-66	849	218	1067	20.40
1970-71	1563	391	1954	20.00
1975-76	2131	595	2426	24.50
1980-81	2003	749	2752	27.20
1985-86	2512	1059	3571	29.60
1990-91	1986	1439	4425	32.50
1995-96	4235	2191	6426	34.10
2000-01	4988	3012	8001	37.60
2005-06	6562	4466	11028	40.50
2012-2013*	13468	10687	24180	44.20

Source: Enrolment of women in higher education (selected educational statistics 2005-06; University Grants Commission Annual Report, various years). *Statistical Report-registrar.edu/edu/statistics/reports and Archana-Renju (2014).

Modernisation and scientific development will increasingly demand competencies and pose challenges requiring more vibrant personnel. Higher education needs to be reoriented to increase women's entry to conventionally male dominated courses and equip them to take up entrepreneurial administration.

There has been an 18.2 percent rise in female enrolment from 2015-16 to 2019-20. The Gender Parity Index (GPI) in higher education rose to 1.01 in 2019-20 against 1.00 in 2018-19.

The percentage share of men is higher than women at almost every level, except M.Phil, postgraduate and certificate courses. Women participation in professional courses is lower in comparison to academic courses at both undergraduate and postgraduate levels.

Share of women is the lowest in Institutions of National Importance, followed by Deemed University-Government, State Private University. Distance enrolment constitutes about 11.1 percent of the total enrolment.The man-woman ratio is similar among all social groups. In case of OBCs, its 50.5: 49.5. There are more women students than men among minorities.

Gender inequalities in Higher Education

Probably the most important problem faced by the higher education system in India is the persistence of inequalities in access to higher education. Inequalities in access to higher education result in socio-economic inequalities in the society which in turn accentuate inequalities in education. In fact, it a cyclic chain of inequalities; inequalities in access to higher education result in inequalities in employment and participation in labour market, resulting in inequalities in earnings contribution in turn to socio-economic and political inequalities again are translated into the education sector, resulting in inequalities in education. Inequalities in access to education reflect loss of individual as well as social welfare. That economic returns to their counterparts (Tilak, 1987), implies that inequalities in education would cause huge losses in National output; and that inclusive strategies that contribute to equity should be viewed favourably not only from the point of view of social justice but also even in terms of economic wellbeing as the total equity gains might surpass the losses in efficiently, if any (Patnaik, 2012).

During the post-independence period, there is a significant improvement in women's participation in higher education. Women constitute 43 percent of the total enrolments in higher education in 2011-12, while there were only 14 women per 100 men in higher education in 1950-51, according to the available UGC statistics (UGC, 2013). Thus compared to the earlier decades, this marks a significant improvement. Women students constitute 11 percent in engineering/technology, four percent in medicine and less than five percent in education. Nevertheless, the overall level of participation of women in higher education has improved remarkably and current overall level is quite impressive. Further, research studies (for example, Basant and Sen, 2012), have also shown that after controlling for other factors, the chances of women participation in higher education are higher than men generally observed inequalities by gender in higher education need to be interpreted with caution.

The gross enrollment ratio among men increased from 10.9 percent in 1983-84 to 27 percent in 2009-10. It increased by 2.5 times in about two decades and half. In contrast, only 19 percent of the women in the relevant age group were enrolled in higher education in 2009-10. But what is strikingly clear that there has been a rapid progress in the enrolment ratio among women increased by more than four times. As a result gender inequalities in gross enrolment ratio have come down very significantly during this period. A simple coefficient of inequality (ratio of male enrolment ratio over female enrolment ratio) declined from 2.4 in 1983-84 to 1.4 in 2009-10.

Table 4: Enrolment Ratios in Higher Education, by Gender

	Women	Men	Coefficient of Inequality
Gross Enrolment Ratio			
1983-84	4.49	10.87	2.4209
1987-88	5.37	11.82	2.2011
1993-94	5.9	11.7	1.9831
1999-2000	8.0	12.1	1.5125
2004-05	10.4	14.8	1.4231
2009-10	18.7	27.0	1.4402
Net Enrolment Ratio			
1999-2000	6.8	9.4	1.3905
2004-05	8.5	11.8	13.905
Eligible Enrolment Ratio			
2004-05	48.6	19.7	1.1440
Transmission Ratio			
2009-10	19.0	19.7	1.0374

Note: Coefficient of inequality in simply the male - female ratio.

The enrolment rate of women in higher education clearly shows that there has been development over the years in considering special education as an important part of 'women's development'. But the picture is still vague. Real indicators such as the gross enrolment ratio make it clear that women are on the path to higher education, but the rate at which it is happening is not strong enough to cover gender inequality and lead the country towards sustainable development. Only a few of the literate women received special education to gain financial independence, while the majority of literate women received education only to qualify further for marriage. The rural and urban society needs to understand that women constitute 48 percent of the total population today and if these 48 percent are prevented from developing specialised skills, knowledge and expertise to provide their best, huge amounts of human resources will be wasted and this will ultimately serve as a major obstacle to national development. It is imperative that every girl be provided with a full school education and thereby enrolled for timely higher education in accordance with her qualifications and interests. It is a prerequisite for the socio-economic development of women and society as a whole. Fully aware of the need for effective human resources for national development, the Government and allied Ministries are doing their best to provide ample opportunities for higher education to Young India. And then preventing our women from enrolling for higher education and giving them more meaning is their life when we can do the same in our men.

Conclusion

Higher education is the best tool to achieve the cherished goal of women empowerment in the Indian context. But if it is to become a vigorous agent for ending gender discrimination, it requires a new perception and understanding about the origin of women's subordination. It is not class room transaction only, but the combined mobilisation of community, political vision and bureaucratic will that hold the key. The bedrock of such a road map should be a gender sensitive approach aimed at correcting the imbalances in our educational landscape. But in a country like India where in the people gave themselves the Constitution but not the ability to keep it, inherited a resplendent heritage but not the wisdom to cherish it and suffer and endure in patience without the perception of their potential. Attaining this goal needs proactive strategies and administrative competence.

It is said that women do three-ifths of the world's work, earn one-tenth of the World's income and own one-hundredth of the world's asset (Harsh Gandhar). Empowerment requires self-help, confidence, daring, knowledge and skill. All these are facilitated by education especially the higher education. Thus, higher education is a pathway of women empowerment. Institution of higher education should cross their traditional border of teaching only the designed curriculum of traditional courses. National Policy for women includes social empowerment, economic empowerment and gender justice. It is the duty of higher education institutions to make provision of training, employment and income generation activities for women. This would help women to take off themselves. The path is clear for only strong and positive attitude with assertive efforts on the part of higher education sector and society at large are needed. Then there will be no limit for women except the sky.

References

1. Azam, M., and Blom, A. (2009, April). Progress in participation in teritiary education in India from 1983 to 2004. Journal of Educational Planning land Administration. 23 (2:125-67)

2. UNDP (1997). Human Development Report, Oxford University Press, New York.
3. Mc Mohan, Walter W. (1999). Education and Development. New York: Oxford University Press.
4. Tilak, Jandhyala B.G (1987), Economic of inequality in education, New Delhi: Sage Publications.
5. Singh, Ayesha, (2014). "Higher Education: A Dream Too High". The New Indian Express.
6. Davies (2001). "Women and Work" in Anderson Margart (ed.), Thinking about Women: Sociological Perspectives on sex and Gender, Allyn and Bacon, London.
7. Taxak, Pratima. (2013). "Women Empowerment through Higher Education". International Indexed and Referred Research Journal, Vol. IV (4), January.
8. Begum, Syed Mehartaj (2010). 'Women Empowerment through Higher Education' University News, October.
9. Agarwal. (2006). 'Higher Education in India: The Need for Change', Indian Council of Research on International Economic Relations. Working paper No. 180.
10. Indian Planning Commission (2012). Higher Education in India: Twelth Five Year Plan (2012-2017) and Beyond, New Delhi.
11. Shetty, P.K. and other (2010). 'Research and Higher Education in select Indian State Universities an analysis'. Indian Journal of Science and Technology, 3(3).
12. Basant, Rakesh, and Sen, Gitanjali (2010, 25 September). Who participates in Higher education in India? Rethinking the role of affirmative action. Economic and Political Weekly, 45(39):62-70.
13. Weiss Kopf, 'Thomas E. (2004, 25 September). Impact of reservation on admission to higher education in India. Economic and Political Weekly, 39:4339-49.
14. Janaki, K (2005). 'Universities as Boundary Breakers for Empowerment of the Socio-economically Weak in Indai'. University News, Vol.43 N.47, Nov.21-27.
15. Srivastava, Nailing (2005). 'Empowerment of Women through Higher Education', University News, Vol. 43. No.47, Nov. 21-27.
16. Pillai, V.N.Rajasekharan (2005). 'Role of Universities in the Empowerment of Women through Education', University News, Vol. 43. No. 03, Jan. 17-23.
17. Bhadauria, Mridula (2005). 'Access of Women to Higher Education'. University New, Vol.43. No.06. Feb. 07-13.
18. Gandhar, Harsh (2005). 'Gender Disparity in Higher Education in Independent India'. University News, Vol.43. No.42, Oct. 17-13, 2005.

18

Revisiting Gurukul Pedagogue - A Forgotten Pathway to Make Virtual Learning Viable and Wholesome

M. Samuel Praveen Kumar

Abstract

Education from time immemorial, continue to be the most integral aspect of any civilisation. Over the years, it has adapted itself to the changing needs of time and to keep abreast with evolutionary changes and steering towards becoming a meaningful process and promoting lifelong learning. An education system that originated in the eastern world and continues to be a source of inspiration is the ancient Gurukul education system of India.

During the modern times, one aspect which halted every walk of human life in every corner of the world, but at the same time, opened up new perspective and orientation of life, which otherwise would never have been explored is Novel Covid - 19 pandemic. Pedagogue and teaching-learning process too received intellectual churning during pandemic which resulted in surfacing of a cream of innovative and technology based teaching - learning practices. Online or virtual mode of teaching which emerged as a boon during the lockdown, took over the baton to continue the rally of education to the next level. The process of transitioning from a traditional teaching method to the innovative online method requires the academic institution in general and the faculty in particular to meticulously plan activities, tasks, and evaluation methods. This also requires the formulation of a supportive policy by the government with scope for alterations with the changing tides. Despite the challenges faced, online platforms facilitated the continuity of learning process during lockdown and salvaged the education system from the loss of an academic year. Choice Based Credit System (CBCS) found a new boat to sail in the form of digital learning mode. The cloud platform made the atlas shrink and helped the students to avail the lectures of experts from any part of the world, which was even unthinkable with traditional learning. Time, space and economy are the other benefits of online education.

The present study endeavours to explore the pros and cons of online mode of learning and also to identify the challenges of assimilating the virtual mode into the physical mode of learning. This paper also endeavours to trace the relevance of reassertion of Gurukul Pedagogue through virtual channels. Ancient Indian indigenous education, through gurukuls facilitated activity based learning, focused on applied knowledge, enriched with values and ethics, and aimed at holistic development of the student. The present paper attempts to ponder the feasibility of reviving gurukul pedagogue and to identify the possibilities of blending it with modern education through the virtual platforms.

Keywords: Pedagogue, Gurukul, Virtual, Credit System.

'Change is the only constant' said Heraclitus. Change could be either evolutionary or revolutionary. Right from the days of Sophists in Greece and oral culture in India to the modern times, pedagogue underwent a gradual and a progressive change playing its role in moulding the human civilisation. But, for the first time in history, humankind has witnessed a paradigm change in pedagogue during the initial decades of twenty first century because of the novel Covid-19 pandemic. This unforeseen situation has thrown the education system into a furnace to emerge out in new shape demanded by the situation. As quoted by Neel Burton "the highest purpose of education is to unlearn what we once took for granted, to replace certainty with subtlety, prejudice with compassion, and destiny with possibility", the Covid-19 pandemic situations has triggered a fission process in the intellectual corridors to reorient the education system so as to traverse through the odds unleashed by the pandemic and identify the possibilities of navigating new trends in teaching and learning process. For the first time in the human history, all the nations are compelled to gear up for the same cause. India being no exception and with 130 crore population, rose to the occasion and manoeuvred to take teaching and learning process from between the four walls of the class room to the doorsteps of the students during the lockdown.

24th March 2020, the day lockdown was imposed in India, remains as an epoch in Indian history, for the reason that, though the dark clouds of Covid hovered over the country, it heralded the new beginning of exploring the untraveled avenues of all walks of life including the education system thereby developing alternatives to the frontal teaching mode.

Changing Contours of Virtual Learning in Higher Education

Distance learning is not a new concept in India. Different models of learning beyond the class room like MOOCS (Massive Open Online Courses), Open Universities, Distance Learning schools etc have coexisted with conventional learning for many years. But, the Covid-19 pandemic has completely halted the conventional way of learning, opening the new gates for digital or online education.

Lockdown and social distancing measures due to the Covid-19 pandemic have led to closures of schools, training institutes and higher education facilities in whole of the country. There is a paradigm shift in learning process from class room learning to cloud learning. The online learning, distance and continuing education have become a panacea for this unprecedented global pandemic. E-learning tools such as Google Class Room, ZOOM, Microsoft Teams, YouTube links have played a crucial role during this pandemic, helping schools and universities facilitate student learning during the closure of universities and schools. But, as every change comes with its own advantages and disadvantages, so is the case with online learning process.

Origin of Research Problem

The practical experience of all the educators suggests that, initially great enthusiasm was noted among the learners. But in later stages students developed apathy and lackadaisical attitude towards online learning. It is noted that the percentage of students attending online classes has declined drastically. To address this issue is inescapable imperative. Thorough research need to be done on the psychological and emotional traits of students and accordingly pedagogue has to be modified to make it more effective and less burdensome. The researcher also identified that the present system of education failed in promoting holistic development of the students. Gaining of knowledge occupied the centre stage in education process, pushing virtue and values to the periphery.

Research Methodology

In completion of this paper the researcher adopted empirical and analytical methods.

The research is based on primary data collected through Google Forms from students of Under Graduate Colleges of Telangana. The secondary data is procured from Journals, Magazines and Internet.

Significance of Online Learning

The process of transitioning from a traditional teaching method to the innovative online method requires the academic institution in general and the faculty in particular to meticulously plan activities, tasks, and evaluation methods. This also requires the formulation of a supportive policy by the government with scope for alterations with the changing tides. Despite the challenges faced, the significance of online learning can be as follows:

1. Online platforms facilitated the continuity of learning process during lockdown. It also salvaged the education system from the loss of an academic year. Absence of this facility would have resulted in a sudden halt in learning process leading to irreparable catastrophe.
2. Choice Based Credit System (CBCS) found a new boat to sail in the form of digital learning mode. CBCS facilitates the students to score credits in different subjects and in different institutions spread out in the country. But, the students were required to travel long distances and had to face difficulty in finding the hostel facility. Thanks to online mode of learning that it eased the implementation of CBCS.
3. The introduction of myriad digital and online tools facilitated 'Blended Learning' in education process. It is a teaching and learning approach, instructional methodology that combines both physical class room teaching and digital tools to transfer knowledge. This facility has opened new channels for transfer of instructions and made learning process more interesting and less burdensome. The disadvantages of face-to-face learning are to a maximum extent mitigated by computer mediated learning and vice-versa.
4. Online learning allows differently-abled students with more freedom to participate in learning in the virtual environment, requiring limited movement.
5. Pandemic has caused lot of psychological trauma and emotional stress to the vast majority of population in general and to the students in particular. Uncertainty, fear of death, and bleak future created havoc on the psyche of the students. This problem to the maximum was mitigated by the online education, which engaged the students and kept their hopes alive by keeping them in touch with their teachers and peer circle.
6. Online platforms widened the scope of acquiring knowledge. It helped to make available to the students, the lectures of experts from any part of the country, rather any part of the world, which was even unthinkable with traditional learning.
7. Online learning offers teachers an efficient way to deliver lessons to students. Online learning has number of tools such as videos,

PPTs, PDFs, podcasts etc which a teacher can use as part of their lesson plans.

8. Time, space and economy are the other advantages of online education. This system provides for the travel less learning process, allowing the students to attend classes from their homes, which saves their travel time. It is economical too because it saves the travel expenses and online material will bring down the paper cost.

Challenges of Online Learning

Though online technology ushered new paradigm of learning, it cannot be adjudged as the paragon of learning initiatives. It has its own drawbacks which can be summarised with the following reasons:

1. Online learning technology is a paradigm change that engulfed the education system, world over, as a desert storm, for which the phalanx of educators and students in all countries were unprepared and unequipped. Standing on the frontline, facing new challenge, the educators could only replace chalk and black board with smart phones, but continued with same time table and teaching methods. Though, initially enthusiasm was noted among the learners, many studies reported that gradually the students developed apathy and lackadaisical attitude towards online learning. To address this issue is inescapable imperative. Thorough research need to be done on the psychological and emotional traits of students and accordingly pedagogue has to be modified to make it more effective and less burdensome.
2. There is no one-size-fits-all pedagogy for online learning. There are a variety of subjects with varying needs. Different subjects and age groups require different approaches to online learning. The online teaching infrastructure presently used could not be mastered to adopt it to different situations. The limited exposure of teachers to online teaching, the information gap, non-conducive environment for learning at home could be seen as the drawbacks of online teaching.
3. One of the biggest drawbacks of online learning is that the students find it hard to focus on the screen for a longer duration. Social media on the other side adds fuel to the fire. The academic literature is replete with research findings that lectures adhere to the 10 to 15 min attention span. Davis Barbara Gross in his book "Tools of Teaching" stated that "...student attention during lectures tends

to wane after approximately 10 - 15 minutes. The over ambitious mechanism of adopting the same timings of physical classes to virtual mode was taxing on the students.

4. Sense of isolation is also one of the key challenges of virtual class room. Joseph Powell rightly stated that "it is absolutely human certainty that no one can know his own beauty or perceive a sense of his own worth until it has been reflected back to him in the mirror of another loving, caring human being". Very truly, in an online class, there are minimal physical interactions between students and teachers. Peer affinity that used to give confidence and comfort is missing in the virtual class room.
5. Internet connectivity is one of the major challenges of online learning. While internet penetration has reached the major cities and towns in India, in rural areas internet connection with required speed is still a long time dream. According to a report by Deloitte, the Broadband penetration in India's rural areas continues to be poor at 29.1 percent against national average of 51 percent with 687 million subscribers as of March 20202. This gap has to be bridged for the successful implementation of online learning.
6. Mahatma Gandhi stated, "By education I mean an all-round drawing out of the best in the child and man; body, mind and spirit". All-round development, which is the primary goal of education, is possible only through face-to-face learning process. Online mode facilitates the communication of subject knowledge to the students, but falls short in ushering the holistic development of the student.

Gurukul Pedagogue

'Gurukul' or 'gurukula' system of education is the epitome of Indian style of learning. It is a system in ancient India with students called as shishya living and pursuing his education with the teacher who is called as guru, in the same house. The word gurukula is a combination of the Sanskrit words guru ('teacher' or 'master') and kula ('family' or 'home'). It was a residential schooling system whose origin dates back to around 5000 BC in the Indian subcontinent. It was more prevalent during the Vedic age where students were taught various subjects and about how to live a cultured and disciplined life. The epics of Ramayana and Mahabharata; Buddhist and Jain literature have many references of students having their education at Gurukul. The students learn from the guru and help the guru in his everyday life, including carrying out of mundane daily household chores, which is essential to inculcate qualities like self-discipline, self-help, social consciousness among students.

The Gurukul pedagogue was a comprehensive, inclusive and wholesome education system. It focused not only on imparting knowledge, but also on character building of students. The significant features of Gurukul education are:

1. **Applied Knowledge:** Ancient indigenous education system of India was not confined to four walls and restricted curriculum, rather it treated society as enlarged class room. It focused on applied knowledge and offered an education system that prepares students for all fields of life. The students were motivated to have hands on experience of all disciplines of knowledge by enabling them to have practical experience.
2. **Activity Based Learning:** "Education is the knowledge of how to use the whole of one self. Many men use but one or two faculties out of the score with which they are endowed. A man is educated who knows how to make a tool of every faculty, how to open it, how to keep it sharp, and how to apply it to all practical purposes" said Henry Ward Beecher, an American Social Reformer. The ancient Gurukul education system of India was multi - dimensional and multi - disciplinary providing wider opportunities for the students to develop their faculties. Activity based learning impart creative thinking among students; and learning by doing will enhance the rate of retention of knowledge among students.
3. **Value-based Learning:** 'Virtue is Knowledge' is the philosophy that separate Socrates from Sophists, the first teachers in ancient Greece. During the same period in India, Gurukul institutions too offered value-based education to the students and nourished them with qualities like self-discipline, character building, social consciousness, respect towards elders and teachers, tolerance and other moral and ethical qualities. Education bereft of values is purposeless and will be a catastrophe in the long run.
4. **Holistic Development of Student:** Plato, Greek political philosopher discussed vividly on the system of education to be adopted to realise an 'Ideal State'. The Primary and Higher Education proposed by Plato in his Socratic dialogue "The Republic", is a holistic entity including the subjects like basics of religion, physical culture, music, geometry and literature to be

taught at initial stages to the subjects like art of governance, warfare, astronomy, dialectics to be taught in the later stages. So also, the ancient Indian indigenous education was wider and universal in its vision and facilitated wholesome development of the student.

5. **Student-teacher relationship:** Gurukul facilitated a teacher and student relationship that creates a secure learning environment. In this system, the teacher is accountable and responsible for students performance and his future. A sense of belongingness and parental atmosphere between the teacher and student will act as catalyst in exchange of knowledge and makes learning process more comfortable and flexible.

Gurukul Pedagogue through Virtual Learning

For years few sections of people in India believed that Gurukul mode of education is the panacea for all the ills in the present education system. Though, this argument holds ground, the structural design of modern education system had no place to accommodate Gurukul pedagogue. The Residential Education system had the scope to imbibe the features of gurukul model, but unfortunately it too got engulfed in the tide of Corporate model of education, whose primary goal is to run for the ranks, and produce human machines conducive for the industry. As the disproportionate cultivation of commercial crops, in the long run, made the soil lifeless and barren, so also, the made craze for buyers ready subjects at Plus Two and Under Graduate level, made education system market friendly, devoid of values and social consciousness. This resulted in the gradual erosion of values in the society, which the education system was expected to nurture and protect. This deteriorating value system can be addressed and mitigated by the adoption of Gurukul Pedagogue, which is made easy and feasible by Virtual Platform.

The Cloud Channel of instructions or Online Learning can be made more interesting and relevant by adopting the below summarisd Gurukul pedagogue:

1. Virtual Platforms have brought the students to the home of the teacher, which is the primary feature of Gurukul model of education.
2. The centre of accountability, which is seldom found in modern education system, amply exists in Gurukul mode of education. Teachers in present system of education are accountable only for the marks scored and rank secured by the student. The avowed objectives of education like wholesome development of

student, inculcation of ethical values, and promotion of rationalistic outlook among them are disposed as achieves and obsolete. This vacuum can be filled by assimilating conventional education with Gurukul pedagogue.

3. Education is not time bound; rather it is a continuous process. The conventional model restricted education to a fixed curriculum and time. On the other side, through online learning the availability of the student to the teacher is more, like in gurukul system of education. This dividend can be utilised by the teacher to concentrate on the holistic development of student. The day of the student can start with meditation and Yoga and end with personality development class. This needs the complete overhaul of current pedagogue and redesign of curriculum to make online learning complete, meaningful and relevant.
4. One reason for the students developing apathy towards online learning is the indiscriminate dumping of conventional teaching practices like Lecture Method of teaching, 50 minutes' class, time table from 10.00 am to 4.00 pm etc onto the online platforms. This made online learning tedious, burdensome and insipid. Every channel of learning requires tailor made curriculum design so as to make it run. This lacuna can be addressed by the adoption of Gurukul pedagogue which is activity based, flexible hours of instruction and it facilitates applied knowledge by practical experiences. Activity based strategies like collaborative learning; cooperative learning and problem solving learning positively affect student retention.
5. Mentor - mentee system, where a teacher is supposed to play the role of a counselor and guide to the students, remained only on the paper and failed to bear fruits. The growing number of suicides among students in recent times because of the stress of competition is alarming, which highlights the dire need for the teacher to play a proactive role in guiding, counseling and supporting the students. This is possible by the adoption of gurukul pedagogue through online platforms. The teacher is the centre of this system. The hotline between the teacher and the student always has to be available, to give emotional support to the student when needed. This makes online learning student - centered and learner friendly.
6. Blended learning, a new inclusion in the education system, is a blend of conventional and virtual models of learning. Both platforms

require different methods of learning to suit their requirements. Gurukul pedagogue is handy in adopting blended learning, Activity based learning which is one of the features of Gurukul model of learning can be best adapted for online learning. Conventional lecturing method is better suitable for offline platform.

Conclusion

The one factor that influenced every aspect of human life in every country is the Novel Covid - 19 pandemics. Education Sector too was unprepared for the unforeseen situations caused by the pandemic. But, history since five million years has shown the adaptability capability of human beings. Accordingly, the pedagogue too, with the initial hiccups, has adapted to the changing scenario by coming out with alternative sources of learning. Online initiatives were successful in keeping the gates of education open during lockdown. The experience with online infrastructure has enriched the teaching - learning process by bringing in innovative practices like Webinars, Online examination and evaluation, MOOCs etc. Online learning process has been so deeply assimilated into the education system, that the Post-Covid situation demands for a well-articulated curriculum plan to embrace both physical and virtual learning. Different teaching platforms need different types of techniques to communicate the subject. The experience of online teaching during the lockdown brought to light certain challenges like student attention capacity, health hazards of viewing the screen for longer duration, internet connectivity etc that need to be addressed. A thorough research is imperative on the impact of online teaching on emotional, physical and psychological health of the students. eLearning doesn't just happen; it requires careful planning and implementation.

Online learning can be made more viable and purposeful by adopting ancient Indian Gurukul model of education. As it is said, 'Old wine cannot be poured in new bottles' so also, conventional methods of teaching cannot be adapted in new and technology based cloud learning platforms. At the same time, it is dire necessity to blend values with technology so as to make education system a strong substructure to build a just, equitable, healthy and knowledgeable society. Under the circumstances, revisiting of Gurukul pedagogue is an unavoidable imperative. Ancient Indian indigenous education, through gurukuls facilitated activity based learning, focused on applied knowledge, enriched with values and ethics, and aimed at holistic development of the student, which is the need of the century.

References

1. Tools of Teaching' by Barbara Gross Davis, Jossey-Bass edition (13 February 2009).
2. The Economic Times - Indian rural broadband penetration at 29.1% vs national average of 51.1 percent: Report, dated Nov 06, 2020.
3. Blended Model of Teaching and Learning: Concept Note; UGC New Delhi.
4. The influence of Activity Based teaching method used in teaching Social Studies on Student Retention and Academic Performance: a Quasi-experimental study of selected Junior High School Students in Sekyere South District of Ashanthi Region, Ghana - by Thomas Sarpong, Francis Atta Sarpong, Angelina Osei Asor' - In Scientific Research Publishing, Open Journal of Social Sciences.
5. The Influence of Activity-Based Teaching
6. Method Used in Teaching Social Studies on
7. Students Retention and Academic
8. Performance: A Quasi-Experimental Study of
9. Selected Junior High School Students in Sekyere
10. South District of Ashanti Region.

19

After Covid- 19 Professors Evergreen Role in Higher Education

Dr Md. Shafiq Ahmed

Abstract

Changes around the world are taking place in higher education. What kind of changes are needed in the state and country where the professor is working at the same time. What is the current state of education in the country? How people's traditions and economic conditions contribute to higher education. Take a closer look at these and teach why backward areas do not grow into developed areas. Political factors are analyzed as reasons for this or the role that educated people have to play.

Introduction

II. The Ever-Present Professional Perspective of Higher Education Professors

1. A subtle understanding of higher education.
2. Assessing and teaching the impact of traditions on higher education.
3. Assessing and teaching political issues on higher education.
4. Assessing and teaching social aspects of higher education.
5. Assessing and teaching the conditions of backward people in backward areas.
6. It is very important to teach how the impact of higher educated people can have on society.
7. On the subject of how a student should be obedient to the law rather than under the influence of the media. Teaching is the minimum duty of rituals.

8. It is very important to prepare the students to mature in the way of thinking.
9. Introducing students to the research vision, vision, and sacrifice of intellectuals is like a challenge for professors.
10. Strive to provide teaching at the field level to students as well as make them patriotic. Styling is very intimate.
11. Explain to students the real picture of current media.
12. Lead students from the information community to the knowledge community.
13. Explain how individuals and organisations can be held accountable.
14. Explain how education contributes to the average person.
15. Efforts should be made to link professionals from different fields to educational institutions.
16. The role of professors is crucial in the design and implementation of government schemes.

III. Higher education issue

1. Poor students cannot pursue higher education.
2. Outlying students cannot pursue higher education.
3. Those who follow more traditions are more likely to stay away from higher education.
4. Girls did not pursue higher education for security reasons.
5. There are also those who are deprived of higher education due to lack of information.
6. Lack of solid buildings, continuing in other rental buildings is also a problem.
7. Awareness should be created among the people on schemes like RUSA.
8. The lack of practices in higher education is also a problem across India.
9. Another problem is that the highly educated do not have a superior way of thinking.
10. We are failing to identify intelligent students in every educational institution.

IV. Suggestions for the development of higher education

1. Appoint dedicated professors.

2. Higher education should be properly spent.
3. Sturdy buildings, technology should be formed.
4. Continuous research should take place. For example, at universities, at the field level.
5. Establishment of the position of Academic General at the State and Central levels, such as the Advocate General and the Attorney General. Should do.
6. A section called "Visionery Approach" wing should be established in every educational institution, for which professors should take the lead.
7. The award should be instituted for the sake of new reforms in higher education.
8. Professors should train students to adapt to change.
9. The Chancellor of the University must spend some time during the year at the University. For that, the professors should be consulted and persuaded.
10. It is very important for the sponsors to act in a clear manner on each top.

V. Conclusion

A teacher should act as a guide. As a running library should have been. In a constantly changing society, students need to be trained to become full-fledged personalities / citizens. It is imperative that students from the student stage be judged as citizens with the best qualities. In the changing age of speed, the role of professors has become very crucial in shaping the personality of students as parents give less time to their children.

References

Christophe Jaffrelot, India's Silent Revolution : The Rise of the low castes in North Indian politics, Delhi, 2003.

David Moss, Caste and Development: Contemporary perspectives on a structure of discrimination and advantage, World Development, Vol. 110, 2018, pp. 422-436.

Dinkar Gupta, Caste in Question: Identity or Hierarchy? Institute of Economic Growth, Sage Publications, New Delhi, 2004.

Farhana Khatoon, A Regional Analysis of Literacy and Educational Levels of Scheduled Caste in Uttar Pradesh, Journal of Humanities and Social Sciences, 6 (4), 2013, pp. 08-19.

Frankel and Rao, "Dominance and State Policies in Modern India - Decline of a Social Order", Oxford University Press, New Delhi, 1989.

Irshick, E. F., Politics and Social Conflict in South India: The Non-Brahman Movement and Tamil Separatism, 1916-1929, University of California Press, Berkeley and Los Angeles, 1969, p. 115.

Kancha Ilaiah, "Why I am not a Hindu", Samya, Calcatta, 1969.

Kooiman, D., Political Rivalry among Religious Communities: A Case-Study of Communal Reservations in India, Economic and Political Weekly, February 13, 1993, pp. 287-295.

Krishna Reddy G., "Backward Classes and Political power Structure in Andhra Pradesh", Unpublished Ph.D. thesis submitted to Osmania University, 1993.

Illaiah, Kancha, Caste or Class or Caste Class a Study in Dalit Bahujan Consciousness and Struggles in Andhra Pradesh in 1980's, Unpublished PhD Thesis, Nehru Memorial Museum and Library, New Delhi, 1978, p. 1.

Pauline Kolenda, "Caste in Contemporary India", Rawat Publication, New Delhi, 1997.

Ponna Wignaraja (ed 1993), "Social Movements in the South - Empowerment of the People", Vistaar Publications, New Delhi, 1993.

Ramachandram Valluri, "Rural Political Leadership among Scheduled Castes - A Study in Telangana Region", Unpublished Ph.D. thesis submitted to Osmania University, 1998.

Ramaswamy, U., The Belief System of the Non-Brahmin Movement in India: The Andhra Case, Asian Survey, Mar., 1978, Vol. 18, No. 3, 1978, pp. 290-300.

Rao, M.S.A., Social Movements among the Backward classes and Blacks: Homology in the sources of identity, in Social movements in India, Monohar Publication, Delhi, 1979.

Steinberg, D.M., The social work student's handbook, The Haworth Social Work Practice Press, New York, 2004, p. 15.

20

Social and Economic Impact of Covid-19

Shaveta Thakur, Vishali Mahajan and Sapna Chadha

Abstract

Corona has made a great impact on different aspects of human life around the world and different theories have been put forward for further life. The Covid-19 pandemic has prompted an emotional loss of human existence worldwide and presents a phenomenal test to general wellbeing, food frameworks and the universe of work. It has not only distressed human health and relations but has also changed other important domains. It has uplifted human misery, undermined the economy, turned the existence of many individuals all over the planet upside down and altogether impacted the wellbeing, monetary, natural and social areas. Through the study, an attempt has been made to highlight the impact of the Covid-19 on human's social and economic life. In response to this global outbreak, we summarise the socioeconomic effects of Covid-19 on individual aspects of world economy.

Keywords : Coronavirus, Covid-19, social life, economic life.

Introduction

Coronavirus has led to acute and severe losses in numerous around the globe due to ailment and government-commanded social distancing orders. The outbreak of Covid-19 has negatively affected worldwide medical care systems with a ripple effect on every aspect of human life. Catrin et al (2020) stated that the extent of the outbreak with the World Health Organisation (WHO) declaring the Covid-19 outbreak as a global emergency on January 30. Andi and Avi (2020) studied that in response to 'flatten the curve', governments have enforced border shutdowns, travel restrictions and quarantine in countries which constitute the world's largest economies, sparking fears of an impending economic crisis and recession has negatively affected worldwide medical care frameworks mind a far reaching influence on each part of human life.

Impact on Agriculture

Agribusiness contributes a significant part in the economy of developing nations, and provides the main source of food, salary and work to their rural populaces. As indicated by Food and Agriculture Organisation (2000), it has been set up that the portion of the farming populace of the total people is 67 percent that agriculture accounts for 39.4 percent of the GDP and 43 percent of all exports consist of agricultural goods. FAO has also assessed that over 60 percent of the total populace depends on agriculture for their living. According to International Labour Organisation (ILO), out of total employer population in 2019, 26.85 percent of employers are in agricultural sector. Coronavirus has influenced all the routes which join farm production to final consumer. China is one of the significant manure producing country and exporter in the world. Due to worldwide trade disturbance, farmers are confronting with shortage of farming sources like seed, manure and pesticides. Marlow (2020) stated that the lockdown in China have extremely influenced the worldwide fertilizer exchange. As per Singh (2020), India alone need 250 lakh quintals of seed for crop production in kharif season. If the pandemic prolonged import dependent countries seem to be highly affected by pandemic. In poor countries, farm production is mostly much more labour intensive, with many processes such as rice planting and harvesting of staple crops bringing workers close together. Workers in these countries lack proper health services and social protection and due to slight saving or no saving, many informal workers in agriculture are obligate to work regardless of the self-isolation protocol during Covid-19 pandemic. Hence, these workers are at high risk of virus. Most of the farm producers are facing the manpower scarcity. According to Hans and Guillaume (2020), travel ban have made the shortage of seasonal and informal farm workers. There is rapid increase in employment losses around the world. International Labour Organisation (2020) estimated that Covid-19 has affected the 81 percent (2.7 billion workers) global work power due to full or partial closure of the work place.

Impact on manufacturing sector

The manufacturing industry is a significant aspect of the economy as it represents almost 16 percent of the worldwide GDP in 2018. According to the assessment by United Nations Conference on Trade and Development (UNCTAD), the COVID-19 flare-up could cause worldwide FDI to contract by 5 percent-15 percent, because of the destruction in assembling segment combined with industrial facility closure. The negative impacts of COVID-19 on FDI investments are estimated to be high in the energy, airline and automobile industry. According to WHO (2020), because of the Covid-19 pandemic over the globe, the makers of the vehicle, synthetic, hardware, and airplane are confronting concerns with respect to the accessibility of crude material. The tale Coronavirus started in China, which is home to most of the production lines that supply crude materials to manufacturing units over the world. The USA and other significant drug and clinical gadget fabricating countries depend intensely on sourcing material straightforwardly and by implication from China, where the infection began. The USA, for instance, gets 13 percent of its clinical items made in China. India, as well, depends for around 80 percent of dynamic drug fixings (API) on China, which is the world's driving maker and exporter of APIs by volume. Additionally, India, another driving API producer, has ended the fare of 26 fixings ordinarily utilised in drugs in its endeavours to guarantee continuous accessibility of basic APIs. According to the data from Batchmaster (2020), the supply of raw materials and ingredients to the manufacturing sites has been badly affected, which has hampered production, driving makers to avoid activities.

Impact on tourism sector

The travel industry segment is right now one of the hardest-hit by the flare-up of Covid-19, with impacts on both travel supply and demand. As indicated by the Mobility Market Outlook (2020) on Covid-19, the worldwide income for the travel industry will be an expected 447.4 billion U.S. dollars in 2020 - a reduction of around 34.7 percent from the earlier year. As an immediate outcome of Covid-19, The World Travel and Tourism Committee (2020) has cautioned that 50 million positions in the worldwide travel and the travel industry part might be in danger. The progressing pandemic, travel limitations, and the nation wide lockdown in many countries have carried the whole the travel industry to a halt, the travel industry will take more time to recuperate, particularly recreation the travel industry. Asia is likely to be the worst affected. Once the pandemic is over, it could take as long as 10 months for the business to recover. The travel industry right now represents 10 percent of worldwide GDP. The pandemic is putting up to 50 million positions in the worldwide travel and the travel industry part in danger, with make a trip prone to droop by a quarter this year, Asia being the most influenced continent, the World Travel and Tourism Council has said.

Impact on IT sector

The huge shortcomings the IT business is confronting now is because of the fall in the economy, as a lot of companies are forced to ask their employees to work from home keeping in the account of the communal health concerns. Apple Inc. is assessed to have at least 10 percent fall in its shares due to the absence of accessibility of iPhones in the market. The parts that are required to build the iPhones are, and it is facing a major lockdown. According to Market Data Forecast (2020), the parts that are needed in building the iPhones supposed to come from China, and it is confronting a significant lockdown. With the beginning of Coronavirus ailment (Covid-19) emergency in January 2020, dominant part of worldwide ICT occasions, social affairs, gatherings were dropped. Significant worldwide occasions for the ICT business, for example, Mobile World Conference 2020, Game Developers Conference 2020, MTN Global Connect and other conspicuous ICT social affairs and gatherings faced the fate of cancellation. Likewise, tech pioneers including Google, Microsoft, Adobe, Facebook, NVidia, Cisco, and Sales force among others were additionally compelled to cancel their yearly occasions. Such occasions and get-togethers offer imperative business chances to ICT organisations to feature their items and arrangements. Cancellation of such events has certainly affected the upcoming opportunities for market players, making recovery of the industry more troublesome.

Impact on Education

The Covid-19 pandemic has caused the biggest disturbance of education ever, which have general effect on students and educators around the globe, from pre-primary to secondary schools, colleges, technical and vocational education and training (TVET) institutions, grown-up learning, and aptitudes improvement institutions. By the mid-April 2020, 94 percent of students overall were influenced by the pandemic, representing 1.58 billion kids and youth, from pre-primary to advanced education, in 200 nations. Gromada et al (2020) published that the interruptions brought about by Covid-19 to regular day-to-day existence implied that above 40 million kids around worldwide have lost out early childhood education in their pre-school. They subsequently missed an energising and improving condition, learning openings, social. This is probably going to bargain with their longer-term healthy development particularly those youngsters from poor and deprived families. In the higher education sub-sector, while internet learning has commonly take place through recorded talks and online platforms. According to UNESCO (2020), 40 percent of the poor countries are unsuccessful to support learners in danger during the Covid-19 crisis and past practices show that both education and sex inequalities will tend to be ignored in reactions to disease outbreaks. Kids with special needs are not generally included in plans of distance learning. Domestic tasks, particularly for girls, and the work needed to run families or farms, can prevent the children from getting adequate learning time. Refugee and forcibly uprooted children are additionally denied of access to support facilities offered through schools, for example, school meals and psychosocial uphold programme. The learning harm, in the short and long tenure, is relied upon to be extraordinary. Scientists in Canada estimate that the socio-economic skills gap could increase by increment by more than 30 percent due to the Covid crisis. Syedah et al. (2020) recognizes three potential situations for the loss of learning: a decrease in normal learning levels for all students, an extending appropriation of learning accomplishments because of exceptionally inconsistent impacts of the crisis on different populaces, or a noteworthy increment of students with extremely low degree of achievement due partially to large number of dropouts. According to World Bank (2020), 25 percent more students may fall under a standard level of proficiency needed to partake successfully and gainfully in the public arena, and in future learning, a consequence of the school terminations only.

Impact on oil petroleum

In early 2020, the cost of oil fell because of the oil price war among Russia and Saudi Arabia. The Covid pandemic make worse the circumstance through the drop in the interest for oil due to lockdown. The forced travel limitations during the pandemic, which prompted a decrease in the development of individuals and merchandise, brought about a fall in the demand for flight fuel, coal and other products, which consequently led to a fall in oil cost because of low interest. The Covid emergency influenced a wide scope of energy markets, for example, the coal, gas and sustainable power source markets, however its effect on oil markets was more serious in light of the fact that it halted the movement of individuals and goods, which led to a drastic decrease in the demand for transport fuels. The Covid-19 pandemic is required to prompt an entire year volume request drop of up to 10 percent all things considered, contingent upon application markets i.e. more demand decrease in industrial and infrastructure, restricted or none for bundling and the production continuity and working rates are additionally influenced. The oil price drop is dragging the pricing of most of the petrochemical materials down (e.g., PP pricing in China is down on average by 20 percent, PE is down by 15 percent on China ex-warehouse prices for Dec 2019 - Apr 2020) and bringing a major feedstock price disruption (naphtha price collapsed by 70 percent in line with crude oil). Mirko (2020) stated that financial market collapse combined with the fluctuating share prices of oil, gas, and petrochemicals, with the valuation of petrochemicals, many players going down by 20-30 percent.

Impact on sports industry

Sport industry is a significant contributor to financial and social developments. The worldwide value of the sports business is estimated at US$756 billion yearly. The sports industry was severely affected during the coronavirus outbreak. To protect the health of competitors and others included, most major games at worldwide, regional and public levels have been dropped or suspended from long races to football competitions, games titles to basketball games, handball to ice hockey, rugby, cricket, cruising, skiing, weightlifting to wrestling and more. The Olympics and Paralympics, for the first time in the history of modern games, have been deferred, and will be held in 2021. In the football section, European football associations in England and Scotland declared the prompt suspension of football matches for about a month and a half until 30th April. The Turkish super league was the last European association to suspend its matches. The Monaco Grand Prix, in Formula One was also cancelled. In the hockey, the 2020 hockey games in England were postponed. Britain's FIH Pro League games were also delayed. In rugby matches, the Pro14 final planned for 20th June at the Cardiff City Stadium was cancelled. The major league rugby (MLR) was cancelled for 2020 season. In the baseball segment, all the baseball league season games were cancelled in Mexico and Puerto Rico. According to Ozli and Arun (2020), the Motorsport game in Portugal was delayed after the Portuguese government declared a highly sensitive situation and suspended all games in the nation. In the snooker portion, the World snooker title to be held in Sheffield from 18th April to 4th May, was delayed. One of India's most loved games, the Indian Premier League, was dropped for the current year because of the Covid-19 pandemic. The cricket competition, which has sold its telecom rights for over Rs16,000 crore ($2.55 billion) to Star India for a very long time (2018-2022), would have potentially discovered more eyeballs this time than any other time in recent memory as most pieces of the nation are under lockdown with TV being the essential wellspring of diversion. The subsequent loss in income to the organisers and sponsors of the cancelled games ran into billions of dollars.

Impact on social life

June and Tomos (2020) stated that lockdown and social distancing measures to inhibit the spread of Coronavirus have elevated fears of domestic violence, which incorporates physical, emotional and sexual maltreatment. The constrained sharing of numerous families around the globe has given indications of a genuine 'crisis in a crisis'. The factual information that rose up out of China, presently toward the end of the remarkable isolation measures, have provoked brought expanded examples of reports of domestic maltreatment, particularly of ladies who had to live for quite a long time inside an abusive relationship. Numerous papers announced scenes of couple brutality that followed with emotional maltreatment vented on their kids. One of the UK's domestic abuse charities, has reported a 25 percent expansion in calls made to its helpline since lockdown measures were stated. The closure of schools, colleges, and different foundations to prevent the spread of Covid has made individuals invest a great deal of energy at home, which can lead individuals to gain abilities and side interests, for example, perusing, painting, music, sewing, cooking, engage, etc. There is no uncertainty that isolation and distance from society can have many negative impacts, and not going to school for long periods diminishes students' capacity to learn. Furthermore, a critical effect of the Covid-19 pandemic has been seen inside the video-gaming industry. According to Amiri and Pagheh (2020), with numerous people self-disengaging and additionally staying home under strict government guidelines, web based gaming has seen the rise of record numbers of players, which has encouraged a lift in income for some organisations.

Conclusion

In the present study, the effect of Covid-19 on Indian economic and social life is studied. It has also sparked fears of an impending economic crisis and recession. Self-isolation, social distancing and travel restrictions have prompted to a diminished workforce across all every financial division and numerous positions to be lost. Schools have shut down and need of items and manufactured products has decreased.

References

Sohrabi, C., Alsafi, Z., O'Neill, N., Khan, M., Kerwan, A., Al-Jabir, A. et al., World Health Organisation declares global emergency: a review of the 2019 novel coronavirus (COVID-19), Int. J. Surg. 76 (2020 Apr) 71-76.

Burkert, A., Loeb, A., Flattening the COVID-19 curves, [Internet]. Scientific American Blog Network, 2020.

Marlow, S. COVID-19: Effects on the Fertilizer Industry. IHS Markit. 2020.

Singh, IS. Agriculture in the time of Covid-19. The Hindu Business Line. 2020.

Brelie, H., Petit, G. French farm producers suffer during the COVID-19 restrictions. Euronews. 2020.

ILO. ILO: COVID-19 causes devastating losses in working hours and employment. 2020.

BatchMaster ERP 2020 article https://www.manufacturingtomorrow.com/article/2020/06/impact-of-covid-19-on-the-process-manufacturing-industry-2020/15487

Statista article: Global change in travel and tourism revenue due to COVID-19 2019-2020 https://www.statista.com/forecasts/1103426/covid-19-revenue-travel-tourism-industry-forecast

World Travel and Tourism Council https://www.weforum.org/agenda/2020/03/world-travel-coronavirus-covid19-jobs-pandemic-tourism-aviation/

Market data forecast, Impacts of COVID-19 on the Information Technology (IT) industry. 2020.

Anna, G., Richardson, D., Rees, G., Childcare in a global crisis: the impact of COVID-19 on work and family life. 2020.

UNESCO, Global Education Monitoring (GEM) Report, 2020: Inclusion and education: all means all, 2020.

Iqbal, S.A., Azevedo, J.P., Geven, K., Hasan, A. We should avoid flattening the curve in education - Possible scenarios for learning lose during the school lockdowns. 2020.

World Bank, Simulating the Potential Impacts of the COVID-19 School Closures on Schooling and Learning Outcomes: A set of Global Estimates. 2020.

Rubeis, M., Jedrzejewski, M., COVID-19's Impact on the peterochemical Industry. 2020.

Peterson, O., Thankom, A. Spillover of COVID-19: Impact on the Global Economy. 2020.

Kaley, J., Morgan, T., Coronavirus: domestic abuse calls up 25 percent since lockdown, charity. 2020.

Amiri, M., Pagheh, M., Amiri, M. The impact of the coronavirus crisis on human social life. 2020.

21

Impact of Covid-19 on Higher Education-Challenges and Opportunities

Dr G. Sreenivasulu

Introduction

The global outbreak of the Covid-19 pandemic has spread worldwide, affecting almost all countries and territories. The outbreak was first identified in December 2019 in Wuhan, China. The countries around the world cautioned the public to take responsive care. The public care strategies have included handwashing, wearing face masks, physical distancing, and avoiding mass gathering and assemblies. Lockdown and staying home strategies have been put in place as the needed action to flatten the curve and control the transmission of the disease.

Bhutan first declared closing of schools and institutions and reduction of business hours during the second week of March 2020. The complete nationwide lockdown was implemented from 1 August 2020. In between, movements were allowed, offices began functioning, schools and colleges reopened for selected levels and continued with online class for others. More than 170,000 children in Bhutan from classes PP-XII are, today, affected by the school closure. The impact is far reaching and has affected learning during this academic year or even more in the coming days. Several schools, colleges and universities have discontinued face-to-face teaching. There is a pressing need to innovate and implement alternative educational and assessment strategies. The Covid-19 pandemic has provided us with an opportunity to pave the way for introducing digital learning.

Research highlights certain dearth such as the weakness of online teaching infrastructure, the limited exposure of teachers to online teaching, the information gap, non-conducive environment for learning at home, equity and academic excellence in terms of higher education. This article evaluates the impact of the Covid-19 pandemic on teaching and learning process across the world. The challenges and opportunities of online and continuing education during the Covid-19 pandemic is summarised and way forward suggested.

Impact of COVID-19 on higher education in India

The Covid-19 crisis has resulted in India going into an unprecedented nation-wide lockdown in the months of March and April 2020. The effect of the pandemic is being felt across all aspects of the economy with multiple agencies such as Moody's expecting GDP growth to fall to as low as 2.5 percent[1] in this calendar year. The Indian government has responded to this by providing several guidelines including restricting movement of people and social distancing.

University Grants Commission (UGC) and other apex education bodies have also issued Covid-19 specific guidelines for Indian higher education institutions (HEIs) resulting in ~1000 universities and ~40,0002 colleges temporarily closing, students being asked to go home, and efforts being undertaken to move classes online. These measures will have varying degrees of impact on ~3.75 crore students enrolled in and ~14 lakh faculty[2] employed by the system.

Higher education leaders are also concerned that an extended lockdown due to the pandemic could have a deeper impact for the sector, as Covid-19 has disrupted the current admissions cycle and might have an effect on enrolments, create a cash flow crunch, slowdown research and consulting activities.

This year, close to 1.44 crore students[3] are appearing for their school leaving exams and close to 50 lakh[4] of these students will be looking to enrol in a higher education institution in this academic session. Institutions planning for their admissions cycle will need to muster their limited resources, have an agile response plan to Covid-19, and build resilience to minimise the impact on their enrolments, diversity of students, and revenues.

The emergence of Information and Communication Technology (ICT) has fundamentally changed the practices of not only business, governance or education but every spheres of human endeavour. As the world population edged to seven billion in 2011, it has profound implications in every sphere (UN, 2013). India has a massive 1.2 billion population (Census, 2011) of which a high proportion of them are young. The demand for education in developing countries like India has skyrocketed as education is still regarded as an important bridge of social, economic and political mobility. India has innumerable challenges in terms of infrastructure, socio-economic, linguistic and physical barriers for people who wish to access education (Bhattacharya and Sharma, 2007). However, it is hoped that ICT can transform the educational scenario in the country.

The emancipatory and transformative potentials of ICT in higher education in India has helped increase the country's requirement of higher education through part-time and distance-learning schemes. It can be used as a tool to overcome the issues of cost, less number of teachers, and poor quality of education as well as to overcome time and distance barriers (McGorry, 2002). Mooij (2007) states that differentiated ICT based education can be expected to provide greater reliability, validity, and efficiency of data collection and greater ease of analysis, evaluation, and interpretation at any educational level. While the world is moving rapidly towards digital media, the role of ICT in education has become increasingly important.

Changing student needs

The progress made by HEIs has been remarkable across the different education paradigms, but it is not the end of the journey. The education sector around the world and more so in India has seen and is still undergoing the biggest shift ever.The year 2020 has been like no other in history. Although the education system has been gradually evolving and responding to triggers such as the changing learner needs and emerging technologies the pace of change has accelerated with the unforeseen situation created by the pandemic and the approval of the NEP.

Student needs are continuously evolving, this can be attributed to the new student majority of non-traditional students, who juggle their studies with work or caregiving responsibilities. The new learner yearns for personal and adaptive learning paths based on competency levels.

Acceptance of online learning

The online learning environment has undergone a change both in India and globally. In India, regulators have started accepting online degrees as a substitute to classroom learning and have provided more flexibility to HEIs to increase component on online learning in regular programme as well. Many online learning companies and global universities are now innovating to develop online learning programme, associated pedagogies and content that deliver on unique student experience.

The Covid-19 pandemic

The current situation of higher education across the world is similar. The pandemic has brought about unprecedented changes and transformed the face of education in 2020. It has accelerated the trends, notably the transition to a digital economy. It has acted as a test bed for Education 4.0 by transforming concepts of personalised learning and integration of technology to reality.

NEP 2020 proposes the revision and revamping of all aspects of the education structure, including its regulation and governance, to create a new system that is aligned with the aspirational goals of twenty first century education, while remaining consistent with India's traditions and value systems.

Programmes and policy of the government of India on online teaching-learning in HEIs

The government of India started thinking gravely on this matter with emphasizing on ICT and use of online education as the part of compulsory teaching-learning process at tertiary level. Moreover, it is reflected on preparing draft new education policy 2019 that has been regarded as a proactive and highly techno-efficient step in the time of this pandemic. Study Webs of Active-Learning for Young Aspiring Minds (SWAYAM) is a programme or Massive Open Online Courses (MOOC) platform initiated by the government of India hosted online courses in different quadrants. The SWAYAM PRABHA is a group of 32 DTH channels dedicated to telecasting of high-quality educational programmes throughout the week. Annual Refresher Programme in Teaching (ARPIT) is an online professional development programme launched by the MHRD on November 13, 2018 using SWAYAM platform. Another initiative of MHRD was e-PG Pathshala run by the University Grants Commission (UGC) that provided high-quality curriculum-based and interactive e-content in 70 subjects across all disciplines. e-Pathshala is a portal jointly run by the MHRD and National Council of Educational Research and Training (NCERT) launched on November 7, 2015, that provided educational resources for teacher educators, teachers, research scholars, students and parents through an online learning platform. Therefore, it can be said that we were not unaware of the challenges and prospects of online education.

Implementation of online teaching-learning in HEIs

There are some difficulties felt in the implementation of the change process in the education system that has been arisen after Covid-19 crisis; these difficulties are related with the novel perspectives of online education and their technological complexities. Earlier to this pandemic, online education is considered as the education provided by the open universities in India. But in Covid-19 induced time, online teaching-learning became a massive challenge to deal with, and stakeholders are not potentially fit to adjust with the sudden educational change as they are not technologically competent to embrace the current situation. Therefore, for successful implementation of educational change (in this case, it refers to the shift from traditional teaching-learning methods to online teaching-learning methods), implications of change need to be addressed.

The journey begins from the collective vision of UGC and MHRD (supra-system), University and Colleges (system), and different academic departments (sub-system) in favour of implementing online teaching-learning in the education system. In the face of Covid-19, the shared vision of education system realised that during the pandemic period, teachers and students are motivated to adapt online teaching-learning platforms in fulfilling the current educational needs. Everyone, either teachers or students, were friendly skilled in using social media app viz. WhatsApp, Facebook, Twitter, Instagram, which turned into smooth facilitation of using online educational platforms such as ZOOM, Cisco WebEx, Google Meet etc. as a sign of positive transfer of learning. Also, there are some useful educational apps such as Office 365, Google classroom and much more user-friendly videoconferencing app that can be downloaded free of cost and easy to use (FutureLearn, 2020); so to some extent, it seems that there is no reason to get into a panic to get new technology all of sudden as some of the apps are already embedded in our HEIs. Majority of stakeholders possessed smartphones and only considerable numbers having laptops are the needed resources to implement online teaching-learning. Mizoram University has its ICT centre and LMS that helps in seamless monitoring of online teaching-learning modes.

Technology Trends in Indian Universities

Educational technology has successfully been used for improving the quality as well as expanding the frontiers of higher education in the country. The tools help to create a social, highly collaborative and personalised environment with innovative solutions that will enhance the way students learn, communicate and collaborate and study both on and off campus. It has broken the monopoly of oral communication and invaded the classrooms of the colleges and universities.

Since August 15, 1984, the University Grants Commission launched the project "Countrywide Classrooms" and has been investing huge amount on establishing production centers providing TV sets, producing and purchasing suitable Educational Television (ETV) programme.

The ETV programme are produced at the different media centers, namely, Educational Media Resources Centers (EMRCs) located at Ahmedabad, Hyderabad, Pune, MCRC situated at Jamia Millia Islamia, New Delhi.

A Mass Communication Bureau has also been functioning at the UGC New Delhi and ETV production facilities have also been developed in the Technical Teachers Training Institute (TTTIs) located at different cities of the country.

Indira Gandhi National Open University (IGNOU) has been set up as an effective alternative model of higher education on September 20, 1985 by an Act of Parliament. The instructional system of IGNOU is different from that of conventional universities as it adopts a multimedia approach to education.

Some of the exciting technology trends in Indian Universities are:

Mobility

With the proliferation of mobile phones on campus, colleges everywhere are compelled to capitalise on feature-rich phones that are capable of much more than just voice calls. Adoption of the BlackBerry, iPhone and other smart devices that have Internet access allows students and faculty to perform a wide range of assignments. Tasks like administration, sharing class notes, downloading lectures, instant messaging, etc., are possible anywhere cell phone service is available.

Mobile phones are also being used to access computer files from remote locations. With services like "Soonr", students who have forgotten to bring an assignment to class can use their cell phone to access the completed work on their home computer and show it to the professor.

Digitisation of Books (E-Text Books)

There is an increased trend towards creation of a digital repository of books to create a digital learning environment for students. The digital version of the books embedded with text, pictures along with video, simulations and visualisations help students learn the concepts in an interactive way.

The National mission on Education through ICT plans to generate new online course content for UG, PG and Doctoral education. Efforts are already underway to prepare course content for 130 courses (UG and PG).

Content Delivery using IT/ICT

Higher Education is purely a content driven play where educational content is delivered through innovative use of ICT. There is an increased trend in higher education institutes to render content through Radio, TV and Satellite.

Open Education Resources

Many Indian universities are contemplating Technology enabled free access of education resources. AICTE - Indian National Digital Library in Engineering and Technology (AICTE - INDEST) is a consortium set up by the Ministry of Human Resource to enhance greater access and generate annual savings in access of bibliographic databases.

The University Grants Commission (UGC) has also launched its Digital Library Consortium to provide access to peer reviewed journals and bibliographic databases covering subjects such as arts, humanities, technology and sciences.

Virtual Technical University

The National mission on Education through ICT is working on a war foot to establish a virtual technical university to impart training to UG/PG students along with new teachers.

Social Learning

The emergence of Web 2.0 and social networking such as blogs and wikis, as well as new online video repository and delivery websites such as YouTube, iTunes U and Big Think is influencing a new trend in higher education.

The emergence of smartphones such as the iPhone and other intelligent devices has enhanced mobile learning (referred to as m-learning). These technologies create new channels for content delivery, online video expansion and podcasting. Also, the adoption of virtual reality websites such as "Second Life" has provided higher-education institutions with new venues for class gatherings and learning.

A combination of Web 2.0 tools viz., Blogs, Wikis, Podcasts, Mashups, and Social Networking Communities are transforming the traditional learning environment into something more social and personalised. While traditional Learning Management Systems (LMS) like Blackboard, Sakai, Moodle or Web CT are course-centered and driven by faculty, the new trend in education is to create a "learner-centric" system.

Challenges in India's Higher Education

With the urban and the rural divide having significantly narrowed due to the onset of technology, communication and better infrastructure over the last two decades, there has been an appreciable improvement in the reach of better higher education to several under-represented groups across the country.

However, the need of the hour is a provision of high quality education across all sectors to match the requirements of a growing Indian economy. The suffering of the under-represented communities has not been appreciably alleviated as unemployment, inflation, low income and lack of adequate access to quality education continue to plague them.

Some of the key challenges for India in terms of access and quality of higher education are the following:

Poor Infrastructure - This shortcoming is perhaps the chief of all in delivery of quality education. While focus on the urban segment has been heavy, the same is not replicated in most of the rural areas. Establishment of quality higher education institutes in the rural sector has not been significant, which is a serious deterrent for the rural community in general.

There is wide disparity in higher education GER across states, urban versus rural areas, gender and communities that have to be bridged.

Inadequate faculty - The student teacher ratio on the whole is at a lamentable state. While it is still lower in the urban areas, the rural areas take the brunt of the scene with the ratios being at very high rate.

Unqualified or untrained faculty-- Even as the woes of inadequate faculty remain, a major part of the ones who are present to impart higher education are woefully unequipped in terms of either.

Challenges in Teaching and Learning

With the availability of a sea of platforms and online educational tools, the users-both educators and learners-face frequent hiccups while using it or referring to these tools. Some of the challenges identified and highlighted by many researchers are summarised as follows:

Broadly identified challenges with e-learning are accessibility, affordability, flexibility, learning pedagogy, life-long learning and educational policy. Many countries have substantial issues with a reliable Internet connection and access to digital devices. While, in many developing countries, the economically backward children are unable to afford online learning devices, the online education poses a risk of exposure to increased screen time for the learner. Therefore, it has become essential for students to engage in offline activities and self-exploratory learning. Lack of parental guidance, especially for young learners, is another challenge, as both parents are working. There are practical issues around physical workspaces conducive to different ways of learning.

The innately motivated learners are relatively unaffected in their learning as they need minimum supervision and guidance, while the vulnerable group consisting of students who are weak in learning face difficulties. Some academically competent learners from economically disadvantaged background are unable to access and afford online learning.

School time also raises social skills and awareness besides being fun for the children. There are economic, social and psychological repercussions on the life of students while they are away from the normal schedule of schools. Many of these students have now taken online classes, spending additional time on virtual platforms, which have left children vulnerable to online exploitation. Increased and unstructured time spent on online learning has exposed children to potentially harmful and violent content as well as greater risk of cyberbullying. School closures and strict containment measures mean more families have been relying on technology and digital solutions to keep children engaged in learning, entertained and connected to the outside world, but not all children have the necessary knowledge, skills and resources to keep themselves safe online.

Some students expressed that they had to attend to their ailing parents/grandparents/family members and take them to hospitals. By evening, when they are back home, it becomes difficult for them to keep abreast with the lessons. Parents whose children are in lower grades feel that it would be better to let the children repeat the next academic year. Majority of students do not have access to smartphones or TV at home in addition to poor Internet connectivity. There is no or less income for huge population due to closure of business and offices. The data package (costs) is comparatively high against average income earned, and continuous access to Internet is a costly business for the farming community. Online face-to-face classes (video) is encouraged by most; however, some students (economically disadvantaged) have expressed that the face-to-face online class consumes more data packages.

Opportunities for Teaching and Learning

Although there have been overwhelming challenges for educators, schools, institutes and the government regarding online education from a different angle, there are several opportunities created by the Covid-19 pandemic for the unprepared and the distant plans of implementing e-learning system.

It has forged a strong connection between teachers and parents than ever before. The homeschooling requires parents to support the students' learning academically and economically. Children with disabilities need additional and special support during this ongoing emergency.

The use of online platforms such as Google Classroom, Zoom, virtual learning environment and social media and various group forums like Telegram, Messenger, WhatsApp and WeChat are explored and tried for teaching and learning for the first time ever to continue education. This can be explored further even after face-to-face teaching resumes, and these platforms can provide additional resources and coaching to the learners.

Teachers are obliged to develop creative initiatives that assist to overcome the limitations of virtual teaching. Teachers are actively collaborating with one another at a local level to improve online teaching methods. There are incomparable opportunities for cooperation, creative solutions and willingness to learn from others and try new tools as educators, parents and students share similar experiences (Doucet et al., 2020). Many educational organisations are offering their tools and solutions for free to help and support teaching and learning in a more interactive and engaging environment. Online learning has provided the opportunity to teach and learn in innovative ways unlike the teaching and learning experiences in the normal classroom setting.

Conclusion

The recent pandemic created an opportunity for change in pedagogical approaches and introduction of virtual education in all levels of education. As we do not know how long the pandemic situation will continue, a gradual move towards the online/virtual education is the demand of the current crisis. UGC and MHRD have lunched many virtual platforms with online depositories, e-books and other online teaching/learning materials. Combination of the traditional technologies (radio, TV, landline phones) with mobile/web technologies to a single platform with all depositories would enhance better accessibility and flexibility to education. This would involve upgrading the service platform to enable it to meet the required volume of educational demands of students.

References

Covid-19 and Higher Education: Today and Tomorrow - Impact Analysis, Policy Responses and Recommendation", United Nations Educational, Scientific and Cultural Organisation,International Institute for Higher Education in Latin America and the Caribbean (IESALC), UNESCO (2020).

K. Jain, D. Makkar, J. Ng, N. Makkar, T. Gupta, Covid-19: Assessing the Impact on the Education Sector and Looking ahead, Ey Parthenon, 2020.

P. Sahu, Closure of Universities Due to Coronavirus Disease 2019 (COVID-19): Impact on Education and Mental Healthof Students and Academic Staff, Cureus 12 (4)(2020) 1-6. doi:10.7759/cureus.7541

J. Crawford, K. B. Henderson, Rudolph, M. Malkawi, R. Glowatz, P. A. Burton, S. Magni, Lam, COVID-19: 20 Countries' Higher Education intra-period Digital Pedagogy Responses", Journal of Applied Learning and Teaching 3 (1) (2020) 1-28.

J. Josh, Anna University Final Semester Exam 2020 to be held Online by end of August, Offline Exams Later (August 2020).

Savitha, Madras University UG Final year Exams Likely to be conducted from 21 to, Getmyuni, 2020.

Wikipedia. Covid-19 Pandemic in India. Retrieved on May 20, 2020 from https://en.wikipedia.org/wiki/COVID19_pandemic_in_India 3.

Wikipedia, Education in India Retrieved on May 24, 2020. from https://en.wikipedia.org/wiki/Education_in_India

UNESCO. COVID-19 Educational Disruption and Response. Retrieved on June 3, 2020 from https://en.unesco.org/covid19/educationresponse 5. DNS Kumar (29 April 2020).

Impact of COVID-19 on Higher Education. Retrieved on May 25, 2020 from https://www.highereducationdigest.com/impact-ofcovid-19-on-higher-education/

Ravat Ku Jena. Challenges and Opportunities created by Covid-19 for ODL: A case study of IGNOU. International Journal for Innovative Research in Multi-disciplinary Filed. 2020a; 6(5):217-222.

22

Multilingual Assets: Exploring Writing Summaries

M. Srilatha and Dr Shree Deepa

Abstract

This paper reports a study that was conducted on a group of undergraduate students whose dominant language was Telugu who had enrolled themselves for a proficiency course in English. The researcher used three stories in both English and Telugu and activated the meta strategies of summary writing and enabled the students to apply them to the summary writing in English. It qualitatively analyses the data and documents the growth in proficiency in writing summaries in English when the dominant language is used as an asset rather than an interference.

Key words: Dominant language, Language learning strategies, under-graduation, short stories, summary writing.

The present research was focused on improvement of writing skills of Telugu medium students, who completed their higher secondary education in Telugu medium and joined in English medium for their graduation. To improve their writing skills, the researcher used story telling as a teaching tool at undergraduate education level in Telangana. Writing skill is something that is not acquired naturally by humans but is to be learnt under the tutorship of a learnt person (Nagaraj, 2008). Writing is a difficult skill that any ESL learners are expected to "acquire, requiring the mastery of linguistic, cognitive and socio-cultural competencies" (Khaled, 2013.p:1). The study examined the methods employed by teachers to teach writing to learners from multilingual, multicultural background. Culturally unfamiliar English syllabus and the ineffective bilingual method of teaching writing might have caused poor writing in English. The students have Telugu as their dominant langauge, they donot have knowledge in English. They thought that they are unable to learn English language without prior knowledge about it.

The knowledge of the mother tongue is an important cognitive element which decisively affects the order of the second language learning process (Corder, 1992, Gass and Selinker 1992). Thus, the Basic Interpersonal Communication Skills (BICS) in their first language does help them much in learning English language. Similarly, the transferability of Cognitive Academic Language Proficiency (CALP) from source language to target language, as per Jim Cummins's (1979) claim, also does occur in case of the English language learners due to their strong foundation in L1 i.e. Telugu. Krashen (1985) believed that ineffective bilingual/multilingual teaching due to concurrent translation, blocks the meaningful comprehensible input in the first language due to which attaining a solid foundation in the target language is obstructed. Thus, the Telugu medium learners' writing skill was poorer compared to that of English medium students. However, recent research which investigated the effects of knowledge of one language on the learning of another suggested that, regardless of the relationship across the two languages, there can be a positive influence exerted by any known language on the learning of any unknown language (Garcia, 2009). Aggarwal (2013) makes an argument. She proposes that even when the language teacher does not share a common first language with learners, she or he can encourage the students to use their L1, and the teacher can also be a learner of their first language. Importantly, she concludes that, "the freedom given to children to answer/ speak in their L1 (Gondi) led them to think and answer more freely" (Aggarwal, 2013, p.62). The first, or more enabled language in the classroom, can also be the language or resource of metacognitive practices of language learners; it can be "the language of discussion to enable thinking and reflection" (Durairajan, 2012, p.4). This implies that the first language can not only act as a scaffold but can enable the transfer of capabilities across languages.

Brown (2001, p. 335) stated that writing is "as different from speaking as swimming is from walking". Stressing on the importance of writing in the present globalised context, Lindermann (1987) has referred to writing as an economic power that creates impressions, adverse or otherwise, in an individual's professional field since it is the only established mode of communication which is considered official in social life. To enable writing ability, "brainstorming, planning and organising can be done in homogeneous L1 classroom", with the whole class. Students can be encouraged to search for equivalent words in English, once the ideational planning is done, and then asked to compose their essays in English. Feedback, if needed, may also be given in the first language (Durairajan, 2016, pp.11-12). To enable reading ability, students can be given texts in English but asked to write their answers in their L1. "To augment their listening skills they could be encouraged to mind map the texts they hear in their L1" (Durairajan, 2016, p.12). The learners' first language can also be used to enable higher order thinking skills. Cognitively demanding tasks, if they get done first in the first language and then in the target language, can actually function as a "prop" to transfer ideas, strategies and later capabilities (Durairajan, 2016, p.12).

The study adopted story-telling as a research tool based on culture relevant to learners. Story-telling is defined as, "relating a tale to one or more listeners through voice and gesture" (National Council of Teachers of English, 1992, p. 1). No matter how different the stories are from varied cultural backgrounds, by way of telling those breaks the barriers of language and facilitates meaningful communication, where students can hear and understand each other's stories and generally they recognize themselves in the stories of others (Wallace, 2000). In this paper, the pre-experimental research design was used and it mainly focued on Telugu medium students to about their strategies, which they are used in summary writing in Telugu. Another purpose of this paper is to check whether the students used the same strategies in English as well. And the final aim of it is to identify whether the students are able to transfer strategies from Telugu to English through intervention.

The study conducted on undergraduate students, who completed their higher secondary education in Telugu medium and they joined in English medium for their undergraduation at Suryapet district, Telangana.The researcher went to the Telugu medium students, asked their permission to conduct this study on them. To improve writing skills in Telugu medium students, the researcher had taken the short stories were as a research tool. These are the similar stories in both Telugu and English langauges. These stories had taken from Vikram Bhetala story book. Because, these stories have adult characters in it and undergraduate students can get more interest with these stories. These are similar in English and Telugu story books not exactly the same stories. After completion of story telling, the writing tasks given to the students, to improve their usage of the strategies in summary writing in both languages.

First, in the part of intervention, the strength of the classroom was 15. The researcher had two hour class to teach the students. In first two hour class, the researcher taught story in Telugu as "Vikramarkudu-Mantrikudu" in Telugu langauge to the students around one hour and gave them half an hour time for preparation, within last half an hour they completed ttheir summary writing in Telugu. In next class, the researcher, first one hour taught the short story "The tales of bhetala- the Vampire" for the students in English and next one hour clarify their doubts regards subject and in general. When they were listening to the story, they showed their enthusiasm to know about the story completely. Based on this story the researcher asked the students to write summary of it. In this task, before starting the task the researcher gave them one day time to prepare for the task, after checking the tasks, all the students didnot follow any strategy like advance gathering and sequencing of information, thinking about main and supporting ideas of the story. They did not maintain any strategy like note making, sequencial order, usage of their words in summary writing task. Five of the students had written it as in bullet points and few of them wrote it as like small paragraph and few of them completed it as they simply copy pasted the sentences from the text itself. Three of them, wrote the summary just in two lines, basically they did not know how to write summary in English. They did not use their own words in a proper way and they did not correct words from the text too. In that one day gap, they did not arranging or note taking the story, they did not practice any difficult words from the story. Few of them practiced few words, which are difficult for them but when it comes to summary writing they were unable to use those in a particular sentence. Comparatively, they performed much better in Telugu summary writing with English summary writing. Most of them used their own words and sentences to convey the story, sequencing of the story was maintained. They started summary writing with the main ideas of the story. Followed the process of summary writing like parts wise, i.e. introduction, Body and conclusion. They conveyed the story with their dominant language knowledge.

After completion of the first story tasks in English and Telugu languages, the researcher checked their summary writing tasks of first story and explained everything about their usage of the strategies in Telugu language and about which were absent in English summary writitng. Suggested them follow the process of usage of strategies in English language. The researcher taught the second story "Adbhuta Vidyalu" to them in Telugu language and gave them the summary writing task. They followed the steps of sequencing, finding out the main and supportive ideas, all the students maintained the proper structure of summary writing in Telugu langauge.

After that, the similar story "Whose fault is it?" in English language taught to them and had given one day time to prepare for the task. Next day, the students completed the task of summary writing. Eight members of them tried to follow the strategies which are used in Telugu and they prepared note-taking, sequencing the sentences and they tried to convey the main ideas and supportive ideas in the text. Five of the students tried to sequence the summary with introduction, body and conclusion. But they did not maintain relevant matter in those sub-headings. They just tried used to get the process and practice of summary writing. Two of them did not follow any particular process. They just wrote it as it was in the text. But comparatively, the students somewhat changed the way of writing summary in English. Here, the students tried to transfer the strategies from Telugu language.

After completion of the second story tasks, the researcher taught the third story "Mugguru Yuvakulu" to the students. After completion of story telling, the students had taken task within half an hour, they completed the task very quickly and with a lot of confidence. The students followed sequencing the text for summary writing, arranging the main ideas and the supproting ideas, and followed proper way of writing summary in Telugu with introduction, body and conclusion. They used their dominant language knowledge to convey the story with their own words and sentences.

After that, the researcher taught the story "Whom should She Marry?" in English to the students. After one day, the students completed the task in English language. All of them used the strategies, which are used in Telugu. They found out the main ideas and the supporting ideas, prepared note-taking, arranged the sentences according to sequence of the text. They followed the proper way of writing summary like introduction, body and conclusion. Nine of them tried to use their own words to convey the story. They used their dominant language knowledge to convey the story in proper way. They did not use the exact sentences from the text in summary writing. Almost all of them comletely tried to transfer the strategies from Telugu to English.

The researcher first interacted with the students about the study and started the study. The study has to conduct summary writing tasks in Telugu and English langauges.

To find out the strategies, which are used Telugu summary writing

After researcher taught the short story in English and asked them to prepare for the task by next day. First, English task conducted, before conducting the task in English the students have one day for preparation of it. After completion of English task, similar story in Telugu language taught to them by the researcher. After completion of first story task in

Telugu, the researcher found out the strategies usage of the Telugu medium students in summary writing in Telugu language. The students used the strategies like thinking about the main ideas and the supportive ideas, arrangement of the sequences of the text, practice of difficult words within the text, and the proper way of writing summary like introduction, body and conclusion. The students have strategy knowledge in their dominant language, but they donot know the exact word "strategy" and they donot know about usage of it in particular way too, the researcher explained about the strategies usage and the knowledge, they have about it in their dominant language and made them know about strategy usage in Telugu, and explained the possibilities of transfer of the strategies from dominant language English as well.

To check whether the same strategies are used in summary writing in English

In first task of English language, the students did not follow any those strategies and they had written the same sentences from the text itself. Few of them wrote it in three, four lines only. After the researcher's explanation about the strategies usage and the possibility of transfer of it from dominant language to English. The students tried to follow those strategies in English language. They followed thinking about the main ideas and the supporting ideas, sequencing the points, and they tried to follow the proper way of summary writing but they did not connect the exact composition for the text and few of them did not use their own words in summary writing. Few of them tried to their own words but there was no progress in conveying the story exactly. When first task completion in English, the researcher did not find any strategy usage in summary writing in English.

After second tasks in both languages, the researcher explained their mistakes in summary writing in English like using their own words in proper places of the sentences to convey exact meaning of the text, the usage of proper way of summary writing, and about practicing difficult in the text, using of similar words of the text from their own words. And in Telugu, they performed well with their dominant language knowledge. Before third task in English, the students have one day for preparation as usual for other two stories too.

To get clarification about there is any transfer of writing strategies from Telugu to English through Intervention

After completion of third task in English, the researcher felt good for the improvement of the students in summary writing. They followed thinking the main ideas and the supporting ideas, they arranged the sequencing of the sentences, and they practiced difficult words of the text. And they tried write the summary in own words in the proper way like introduction, body and conclusion, which are the strategies they used in Telugu summary, they simply transfer those and improved their summary writing skills in English. Through the intervention, from first to third tasks in English the researcher and the students got to know the change in summary writing in English. The students tried and succeed in transferring strategies from dominant language to English.

The students felt happy for improving their knowledge in the strategies usage and transfer of those into English language. And they said that through the short stories they got more interest to learn English language, with the regular syllabus they have to follow those rules and that syllabus is not relevant to the students who came from Telugu medium background.

The researcher found out that the students are able to transfer strategies from dominant language to English through the short stories as an intervention. An irrelevant of syllabus to the students, made them more frighten in the learning process of English. They thought that they donot anything in English language, they donot understand all these rules and structures of the language itself. By changing the way of teaching English to them, they can more interest in the language, they can give their efforts towards English language learning.

References

Aggarwal, N. (2013). Teaching English using multilinguality in the classroom: the teacher's role as learner. In P Powell-Davies, and Paul.Gunashekar (Eds.), English language teacher education in a diverse environment: selected papers from the third international teacher educators conference, Hyderabad, India (pp. 58-63). British Council Pvt. Ltd.

Brown, J.D. Using Surveys in Language Programmes. Cambridge: Cambridge U P, 2001. Print.

Corder, P. (1992). 'A Role for the Mother Tongue'. In S.Gass and L. Selinker. (Eds), Language Transfer in Language Learning (pp.18-31). Amsterdam: John Benjamins Publishing Company.

Durairajan,G. (2016). 'Language Teaching in Multilingual Contexts: Using First/ More Enabled Language as a Positive Resource in the English Classroom'. FORTELL. 32, 10-12.

Durairajan, G. (2012). Evaluation: Is It the Cane that Guides or the Dog that Guards? Language and Language Teaching. 1(2), pp.1-4. Retrieved

https://www.academia.edu/3408265/evaluation_is_it_the_cane_that_guides_or_the_dog_that_guards

Garcia, O. (2009). Education, multilingualism and translanguaging in the 21st century.

Nagaraja, G. (2008). English Language Teaching: Approaches, Methods, Techniques, second Edition. India: Orient Longman Private limited.

Khaled Barkaoui (2007). Teaching Writing to Second Language Learners: Insights from Theory and Research. TESL Reporter 40, 1 (2007), pp. 35-48.

Krashen, S. D. (1985). The input hypothesis: Issues and implications. London: Longman and New York.

Lindermann Erika (1987). A Rhetoric for Writing Teachers by Erika Lindemann. Oxford University Press; 2 edition.

Sara Miller and Lisa Pennycuff (2008). Journal of Cross-Disciplinary Perspectives in Education Vol. 1, No. 1: 36 - 43.

Wallace, M. J. (2000). Action research for language teachers: Cambridge University Press.

23

Impact of Women Entrepreneurship Education on Economic Development in India

B. Suchetha

Introduction

Entrepreneurship is the process of starting a business or an organisation. It is a dynamic socio-economic process which makes unemployed as self employee and even as employer in the society. The entrepreneur develops a business model to meet needs and wants of society, mobilise resources and use them properly and endeavours until get success. Entrepreneurship within an existing firm or large organisation has been referred to as intrapreneurship and may include corporate ventures where large entities spin off subsidiary organisations. Entrepreneurs are leaders willing to take risk and exercise initiative, taking advantage of market opportunities by planning, organising, and employing resources often by innovating new or improving existing products. More recently, the term entrepreneurship has been extended to include a specific mindset (see also entrepreneurial mindset) resulting in entrepreneurial initiatives, e.g. in the form of social entrepreneurship, political entrepreneurship, or knowledge entrepreneurship. According to Paul Reynolds, founder of the Global Entrepreneurship Monitor, "by the time they reach their retirement years, half of all working men in the United States probably have a period of self-employment of one or more years; one in four may have engaged in self-employment for six or more years. Participating in a new business creation is a common activity among U.S. workers over the course of their careers". According to Schumpeter, an entrepreneur is willing and able to convert a new idea or invention into a successful innovation. The entrepreneur is commonly seen as an innovator - a generator of new ideas and business processes. Management skill and strong team building abilities are often perceived as essential leadership attributes for successful entrepreneurs.

Entrepreneurship Education

Education is an important factor in determining the entrepreneurial orientation in individuals. Education may be in the form of informal or formal. The informal form of learning stresses the importance of early role models and reinforcement patterns on the acquisition and maintenance of entrepreneurial behaviour. If India wants to be a developed country, the government should realise that only entrepreneurs can help it to grow at the desired rate. The government should frame its policies to nurture and promote budding entrepreneurs. So, there is a need for Indians to venture out into the world of entrepreneurship, build intellectual property and create wealth, which hopefully will find its way back into the system to fund more start-ups. India may be becoming a hotbed of innovation as an increasing share of global research and development shifts here. But Indians are still not making the shift to entrepreneurship and aiming to build the next Microsofts, Ciscos and Googles. We seem to be content working for them. India needs Entrepreneurs. Together, the new entrepreneurs will inspire the next generation. That will be the real coming of age of Indian technology and entrepreneurship. To do this, the government needs to focus on Entrepreneurship education to create a pool of trained and highly skilled entrepreneurs. During liberalisation, which started in India in 1991, India exerted greater effort to promote and nurture entrepreneurship. Attempts at various levels have taken place to directly or indirectly promote entrepreneurship. Over the past two decades there has been a growing debate about how well educational systems prepare young people for adult life in general and 'enterprise' in the world of work in particular. In the present scenario this debate becomes large.

Women Entrepreneurship

Entrepreneurship among women is a vital component of the over all solution. It not only boosts the economy through job creation, but also delivers transformational social and personal outcomes for women. Today India has 13.5 - 15.7 million women owned entrepreneurship representing 20 percent of all enterprises. Many women entrepreneurs are successful because they are trusted ones in the community. Despite several hurdles like family obligations and funding issues etc women successfully challenged the world and made their own identity. The hidden talents and creativity of young women can be identified, trained with different skill enhancing programmes and used for various types of industries to increase the productivity in the industrial sector.

Strategies for Development of Entrepreneurship Education in India

(a) Embcdding entrepreneurship into education and training;
(b) Curriculum development
(c) Teacher development; and
(d) Engagement with the private sector.
(e) Providing venture capital to college student who have innovative business ideas
(f) Implementation of Project Bases learning system
(g) Implementation of Design Based Learning System

Significance of Entrepreneurship Education

- The global economy is changing rapidly, with tech transformations ruling every industry. With entrepreneurship education, schools and colleges can prepare the students for the unmapped road.
- Learning about entrepreneurship encourages collaboration and teamwork. It fosters a mindset where students depend on one another for creative reasons instead of merely competing in the classroom.
- Students are future entrepreneurs, and by giving them the tools, resources, and expertise for learning about enterprise management, institutions can make a difference in the learning process.
- A key aspect of entrepreneurship education is about imparting problem-solving skills. Beyond the world of jobs and businesses, these skills allow students to cope better with challenges in regular life.
- Nurturing a culture of entrepreneurship spirit also helps students in creating and achieving realistic goals. Young minds can be trained about long-term and short-term goal achievements.
- Every student is creative and has unique capabilities. With smart training, they can do better with their talents and imaginative ideas. For schools, universities and colleges, this would mean having more students doing well in the practical world.

- Besides students, educational institutions can also gain huge by including entrepreneurship education in their curriculum. Considering the relevance of the subject, more students and parents are likely to be interested.

Challenges Faced By Entrepreneurship Education In India

The present entrepreneurship education in India just concentrates on courses which are similar to the general business courses. There is a demand for education programme specifically designed to expand students' knowledge and experience in entrepreneurship. Entrepreneurship education in India faces cultural and financial constraints along with insufficient government capacity. The significant challenges faced by entrepreneurship education in India are given below:

1. **Cultural barriers:** Entrepreneurship can develop only in a society in which cultural norms permit variability in the choice of paths of life. Unfortunately, the Indian culture consists of a network of benefits that in many ways run counter to entrepreneurship. For example, Indians believe that being passive and content with the status quo is healthier for the inner soul than striving to improve one's situation. They believe that peace of mind can be achieved from spiritual calm rather than from materialism. People in India are more sensitive to emotional affinity in the workplace than to work and productivity. An entrepreneur needs to work around the clock and this has kept some people away from their own start-ups. After all, compared with other countries, family life in India is more important.
2. **Difficulties towards Start-ups:** Starting a business in India is costly in terms of the time required and the cost involved. While it takes just five days to start a business in the United States and just two days in Australia, in India it takes as long as 89 days. What really hurts is that even in neighbours Pakistan, Nepal, and Bangladesh, it takes just 24, 21, and 35 days respectively to do so. The reason for such delay is bureaucratic - too many rules and regulations, and too much paperwork. On an average, it would cost an entrepreneur nearly half of his/her total income (49.5 percent of the gross national income per capita) to set up a business, which is 100 times more than what is needed to set up a business in the United States.
3. **Incomplete Entrepreneurship Education:** A survey done by the Entrepreneurship Development Institute, India (EDII) in 2003

shows that young people are afraid to start their own business because they are not confident, not capable, and lack knowledge in starting a business. Many people have the opportunity to change jobs or become an entrepreneur if they are properly trained. The students in India are not confident with the traditional education they receive in the university.

4. **Lack of a standard framework:** Entrepreneurship education is widely spread, has diverse forms and has a large number of stakeholders. But the overall state of affairs is a confused one, one that lacks broad vision, goals, and systematic planning (akin to the 5-year plans for the economy). The lack of a standard framework is a big challenge to the development of entrepreneurship education in India.
5. **Dependence on government:** Higher degree of dependence on government is another challenge before entrepreneurship education in India. Insufficient private-sector participation and lack of sustainable business models in the entrepreneurship education act as barriers to its development in India.

Impact of Entrepreneurship Education on Economic Development

Entrepreneurship development has positive impact the many economic aspects of the nation. Some of them are presented here:

1. Growth of Entrepreneurship.
2. Creation of job opportunities.
3. Innovation.
4. Impact on community development.
5. The consequence of business failure.
6. Political and economic integration of outsiders.
7. Spawns entrepreneurship.
8. Enhances the standard of living of people.
9. Promotes research and development.

Conclusion

The promotion of entrepreneurship in the country increase self employment in the economy. Entrepreneurship should be taught to students in all disciplines in the institution. It is not out of place to say that many business ideas emerge from non-business disciplines but are often waved aside or ignored because students are not sufficiently educated in the knowledge and skills required.

References

- Panigrahi, Ashok and Joshi, Vijay. Entrepreneurship Education and Economic Development: An Indian Perspective (September 30, 2016). Indian Journal of Rural and Urban Development, Volume - 05, Issue - 01, April-September 2016, ISSN 2249-7285, Available at SSRN: https://ssrn.com/abstract=2863818
- D.P.M Johnson, 2005. "A Glossary of Political Economy Terms, 2005". Auburn University.[5] P.D. Reynolds, 2007. Entrepreneurship in the United States: The Future Is Now. Springer. ISBN 978-0-387-45671-3.
- T. Prive, 2012. "Top 10 Qualities That Make A Great Leader". Forbes. Retrieved 1 August 2013.
- Makinde, O. (2013). Curbing the Unemployment Problem in Nigeria through Entrepreneurial Development. African Journal of Business Management, 7(44), 4429-4444.
- Sofoluwe, A. O., Akinsolu, A. T., and Kayode, D. J. (2013). Managing University Education for National Transformation in Nigeria. In A. O. Ayeni, U. G. Emetaron, A. O. Okwori, J. A. Undie, and J. E. Okon (Eds.). Managing Education for National Transformation Nigeria: Nigerian Association for Educational Administration and Planning (NAEAP).
- Garba, A. S. (2012). Entrepreneurship, Public Policy and Poverty Reduction in Nigeria. International Journal of Business and Social Research (IJBSR), Volume 2, No. 2.

24

Impact of Covid on Higher Education and New Education Policy 2020

Dr M. Sudhakar Reddy and Dr T. Vinila

Abstract

Education is the manifestation of perfection already existing in man."
Education is fundamental for achieving full human potential, developing an equitable and just society, and promoting national development. Providing universal access to quality education is the key to economic growth, social justice and equality, scientific advancement, national integration and cultural preservation; and for India's continued ascent, progress, and leadership on the global stage. India will have the highest youth population in the world over the next decade, and our ability to provide high-quality educational opportunities to them will shape the future of our country. The aim must be for India to have an education system that ensures equitable access to the highest-quality education for all learners regardless of social and economic background. To achieve this, actions must be taken now and with urgency.
This National Education Policy is the first education policy of the twenty first century, and aims to address the many growing developmental imperatives of this country. This Policy proposes the revision and revamping of all aspects of the education structure, including its regulation and governance, to create a new system that is aligned with the aspirational goals of twenty first century education, while remaining consistent with India's traditions and value systems.
The National Education Policy lays particular emphasis on the development of the creative potential of each individual, in all its richness and complexity. It is based on the principle that education must develop not only cognitive skills - both 'foundational skills' of literacy and numeracy and 'higher-order' cognitive skills such as critical thinking and problem solving - but also social and emotional skills - also referred to as 'soft skills' - including cultural awareness and empathy, perseverance and grit, teamwork, leadership, communication, among others.
The impact of Covid-19 especially when it comes to education, this is the biggest sector that has been adversely affected by this pandemic. It forced many great nations to enforce lockdown thereby bringing everything to an

abrupt halt for a certain period of time. The educational sector has been fighting to survive the crises. The teaching learning and evaluation methodologies have been completely altered by this pandemic. The digitalisation of education became a necessity in order to provide seamless education. This paper discusses on the impact it had on the teaching, learning and research in higher education in India.

Keywords: Covid19 pandemic, higher education.

Introduction

The outbreak of Covid-19 has forced many countries to enforce lockdowns that brought everything to a standstill including the teaching and learning process. The educational sector suffered the most due to this pandemic. This pandemic has made the world to observe social distancing in the public space. Covid-19 was first identified in Wuhan, China and then it gradually started spreading in other parts of the world. It was only in 2020 the WHO declared it as pandemic. It has claimed millions of lives across the world. According to the UNESCO report more than 90 percent of total student population in the world was affected due to the pandemic during the initial phase of its outbreak. It has caused a serious and very deep rooted impact on the social, economic and also psychological life of people in different parts of the world. The guidelines that were issued by the WHO which we are ratified by the most of the countries across the world compelled the governments to shut down the institutions of mass gatherings. So along with the educational institutions the academic year end exams and also competitive exams were postponed indefinitely. This step was taken in order to slow down and contain the spread of Corona virus in India by segregating the people who were infected with Covid-19. This process came to be known as Lockdown wherein the Govt. had imposed severe restrictions on the movement and the gatherings of the people in order to control the spread of this airborne disease. All the educational institutions in India had to be shut down Right from the primary schools to the universities. The regular classes were suspended citing threat to the lives of the learners and the teachers. It also affected the lives of the aspirants who were preparing for competitive and entrance exams. It has raised multiple issues right from the health to the wealth also affecting the day to day.

The lockdown has compelled many educational institutions to cancel their classes, examinations, internships etc. and to choose the online modes. Initially, the educators and the students were quite confused and didn't understand how to cope up with the situation of this sudden crisis that compelled closure of the educational activities. But latter on all realised that the lockdown has taught so many lessons to manage with the emergence of such pandemics. Thus, Covid created many challenges and opportunities for the educational institutes to strengthen their infrastructure (Pravat, 2020a). The lockdown has given them a ray of hope for teachers and students to continue their educational activities through online. The teachers assigned work to students via internet, delivered lectures video conferencing using different Apps like Zoom, Google meet, Facebook, Youtube, and Skype etc. There are WhatsApp groups of guardians, teachers, students and parents for affective communication through which they are always in touch to share their difficulties through this e-medium.

Objectives

The present paper focused on the following objectives:

- To enlighten on the new education policy 2020 and various measures taken by Govt. of India for education sector
- To discuss on various challenges and opportunities on education system.

Methodology

Data and information is collected from various reports prepared by national and international agencies on Covid-19 pandemic, various authentic websites, journals and e-contents relating to impact of Covid-19 on educational system are referred.

New Education Policy 2020 on Higher Education

Quality Universities and Colleges: A New and Forward-looking Vision for India's Higher Education System.

- Institutional Re-structuring and Consolidation
- More Holistic Education
- Optimal Learning Environments and Support for Students
- Motivated, Energised, and Capable Faculty
- Equity and Inclusion in Higher Education
- Teacher Education
- Re-imagining Vocational Education
- Professional Education
- Promoting high quality research
- National Research Foundation

- Effective Governance and Leadership for Higher Education Institutions
- Transforming the Regulatory System of Higher Education

Initiatives of Govt. of India on education during Covid-19

To prevent spread of pandemic Covid-19, the Government of India has taken number of preventive measures. The Ministry of Human Resource Development (MHRD) has made several arrangements, including online portals and educational channels through Direct to Home TV, Radios for students to continue learning. During lockdown, students are using popular social media tools like WhatsApp, Zoom, Google meet, Telegram, Youtube live, Facebook live etc. for online teaching learning system. ICT initiative of MHRD (e-Broucher-) is a unique platform which combines all digital resources for online education. The digital initiatives of MHRD for secondary as well as higher education during Covid-19 are listed as below:

Diksha portal contains e-Learning content for students, teachers, and parents aligned to the curriculum, including video lessons, worksheets, textbooks and assessments. Under the guidance of its national boards of education (CBSE) and NCERT, the content has been created by more than 250 teachers who teach in multiple languages. The app is available to use offline. It has more than 80,000 e-Books for classes 1 to 12 created by CBSE, NCERT in multiple languages. The contents can also be viewed through QR codes on textbooks. The app can be downloaded from IOS and Google Play Store.

e-Pathshala is an e-Learning app by NCERT for classes 1 to 12 in multiple languages. The app houses books, videos, audio, etc. aimed at students, educators and parents in multiple languages including Hindi, Urdu, and English. In this web portal NCERT has deployed 1886 audios, 2000 videos, 696 e-Books and 504 Flip Books for classes 1 to 12 in different languages. Mobile Apps is available.

National Repository of Open Educational Resources

(NROER) portal provides a host of resources for students and teachers in multiple languages including books, interactive modules and videos including a host of STEM-based games. Content is mapped to the curriculum for classes 1-12, including aligned resources for teachers. It has a total of 14527 files including 401 collections, 2779 documents, 1345 interactive, 1664 audios, 2586 images and 6153 videos on different languages.

Higher Education

Swayam is the national online education platform hosting 1900 courses covering both school (classes 9 to 12) and higher education (under graduate, post graduate programme) in all subjects including engineering, humanities and social sciences, law and management courses. The unique feature is that, it is integrated with the conventional education. Credit transfers are possible for SWAYAM courses (max. 20 percent). Website:https://swayam.gov.in/

Swayam Prabha has 32 DTH TV channels transmitting educational contents on 24 × 7 basis. These channels are available for viewing all across the country using DD Free Dish Set Top Box and Antenna. The channel schedule and other details are available in the portal. The channels cover both school education (classes 9 to 12) and higher education (undergraduate, postgraduate, engineering, Out-of-school children, vocational courses and teacher training) in arts, science, commerce commerce, performing arts, social sciences and humanities subjects, engineering, technology, law, medicine, agriculture.

Website: https://swayamprabha.gov.in/

e-PG Pathshala

Postgraduate students can access this platform for ebooks, online courses and study materials during this lockdown period. The importance of this platform is that students can access these facilities without having internet for the whole day.

Website: https://epgp.inflibnet.ac.in

Opportunities

Move towards Blended Learning: Covid-19 has accelerated adoption of digital technologies to deliver education. Educational institutions moved towards blended mode of learning. It encouraged all teachers and students to become more technology savvy. New ways of delivery and assessments of learning opened immense opportunities for a major transformation in the area of curriculum development and pedagogy. It also gives access to large pools of learners at a time.

Rise in use of Learning Management Systems: Use of learning management systems by educational institutions became a great demand. It opened a great opportunity for the companies those have been developing and strengthening learning management systems for use educational institutions (Misra, 2020).

Enhance the use of soft copy of learning material : In lockdown situation students were not able to collect the hard copies of study materials and hence most of the students used of soft copies materials for reference.

Improvement in collaborative work: There is a new opportunity where collaborative teaching and learning can take on new forms. Collaborations can also happen among faculty/teachers across the world to benefit from each other (Misra, 2020).

Rise in online meetings: The pandemic has created a massive rise in teleconferencing, virtual meetings, webinars and e-conferencing opportunities.

Enhanced Digital Literacy: The pandemic situation induced people to learn and use digital technology and resulted in increasing the digital literacy.

Improved the use of electronic media for sharing information: Learning materials are shared among the students easily and the related queries are resolved through e-mail, SMS, phone calls and using different social Medias like WhatsApp or Facebook.

World wide exposure: Educators and learners are getting opportunities to interact with peers from around the world. Learners adapted to an international community.

Better time management: Students are able to manage their time more efficiently in online education during pandemics.

Demand for Open and Distance Learning (ODL): During the pandemic situation most of the students preferred ODL mode as it encourages self-learning providing opportunities to learn from diverse resources and customised learning as per their needs.

Negative impact of Covid-19 on education

Education sector has suffered a lot due to the outbreak of Covid-19. It has created many negative impacts on education and some of them are as pointed below :

Educational activity hampered: Classes have been suspended and exams at different levels postponed. Different boards have already postponed the annual examinations and entrance tests. Admission process got delayed. Due to continuity in lockdown, student suffered a loss of nearly three months of the full academic year of 2020-21 which is going to further deteriorate the situation of continuity in education and the as students would face much difficulty in resuming schooling again after a huge gap.

Impact on employment: Most of the recruitment got postponed due to Covid-19. Placements for students may also be affected with companies delaying the on board of students. Unemployment rate is expected to be increased due to this pandemic. In India, there is no recruitment in Govt. sector and fresh graduates fear withdrawal of their job offers from private sectors because of the current situation. The Centre for Monitoring Indian Economy's estimates on unemployment shot up from 8.4 percent in mid-March to 23 percent in early April and the urban unemployment rate to 30.9 percent. When the unemployment increases then the education gradually decreases as people struggle for food rather than education.

Unprepared teachers/students for online education: Not all teachers/ students are good at it or at least not all of them were ready for this sudden transition from face-to-face learning to online learning. Most of the teachers are just conducting lectures on video platforms such as Zoom, Google meet etc. which may not be real online learning without any dedicated online learning platform.

Reduced global employment opportunity: Some may lose their jobs from other countries and the pass out students may not get their job outside India due to restrictions caused by Covid-19. Many Indians might have returned home after losing their jobs overseas due to Covid-19. Hence, the fresh students who are likely to enter the job market shortly may face difficulty in getting suitable employment. Many students who have already got jobs through campus interviews may not be able to join their jobs due to lockdown. The Indians who have been doing their jobs abroad may lose their jobs. Recent graduates in India are of also fearing for withdrawal of job offers from corporate sectors because of movement restriction in the current pandemic situation.

Increased responsibility of parents to educate their wards: Some educated parents are able to guide but some may not have the adequate level of education needed to teach children in the house.

Loss of nutrition due to school closure: Mid-day meals is a school meal programme of the Government of India which is designed to provide better the nutritional food to school-age children nationwide. The closure of schools has serious implications on the daily nutrition of students as the mid-day meal schemes have temporarily been shut. Various studies have pointed out that mid-day meals are also an important contributing factor for increased enrolment in the schools.

Access to digital world: As many students have limited or no internet access and many students may not be able to afford computer, laptop or supporting mobile phones in their homes, online teaching-learning may create a digital divide among students. The lockdown has hit the poor students very hard in India as most of them are unable to explore online learning according to various reports. Thus, the online teaching-learning method during pandemic Covid-19 may enhance the gap between rich/poor and urban/rural.

Access to global education: The pandemic has significantly disrupted the higher education sector. A large number of Indian students who are enrolled in many Universities abroad, especially in worst affected countries are now leaving those countries and if the situation persists, in the long run, there will be a significant decline in the demand for international higher education.

Payment of Schools, Colleges fee got delayed: During this lockdown most of the parents will be facing the unemployment situation so they may not be able to pay the fee for that particular time periods which may affect the private institutes.

Problems in Higher Education

Some of the major problems currently plaguing the higher education system in India include:

(i) A severely fragmented higher educational ecosystem, with more than 50,000 higher National Education Policy 2020 education institutions (HEIs), a large proportion of which offer only a single programme and have fewer than 100 students and a large percentage of which are commercial enterprises in which little or no education is taking place;

(ii) Poor learning outcomes and development of cognitive skills of students;

(iii) Rigid separation of disciplines, with too much early specialisation and streaming of students into narrow areas of study;

(iv) A lack of access to higher education, especially in socio-economically disadvantaged areas;

(v) A lack of teacher and institutional autonomy to innovate and excel;

(vi) Inadequate mechanisms for merit-based career management and progression of faculty and institutional leaders;

(vii) a lack of research at most universities and colleges, and transparent and competitive peer-reviewed research funding across disciplines;

(viii) Suboptimal governance and leadership of HEIs;

(ix) A regulatory system that is not empowered to close down fake colleges, while constraining excellent and innovative institutions;

(x) Problems associated with large affiliating universities resulting in poor undergraduate education in colleges. This policy envisions a complete overhaul and re-energising of the higher education

Suggestions

- India should develop creative strategies to ensure that all children must have sustainable access to learning during pandemic Covid-19. The Indian policies must include various individuals from diverse backgrounds including remote regions, marginalised and minority groups for effective delivery.
- Immediate measures are required to lessen the effects of the pandemic on job offers, internship programme, and research projects.
- Many online learning platforms offer multiple programmes on the same subjects with different levels of certifications, methodology and assessment parameters. So, the quality of programmes may differ across different online learning platforms. Therefore, establishment of quality assurance mechanisms and quality benchmark for online learning programmes must be developed and offered by Higher Education Institutions (HEIs) in India keeping in view of rapid growth of the online learning platforms.
- Across the globe, Indian traditional knowledge is well known for its scientific innovations, values and benefits to develop sustainable technologies and medicines and this knowledge systems in different fields should be integrated with a present-day mainstream higher education system.
- Govt and educational institutes should plan to continue the educational activities maintaining social distancing. 30-40 percent students and teachers may attend schools/colleges in two shifts per day to carry on educational activities by obeying guidelines for Covid-19.

- At current times, access to technology and internet is an urgent requirement. So, the digital capabilities and the required infra-structure must reach to the remotest and poorest communities to facilitate the students to continue their education during the pandemics. There is a need to deploy public funds to fix the internet gap and ensure that students continue to learn digitally. The state governments/private organisations should come up with ideas to address this issue of digital education. Some significant issues associated with distance learning strategies like the availability and access to digital devices with internet connectivity, the need for safe learning spaces, creating capabilities for teachers, families and students to operate and navigate digital devices, and engaging lesson plans for disabled students and other marginalised groups should be addressed by Govt. and the stakeholders.

Conclusion

Covid-19 has impacted immensely to the education sector of India. Though it has created many challenges, various opportunities are also evolved. The Indian Govt. and different stakeholders of education have explored the possibility of Open and Distance Learning (ODL) by adopting different digital technologies to cope up with the present crisis of Covid-19. India is not fully equipped to make education reach all corners of the nation via digital platforms. Thc students who aren't privileged like the others will suffer due to the present choice of digital platforms. But universities and the government of India are relentlessly trying to come up with a solution to resolve this problem. The priority should be to utilise digital technology to create an advantageous position for millions of young students in India. It is need of the hour for the educational institutions to strengthen their knowledge and Information Technology infrastructure to be ready for facing Covid-19 like situations.

Even if the Covid-19 crisis stretches longer, there is an urgent need to take efforts on maximum utilisation of online platforms so that students not only complete their degree in this academic year but also to get ready for the future digital oriented environment. The concept of "work from home" has greater relevance in such pandemic situation to reduce spread of Covid-19. India should develop creative strategies to ensure that all children must have sustainable access to learning during pandemic Covid-19. The Indian policies must include various individuals from diverse backgrounds including remote regions, marginalised and minority groups for effective delivery of education. As online practice is benefitting the students immensely, it should be continued after the lockdown. Further detailed statistical study may be undertaken to explore the impact of Covid-19 on education system of India.

References

Jena, P. K. (18-06-2020). Impact of COVID-19 on Higher Education in India. International Journal of Advance Education and Research, 77-81.

Covid-19 crisis brings opportunity to expand the autonomy of public universities. The Indian Express. 5-Gopinathan, K. R. (2015 , April 19). Is online the way forward? The Hindu.

International Journal for Innovative Research in Multidisciplinary Filed, Volume-6, Issue- 5, pp. 217-222. Study Abroad Life (2020). How Covid-19 will affect the Indian education system.

Dishtavo. (2020). Retrieved from Digital Integrated System for Holistic Teaching and Virtual Orientations: http://dishtavo.dhe.goa.gov.in/index.php

Dr. Priyanka Dhoot. (2020). Impact of COVID-19 on Higher Education in India. International Journal of Creative Research Thoughts (IJCRT), 6-7. 4-Gopinath, M. (2020, June 10).

25

Educational Enrichment in India: Issues and Challenges

Sukka Kiran Kumar

Abstract

In our national development process, education system has a very important role to play, especially the higher education. Higher education faces various challenges in all areas of development. After independence, we wanted to build a modern, strong dynamic and self - reliant India which could stand abreast with the developed nations. While working towards this end, the country had faced the greater challenge of rapidly industrialising the then predominantly agricultural economy and in the process it had to create wide - based infrastructure in higher and technical education institutions, research laboratories and industries, covering a wide spectrum of disciplines and capabilities. The higher education system of the twenty first century should accept the challenges of change and motivate their faculty and the society to do the same. The institutions of higher learning preparing to enter the new era will have to accept the fact that the systems of today are demanding, competitive and accountable. The higher education system in the country is now being put to test. University should undertake intensive introspection and reorient them to respond adequately to the emerging challenges to the changed economic scenario in the country. In addition, it has the added responsibility to strengthen the value system in the society. At the same time, one should keep in mind it is important to free the system from unnecessary constrains and political interference and provide the needed academic and administrative system which is accountable.

Key Words : Educational Enrichment, Global Era, Raw Materials, Inadequate, Poor massess, added Responsibility.

Introduction

In our national development process, education system has a very important role to play, especially the higher education. Higher education faces various challenges in all areas of development. After independence, we wanted to build a modern, strong dynamic and self-reliant India which could stand abreast with the developed nations. While working towards this end, the country had faced the greater challenge of rapidly industrialising the then predominantly agricultural economy and in the process it had to create wide - based infrastructure in higher and technical education institutions, research laboratories and industries, covering a wide spectrum of disciplines and capabilities. During the 90's, the country was becoming progressively more integrated into the global economy. With the restructuring of the economy, new industrial and trade policies and liberalisation, the Indian industry was exposed to domestic and global competition. Knowledge based industries was on the increase. We have to increase research efforts to catch up with the rest of the world in frontier areas of knowledge which will dominate and determine the course of the twenty first century. According to University Education Commission "Education is a great instrument of social emancipation by which a democracy establishes, maintains and protects the spirit of equality among its members".

The higher education system of a country plays a significant role in the creation of skilled human resources. In the emerging scenario of knowledge based on society across the globe, India is well placed with Potential brains needed for the revolutionary changes. According to Swami Vivekananda, "We want that education by which character is formed, strength of mind is increased, intellect is expanded and by which one can stand on one's own feet". The new generation of students have new challenges and goals. These challenges involving independent living, juggling with family or a work commitment or grasping new ideas and concept, is obviously a very individual issue. The foremost feature of our educational system should be to train the youth to see the good in every human being and take the best out of each individual. Our educational system still continues to be dominated by model and values of colonial regime, of the system that emphasizes on narrow individualism, verbal fluency especially in English.

Competitive life and mere acquisition of knowledge neglecting national objectives skill development and character building is ineffective in making students face challenges of the fast growing world and stand on their own legs. India is to grow to her full potential as a strong, united, prosperous nation, and to attain the highest ethical moral values, true to the genius of her cultural and spiritual heritage. It is only transformation and education which can unlock all doors for a progress as, "A nation advances in proportion to education and intelligence spread among masses". Higher education experience has brought about a greater feeling of Independence, self-discipline and growing confidence. For most it is about realising one's full potential. In an international study of University a student, described,

Education in the Global Era

Indian higher education institutions also produced world beating scientists and engineers, lawyers, and doctors, managers and technocrats. To locate the area of education in which we have expertise such as alternate system of medicine, yoga, traditional wisdom and culture where we can develop courses of international standards in order to attract international students and to meet the much needed financial resources. The advent of globalisation in the area of education as in other services called, for the internationalisation of Higher Education in India. The important concept implies the acceptance of a World Wide Quality Label (WQL) of quality assurance in higher education. A system of education is expected to be responsible and to meet the needs of a student. One of the activities of Global Alliance of Traditional Education (GATE) is to establish principles and policies for evaluating quality of Education. The Kothari Commission has beautifully said, "The destiny of India is now being shaped in her class rooms. This we believe is no mere rhetoric. In a world based on science technology, it is education that determines the level of prosperity, welfare and security of people. The Quality will depend on our success in the great enterprise of national construction whose main objective is to raise the standard of living of our people".

We cannot also ignore basic research. Erosion in human values is another area causing concern. In this situation, the higher education system should identify the emerging challenges and respond to them adequately. In our national developmental process, education system has a very important role to play, especially the higher education. Higher education faces various challenges in all areas of development. The twenty first century is the age of liberalisation, privatisation and globalisation. Knowledge is the key to this age. Fundamental sources of wealth is know ledge and information rather than raw '(materials and labour. Tomorrow's industry will be Knowledge industry where knowledge workers may be quite expensive, but most expendable of all.

There are many drawbacks in the affiliating system of higher education. Despite spectacular growth of educational institutions, the present scenario. The basic strategy to make our products current and quality sound is basically curricular and pedagogic reformation. The battle of quality has to be fought in the minds of all men and women connected with education. Quality can be assured by making everybody in the system accountable and responsible to everyone else. Everybody should become a watchdog on the quality of the educational system. The students and administrators should monitor the quality of teaching and teachers and the parents must monitor the quality or learning.

Higher Education Scenario in India

We have built a vast higher education system which is one of the largest in the world as of 2015. There are at present more than 650 universities, 120 deemed to be universities, 50 Central Universities, 38,000 colleges, more than 2000 exclusive Women Colleges and the total enrolment in higher education system is around 60 lakhs. It is estimated that the total student enrolment at the end of 2020 will be around 150 lakhs. In addition, there is a vast network of technical education, including colleges institutions, offering courses in engineering, Management, pharmacology, etc. It on account of this extensive higher and technical education system and the human resource graduating from them that India is perceived to the biggest producers of scientific and technical manpower. Planwise approved outlays for education is including general higher and technical education, it may be seen that the percentage of higher education out of the total allocation to education varied from 20.89 percent in the Sixth Plan and 11.20 percent in the Eight Plan. The higher education system has done a commendable job with all limitations, in fulfilling its role as a powerful for social, political, and economic change in the source of new knowledge, and manpower generator for all sectors of the economy. While dealing with the problems and challenges in the field of higher education one has to perceive the entire scenario in totality. The socio-cultural, political economic and technological advancements are to be considered and analyzed while viewing the prospects of higher education in our country.

There are different sources of educational finance in India-Central and State governments, local bodies, and private sector including the students who are its potential beneficiaries. As the system of higher education grew in size, it required increased funds even for its maintenance. Simultaneously, due to successive reduction in the private contribution, its dependence on government for funds also increased. Consequently, the government contribution to educational finance increased from about 57 percent in 1950-51 to about 90-95 percent during 2000s.. During the same period the contribution, of students in terms of fees decreased from about 20 percent to less than five percent. Moreover, the allocation of funds for education over the different five year plans has not shown noticeable improvement, rather, in relative terms, it has been declining continuously. In the developing societies, higher education is considered a speedy vehicle for upward social mobility, especially by the socially and economically deprived and underprivileged sections. Poor people do not demand better quality because they are not paying for it. The more expensive course such as medicine, engineering and management. Here in a case for increasing fees so as to cover at least 50 percent of the cost in general education. In professional education, the fee may be even higher because these courses lead to higher personal returns. One can see the difference in the fee structure as well as in the facilities provided by the different institutions because of financial crisis.

As we can see, the Indian higher education system is one of the largest in the world, but still it is inadequate for meeting the increasing demand for private college. Privatisation of higher education is inevitable India's school education is already partially privatised with a large number of high - fee charging public schools functioning all over the country. The dual system of school education, one for the privileged few and the other for the poor masses, has already caused considerable damage to the social fabric of the nation. But, university system has so far been common to all capable and motivated youths, and to some extent has been instrumental in making up for this damage. If private universities proposed to be set up also follow the policy of public schools, the social gulf between the dual and the poor will further widen, and damage thus caused will be irreparable. In that case we will have dual higher education system also, one for the rich and other for the poor. The net result will be that poor and deprived sections of the society will be further marginalised. We have to safeguard the interests of the people through an adequate state policy.

Educational Development in India

Universities and Colleges do not have adequate facilities. In the outer world there is a move from primitive and print media to modern electronic and multimedia. Our colleges· are still compromising with chalk and talk. Computers, computer labs, ICT labs, media are not properly utilised. It is because there is very little convergence of perspectives of higher education among the Governments and Central Government. Rarely the academic staff colleges have inputs of ICT for orienting and refreshing higher education teachers. Through UGC as approved actual position of lecturers in computer education in the Twelfth Five Year Plan, there is no concurrence from different State Governments. The institutions of higher education that can accept the challenges and implement the process of change will lead the system in the twenty first century. Once this change is accepted the institutions of learning in the years to come. It will be a paradigm shift for most of the traditional universities in terms of its functioning and activities - its teaching and research, its service to the society, its financing mechanisms. Thus a concerted effort is needed on the part of higher learning institution to make a transition from the traditions of the past to the challenges of the present, and ensure the entry into the future success will lie only with such institutions. These institutions will be necessitated to adopt the modern mechanism of change in terms of the higher education system of the twenty first Century should accept the challenges of change and motivate their faculty and the society to do the same. The institutions of higher learning preparing to enter the new era will have to accept the fact that the systems of today are demanding, competitive and accountable. The higher education system in the country is now being put to test. University should undertake intensive introspection and reorient them to respond adequately to the emerging challenges to the changed economic scenario in the country. In addition, it has the added responsibility to strengthen the value system in the society. At the same time, one should keep in mind it is important to free the system from unnecessary constrains and political interference and provide the needed academic and administrative system which is accountable.

Higher education and learning has always had a strong international flavour. Where political constraints make any change unfeasible and the supply of higher education institutions with any signaling effect is severely limited, there is an increasing tendency to purchase higher education overseas. Since the late 1990s, the number of students crossing borders to receive education has increased by more than 50 percent. It is estimated that the number of students from developing countries studying abroad is likely to double before 2015 and double again by 2025. While China has emerged as the largest country of origin for international students, there has been a surge of students from India as well. International student outflows from India have been growing rapidly. In contrast to past decades when these outflows were more the result of low payoffs to skill rather than underinvestment in higher education capacity, with the rapid rise in skill premiums and the difficulties of access to quality institutions within the country, the latter has become more important. There has been a substantial Development in higher education in India, whether measured by the number of students or expenditures, serious governance issues have hobbled the Indian university system. As a result, it continues to provide graduates that are unemployable despite emerging shortages of skilled manpower in an increasing number of sectors. The standards of academic research are low and declining. Some of the problems of the Indian higher education, such as - the unwieldy affiliating system, inflexible academic structure, uneven capacity across various subjects, eroding autonomy of academic institutions, and the low level of public funding are well known. Many other concerns relating to the dysfunctional regulatory environment, the accreditation system that has low coverage and no consequences, absence of incentives for performing well, and the unjust public funding policies are not well recognised. Considering both the multitude and the magnitude of the difficulties that Indian higher education faces, it would be easy to be overwhelmed by the problems and to despair of finding solutions. At the same time, given the tremendous potential of India's booming industry and technology and the considerable progress made in higher education and research in recent decades, it would also be easy to reach a state of exuberance and expect that, somehow, India will surmount these difficulties.

Conclusion

Thus, our Education System is famous for its Qualitative teaching which has to be continued in future. As John Dewey stated, a socially efficient individual should be able to control to environment and fulfill his possibilities. All education proceeds by the participation of individuals in the social consciousness of the race". Higher Education, ultimately is to be directed to the intellectual maturity and flowering of the soul. It is the duty of all sections of society to protect and promote Education as the fundamental human right.

The Education system should develop necessary infrastructure for the evolution of "Knowledge Society". It is also aimed at imparting Quality to the teaching - learning process and develop a purposeful "Research Culture" in India. In the emerging scenario of knowledge-based society across the globe, India is well placed with potential brains needed for revolutionary changes. Government of India has announced the national goal to become a developed nation by the year 2020. India aspires to be free from poverty and to sit in line with G-8 nations. Honourable former President, Dr. Abdul Kalam wrote, "A developed India by 2020 or even earlier, is not a dream. It need not even be a mere vision in the mind of many Indians. It is mission we can all take up". By 2020, the people of India will be better educated, healthier and more prosperous than at anytime in our long history. Goldman and Sachs predictions of 2050 are that India along with China and USA will be the three top economies of the world. One can confidently predict that if India plays its card right, by 2020 it can become the number one "knowledge production" Centre of the world.

I conclude with the wording of Pt. Jawaharlal Nehru, "A moment comes, which comes but rarely in history, when we set out from the old to the new". An essential requirement for envisioning India's future in the new century is to recognise that the parameters which determines national development have changed in recent years and will change further in future. This will certainly include rapid rise in levels of education.

References

1. Communication, (2019). New Challenges, Before Indian Higher Education, University News, 46(15) April 14-20.
2. Dhar, B.B. (2021). Higher Education Scenario in the 21st Century. Accepting Challenges to Change. University News, 39(35), August 27 - September 2.
3. Gamble, and Bloom, From Ideas to Action on Higher Education Reform Harvard University (http://"www.www.bi.ulaval.ca/ Globalisation Universities/Pages/ actes/ BloomDavid.pdf). dt: 20-02-2005.
4. Kapur, Devesh and Crowley Megan. "Beyond the ABCs Higher Education and Developing Countries." Center for Global Development Working Paper. 2010.
5. Knight, J. and H. De.Wit (eds). Internationalisation of Higher Education in Asia Pacific. Amsterdam. European Association for International Education, p. 8, 1995.
6. Knight, J. Internationalisation remodeled: Responding to new realities and challenges. 2004.
7. Patil, L.A., (2020). Higher Education Challenges, Excellence and Future, Pratap College, Amainer, University News, 40(27), July 8-14.
8. Shamshad, H (2019). Challenges Before Higher Education, University News 38 (38). September, 18.
9. Sinha, A. India Tech: What's the Matter U? Wired (http://wwww.wired. com/ techbiz/media/news/2002/06/52942). 2005.
10. Soundararaj, F. (2020). Privatisation of Education, Kodaikanal Christian Colleges, Kodaikanal University News. Monday News, September, 30.
11. Swaminadhan, D (2020). Challenges to Higher Education and Research in India, University News, February, 27, 1995.
12. Swaminathan D. Challenges to Higher Education and Research in India, University News, February 27, 2015.

26

Holistic Entrepreneurial Education and Budding Entrepreneurs

Dr Susmita Banerjee and Saikat Majumder

Abstract

In last few decades the rapid development of Entrepreneurship education help our society with generating further dimensions in Entrepreneurship. The new era of tackling unemployment problem is also associated with new dimensions of entrepreneurship. We are now in fact in the age of knowledge explosion. In the process of rapid development the exhaustive use of readily available information and other resources if associated with narrow interest is some time hindering the sustainability of development. Budding entrepreneur's needs skill and quality based entrepreneurship education.

So, entrepreneurs need holistic all-round training development with soft skills for serving the society. Needs attention on the purpose and it should be focused on sustainable holistic development of the society and the mankind. The enhanced conscience of the Policy maker and Strategic leader can influence a lot on the use of value consciousness in business innovation.

Entrepreneurship activity, profit making purpose must be purified with spirituality to solve the crisis of values in knowledge based society. It is felt that universal human values must be incorporated in the use of Knowledge for sustainable economic and holistic development. This paper is a qualitative study of holistic entrepreneurial education and management for better performance of Entrepreneurs. Secondary data analysis will fill up the information gap. It is important for new age sustainable development; it will help poverty eradication, employment generation, income generation, empowerment, capacity building, confidence building, disease prevention, health improvement, safety and environment preservation.

Keywords: entrepreneurship education, Budding entrepreneurs, Strategic leader, universal human values.

Introduction

Small business development and entrepreneurial growth are considered as associated with economic recovery and growth. Consequently, in recent years entrepreneurship has ascended progressively towards the top of political agendas in Eastern, Central and Western Europe.

As a result, entrepreneurship education has emerged as the most cost-effective and time-efficient method of increasing the quality and number of entrepreneurs entering a market.

Despite the conceptual ambiguity and problematic features emphasised by entrepreneurship education experts, the teaching and development of entrepreneurial students has become a hotly disputed European topic.

The writers of an article argue that entrepreneurship is more than a collection of applicable information, skills, and attitudes (Oganisjana, et.el. 2012).

We tend to have a single focus in entrepreneurship education, such as "motivation," "self-directed learning," "learning goals," and so on, but perhaps we need to extend our focus and look at the wider picture. Davidsen, H et.el 2017)

The key question of this study is: how can we comprehend the challenges that entrepreneurial learning brings to the teacher's position and the learning culture in schools, as well as how can we develop entrepreneurial learning?

Main activity of the entrepreneur is facilitating new ways of innovation, new dimensions of job creation and overall national prosperity.

When an entrepreneur is starting a business for the greater social benefit he is a social entrepreneur. Social entrepreneurs may aim to create environmentally friendly products, provide services to marginalised communities, or engage in philanthropic endeavours.

They are linked to the foundational ideas of the information based economy.

The current Knowledge Economy is founded on writer Disposes creating, evaluating, and trading knowledge. (Despress, 1999).

Individual, community, and corporate social responsibility is defined as societal awareness.

There are few contexts which could be understood by individual, group and organisation.

Different activities involved in knowledge mapping in general are as follows:

- Proper scanning of knowledge and mapping it for better concept formation.

- Continuous capturing and Creation of new era of knowledge.
- Further wrapping Storing.

Constant gathering of Information is the base for knowledge societies. The concept of Information society as correlated to the idea of technological progress. The perception of Knowledge societies includes a measurement of "social, cultural, economic and political transformation" (Khan, 2003)

There is a relationship between the qualities of leadership and knowledge economy for better entrepreneurial commitment and productivity.

In ancient days knowledge was for the following objectives:

- The main objectives of the gurukul system in ancient Indian system are as follows:
- Self-control faith in Divinity, including control of thoughts, feelings, senses, emotions, character development and personality development through working on oneself.

Budding entrepreneurs and knowledge with culture

According to Khan 2003, he explains that education - both in traditional and in new settings - is the key to creating rational knowledge societies. identified two types of linkages between ICTs and education.

There is a relationship between the qualities of leadership and entrepreneurship for the first is the use of formal and informal learning and exercise to develop IT-literate individuals who can confidently use ICTs in their personal life and professional contexts. This is a declared policy in some nations." (Khan, 2003). Better entrepreneurial commitment and productivity. (Fairholm 1998) -"Do what it takes" in pursuit of the vision to continuously improve and be more hard-working.

Negative mental conditions are

- Greed - for authority, position, status and wealth.
- Envy - concerning others' achievements, triumph, rewards.
- Egotism - about one's personal activities.
- Disbelief, irritation and annoyance.
- Suffering through comparisons
- Teaching from major Indian Scriptures

The main thoughts in the Vedas is a spiritualist notion of the cosmos. To achieve union of the individual Self (Atman) with the world Self (Brahma) is the (God or supreme consciousness). Vedanta Upanishads according to Vivekananda and Aurobindo is realising self within and continuous.

Love that drives out and removes fears associated with worry, anger, jealousy, selfishness, failure, guilt, back biting, irritation, agitation and gives one a sense of devotion - that part of spiritual survival that gives one an consciousness of being understood and appreciated. According to ancient spirituality realising the truth is the ultimate goal of life. The four areas is to be understood. Dharma artha kama moksha.

Statement of the problem

There has been very less amount of studies done in this area of Entrepreneurship and his spiritual and holistic development. This study is thereby an attempt to provide awareness into this area and analyse it as a part and parcel of every group which contributes. Meaningful for the entrepreneur's persistence and sustenance, for individual psychological development, better productivity, better emotional intelligence, and for better spiritual quotient. The study shows the fact that very urgency in the concept is understood. The study tries to relate. The past with the present. It is leading to better performance of budding entrepreneurs.

Review of literature and analysis

- Knowledge can be used by decision support systems in various fields to create economic value.
- Drucker as the heading of Chapter 12 in his book The Age of Discontinuity.
- The entrepreneurship in knowledge economy is spreading to shape business and educational policy in the United Kingdom.
- Interdisciplinary Nature of Knowledge Management gives various articles.
- We can refer the enhancement of knowledge management presentation by Christina Ling- hsing Chang. (Christina Ling-hsing Chang, 2015)
- Database technologies are used in knowledge management and knowledge economy for better result.
- Using Entrepreneurs intelligence and skill to conquer difficulties and challenges on the way to success.

Our real life is not always smooth enough so hurdles are obvious. Hopeful able entrepreneurs in India decide to take the thrust and start up a business of their own. (Bridge, 2005).

The study of entrepreneurial knowledge was based on the theory of the entrepreneurial concern which was based on organisational economics and was bounded by the generation of rent and the appropriation of entrepreneurial knowledge. (Alvarez, 2004)

Help Desk Systems are used in database technologies. Collaborative technologies is also very significant in database technologies Cognitive science is applicable and frequently used.

Technical Writing is used for database technologies. Artificial Intelligence is giving new dimension in database technologies. Organisational sciences also need to be including in knowledge management areas as described by Pratyush Bharti. (Pratyush Bharati, 2015)

Cognitive background of knowledge sharing in an organisationally relevant context, is given by Minna Stenius..." (Minna Stenius, 2015)

Pratyush Bharti gives the idea that social media affects relational prosperity ultimately through structural and cognitive capital. (Pratyush Bharati, 2015) Psychological dimensions given by (Brockhaus, 1982).

A deeper knowledge of the learning consequences caused by notable, alternating occurrences is required for the entrepreneurial process. The field of entrepreneurship provides a unique and special framework for studying management learning.

Learning from discontinuous encounters is more than the incremental accumulation of increasingly routinised situations, according to one theory (Cope, 2003).

Entrepreneurs have an attitude to change: 'the entrepreneur always searches for change, responds to it and exploits it as an opportunity'. (Drucker, 2014).

Measuring personality, personal resources, environment, and organizing activities through questionnaire was done . A representative sample of 1,169 nascent entrepreneurs and new business owner-managers was examined (Korunka et el 2003).

"Entrepreneurship" and "Entrepreneurship Education" are two terms that are to conduct a critical assessment of entrepreneurship education and its impact on graduate entrepreneurship in the United Kingdom according to Matlay (2006).

The Bhagvad Gita places a strong emphasis on developing holistic knowledge and universal understanding.

This is also reflected in the Biswa Roop Darshan.

This darshan exemplifies a comprehensive viewpoint that transcends life's earthly and spatial boundaries. Each person needs this comprehensive perspective and comprehension to be successful, to be a true leader in any profession, to be truly knowledgeable, and to get true insight. (Acharya, 2015)

Further Acharya highlights 'Man-management involves recognition psychological-behavioural problem, industrializsation, globalisation.

- These problems are of isolation, loss of goals of life, - IT communication revolution, social medias problems arising out of modernisation.

Need of material goals, lack of spiritual values and concerns. Modern problems of anxiety, nervous tension hopelessness etc. effect health and life of individuals, society and mankind (Acharya, 2015).

Ancient wisdom distinguishes between subject and object.

In Ramayan knowledge based good manager in the viewpoint of management manager is one who can even get his work done from the rivals as we can take for instance Angad (whose father was killed by Rama) actually helped in battle.

This shows the splendid administrative skill of Rama and Sughriva while Ravana selected wrong path continuously ignored the suggestions, advices of his fellow people and good managers.

The holy Quran explains ethical concepts are implied in modern-day management. Surrender and Respect with unquestionable recognition is the basic requirement of business activity. Bible has impact. And direction on ethical business practices, is also dependent upon the individuals who lead the business. Christianity also studies as a voyage of life and will end with the union of Celestial divinity. Becoming humble heartfelt and devoted with love and affection. or a better understanding, there are two ways to look at entrepreneur education.

For a better understanding, there are two ways to look at entrepreneur education. There is a distinction between tacit and explicit knowledge:

- Tacit Knowledge, the word tacit means understood and implied without being stated. The tacit knowledge is distinctive. That which the general public acquires is not easy to Communicate.
- The cognitive skills of an area standard example of tacit knowledge. The tacit knowledge can be explained as personal and it varies depending upon the learning.
- Thoughts and awareness, observation, attitude of the individual.
- This is impossible to communicative because every so often the implicit knowledge may be even subconscious.

- This tacit knowledge is also not discussed it is private. This knowledge is exhibited by the human being routinely. People utilise this knowledge without proper understanding.

The word explicit means confirmed evidently and in detail with no confusion.

- The explicit knowledge is easy to communicative and they are not biased.
- This is also not exclusive and it will not be different upon persons.
- It is also impersonal in nature.
- The explicit knowledge is straightforward to share with others.
- Technology influences business transfer of new technology is also required.
- New Products for use in daily life.
- Demand for more skilled employees.
- Demand for more capital enriching capital formation.
- Rise in Productivity better quality of job.
- Social Change Expectations of the customers.
- Organisation structure usually becomes as follows.
- Techno-structure policy and needs implementation.
- The control of Technology over company.

The international institute for sustainable development in the year 1997 suggested that the Knowledge management comprises of five activities namely

- Knowledge creation,
- Knowledge acquisition,
- Knowledge assimilation,
- Knowledge use,
- Knowledge dissemination.

We know that economic development can be observed in modern context. School education higher education and maintaining quality, human development index improvement GDP improvement.. Though population increase is a severe obstacle to our country still we are progressing.

The knowledge formation is very important for any knowledge based organisation.

Bhagavad Gita's teaching would be beneficial for the inculcating value inclined knowledge for the batterment of the society as a whole. The article 'An Enquiry into extraction of the implicit knowledge' the author aims to provide a brief enquiry into the nature of implicit knowledge and what is implicit knowledge.

Taggerin 2006 provides a brief of some methods currently used in the extraction of implicit knowledge. (Tagger, 2005)

Haron 2006, found that basically there are two issues concerning tacit knowledge. First, whether tacit knowledge individual can use - or is it owned by society and secondly can this knowledge becomes explicit. (Haron, 2006)

The author, Rebecca McNeilin his article 'Application of Knowledge Management for Sustainable Development in Institutions of Higher Education' suggests that sustainability in world in recent years (Rebecca McNeil, 2011) Nonaka explained scientific, and explicit knowledge, by admitting that "knowing" requires the commitment of the individual (Nonaka) Ipeandamp; Minu (2003) showed in their research paper that knowledge was the organisation's most important strategic resource; (Ipe, 2003)

Objective of the studies

The study aims to achieve three main goals:

1 To describe the entrepreneurs' education and observing necessity of quality and quantity of knowledge for budding entrepreneurs.

2 To find proper mind set for enhancing knowledge management and better quality budding entrepreneurs.

3 To include spiritual dimensions for complete value based peaceful knowledge Management.

Hypothesis to be tested on qualitative inference

H1 Holistic Entrepreneurial education improves quality of budding entrepreneurs.

H2 There should be a trade-off between Entrepreneurial development and quality of education in cultivating human values for budding entrepreneurs.

Methodology

The study's methodology is both descriptive and analytical in nature.

The substance of the paper is based on secondary analysis.

As a result, the research is focused on secondary data found in ancient and current literature.

Literature review and inductive qualitative content analysis are part of the process. Wang, 2010, explained knowledge sharing behaviour was the basis means that employees can contribute to the application of knowledge, innovation and optimisation of the resources (Wang, (2010).

To make swift and perfect decisions, they need to learn critical thinking and interpersonal skills as quickly is required today. (Sogunro 2004).

Indian spiritual knowledge is explained in Bhagavad-Gita. Bhagavad Gita's teaching influence

- A variety of circumstances necessitate value-oriented education.
- Physical value, mental value, moral value, discipline value, national value, cultural value, ethical value, aesthetic value, spiritual value, economical value, educational value, cognitive value, religious value, individual value, societal value, organisational values, intellectual values, and so on are all examples of value.
- According to Ramakrishna, "However, Vedanta's essence is: 'Brahman alone is real, and the universe is illusory; I have no distinct existence; I am that Brahman alone.'"
- Swami Vivekananda emphasised that "religion is realisation" and that "everything is for the realisation."
- In the universe, there is only one truth: monism Adwitabad.
- Bhakti Yoga is the practise of loving God; GyanYoga is the practise of intellectual knowledge; Kormoyoga is the practise of working for him; and Rajjoga is the practise of managing one's mind.
- Someswarananda suggested "that in India a leader can be successful when he knows his subordinates well and for that he has to understand the characteristics of Indian psyche and the focus should be on workmen and masses. (Someswarananda, 2005)
- One of the most well-known Upanishads is the Kathopanishad.
- The fundamental test of a manager's competence is his or her capacity to make decisions.
- According to the mantra in this Upanishad, a man must choose between two paths of action at every stage of his life.
- One is sreyas (beneficial), which is initially painful but ultimately beneficial.
- In terms of management, sreyas (hard) is the hard option, whereas preyas (enjoyable) is the soft one.

- The Taittiriya Upanishads establishes the qualifications of individuals who are worthy of being held up as examples.
- (Gambhirananda)
- In the YakshaPrashana episode, Yaksha asks which path to choose? And answer was : The path that great men of yore had traversed in the past is the path we should follow.
- Top executive having firm conviction in value-oriented holistic organisation. Profit is earned through service and fulfilment of all stakeholders - employees, customers, shareholders and citizens. Man-machine interaction, human centric interaction, ergonomics should be taken care.

On the basis of present analysis hypotheses are accepted and main findings are as follows:

Findings

1. Entrepreneurs knowledge is a resource for both Physical and Psychological purpose in the area of entrepreneurs innovation for budding entrepreneurs.
2. Knowledge acquired both modern and ancient days were needed to be practiced in. Effective strategies are needed for better utilisation of capacity and socio-economic reflections.
3. Personal spiritual development for total quality management. As Swami Vivekananda says "AtmanoMokshartham, Jagathitayacha". All effort is an opportunity for taking responsibility for excellence to the world and thus gaining materially and spiritually in our lives. This will generate more organisational values in modern life creating peace and bliss.

Conclusion

The study proves with the various examples that holistic entrepreneurship education for budding entrepreneurs in achieving Success are not age old or out of date. Budding entrepreneurs can be a resource for the mankind. Knowledge in fact is very sophisticated techniques of gaining a competitive Advantage. Therefore, it states our second objective the perspective for development should be effective in present day time and is relevant. Indian scripture Gita supports and cultivates definite vision and thoughts, which has created a target in the modern world as a key base for accomplishment of an entrepreneur as an individual. A person's values in individual social, family and spiritual level must be unchanged irrespective of his attitude and other factors for moral intellect, strong personal values are an essential tool for budding entrepreneurs.

Bibliography

1. Alvarez, S. A., and Barney, J. B. (2004). Organizing rent generation and appropriation: Toward a theory of the entrepreneurial firm. Journal of Business Venturing, 19(5), 621-635.
2. Bharati, P., Zhang, W., and Chaudhury, A. (2015). Better knowledge with social media? Exploring the roles of social capital and organisational knowledge management. Journal of Knowledge Management.
3. Bridge, R. (2005). How I made it: 40 successful entrepreneurs reveal all. Kogan Page Publishers.
4. Brockhaus, R. H., and Kent, C. A. (1982). Encyclopedia of entrepreneurship. Available at SSRN.
5. Chang, C. L. H., and Lin, T. C. (2015). The role of organisational culture in the knowledge management process. Journal of Knowledge management.
6. Cope, J. (2003). Entrepreneurial learning and critical reflection: Discontinuous events as triggers for 'higher-level'learning. Management learning, 34(4), 429-450.
7. Drucker, P. (2014). Innovation and entrepreneurship. Routledge.
8. Davidsen, H. M., and Sørensen, K. B. (2017). A holistic design perspective on entrepreneurship education. Universal Journal of Educational Research, 5(10), 1818-1826.
9. Despress. (1999). Managing_in_the_Age_of_Sand... Retrieved April 18, 2019, from https://www.academia.edu/339671: https://www.academia.edu
10. Fairholm, G. W. (1998). Leadership as an exercise in virtual reality. Leadership and Organisation Development Journal.
11. Gambhirananda, S. (1980). Katha Upanishad: With the Commentary of Shankaracharya. Advaita Ashrama (A Publication House of Ramakrishna Math, Belur Math).
12. Gupta, M. Ramkrishna Kathamrita. Udbodhon.
13. Haron, H. (2006). Proceedings of the Postgraduate Annual Research Seminar 2005.
14. Conceptualisation of Tacit Knowledge Dimension.
15. https://www.investopedia.com/terms/k/knowledge-economy.asp. (n.d.). Retrieved 04 20, 2019, from knowledge-economy
16. Ipe, M. (2003). Knowledge sharing in organisations: A conceptual framework. Human resource development review, 2(4), 337-359.
17. Khan, A. W. (2003, 07. 18). Towards Knowledge Societies. An Interview with Abdul Waheed Khan. Retrieved 04 18, 2019, from
18. Korunka, C., Frank, H., Lueger, M., and Mugler, J. (2003). The entrepreneurial personality in the context of resources, environment, and the startup process-A configurational approach. Entrepreneurship theory and practice, 28(1), 23-42.

19. Matlay, H. (2006). Researching entrepreneurship and education: Part 2: what is entrepreneurship education and does it matter?. Education+ Training.
20. Oganisjana, K., and Matlay, H. (2012). Entrepreneurship as a dynamic system: a holistic approach to the development of entrepreneurship education. Industry and Higher Education, 26(3), 207-216.
21. McNeil, R. (2011). Application of knowledge management for sustainable development in institutions of higher education.
22. Nonaka, I. (n.d.). Leadership in Knowledge based Organisation.
23. oxforddictionaries.com. (n.d.). knowledge_economy. Retrieved April 18, 2019, from
24. https://en.oxforddictionaries.com/definition/knowledge_economy:
25. wikipedia. (n.d.). Retrieved 04 20, 2019, from
26. https://en.wikipedia.org/wiki/Knowledge_economy.
27. Businessdictionary.com. (n.d.). knowledge-economy.html. Retrieved April 18, 2019,
28. from www.businessdictionary.com/definition/knowledge-economy.html:
29. www.businessdictionary.com
30. Primo, N., and Khan, A. W. (2003). Gender issues in the information society (pp. 81-85). Paris: Unesco.
31. Sivaraman, M. A. F., and Noor, S. N. M. (2016). Human embryonic stem cell research: ethical views of Buddhist, Hindu and Catholic Leaders in Malaysia. Science and engineering ethics, 22(2), 467-485.
32. Sogunro, O. A. (2004). Efficacy of role playing pedagogy in training leaders: some reflections. Journal of management development.
33. Sogunro, O. A. (2004). Efficacy of role playing pedagogy in training leaders: some reflections. Journal of management development.
34. Someswarananda, S. (2005). Business Management the Gita Way. Mumbai,. Jaico.
35. Stenius, M., Hankonen, N., Haukkala, A., and Ravaja, N. (2015). Understanding knowledge sharing in the work context by applying a belief elicitation study. Journal of Knowledge Management. Vol. 19, Issue: 3, pp, 497-513.
36. Tagger, B. (2005). An enquiry into the extraction of tacit knowledge. Retrieved April, 30, 2006.
37. Tagger, B. (2005). https://www.researchgate.net/publication/242306005_An_Enquiry_into_the_Extraction_of_Tacit_Knowledge
38. Von Krogh, G., Nonaka, I., and Rechsteiner, L. (2012). Leadership in organisational knowledge creation: A review and framework. Journal of management studies, 49(1), 240-277.
39. http://www.unesco.org/new/en/communication-and-information/resources/news-and-in-focus-articles/all-news/news/towa : en/communication-and-informatio
40. Wang, S., and Noe, R. A. (2010). Knowledge sharing: A review and directions for future research. Human resource management review, 20(2), 115-131.

27

Professional Agriculture Students-Curriculum and Syllabus for Betterment of Farmers in Post-Covid Era

Thota Suresh

Abstract

Covid turned the entire world life in all fields. Agricultural area is no more exemption on this account. Agricultural field was also interrupted with no proper guidance for cultivation. In no way it is an undeniable fact that governments tried to improve the communication and information in guiding farmers by various electronic means and field work assigned to novitiate participants and scholars through their projects. In this regard it is an appreciable task by agricultural colleges and universities. In this concern the bridge between farmers and students was not delinked instead it made possible in ways to assist the farmers of India and especially in Telugu States. As everybody knows in India the backbone of Indian economy is agriculture in this case students, scholars, scientists' role is unimaginable and more significant. On this account the students' syllabus was framed as per the importance and cope up with the worldly standards and for the better products of agriculture and continue the exporting the quality foodgrains by Indian farmers as the world needs.

Hypothesis

The present research focuses on the post Covid Higher Education and changes in agriculture students' curriculum and syllabus.

Objectives

- The research explores education system in pre- and post-independent era.
- The agriculture students' curriculum and syllabus change due to Covid-19.

- The use of new methods and technology in higher education agriculture universities.
- The virtual teaching for agriculture students (BSc, MSc, MPhil and PhD) and other research projects in national and international levels.
- The alternative curriculum and syllabus frame during Covid-19.

Research Methodology

The research methodology used for this purpose is Historical method, Historical Cross study method, Observation method and Comparative method.

The use of technology in the field of agriculture to impart the knowledge of agriculture to peasants India is the land of fertile and rich in all crops since ancient days. The same traditional agriculture was continued. The conditions which prevailed in pre Independence the like wise practices continued. When new industries developed by govt of India formers were encouraged to apply them in the agriculture formal education was encouraged. At that movement onwards, the formers encountered grave problems in India, as a result of it, the guidance from agricultural scientists, advisors and academic students sought prominent. The post-Covid conditions differed from the Covid time conditions.

During the Covid the students of agriculture remained at home due to severe raise of Covid cases. Even the students learnt to have virtual classes. However, their practices are merely conducted with the basic fulfilments. In Indian agriculture government of India has specific administration to guide the formers. The students got struggled to participate in project works. It became more informative to the formers were disconnected with the administrative offices-officers to resolve their agricultural problems due to Covid. In some extent the students' syllabus and classes are managed for continuity of their education so that their academic year will not be in futile, so that students can advance for higher education in the same field. However, the farmers were disconnected with agriculture development for any guidance regarding grooving crops, solutions for deceases of crops and remedies. Some of the local offices were away to protect them.

Further the research, innovation and development sector fall down during the Covid, the exact conditions provided in the world. The formers were also in loss due in sufficient knowledge. There are some concepts of agriculture General Conditions for Cultivation of Crops, Soil and Plant

Nutrition, Plant Protection, Categories of Pesticides and Precautions, Farm Management and Occupational Health and Safety. The implications for this purpose are as followed, the agriculture department must investigate to encounter any problems teaching instruction and practice.

To conclude the research analyzed about the significance agriculture and imparting of information and education peasants for better growth during Covid and post-Covid and its impact on the world, it also examined the students learning and teaching through virtual mode for growth of research and innovation in the same area. It also considered the key concepts of agriculture and learnt by students and higher education how to handle the adverse conditions and retain sustainable progress in the same field.

References

Balasubramanyan T., (2001). A Text of Phonetics for Indian Students, Macmillan Publication, Delhi.

Cutts Martin, (2013). Oxford Guide to Plain English, OUP, New Delhi.

Misra, Partha Sarathi, (2016). An Introduction to Stylistics, Orient Black Swan, Hyderabad.

Sadhu, M.S., (2012). Aspects of Linguistics, Rastogi Press, Bareilly.

Hornby, A. S. (2012). Oxford Advance Learner's Dictionary of Current English. Indira printers: India

Vijay Kumar, T. (2016). Perspectives in Education. Telugu Akademi: Delhi, 2016.

Mabgal, S K. 2008. General Psychology. Sterling Publishers Private Limited: New Delhi.

Dr. P. Chandra Shekara (2016). Farmer's Handbook on Basic Agriculture, Desai Fruits and Vegetables Pvt. Ltd.

Padma, T., Rao, K P C, (2013). Legal Research Methodology. Haritha Graphics: Hyderabad.

Vishwanadham. (2014). Jurisprudence and Legal Theory. Haritha Graphics: Hyderabad.

28

New Education Policy 2020 - Holistic, Multidisciplinary and Futuristic Aspects

Dr K.V. Vijayaveni

Abstract

The main emphasis of NEP - 2020 is to bring in " Quality in Education", access scope for the high aspirations. As the teacher needs to be resourceful to engage students in the new methods, the New policy enshrines a provision in its policy for continuous professional development (CPD) programme, to equip educators. Multidisciplinary and Holistic learning is an ancient method used in Indian Education system as well as the other parts of the world. The multidisciplinary education is extremely significant in this post-modern society of twenty first century. In Indian Gurukul system where the students had to learn Science, Mathematics, Geometry along with vocational skills, professional skills, soft skills, Ethics, morality, Human values and so on. Holistic development and a wide choice of subjects and courses year to year will be the new distinguishing feature of secondary school education. The NEP 2020 is the outcome of extensive and comprehensive consultations aimed to make India, a knowledge superpower, by equipping its students with the appropriate knowledge capabilities and skills. Energised, Motivated and capable faculty will have the autonomy to innovate on curriculum, Pedagogy and assessment within a broad NHEQF. Promotion of Indian languages, arts and culture establish Academies for different languages, departments in HEIs for Indology, Arts, Translation and interpretation, museum administration, Indian languages etc. Evaluation studies must feedback into the implementation cycle to make mid - course corrections for smoothening any rough stumbling blocks.

Key words : NEP - 2020, Holistic education, Multidisciplinary, Futuristic.

Introduction

Education Policy consists of the principles and policy decisions that influence the field of Education, as well as collection of laws and rules that govern the operation of education systems. Education, according to Merriam Webster, is "the knowledge and development coming from the process of being educated". The primary outcomes of Education are knowledge and progress- you learn how to apply what you are learning to your life during the Educational process. Education can be achieved through a formal procedure such as going to school or reading carefully selected literature but it can also be earned through real- life experience. Education gives stability in life by giving financial benefits by job or business, assist in evaluating the information which receive and determining whether the sources are likely to be trust worthy, allows to continue to develop as a person throughout the life, can help to explore and answer the questions about the world today and in the future. The productivity will increase because Education will help to manage several projects to maintain the high level of quality, when use in the work place, the output will be good. And also Education exposes the ideas and cultures, may have only been exposed to certain forms of music, art or literature as a child, it exposes to a wide range of issues and cultural expressions broadening and understanding of the world's contributions. We can hear new kinds of music or see art work created by people even though unfamiliar with the scientific discovery process. And finally, Education allows to appreciate the beauty of life and can see the special creation of the Globe.

Etymologically, the word "Education" is derived from the Latin word 'educatio' (A breeding, a bringing up, a rearing) from educo (I educate, I train) which is related to the homonym educo (I lead forth, I takeout, I raise up, I erect) frame - ("from,Out of") and duco (I lead, I conduct)

Education has no specifications or boundaries assigned to it. Therefore, it can be broadly classified into three categories - Formal, Informal and Non-Formal. Education forms a Holistic and significant part of any individual life. It is the process of gaining or imparting knowledge that aids in building a proficient personality, ultimately improving the quality of life. 'Formal education' is the one that works under the framework set by individual boards of education. The orderly learning environment includes educational institutions, classrooms, specially trained teachers, teaching equipment, extracurricular activities, competitions, examinations and a curriculum or syllabus. It is very structured in natures as proper guidelines are laid, and the students are expected to work under these guidelines. 'Informal education' is the type of knowledge that one gains through several life experiences. Ex: learning to cook, Arts and crafts, make specific arrangements - gained under the influence of society and community. And the third type is 'Non-Formal' education is one that is framed according to the requirement of a particular job. Ex: fitness programme, software, technical works, tailoring etc.

Education during childhood and early adulthood is typically provided through either a two- or- three stage system of childhood school, followed by additional stages of higher education or vocational education for those which continue their formal education.

Holistic Education

Holistic education is a philosophy of education based on the premise that each person finds identity, meaning and purpose in life through connections to the community, to the natural world and to spiritual values such as compassion and peace. Robin Ann Martin (2003) describes this further by stating "At its most general level, what distinguishes Holistic education from other forms of Education are its goals, its attention to experimental learning, and the significance that it places on relationships and primary human values with in the learning environment". The concept of Holism refers to the idea that all the properties of a given system in any field of study cannot be determined or explained by the sum of its component parts. Instead, the system as a whole determines how its parts behave. A Holistic way of thinking tries to encompass and integrate multiple layers of meaning and experience rather than defining human possibilities narrowly. Ron Miller, Founder of the journal Holistic education review defined that Holistic education aims to call forth from people an intrinsic reverence for life and a passionate love of learning". The aim of this Education is to prepare students to meet the challenges of living as well as academics. And it belives it is important for young people to learn:

- About themselves
- About healthy relationships and pro-social behaviour
- Social development
- Emotional development
- Resilience
- To see beauty have awe, experience transcendence, and appreciate some sense of 'truths'

The four pillars of education all started with the report entitled "Learning the treasure with in" of the International commission of education for the twenty first century. It was published by the UNESCO. The pillars are "To know", "to be", "to live together" and "to do".

Learning to know involves the development of knowledge and skills that are needed to function in the world. These skills include Literacy, Numeracy and critical thinking, 'Learning to be relates to self-management like skills related to self-awareness, self-esteem, self-confidence and coping skills. "Learning to live together" involves the development of social skills and values such as respect and concern for others, social and inter - personal skills and an appreciation of the diversity of the world. And the last one is 'Learning to do' describes putting knowledge and learning into practice innovatively through skill development, practical (know-how), development of competence, life skills, personal qualities and attitudes.

Advantages of Holistic education

Over the courses of time, we have gone through a number of changes in the systems of education. Each system has its own unique set of advantages. These systems have evolved over time giving way to the modern education system as we know it.The modern education system is the widely accepted standard throughout the industry and is known by many names. Some call it traditional education, but unlike the traditional education system, this Holistic in nature. The primary focus is on the individual student's needs along with ample freedom for self-expression. The phrase Holistic education refers to the inclusion of multiple facets of life like livehood skills, economics, health and nutrition into education. It is a progressive education system.

Holistic education is a personalised learning pathway which changes from student to student. The system takes into an account that no two individuals are the same. Some students are fast learners and some are slow picks up the subject. This type of education is important today than ever before because of the ease with which students can access information. The sheer quantity of information present online can be over whelming but then students who have gained experience at accessing it can easily filter out those that are relevant from those that are not. This system focuses immensely on each student discovering their unique pathway. In simple, this form of education can be called 'whole child education'. The development of emotional, intellectual physical, spiritual and social aspects of the student are the main focus areas of Holistic education.

Multidisciplinary education is a unique educational approach that allows the students to learn and explore distinct subjects or curriculum from various disciplines. Education is not limited to a particular discipline ex: a student of engineering can take a subject from Humanities. This education approach offers student, the flexibility of choosing subjects, helps students to pursue their passions along with mainstream education helps to develop pragmatic attitude and helps to develop collaborative teacher - student relationship. Students get to choose their subjects, courses and programme from different institutes, they can discover their interests during teaching - learning journey and it enables students to crave their ownpath.

Futuristic: As per Stevenson study brings a right conclusion stating that all that we have learned make our future shine beyond the imagination. The courses being included may not be always the understanding of the past but the application in the future makes it wholesome. The existing education and its operating procedures must make the future worthy. The implication of the (Development, 2019) National education policy (2020) must also make a change and brings in a positive impact.

Role of a Teacher : In the regular classroom system the teacher is a person of tremendous authority who controls every aspect of education in the classroom. But in the case of Holistic education the teacher is perceived as a mentor, a friend, a facilitator or as a companion with considerable experience. This helps students get rid of fear and creates a lot of openness when dealing with teaches. Especially, this Holistic education tries to promote open and honest communication between people and teaches to respect and appreciate individual differences. Competition is replaced by co-operation which is the reason why most schools under the system do not choose to give grades or rewards. Students start developing a cooperative mind set from a young age that they carry on to their professional lives as an adult. Teacher try to promote the concept of reward by helping one another rather than being at the top of the class. This helps in fostering a much more positive atmosphere at school.

Prof. Najma Akhtar, vice chancellor of Jamia Millia Islamia university (JMI), New Delhi said that "The NEP will create new opportunities for students in the domain of higher education, more over, they can pursue education with greater flexibility in a seamless learning - environment. They can enter, exit and re-enter as per their convenience and career choices, "the Higher education now be holistic and multidisciplinary with a shared focus on Science, Arts and Humanities". And also she expresses that The vision of Holistic, multidisciplinary and futuristic education" in NEP 2020 will create 'sound mind in sound body'. The policy seeks to cultivate minds, build character and prepare eminent researches and teachers and also aspires to provide freedom to students and transform the education system to meet twenty first century needs through "proper solution to the multiple pedagogical problems and' eradication of structural inequities and asymmetries". An official statement of Prof. Akhtar is 'NEP -2020 wants to end the fragmentation of higher education by moving higher education into large multidisciplinary universities and colleges'. For this she added the statement 'Multidisciplinary education and research universities will be founded for multi disciplinary education and research well equipped, they will compete with the best multidisciplinary education and research universities in the world'.

Conclusion

By observing all the above features aims, advantages of holistic, multidisciplinary and futuristic aspects of NEP-2020 has given an immense pleasure in learning multiple subjects/ aspects as per the present societical conditions. Because, the qualification of a job included of computer knowledge even to the B.A,/B.Com Arts student. It is a technical education who can study in their subject like computers. So, the multidisciplinary education which helps to gain knowledge in different fields along with their main stream which are helpful to the student at anytime in their life. For example, As a Performing Arts student (Dance) I have completed Masters in English (Literature), Praveen (Hindi Literature), Diploma in Music, Diploma in Theater Arts (Direction) and Masters in Journalism and Mass communication. When I was in Masters in Dance, I know that the Dance is the combination of Literature, music, Drama and paintings. So, by completion of my Ph.D. in Dance I have completed these courses to get good knowledge and to express the importance of the fine arts. I used to write the articles in a proper way to publish in books the Masters in Journalism was helped me. To type and prepare my articles and Thesis of M.Phil. and Ph.D. I did the course of D.T.P. and Multimedia in computers to get good output in soft copy. Now I want to forward the history and importance of our Fine Arts which are also helping for communication I am pursuing Ph.D. in journalism, when I saw the NEP-2020 policy felt very happy because I have already getting the fruits from it. Now I am applying in my teaching as a teacher/instructor in performing arts to build the students with multiple challenges and achieve a high position in their lives.

The new education changes are essential to our country like developing country. Because, with one qualification the possibility of job opportunity is difficult to create. If the students trained with multiple aspects the job opportunities are more optional. For example, Now I have options teaching English, Dance, Journalism, Drama and Music. So the NEP - 2020 is very useful to develop country along with individual development.

References

1. Liveedu.xyz/significance of -education
2. Ecoleglobale101.medium.com
3. Licet.ac.in
4. The four pillars of Education book - UNESCO
5. Blog.byjus.com/trending
6. Ndtv.com/education/new-education policy - promote- holistic- multidisciplinary and futuristic- education-jmi-vice chancellor
7. Stevenson,L.B.(2006). Education policy process, themes and Impact. London and New York : Routledge.

29

Incorporating Technology into Teaching and Learning Process During Pandemic Period

Yedavelly Srinivas Reddy

Abstract

The Indian education system has been subject to tremendous change, especially throughout the twenty first century. Perhaps quite unlike any other discipline, this tradition has been practiced, in various adaptations, in language classrooms all around the world for hundreds of years. As will become evident during this short paper, there are some milestones within the development of this tradition, which we'll briefly touch upon in an effort to reveal the importance of research within the selection and implementation of the optimal methods and techniques for teaching and learning. The twenty first century is discovered among tools and technological revolutions. The century has shown the universe a new world filled with creativity, innovation, and a desire to progress toward technology. It's proven how things might be done more easily, with more efficiency and quality, instead of manually by men. This technology has entered into every walk of human life. It's quite undeniable to imagine a life without technology. The world has been watching through a technological eye rather than a person's brain. This technology is being adopted regardless of whether one is literate or illiterate. This paper explains the incorporation of technology into teaching and learning and various opportunities in a pandemic situation.

Keywords : teaching and learning, technology, tradition, creativity, innovation and pandemic.

1. Introduction

Although initially, the importance that twenty first century education technology adds to the training setting is vital to explore. Four main areas are in place:

The first area: Incorporating technology into the classroom will help to turn the classroom experience from a classic teacher-centered one into a student-centered one, with students playing a lively role in their learning. The trainer becomes something of a reference during a student-centric classroom and is granted meaning once they communicate with the teacher and discuss the day's lesson. And nothing relaxes me more than seeing the scholars take an interest. It is essential to understand that its by no means a substitute for a successful instructor to bring technology into the classroom. To put it clearly, the perfect classroom setting is going to be student-centered and requires a carefully chosen method of teaching technology through face-to-face contact.

The second area: Technology offers access to a variety of educational opportunities for teachers and students that encourage imagination, analytical thought, engagement and teamwork

- It promotes participation and, as a result, the development of digital literacy skills. Even a two-year-old is more drawn to studying technical aids.
- It extends learning beyond the meaning of the lesson and beyond the four walls of the classroom. In an easy way, technology lets students imagine more and capture more things.

Finally, it introduces students and educators to time-based cultures online. This successively facilitates global comprehension which is an integral component of twenty first century schooling.

The third area: We all recognize that various scholars are, and may still be, in our classrooms, with different essential learning needs. Differentiated directions are also made even easier by the utilisation of instructional technologies. It would become more of a reality. Students are given a customised curriculum with differentiated learning that reaches them where they are at in a developed manner. Most students are prepared to enjoy this sort of teaching. The usage of technology often allows students outside of the classroom access to vibrant learning resources. Technology gives a standard location to the entire globe.

Finally, it gives utmost significance for college kids to use instruments that better to train them in school for their potential learning experiences. This needs a mixture of traditional software and, therefore, new technology. Integrating technology into the curriculum offers students a variety of skills to figure out the variability of today's online technologies. It also gives teachers the power to model digital citizenship for students and thus, meet the fashionable demands of educational ethics.

2. Impact of online teaching and learning on learners and teachers of twenty first century

Information is out there exponentially because of all the innovations. Younger generations accept modern learning approaches with barely a problem because they are applied earlier and in graded school to advanced technologies. Students from tomorrow are going to be expected to develop and learn different learning methods at a much quicker and earlier pace. Even pedagogical learning is going to be revised.

Contrarily, some academics (See Crook, 2012; Selwyn, 2012) involved departing from the "Ed-tech bubble and blaming academics within the field of educational technology for being "inward-looking and not interacting with academics and practitioners in various levels of education. The necessity is stressed for educational technology academics to interact with debate about e-learning's challenges and hot topics. Critical and doubtless undisciplined discussion is required more now than ever with the spread of the latest beginnings like massive open online courses (MOOCs), Khan Academy, and therefore the strength of using social media in learning.

The important point within the consideration is that online teaching and learning have moved beyond a fascination with technology and feasible applications to a more full-fledged review of its impact and therefore the consideration of pedagogical success and failures of a number of fanciful dreams that were bound up within the excitement of the fast technological advances from the 1990s to 2010 (Carrson, 2011; Rudest, 2010).

It is proposed that online teaching and learning have reached a state in the development of theory, research, and practice integration. There is sturdiness and comprehension of the impact of the variety of encounters that more and more people around the world have within their lebensraum.

Firstly, problems with access, equity, and a replacement sort of poverty with reference to involvement within the online community raised issues about the haves and have-nots. While this thing has not been solved globally, the spread and coverage of online potential has begun to become more universal at a greater rate in one century than the spread of literacy did over many centuries. The historical parallels with the arrival of the printed word and, therefore, the spread of literacy rate for the purpose of an almost assumed fundamental right should not be lost during this electronic era.

Many learning areas are suffering from the overall conceptualisation of what has become abridged within the term "online" training schools.

Learning schools' action expansion and application are one area of learning schools' action. Less well-known, but no less significant, has been the impact and activity in vocational and workplace learning. However, online technology and related applications have long been a staple of the business world, especially within the information technological (IT) areas, a number of which support developments in online learning, others in software and hardware development for applications.

A further related application has been in training (Driscoll, 1998), where aspects of online and Web-related planning, design, and delivery of adult training programmes have increased over the past fifteen to twenty years. This areas impression has led many organisations to specialise in corporate training and support systems online where employees can take personality profiles, tests about their learning styles, and more improved psychometric analysis.

The impact of online teaching and learning on teachers and students during the pandemic period

For the upper education sector worldwide, the Covid-19 pandemic has posed significant obstacles. Our results point to the preparation of learning experiences with particular elements, namely the synthesis of three sorts of involvement (social, cognitive, and facilitator). As a result, there is a need to tailor the test to the current state of learning. Online learning is an instructional method that takes place as a sort of distance learning through the web. As a result of the Covid-19 pandemic in 2020, distance education has become widespread. Thanks to these conditions, online training and learning have played a crucial part in early education schemes, while discussions are still useful for young children.

This descriptive research illustrates how a retained teacher education course in childhood education has been revamped to incorporate online learning and teaching resources for student teachers. It defines three stages of the experience of web student teachers: planning, execution, and contemplation. Tasks wiped out by each process are recorded.

During the second week of March, schools and colleges were packed up to contain the Covid-19 outbreak. This has also driven educators to reshape the method of teaching and influence the long run of 32 crore children. Students in Network World are bridging the gap between a patchy and impersonal internet experience, increased screen time, and a lack of regional language content-creation resources.

Another task is to ensure that when classes resume, students return and continue their studies. This is often very true with extended closures and where economic disruptions bring a strain on children to acknowledge financially vulnerable households and lift revenue.

Dede (1998), in Six Challenges for Educational Technology, explains that a lot of exciting information technology applications in schools confirm that emerging technology based teaching and learning models have the potential to vary educational results significantly. Consequently, more people are telling the fragmented, wealthy islands of creativity the way to proportion. Instructional technology has made universal advancements in education feasible through dramatic developments in traditional teaching activities.

He then explains that changing techniques successfully without undercutting their influence, as pioneered by the pioneers of instructional advancement, must be changed to be adopted by traditional educators. During this "scaling-up" phase, technology based developments bring unique challenges and opportunities. Without leveraging the utmost force of high performance computing and communications to spice up curriculum architecture is reshaping in classrooms. I feel structural change is unlikely. However, the expense of technology, its accelerated development, and its users' unique expertise and skills pose considerable obstacles to productive usage.

According to Schank and Jones (1991), substantial study papers that help students add up something they need to understand but do not yet understand are essential to inducing retained and generalised learning (as cited in Dede, 1998). Consistent with (1998), Edelson, Pea, and Gomez (1996) state, "Reflective discussion of everyday interactions from different viewpoints is critical within the transformation of data into information by learners, as well as students mastering the cooperative development of the means and intent" (Edelson et al., 1996). Educational software helps with a number of these interpretative and communicative tasks. Most justifications are better done by face-to-face contact, whereas the computer mediated contact buffer and mask aren't involved. (Brown and Campione, 1994).

However, more educators should adjust their educational methods and achieve large-scale improvements in conventional teaching practices; the administration of classrooms, social organisation, and group partnerships should be completed in elementary ways. This suggests that 'settlers' (people who value stability and associate in nursing and don't want valiant attempts to become an everyday requirement) should be convinced to make the jump to a transparent sort of skilled operation, recognizing that their regular work would be property once they use these different methods, though not extra effort. Can it, though, concurrently invoke educators' critical mass during a very district to supply such a shift?

Dede and Dede (1998) jointly articulated research papers that showed that new, technology based educational methods result in a minimum of four sorts of educational outcomes improvements. A variety of those gains are simple to speak to the community; others are tricky, but along with them, they represent a body of evidence which will convince most of the people.

These four types of changes are described below in order to demonstrate:

- Boosted learner motivation
- Advanced topics have been reduced.
- Students are assuming the roles of specialists.
- Providing learners with the ability to use disadvantage finding methods.

Online learning and teaching v/s category area learning and teaching

Online learning is wonderfully flexible. Usually, after studying digitally, it is the asynchronous activities like displays and quizzes that originally come to mind. However, there is another crucial aspect of online learning: the live, synchronous part.

Live learning would improve interaction by incorporating a personality dimension. For beginners, it's handy. WHO is also not an autonomous body, and the WHO squares measure is used in instructor and advanced traditional instructional paradigms. Live square action online lessons, which are especially important during a course, this provides learners the power to realise input on their learning aspects that can't be calculated during a self-marking quiz area unit.

Live online lessons are practically like ancient face-to-face classes in certain respects; a teacher can gift knowledge and behave in real-time with a gaggle of participants-their equitable efforts require some variations in various ways. To get them, let's take it easy.

In schoolroom administration, the primary fundamental difference is the trainer is absolved to pass the learners back, organise them in several respects, and parturition them out of the classroom into an Associate in Nursing offline schoolroom to make the tasks run swimmingly.

A conference software framework is employed for many online categories to create burst out teams and various learner arrangements within the school room. The sole realistic approach to performing online classes is for the trainer or presenter to handle the cluster as a whole. Due to this, until they are unbroken to a smaller group of users, web categories perform best. The category scale is limitless for courses with no instructor involvement, including MOOCs (Massive Open Online Courses).

The usage of back channels may be a further differentiation. In instructional items, like seminars, backchannels are especially standard; everywhere the audience is expected to need a seat and listen for a protracted amount of time. In the past, lecturers from the Lecture Theater typically used smart phones as an audience platform; radical lecturers could also consider a Twitter hash tag as an audience platform. Usually, online lecture rooms have an integral note and can function as a channel for the viewer to make sure they are involved. For this reason it is typical for every presenter and host to possess online lecture style classes.

Conclusion

The absence of visual input in online categories is usually a standard problem for academics. Once we present the associate to the nursing audience within the same region, we attempt to face the measure and adjust our delivery to visual input from the audience. An area filled with bored faces is usually a specific indication that a presenter or instructor wants to feature several interactive events or change their execution to interact more with the peer group. Several sharp presenters will fill in with the resources out there to market similar inputs inside the web schoolroom. Daily requests to the group that they reply with area unit select tools are beneficial since they guarantee that the participants area unit is engaged during a live online session.

Students attending online sessions can often enjoy the obscurity of not being physically talented during a school day. When learners are reluctant to speak or raise their issues during a physical classroom, they will typically feel braver until they realise the category's multiple participants might not see them. To sum up, though there are area unit disparities between physical and online instruction, each area unit of the distribution method is usually designed to accomplish similar objectives in the hands of a well trained instructor. The one you agree on relies on getting the complete sum of your coaching when the material is being tutored.

References

Nguyen Anh. (2017).The Impact of Online Learning Activities on Student Learning Outcome in a blended learning course. 16. In the Journal of Information and Knowledge Management, 10.1142/S021964921750040X.

Arsham, Dr. Hossein (2002). The Impact of the Internet on Learning and Teaching USDLA Journal.

Learning with technology, Dede, C. (Ed.). 1998 Yearbook of the Association for Supervision and Curriculum Development (Alexandria, VA: ASCD), v-x.

Livingston, Kay, and Condie, Rae (2006). The Impact of an Online Learning Programme on Teaching and learning strategies. Theory Into Practice-Theory Pract. 45. 150-158 10.1207/s15430421tip4502_7.

Selwyn, Neil (2012). Bursting out of the "ed-tech" bubble. 10.1080/17439884. 2012.680212. 37: 1-4.

www.cambridge.org/core/journal/journal-

https://journals.sagepub.com

https://www.microsoft.com

https://www.researchgate.net/

https://onlinelibrary.wiley.com

https://en.wikipedia.org/

https://interchopen.com

https://www.quora.com

30

Literature and Literary Theories and Criticism for English Language and Education - ICT

Bolleddu Amruth Kumar

In the history of humanity epidemics were spread many times. Pandemic threw men into chaos and turned no hope in life and faith that was contagious by bioweapon - "Corona". Eventually it led humankind to maintain contacts by communication devices. In this respect in the field academics Virtual Teaching technology was introduced for education purposes in all levels such as schooling, Inter (11 and 12 standard), University and Higher advanced levels. In teaching English and education, the literature and theories and Information and Communication Technology (ICT) was employed.

In fact, mixed response and cope up with prevailing conditions. On this account literary theories are employed in LSRW (Listening, Speaking, Reading and Writing). Along with this, English in various dimensions applied for other subjects. In modern world in entire globe this technology was used for promotion of education, yet there are pros and cons in executing the education system; the delves into deeper details to examine the problems of teachers, students, educations designers, evaluation systems and critical views and downfalls and alternate process.

Hypothesis

The present paper explores literary theory and criticism in English language education and the application of information and communication technology (ICT).

Objectives

- The study investigates the background of English literary theory and ICT

- The study undertakes "Readers Response Theory" - English literary criticism and theory
- The exploration studies in regard of English language education and teaching
- The research analyses the Information and Communication Technology in English Teaching
- The research finds out the merits and demerits in employment of ICT
- The study delves regarding the world conditions about application of literary theory and ICT.

Research Methodology

The research employed the Historical method, Historical Cross study method, Observation method, Comparative Study method.

In the world during Covid many interruptions were occurred in all human fields. On this account all sectors got effected. Accordingly, the field of education is no more exemption. The students were in grave conditions and chaos. Further students were conducted no exams and abruptly some governments declared results.

In case of English language education and teaching the same conditions prevailed. As the other fields English language education sought for new ways to teach English language through new techniques and methods. On this account all education fields choose only the way Virtual teaching and evaluation modes. In English students were taught lessons with limited syllabus that could enable them towards higher education.

In English language education the new modes were adapted, such as Reader response theory and the technique of ICT. This mode was used from school level to advanced studies in universities. Even though the students have interaction the physical absence of teachers disturbed the students' progress in education. In the case of Indian class rooms, the students found technical problems due to out of coverage area and internet weak signals. Further this method could not be up to the educational thinkers' satisfaction. In fact, the times of Corona taught lessons to exist even in the absence of teacher physically. In addition to this in English language the students could not understand to complete assignments. In continuation to this in higher levels of learning the students depended on virtual meetings, symposiums, seminars and lectures.

In "Reader Response" theory the reader or audience will have chance to remember his and blend his personal experiences with the given literary genre. In this view the reader applies his experiences in poetry, prose, drama, and short story, novel and novella. At the same time the ICT application enhances learning. In this regard language education formed it syllabus as per the need of the study and the students could orient themselves towards the English educational expansion.

To conclude in teaching of English and Education the literary theory of Readers Response and language educational technique of Information and Communication Technology enhanced the students' abilities in leaning language and literature with meaning. It was employed during the Covid period. In this connection the Covid-19 taught lessons to seek for alternative sources in importing knowledge and the same can be applied to English language education and teaching. Moreover English critical views and research advocate the enabling English language learning and teaching methods in new education system.

References

Agarwal, Nidhi, (2012). Stylistics: Its Significance and Techniques in English Literature, Varadan Press, Bareilly.

Balasubramanyan, T., (2001). A Text of Phonetics for Indian Students, Macmillan Publication.

Cutts Martin, (2013). Oxford Guide to Plain English, OUP, New Delhi.

Dean, James, Ridgers, S. Theodore, (2016). Doing Language Research, OUP, China.

Griffin Gabriele, (2007). Research Methods for English Studies, Rawat Publicatins, Hyderabad.

Henry Hudson William, (2019). An Introduction to the Study of English Literature, Maple Press,

Misra, Partha Sarathi, (2016). An Introduction to Stylistics, Orient Black Swan, Hyderabad.

Sadhu, M.S., (2012). Aspects of Linguistics, Rastogi Press, Bareilly.

Wood Frederick, T., (2017). An Outline History of English Language, Trinity Publication, New Delhi.

31

Research Article Title: Transforming Teaching Methods during Covid-19 Era : An Overview

K. Ennuyir Kannapiran and Dr P. Saravanakumar

Abstract

Innovative teaching focuses on establishing learning environments that are conducive to success. Teachers that are innovative excel at educating students as well as creating relevant information and new experiences. In many aspects, introducing innovative teaching practices into the classroom shows an implicit understanding that our teaching approaches may be improved. It knows the significance of learning and development, which is exactly what we want of our students. In both urban and rural areas, India's education system is still in its childhood. The afternoon meal is a programme designed to encourage students to receive higher education. Under these conditions, the government's worldwide lockdown, which began on March 25, 2020, to combat Covid-19, has had a significant impact on the educational system. After China, India has the world's second-largest educational system. According to UNESCO, 63 million academics in 165 countries were affected. A total of 1.3 billion pupils were unable to attend schools or institutions around the world, with nearly 320 million students in India alone. It has transformed the traditional educational system into a structure based on educational technologies, in which teaching and assessments are done online. Covid-19 has both beneficial and negative effects on the Indian higher educational system.

This paper aims to analyze the Impact of Covid-19 on the Indian higher Education System, focusing on Transforming Teaching methods during the Covid-19 Era in this pandemic from settings at home.

Keywords : Transforming Teaching methods, Innovative teaching, Covid-19, Indian higher educational system.

Introduction

Covid-19 is a disease spread by the severe acute respiratory syndrome. The corona virus, which originated in the Chinese city of Wuhan, has already reached pandemic proportions, affecting people on all continents and spreading mostly through intimate contact, resulting in millions of deaths. Covid-19 is referred to as a pandemic due to its strength and intensity, as well as the largest worldwide health disaster in human society since the after-centuries. The emergence of the new corona virus changed everything, from the global economy to social rituals. As a result, the International Labour Organisation (ILO) estimates a loss of 195 million jobs. Enacting Covid-19 containment measures in their respective areas is one of the most preferred strategies to reduce the impact of this issue. Lockdown is a popular term nowadays, and it was a topic of discussion during the corona pandemic. In fact, since-March 2020, the appropriate authorities (in this case, the federal and state governments) have established a state of emergency protocol to prevent people from leaving their homes, resulting in mass quarantines and stay-at-home orders around the world.

The corona virus triggered India's first phase nationwide lockdown, which lasted 21 days and was repeated on April 15, 2020, for 19 days; on May 04, 2020, for 14 days as the third phase; on May 18, 2020, for 14 days as the fourth phase; and on June 01, 2020, only for containment zones, which lasted 16 days. People's unbridled resolve of severe preventative measures such as preserving social distance, following medically prescribed quarantine procedures, and embracing hygiene and sanitation would help to contain the Covid-19 pandemic to a larger extent. UNESCO estimates that 264 million students who were enrolled are out of school, and the pandemic has added to the problem. As the Covid-19 pandemic spreads, there has been a growing trend toward teaching online as the only alternative remaining is to close schools, colleges, and institutions for an indefinite period of time. As a result, now is the moment to really rethink, re-vamp, and reinvent our educational system to meet the high demands of our contemporary position. Informal and non-formal schooling is also impacted significantly.

India is a demographically diverse large country with a high population density. Citizens all around the country elected to stay at home and follow the government of India's directives. Individual universities and states in India quickly suspended academic operations in the middle of the year, even before the countrywide lockdown occurred.

According to the University Grant Commission (UGC), India's supreme organisation for higher education, educational institutions must seek to deliver quality education to all students while ensuring uniformity, equity, and universal accessibility. This global crisis has had a significant impact on medical and healthcare education. Furthermore, because most teaching hospitals are entirely occupied by Covid-19 load, healthcare systems will continue to be impacted. The problem of clinical exposure for medical and health profession students will become even more difficult. Face-to-face and small-group tutorials were not permitted due to the rapid spread of Covid-19.

The objectives of the this research article are: (1) To identify the Teaching Methods Higher Education System before Covid-19, (2) To trace the Transforming Teaching methods during Covid-19. The methodology adopted for this present study is, a descriptive method was used to understand the Transforming Teaching methods during Covid-19. The study's data was gathered from books, news stories published in journals, and government documents.

This research article reports the findings of the study describing the rapid Transforming Teaching methods in India during Covid-19. It not only informs the readers about what changed in reference to the past but also appraises how and why the quick adaptation was possible, along with the challenges that are faced during the transition from the educator's perspective.

Teaching Methods in Higher Education System before Covid-19

In the Higher Education system, teaching methods is a process that usually takes place in a classroom setting. It is more of a formal process in which the instructor makes every effort to ensure that the students understand his teaching. His teaching is only successful if the pupils fully comprehend it. The teacher's ability to teach in the classroom is determined by how he or she conducts his or her teaching duties. Teaching has taken on new dimensions in this age of science and technology when there is an explosion of knowledge. "A teacher can never properly teach unless he is still learning himself," Rabindra Nath Tagore says "A lamp can never light another lamp unless it keeps its own flame burning." A good learner can also be an excellent instructor. It is impossible to teach others if one does not learn and acquire current knowledge.

Characteristics of Teaching

The six fundamental characteristics of teaching are as follows:

1. Teaching is a two way traffic
2. Teaching is both a Bipolar and Tripolar process
3. All-round growth of the society
4. It is both formal and informal
5. It is related to time and place
6. It is an art.

Teaching is not a one-way street. Both the teacher and the students must be totally engaged. The adage that teaching is a bi-polar process is correct, implying that it is a two-way street. Teaching is a tri-polar process in the context of modern advances because the environment in which teaching-learning takes place, the surroundings in which the learner is enabled to function successfully in his environment, all play unique roles in the teaching process. Teaching takes place in a social setting, and the teacher's goal is to improve the behaviour of an individual or a group of people.

Formal and informal teaching is both possible. In both cases, it largely achieves the desired results. With the passage of time, society, its values, and ideals change, and as a result, teaching changes as well. The way people are taught differs from location to place. Teaching is a rare art form that only a few people like. Teaching is an alternate vocation for all others who are misfits and unfits.

In olden days, the typical classroom with one teacher teaching 30 or 40 students is no longer effective. In both rich and emerging countries, the two generic elements of "information explosion" and "propulsion explosion" are causing changes. Educational technology, which includes multiple forms of mass communication, an appropriate learning process, and current testing and evaluation procedures, is required to successfully solve these difficulties. With the use of educational technology, both quantitative growth and qualitative improvement of education can be facilitated and hastened in emerging countries like India.

A traditional college must provide good facilities for academic and nonacademic growth competent faculty, resources for career development, and infinite opportunity for experimenting with new and creative ideas to attract the best and brightest students. A prospective student's or his parent's choice of college or university should be based on the quality of programme it offers, the prestige of its faculty, the qualifications of its professors, and the availability of different resources, not on the convenience of being close to the institution from home.

Technology in the classroom

In those days calculators and computers are excellent learning aids. We can make our lessons more lively and relevant by introducing technology into the classroom and completing complex and realistic issues. Math and science lessons aren't made any more interesting by relying solely on chalk, conversation, and the chalkboard for routine tasks. Tables are no longer used for numeric operations, and thus are less precise. Handheld calculators and graphing calculators produce higher levels of accuracy in seconds, speed up the learning process, and make learning fun.

Although educational technology refers to the use of sophisticated hardware in the classroom, such as overhead projectors, tape recorders, televised film cassettes, video discs, and so on, it can also refer to the use of any new technique or method of teaching. For example, the technology of education could refer to the entire process of goal-setting, curriculum renewal, and the use of new methods. It's also associated with a variety of devices and methods for efficiently and quickly recording, storing, manipulating, retrieving, transmitting, and displaying data.

Teaching Techniques

Depending on the number of students, different teaching techniques are used. For example, in a large class of 40 to 50 students or more, the lecture or seminar method works well, whereas, in a small group of 15 to 20 students, role-playing or brainstorming tactics work well. There are several age-old approaches, such as lectures and discussions, that are invariably used in most classrooms, particularly at the higher education level. As the needs and requirements of the period change, a few instructional approaches become prominent. The following are a few examples of teaching methods:

1. Play way Method
2. Dalton Plan
3. The Project Method
4. Heuristic Method
5. Seminar Method and
6. Demonstration Method.

Depending on the teaching methods, any competent teacher can develop his or her unique teaching model during the course of his or her career. Good teaching can occasionally lead to a good teaching model. Students will be more attentive in the classroom if teaching aids and scientific equipment are used.

Transforming Teaching methods during Covid-19

The Indian higher education system is now in transformation. Stages in which positive changes have occurred and more alterations in thinking and processes are desired. Any country's higher education system now needs to be re-examined. Higher education for academic institutions and students must adapt to online teaching aids remains a major concern in the Covid-19 emergency. Covid-19 required academic higher education institutions all over the world to abandon the traditional chalk-and-talk (in-class face-to-face education) technique in favour of online teaching and learning. The shift is the result of the problem of sensitivity in learning and the new options that technology provides.

This transition has been simple for autonomous/deemed and private institutions; nevertheless, it has been difficult for public institutions. As a result of the Covid-19 emergency, numerous Indian colleges have temporarily closed their onsite classes. Furthermore, several institutions have decided to provide online lessons to students in metropolitan areas on a trial basis. This abrupt shift in teaching methods to online classrooms left students and faculty perplexed. The current online classes are increasingly focusing on the issue of learning quality.

Many colleges began stating that they had begun offering online programme and that they had successfully reached 90 percent of students and established online facilities. Some colleges have openly admitted that the transition to a new teaching technique makes communication and internet access difficult. During the shutdown, institutions explored a variety of methods to keep the courses going, including recording classes and publishing them on social media or websites. Students with proper internet access can study; for others, it is a challenging effort. The other option is to take live or online classes. Institutions must have uninterruptible high-speed internet, infrastructure, a software tool to reach students, and comfort in order to reach students through live classes.

Online education is more than just a professor giving an oral presentation on a computer/laptop/mobile phone, or a student listening on the other end. Due to faculty and student inexperience with conducting/attending live sessions, as well as a lack of early preparation or support from educational technical teams, the online teaching style faces numerous obstacles.

Online teaching tools

The bulk of online classes is web-based and relies on the internet/network. Education technology has opened up new doors, allowing everyone to profit from their abilities. Because the world is increasingly reliant on digital technology, a variety of online teaching tools are readily available and extremely beneficial. Many web-based software and apps are developed for this purpose, and students and faculty must learn how to use online teaching aid resources successfully and promptly. In Covid-19 emergency scenarios, these digital resources make learning more convenient and interactive with updated versions of tools, making it easier to teach online.

Recording classes/sessions, sharing voice/text messages, software for recording and editing audios, a tool for making online spoken assignments (including images and videos), offering feedback to students, and so on are all advantages of using online teaching tools. The platform for creating websites, blogs, and e-portfolios using the drag-and-drop

method is limited to five voice threads in the trial run version software, such as the file once created cannot be deleted, zooming and other multi-rich presentations for content delivery options are not available, and the platform for creating websites, blogs, and e-portfolios using the drag-and-drop method is not available.

Conclusion

After China and the United States, India has the world's third-largest higher education system in terms of students. Since independence, India's Higher Education industry has seen a massive expansion in the number of Universities/University level Institutions and Colleges. The Covid-19 pandemic has had a significant impact on India's economic and educational health. In the realm of education, the central government decided to close schools and colleges, including universities. The government and higher educational institutions promptly stated that they would conduct online classes. The paradigm shift from traditional face-to-face education to online teaching creates technical challenges that impede the Teaching-Learning Process' efficacy.

To determine the efficacy of the Teaching-Learning process, the researcher looked at the perspectives of numerous stakeholders on all higher education courses. More than 60 percent of students were unprepared for online lessons (due to a lack of technical, infrastructural, and high-speed internet connectivity, as well as electricity and network data each day). According to the findings, online sessions on tough subjects were difficult, whereas theoretical issues are simple to grasp. The majority of students agreed that the morning hours of 8 to 12 a.m. are the best for holding online classes.

There may be many advantages and disadvantages of online classes for both faculties and students. It is, however, very early to conclude the successful narrative of the transformation of teaching methods during the Covid-19.

References

1. Corona virus Disease 2019. World Health Organisation: 2020. https://www.who.int/emergencies/diseases/novel-coronavirus-2019 (Retrieved on 19.03.2022).
2. UGC Guidelines: UGC issues new calendar for universities; 2020-21 https://timesofindia.indiatimes.com/home/education/news/ugc-issues-new-calendar-for-universities-2020-21-session-to-begin-from-aug-1/articleshow/75453706.cms (Retrieved on 19.03.2022).
3. Teacher Training, Social Distancing: Here's How Indian Universities Will Function Post-Lockdown. The Indian Express; 2020. https://indianexpress.com/article/education/ugc-calendar-2020-how-will-indian-universities-function-post-lockdown-ugc-panel-6385273/ (Retrieved on 20.03.2022).
4. Das, R.C. "Educational Technology. A Basic Text" - Sterling Publishers Pvt. Ltd.
5. Kochhar, S.K. Methods and Techniques of Teaching, Sterling Publisher Pvt. Ltd., New Delhi, 1978.
6. Government of India (1986), "National Policy on Education", New Delhi, Ministry of HRD.

32

National Education Policy 2020 is Transforming the Vision for Education in India

Dr Gopal

Abstract

NEP 2020 was the much-needed silver lining. As we complete a year to this progressive roadmap, let's look at the instructional sensitivity and mounting steps which are accelerating our progress towards the realisation of this omnibus policy. Based on the pillars of "Accessibility, Equity, Quality, Affordability, Accountability", NEP aims at transforming India into a vibrant knowledge hub. With almost 85 percent of brain development of children occurring before the age of six, the policy emphasises early childhood care and education with universal provisioning and equipping young children to participate and flourish in the educational ecosystem. Schools are gradually moving towards a flexible, multifaceted, multilevel, play-based, activity-based and inquiry and domain-based learning. With this overarching goal, it has already made headway towards universal access to high-quality ECCE in a phased manner.

In 2021, we have already shifted assessment gears to a diagnostic approach from content-based assessment to competency-based, making Board exams "easier" in the sense that they test primarily core competencies rather than content memorisation. With the ongoing emphasis on transforming assessment for optimising learning and the holistic development of all students in tandem with the environment, the focus is on regular, formative and competency-based learning and development; focus on "assessment for learning", testing of higher-order skills (analysis, critical thinking and conceptual clarity, etc). Today, the school planners and annual calendars are reflecting no hard separation amongst "curricular", "extra-curricular" and "co-curricular" activities among arts, humanities, and science or between vocational or academic streams. With the idea that learning should be child-centric, holistic, integrated, enjoyable and engaging, schools are slowly breaking the straitjackets of arts, commerce and science streams in high school, and aiming to introduce vocational courses with internships. The policy envisages a 100 percent Gross Enrolment Ratio (GER) in school education by 2030.

Key words: NEP, GER, Accessibility, Equity, Quality.

The year 2020 marked a major positive breakthrough in the form of the National Education Policy 2020 re-imagining the educational landscape through equity, inclusion and excellence in education. Though the year started with unprecedented times, NEP 2020 was the much-needed silver lining. As we complete a year to this progressive roadmap, let's look at the instructional sensitivity and mounting steps which are accelerating our progress towards the realisation of this omnibus policy. Based on the pillars of "Accessibility, Equity, Quality, Affordability, Accountability", NEP aims at transforming India into a vibrant knowledge hub.

With almost 85 percent of brain development of children occurring before the age of 6, the policy emphasises early childhood care and education with universal provisioning and equipping young children to participate and flourish in the educational ecosystem. Schools are gradually moving towards a flexible, multifaceted, multilevel, play-based, activity-based and inquiry and domain-based learning.

With this overarching goal, it has already made headway towards universal access to high-quality ECCE in a phased manner. Gradually breaking the shackles of the past in adopting a curricular framework and classroom pedagogy that is based on the 5+3+3+4 system, starting at age three, there is an emphasis on the primacy of the formative years from ages three to eight in shaping the child's future. "If you talk to a man in a language he understands, that goes to his head. If you talk to him in his own language, that goes to his heart." The focus on instruction in the mother tongue is largely to celebrate the idea of being Indian, globalising Indian thoughts, eulogising the rich cultural heritage of our country and bringing it to our classrooms. The policy necessitates the continuation of the three-language formula and its implementation to promote multilingualism a USP of the educated Indian.

In 2021, we have already shifted assessment gears to a diagnostic approach from content-based assessment to competency-based, making Board exams "easier" in the sense that they test primarily core competencies rather than content memorisation. With the ongoing emphasis on transforming assessment for optimising learning and the holistic development of all students in tandem with the environment, the focus is on regular, formative and competency-based learning and development; focus on "assessment for learning", testing of higher-order skills (analysis, critical thinking and conceptual clarity, etc), multimodal assessment through multiple-choice questions to reach the top bracket of Bloom's Taxonomy, learning through reasoning, storytelling, podcasts, puppetry, etc. Report cards are becoming 360-degree holistic progress cards that will give comprehensive feedback on skills and capabilities, substituting the age-old system of marks.

Holistic development and a wide choice of subjects and courses are proposed as the new distinguishing feature of secondary school education. Today, the school planners and annual calendars are reflecting no hard separation amongst "curricular", "extra-curricular" and "co-curricular" activities among arts, humanities, and science or between vocational or academic streams. With the idea that learning should be child-centric, holistic, integrated, enjoyable and engaging, schools are slowly breaking the straitjackets of arts, commerce and science streams in high school, and aiming to introduce vocational courses with internships. The policy envisages a 100 percent Gross Enrolment Ratio (GER) in school education by 2030.

It is said that the jobs of the future are yet to be invented, but with the focus on twenty first century skills scientific temper and evidence-based thinking, creativity and innovativeness, sense of aesthetics and art, oral and written communication, health and nutrition, physical education, wellness, fitness and sports, collaboration and teamwork, problem solving and logical reasoning, coding and computational thinking, environmental awareness, water and resources conservation, etc. we are slowly beginning to resonate with the Fourth Industrial Revolution. Therefore, one of the targets is that curricular and pedagogical initiatives including the introduction of contemporary subjects such as artificial intelligence, design thinking, holistic health, organic living, etc. are integrated.

To ensure the quality of teacher education across all stages, the policy envisions teacher career progression via meritocracy and 360-degree assessments. Aiming for equitable and inclusive education, the policy reaffirms every citizen's right to dream, thrive and contribute to the nation, bridging the social category gaps in access, participation and learning outcomes. To specially address their educational needs, the NEP has clubbed gender identities, socio-cultural identities, geographical identities, disabilities, and socio-economic conditions to create a new social group called SEDGs. More significantly, schools are to be hubs for endorsing resource efficiency and robust governance in the form of school complexes/ clusters which aim to improve support for children where we care and share, collaborate and co-create the best pedagogical practices.

NEP 2020 aims to provide infrastructure support, innovative education centres to bring back dropouts into the mainstream, besides tracking students and their learning levels, facilitating multiple pathways to learning involving both formal and non-formal education modes and association of counsellors or well-trained social workers with schools. Having a single regulator for higher education institutions, multiple entry and exit options in degree courses, the low-stakes board exams, and common entrance exams for universities these are some of the key takeaways from the new policy. Each of these reforms reflects the fact that India is evolving as an economy, and is preparing to be recognised as a force to be reckoned with.

Conclusion

Education is a public good. Everyone is a stakeholder and should therefore be invited to contribute to actualise the vision of the NEP to make India's education system strong, inclusive, and equitable. He new National Education Policy, 2020, which has been approved by the central government to change the Indian education system to meet the needs of twenty first century India, if it is implemented successfully, this new system will make India one of the world's leading countries. Equivalent under the new education policy, 2020, children from three years to 18 years have been placed under the Right to Education Act, 2009. The aim of this new education policy, which came after 34 years, is to provide higher education to all students, which aims to universalise pre-primary education (age range of 3-6 years) by 2025.

References

1. Kumar, K. (2005). Quality of Education at the Beginning of the 21st Century: Lessons from India. Indian Educational Review.
2. Draft National Education Policy 2019, https://innovate.mygov.in/wpcontent/uploads/2019/06/mygov1559651011 1.pdf
3. National Education Policy 2020. https://www.mhrd.gov.in/sites/upload_files/mhrd/files/nep/ NEP_Final_English.pdf referred on 10/08/2020.
4. Yojana Magazine.
5. Other Paper Articles.

33

Social Goals of Collaborative Learning: Special Reference to Indian Education System

Dr Thallapelli Sanjeev

Abstract

Capacity building via participative learning helps students develop critical thinking lest hegemonic forces overpower interpersonal or international discourses and policy-making or decision-making processes. This calls for new pedagogies and new approaches to learning. Traditional educational systems which, in a way, are conducive to the hegemonic trends of market - economy benumb critical sensibilities of students who, in course of time, wittingly or unwittingly contribute to the capitalist modes of accumulation of wealth, clash of civilisations, and to the perpetuation of a world order that does little good to the powerless and the voiceless. We also ought to realise that the world is not competitive enough to glorify competition alone as the value for success or survival. This research article to be critically analysed the importance of Collaborative Learning to be strengthen the Indian Education System.

Key Words: Hegemonic trends, marginalisation, Co-operative Learning behaviour Approach. Identical Object - Global Education.

Introduction

In an era of globalisation where competition and interdependence swing like a pendulum, Collaborative Learning becomes an indispensable value. It projects teaching as an act of learning together - enabling one another to teach themselves so that learning capacitates learners and teachers as well to cultivate positive interdependence. Capacity building via participative learning helps students develop critical thinking lest hegemonic forces overpower interpersonal or international discourses and policy-making or decision-making processes. This calls for new pedagogies and new approaches to learning. Traditional educational systems which, in a way, are conducive to the hegemonic trends of market - economy benumb critical sensibilities of students who, in course of time, wittingly or unwittingly contribute to the capitalist modes of accumulation of wealth, clash of civilisations, and to the perpetuation of a world order that does little good to the powerless and the voiceless. We also ought to realise that the world is not competitive enough to glorify competition alone as the value for success or survival. It has neither the competence nor the wisdom for such a tall claim. Mere bookish knowledge that prepares high achievers and other graded learners to be ready with set solutions makes them feel embarrassed in the face of fast changing situations in the job-market. The presence of a number of university degree holders, unfit for employability in or outside India, should serve as an eye-opener. The question is not merely unemployment but also unemployability. The distance between bookish knowledge and the job-demands is widening day by day.

Indian Higher Education - Progressive Reforms

Urgent and pragmatic overhauling of syllabi and textbooks in our educational systems is the need of the hour if students need to be motivated to be involved in active learning, develop critical thinking, prevent marginalisation, and face the challenges of globalisation. A considerable amount of research, especially psychological research, pertinent to holistic education, has projected a 'cognitive and constructivist approach' as a way of active learning via the power of the mind evident in Collaborative Learning. The preference for this approach stands in contrast to the traditional 'behaviourist approach' evident in the 'factory model of education' in which, as John T. Bruer (1999 and 2006) observes and comments, 'experts create knowledge, teachers disseminate it, and students are graded on how much of it they can absorb and retain' by rote and memory. The result of the factory model of education is that mediocrity is marketed via uninspired teaching as if 'humanity were a business' with mass production of 'identical objects' rather than unique human beings. Against this backdrop, no reasonable parent or educator concerned about better prospects for his/her child/student would grudge any progressive education reforms.

It is time that a revision of curriculum and pedagogy leaning towards cooperative ways of learning is on the top of priority agendas for implementation at all levels - global, national, regional and local. Authorities and agencies behind education and evaluation systems at all graded levels across the globe have a terrific challenge and responsibility in ensuring that all forms and modes of education and evaluation are geared towards a deeper understanding of the vision, theory, research and practices of Collaborative Learning methods. For, Collaborative Learning has sufficient scope for accommodating social goals, goals that could enrich the beauty of human solidarity via celebration of multidimensional perspectives, multiculturalism and interdependence. The world, despite conflicts of interest and brutalities of existence, pines for mutual understanding, cooperation and co-existence, free from hegemony and disharmony.

In a world of cultural diversity, which is not alien to clashes and conflicts, a commitment to promote mutual interaction and working together can be a credible and humanist way of witnessing to the glory of existence, and the glory of existence consists of human capacity to preserve and enhance the dignity of all human beings without discrimination and to celebrate ceaselessly the oneness of humanity. The very nature of the oneness of humanity is its cultural diversity. It means that appreciation of heterogeneity, differences and multiple intelligences reflecting manifold wisdom can be a crucial signifier signifying a collective sense of solidarity which foregrounds positive interdependence as a perennial value. This is a worldview that benefits all and facilitates people to build fellowship despite and beyond borders and boundaries.

Social Goals of Collaborative Learning

In terms of social goals of Collaborative Learning, Kurt Lewin, known as the founding father of modern social and organisational psychology, who influenced the Group Dynamics Movement, may be mentioned here for his pioneering contributions vis-à-vis group processing, psychological ecology of behaviour settings, cooperative experiential learning experiences, action theory, and resolution of social conflicts.

Paulo Freire's (1968) notion of education as a concentrically attuned, democratic, critiquing, and conscientizing experience vis-a-vis the pedagogy of the oppressed and the deprived could be named here as another driving force towards Collaborative Learning that has consciousness raising-significance. Freire was insistent on defeating the 'banking' concept of education which, as an instrument of oppression, tended to transfer facts into the minds of learners as if 'their minds were passive', and on minimizing 'the teacher-student dichotomy'. He believed in Rousseau's idea of the child as an active learner and Franz Fanon's idea of decolonisation of the mind. Based on 'dialogicity' that promotes bi-directional relationship wherein both the teacher and student learn, his method of learning aims at realising the essence of education, namely 'freedom in practice'. In his method, no one 'liberates anyone else, nobody liberates himself all alone, and people liberate themselves in fellowship with one another'. Learning is generative, and learning to realise social goals is a social process of learning together by discovering and understanding each one's reality, of acting together by struggling together so as to transform the reality - when it means oppression, and of experiencing fellowship by enjoying freedom in practice. 'No one can create himself in silence, but through dialogue, reflection and action'. This was how Freire espoused the cause of learning, rather Collaborative Learning by extension.

Practical Views of Cooperative System

Respected Late Kalam's discerned understanding of the realities of India, his vision for a new India, his love for teaching with 'peppered anecdotes' and formula for creative leadership, his interactive crash courses elucidating his concepts of PURA (Providing Urban Facilities in Rural Areas) and NPI (National Prosperity Index) and his interactive learning with students as a socially meaningful collaborative venture indicate not only the fact that he is a man of reasonable and realisable dreams but also justify why students as responsible citizens need to cultivate an interdisciplinary approach to learning, adopt and adapt cooperative ways of learning in order to enrich 'knowledge power', build up 'innovative technology, augment 'management stewardship', accommodate multiple intelligences, and promote collective leadership. All these aspects, as he insists, are fuelled by one another. His vision has the prospect of moulding learners as resources for themselves rather than as mere dependents or recipients of received information, and shaping students as 'job-generators' rather than as 'job-seekers', as he himself articulates.

Both Sen and Kalam are teachers par excellence, adept in managing small groups and mass audience as well. Both can improvise themselves at any instructional situation. The way they interact with students and teachers of different disciplines and of all age groups, is a telling epiphany of how a teacher in a cooperative classroom context performs. Their role as teachers implies by indirection that teachers are there not as information providers but as 'facilitating midwives'. In parenthesis, when one thinks of realising their social vision, it is an uphill task indeed. Towards translating such a vision into action, we need a corruption-free environment and effective dialogical participation, if not political will. For, positive political will for realising social goals and ushering in a new society is becoming a rare and rarer phenomenon. The dynamics of Collaborative Learning are such that they can capacitate learners to usher in a new brand of political class. Cooperative learners are prospective leaders of tomorrow's political or policy - making class, directors and managers of knowledge economy, entrepreneurships, and builders of a new society free from poverty, disparity, discrimination and violence. They can have a big say on the need to promote positive interdependence, international harmony and human fellowship. Ideas do make history, and cooperative learners, as prospective critics and potential builders of a new society, do carry new ideas.

Dynamics of Collaborative Learning

Collaborative Learning is an act of believing in and practising face-to-face interactive learning so as to encourage creativity and foster critical thinking through group processing. In Collaborative Learning, learning is not memorizing a set of truths, or already established or arrived at conclusions. Instead, as Carolyn et al (1992) observe, it hovers around raising the level of 'learners' curiosity' and their 'spirit of questioning', infusing in them a democratic and scientific way of investigation of facts and findings, and facilitating them to integrate critical assimilation and 'multidimensional aesthetic responses'. It organises learners at any graded level in small groups for learning together that aims at contributing to the attainment of shared common goals and a win-win situation for all. With teacher as facilitator performing multiple roles such as 'midwife', 'learning process engineer', 'need detector and analyzer', 'conflict manager' and 'psychologist', learners in groups interact and discuss the given topic - say, a lesson or a particular issue in an anxiety-free ambience wherein 'the affective filter' is lowered to the extent possible. Learning via better understanding and meaning-making via discussion, free from tension, do take place. Discussion that prompts critical thinking, peer-evaluation that minimizes alienation, and collaborative ethic, rather than competitive ethic, that 'promotes mutual respect, trust and altruism' (Goodlad, 1984) may be viewed as core part of this learning together.

In a social set-up where the structures of educational systems are not conducive to Collaborative Learning and wherein evaluation system is more traditional and extrinsic, many children, particularly competitive children, become blind to cooperative solutions. Mere competitive cultural values ingrained within the traditional modes of evaluation may be beneficial to an already privileged sector of urban children but if they, as Kagan and Associates point out, 'do not prepare our future generations to behave rationally across the full range of social situations, and work and interact productively', these generations would be out of step with reality, the reality of the workplace and the indispensable need for cooperative strategies and solutions. It is this realisation that should conscientise educational agencies and authorities even at university level about the relevance and importance of Collaborative Learning. Collaborative Learning can be an educational strategy at all levels from LKG to PG. It can serve both as a temporary strategy and an elongated and enduring one depending on how the groups are formed. It can be extended even beyond formal educational levels and can be applied in manifold life-situations.

Pursuit of Social Goals

Pursuit of excellence is fine but when it happens to be the privilege of a few who outperform, win extra encomiums and receive better teacher approval, and who, in a way, contribute to the elimination of other learners, that too at the cost of national exchequer or limited public resources, it causes disquiet and disparities, and aggravates social tensions. A gifted learner, in all likelihood, is a high achiever by virtue of a sound foundation or innate abilities. A gifted learner's extraordinary academic achievement may give him/ her a personal and individualistic sense of achievement in life. Whether his/her achievements have contributed to eradication of poverty, inequality and societal discrimination, and to the promotion of humane interdependence and solidarity so that occasions for peace are more than occasions for tension, or he/she has become part of the world of cynicism and snobbishness can be a moot point. If seekers and achievers of excellence turn out to be cynics churning out more and more cynics from among the brainy, then it is a sign that our educational systems need comprehensive corrective revamping measures.

The big advantage in Collaborative Learning is that it maximizes group learning not to project individual excellences but to ensure critical thinking and team building. It assumes, as Carolyn Kessler report, that 'learning is NOT necessarily an outcome of teaching', that 'the quality of understanding is more critical than the quantity of information presented by the teacher', and that learning, a moving process from the concrete to the abstract, connotes kinesthetic experience eliciting feedback. Therefore, as Peterson insist, 'the time is ripe for teachers to work relentlessly to create classroom situations in which students are tempted, cajoled, seduced, provoked and firmly rewarded not for being excellent, but for thinking'. The tendency to include competition, 'healthy competition', as part of Collaborative Learning has been discussed in literatures related to Collaborative Learning methods. The research clearly indicates that cooperation, compared with competitive and individualistic efforts, results in '(a) higher achievement and greater productivity, (b) more caring, supportive, and committed relationships, and (c) greater psychological health, social competence, and self-esteem'. Recent research studies have discussed 'the impact of healthy competition' within Collaborative Learning. Staunch advocates of Collaborative Learning have questioned the relevance of healthy competition meaning that it is a myth. Proponents of competitive Collaborative Learning' have their arguments.

Conclusions

Today, the savvy world gives more and more credence and premium to practical cooperative skills. Degrees obtained as part of certification are put to test and scrutiny via face-to-face interview, group discussions and hire and fire system. Proficiency for performance, via team building and cooperative solutions, is valued high. The job-world values, seeks, employs and appreciates performers who could actively participate in its economic life and its knowledge-driven economy. Permanence in postings and jobs is dependent on performance. It tends to nurture competition as proficiency for employability and team-work. India today provides happy times to a miniscule minority but hard times to a great majority of Indian population. What India needs and could aspire is not to become a 'super-power' in the sense that is in vogue today but to ceaselessly expand and enrich the learning curve, the curve that inspires and facilitates the citizenry to promote the art of thinking and living interdependently, and diffuse the fragrance of the same across the globe. Indian poetics and aesthetics have a tradition of implying and diffusing eclectic compassionate humanism, and ways of Collaborative Learning contribute to the conservation and enhancement of this tradition.

References

1. Ausubel, D. P. 1988. Educational Psychology: A Cognitive View. New York: Holt, Rinehart and Winston.
2. Bruner, J. S. 2021. Toward a Theory of Instruction. New York: W. W. Norton.
3. Bruer, T. John. 2013. In Search of Brain-Based Education. Phi Delta Kappan (May 1999), 649-57. http:// www.pdkintl.org/kappan/kbru9905.htm
4. Deutsch, M. 2005. A Theory of Cooperation and Competition. Human Relations, 2: 129-52.
5. Freire, Paulo. 2021. Pedagogy of the Oppressed. New York: Seabury.
6. Gardner, L. Howard. 1993. Frames of Mind: The Theory of Multiple Intelligences. New York: Basic Books.
7. Goodlad, J.I. 2012 - A Place Called School: Prospects for the Future. New York: McGraw -Hill.
8. Johnson, D.W., and R.T. Johnson. 1989. Cooperation and Competition: Theory and Research. Edina, MN Interaction Book Company.

9. Johnson, D.W., R.T. Johnson, and E.J.Holubec. 1986. Circles of Learning: Cooperation in the Classroom. Edina, MN: Interaction Book Company.

10. Kagan, Spencer. 1994. Collaborative Learning. Edina, MN: Interaction Book Company.

11. Kessler, Carolyn. 2018. Cooperative Language Learning. Englewood Cliffs, NJ: Prentice-Hall, INC.

12. Mcgroarty, M. 1989. The Benefits of Collaborative Learning Arrangements in Second Language Instruction. NABE Journal, 13, no. 2 (Winter 1989): 127-43.

Related Websites

www.eduprestine.com

www.zapmate.co.in

34

The Status of Women in Higher Education

Dr M. Ramana

Abstract

Women in the Vedic ages accepted their due acknowledgment in the public arena as well as got equivalent treatment in the question of instructive preparing. Schooling of ladies remained to some degree dismissed during the English time-frame. Be that as it may, as society became conventional, there was change in their status. They were bound to the four dividers of kitchen and involved in raising kids. Men became providers and it was viewed as essential for them to be instructed. The jobs of people were in this way isolated. However, presently the social scene has impressively changed. Ladies all around the world are being taught in pretty much every field that men were so far ordinarily connected with. The information on expressions, science, innovation and governmental issues is at this point not the advantage of men alone. Ladies have started to contemplate these subjects and have carried extraordinary credit to themselves and their country by contributing effectively in those fields. Subsequently every school is currently aware of conferring instruction to young women's.

Keywords: Ladies training; financial; Vedic; UGC; Telangana.

Introduction

Advanced education has a significant job to carry out in the errand of building a country and preparing for generally speaking improvement of a country. The twentieth century has seen a few unrests like Green unrest, White upheaval, IT upset, changing human progress to the period of Data Innovation.

There is a widespread perspective on privatising schooling that can be seen nowadays. As a component of this, administration instructive establishments are being privatised. Private organisations are being allowed an opportunity to give advanced education. The social interest for advanced education, notwithstanding, kept on expanding. The powerlessness of the state to help this developing interest brought about new financing game plans for advanced education. The new changes in this space could be comprehensively isolated into two classifications: the privatisation of public foundations and the foundation of private establishments of advanced education. Privatisation suggests the use of market standards in the activity of public foundations, while possession rests inside the public space. Advancement of the private area suggests the development and extension of the non-state area in advanced education, and regularly this area doesn't depend on state financing for its development and development. Both of these actions have made ready for market activities in advanced education.

In the circumstance, the State needs to assume significant part in schooling through financing it. Government colleges need assistance in advancing instruction, in giving advanced education to helpless understudies. Yet, monetary crunch has prompted decline in the assets for advanced education in numerous nations. Particularly agricultural nations have diminished the assets for instruction among their spending portions.

The state assumed a predominant part in financing monetary turn of events and instructive advancement in the second 50 percent of the previous century. Therefore, state funded colleges turned into the prevailing mode for growing advanced education in many nations of the world. The monetary emergency of 1980s diminished the financial limit of states for kept subsidising of a growing advanced education framework. Besides, underlying change programmes included strategies that supported decreased public consumption on training and redirection of public venture from the more elevated levels to the essential degrees of instruction. The portion of financial plan dispensed to advanced education declined in non-industrial nations during this period and enrolment proportions deteriorated at exceptionally low levels in numerous nations.

The Indian corporate area has found 1,000,000 dollar industry in administrations in training. It is yet to be completely investigated and abused. This industry is the space of instruction as 'administration' with an immense worldwide market wherein understudies, educators and non-showing representatives establish as assets revenue driven making. In this industry understudies are buyers, instructors and the establishments or organisations offering schooling administrations are specialist co-ops and the educating learning measure is no longer for the structure of a country however a business for public showcasing.

Schooling framework in India presently addresses an extraordinary oddity. From one perspective, we have IIMs and IITs that position among the best foundations on the planet and then again there are various schools, and colleges in the country that don't have the fundamental framework. Even after over 60 years of freedom, we are far away from the objective of general education. Be that as it may, on a positive note, the Indian experts are considered among the best on the planet and are in incredible interest. This implies the innate strength of Indian schooling framework.

As of late, the effect of globalisation prompted quick improvement in advanced education area, curiously in South Asian Regions. Advanced education from one side of the planet to the other, in the high level just as the non-industrial nations, is going through huge change. The world is encountering a remarkable development in understudy numbers, yet the fast development popular for advanced education is met rather by inelastic inventory of public advanced education and declining public spending plans in numerous nations. Regardless, the Internationalisation of advanced education is definitely not another wonder. It has been around us for a long time, during the archaic, present day, and contemporary periods, and surprisingly prior. Colleges are general by definition and have consistently been global establishments. The main type of internationalisation used to be trade of researchers. Numerous unfamiliar researchers were on the rolls of antiquated colleges in India, like Nalanda and Takshashila.

Today locally and universally, admittance to advanced education has acquired significance. Created nations give a more prominent significance to admittance to advanced education and have set up establishments for advanced education. Agricultural nations have a low spotlight on advanced education, reasons being destitution, ignorance, and carelessness with respect to governments. In India, there is a less interest for advanced education since it is costly and inaccessible to average person. All nations center around advanced education these days as a result of the effect of globalisation and IT upsets which thus impact advanced education arrangements. Each administration and private organisation currently has an exploration wing for strategy making, which has flagged the need of an advanced education expert to take legitimate choices. Indeed, even the WHO, the UNESCO and different associations are genuinely dealing with advanced education to make a superior society later on.

As indicated by the UNESCO Report on Instruction in the twenty first century, Advanced education is the order to connect the information hole among nations and networks, enhancing exchange among individuals and societies; worldwide connecting and net-working of thoughts, exploration and innovations. Consequently, advanced education gives the capabilities that are needed in various circles of human action, going from organisation to farming, business, industry, wellbeing and correspondence and stretching out to expressions of the human experience and culture. Nonetheless, the value and quality in advanced education are projected as dichotomous in India. Apparently there is almost no reality in it. As per the World Human Advancement report named "Value and Improvement" underlined Human Turn of events and focused on value. The report has stressed the requirement for giving fairness of freedom to accomplish improvement.

It is vital here to attract from this report to comprehend the current issue of advanced education in India, which is enduring with a fear of value and quality controlled by the recorded conditions under which advanced education was created in the nation and its accomplishments. It appears to be that the individuals who are associated with the approach making have neglected to utilise the scholarly data sources given by the World Bank, the UNDP and other autonomous masterminds on this issue to determine the supposed division of value and quality.

The neo-liberal and customary foundations that are available these days are driving in giving more significance to GATS since it opens up new vistas and objectives for advanced education. The revenue driven suppliers treat instruction actually like some other ware exchanged for benefit. The development of private advanced education has relied upon the limit and eagerness of understudies/families to pay for their schooling. The profundity of advancement and its impacts on the design and development of a country's schooling area relies on numerous components. In particular it relies on how the country's approach producers see advanced education. Is it seen as a fundamental assistance for creating HR as an inborn piece of the cycle of improvement Or is it seen uniquely as some other exchange producing administrations reacting to advertise requests? The response to these central inquiries would decide how schooling is seen in the public eye, and how strategy creators outline the country's schooling strategy. This, thus would decide how the schooling area is molded as an outcome of progression.

India has customary establishments with regards to instruction. Indeed, even in the long stretches of BC, there were colleges called Takshashila, Nalanda. As of now, the foundations and colleges offering advanced education are in incredible interest. Notwithstanding, the sad condition of advanced education in India is a direct result of the specialised and business situated schooling being accessible for a minimal price though advanced education being expensive. "Greater work direction or 'expert courses' are seen as a venture for future pay age. Courses that don't ensure business remain somewhat modest and this is the place where the country's financial imbalance is reflected, especially in advanced education. Progressively, training which would create future pay is opening up to the individuals who can bear the cost of it.

In any case, the Indian colleges are the spots for the information and inventiveness for accomplishing social, monetary and political turn of events. Colleges play out a basic job in an economy and society. They make information. They confer information. Furthermore, they scatter information. Colleges should be adaptable, inventive and imaginative. They should have the option to draw in the best ability, be they instructors or understudies. They should/can contend and the inspiration to dominate. We can't examine a change of our advanced education framework without improving in our current colleges. For improving the human limit, there is a need to advanced education for better usage of HR. Especially, the focal and state governments need to assume a dependable part toward this path of advanced education. All things considered, it ought to be connected with the advancement of HR and development of human resources. In the current circumstance, it is seen that lightening of neediness, provide the right guidance to the adolescent and so forth can be guaranteed through creating appropriate labour arranging which will improve the extent of employability of our HR.

In this association, the basic issues concerning advanced education are access and value. While financial reasoning and the abilities plan assume a focal position in the talk on advanced education, the issue of extending access has been personally connected with the rising yearnings in the new years. A youthful populace and enhancements in school training have squeezed the advanced education framework to extend. In the course of recent years, it is the impromptu expansion of colleges and schools, as opposed to proactive, savvy developments that have extended admittance to advanced education. With the new spotlight on comprehensive development, there is presently an unmistakable bearing to the extension of access.

The issue of access is identified with the size and nature of public financing for advanced education. Because of monetary impediments, there are imperatives to the improvement of access. In this manner, access has worked on generally because of extension of private advanced education as of late. The effect of such extension on value and quality are begging to be proven wrong. As the financial real factors change and there is a progressive shift towards supportive of market monetary approaches, public mentalities to private advanced education have changed. Right now, just about 60 percent school pass outs go in for advanced education. Henceforth, there could be pipeline imperative in additional extension of advanced education.

The advanced education framework in India has filled in an astounding way; the framework has numerous issues of worry as of now, such as showcasing, financing and human asset the executives including access. In this way, access, value, responsibility and quality should shape the four core values. These issues are significant for the nation, as it is occupied with the utilisation of advanced education as an incredible asset to construct a left edge-based data society of the twenty first century. Indeed, even India is going to have in excess of 1500 colleges; it needs to foster the instructive framework from the grass roots level itself. "The difficulties that go up against advanced education in India is clear. It needs a huge development of chances for advanced education, to 1500 colleges cross country, that would empower India to accomplish a gross enrolment proportion of no less than 30 percent by 2025. It is comparably significant, to raise the normal nature of advanced education in each circle. Simultaneously, it is fundamental to make organisations that are models of greatness at standard with the best on the planet. Chasing these destinations, furnishing individuals with admittance to higher instruction in a socially comprehensive way is basic. The acknowledgment of these targets, joined with access, would not just foster the abilities and capacities we need for the economy yet would likewise assist with changing India into an information economy and society.

Nowadays, not just is advanced education restricted to the improvement of the people genuinely, intellectually, mentally and profoundly, yet it is additionally a way to give them essential abilities for their prosperity just as for the financial improvement of the general public on the loose. India has the third biggest framework advanced education on the planet after the US and China. In distance mode, India has involved ahead of everyone else on the planet with 3.5 million understudy's enrolment under the Indira Gandhi Public Open College.

As indicated by the insights of 2015, there are 45 Focal colleges, 290 State colleges, 130 Considered colleges and 90 Private colleges in India. Previous Indian Head administrator, Manmohan Singh had said that the India has exceptionally low enrolment in the field of advanced education. 66 percent of our colleges are having level of sub-optimal in their advancement.

The test for Advanced education in India isn't privatising it and not transforming it into a simple business in the open market arranged and making it productive. Corporate schools have transformed advanced degree into a business. Among the agricultural nations, there is an expanding job for private gatherings under GATS. Under its impact privatisation measures have driven public establishments to receive cost-recuperation and cost-sharing techniques and starting pay creating and benefit situated business dares to assemble assets required for the activity of colleges. Private colleges, in numerous occasions, demand high expenses to recuperate the full expense (if not full expense in addition to), particularly in the revenue driven area. The presence of the revenue driven private area in advanced education has given degree for market theory and resultant speculative interest in schooling. A portion of the offices have set up instructive establishments or organisations driven by benefit thought processes.

In this way, the effect of Globalisation has wide going impact on all areas of advancement. Other than its effect on the speed and example of financial turn of events, it has additionally projected its shadow on the arrangement of training. Worldwide training is the one that gives information and comprehension of culture, language, geology and worldwide viewpoints to comprehend the world through the eyes of others and shows them how their activities can influence, and be influenced by individuals all through the world. With more than 200 of the Fortune 500 organisations enlisting from grounds consistently the public authority presently plans to build up India as a brand in the advanced education area and command the notice of worldwide instruction local area under these conditions. India offers a well disposed climate, social variety and best incentive for cash alternative to understudy from SAARC, Center East and South East Asia. As indicated by measurements accessible while India can possibly manage around 50,000 unfamiliar understudies in two or three years, by and by just around 10,000 are concentrating in India.

Privatisation of institution, it is contended, is one of the compelling techniques to upgrade admittance to training, and to further develop value and quality in schooling, other than noting the issues of asset shortage with respect to the public authority. While many will in general concur with the conclusion of the circumstance and the need to extend advanced education, as depicted above, there are contrasts as to the required strategy approaches for such an extension. While some vibe that the public authority can additionally grow the advanced education framework and to work on instructive freedoms for all, some other emphatically accept that the asset position won't permit the public authority to extend public advanced education any further. They even contend that administration appropriations to advanced education should be radically diminished, if not killed through and through. In the present neo-liberal structure, there arises one more solid way of thinking which contends that regardless of whether the public authority has assets, it's anything but a productive proposition for the public authority to grow public advanced education.

Regarding the previous way of thinking, it is contended that it isn't absence of assets, yet absence of political will and absence of confidence in advanced education as an instrument of improvement that is liable for this decrease. The contention that the public authority doesn't have money related assets for schooling acquired help as a critical decrease in broad daylight financial plans for advanced education in the nation turned out to be generally noted. This brought about decay in the nature of instruction, and reception of a few problematic proportions of cost saving, including non-enrolment of educating and non-showing staff in organisations of advanced education. And furthermore endeavours were all the while made to raise the degrees of cost recuperation in schooling, basically through expanding understudy expense. The passage of unfamiliar colleges in India is entirely astounding advance in advanced education framework. Notwithstanding that the "Unfamiliar Instructive Foundations Bill 2010 is viewed as just an authoritative expansion of financial progression to the instructive area. The apparent purposes behind the bill, viz, to address the low gross enrolment rate, and the low quality and deficiency of instructive establishments in the nation comprise the justificatory manner of speaking that conceals the plan of opening the public advanced education area to world exchange."

The Unfamiliar College Bill would work with the interaction. A variation of the parts of unfamiliar colleges is opening up of courses in Indian foundations in a joint effort with unfamiliar colleges. Everything can be said for such an organisation. It will have a synergic impact on the advancement of advanced education in the country. Another method of increasing offices for advanced education is the section of unfamiliar colleges into India. They could set up branches or offices to empower Indian understudies to seek after their course deterring the need of traveling to another country. It is verbalised that before all else like the section of multinationals, the passage of unfamiliar colleges might be taken a gander at with doubt. Be that as it may, with the advantages from such passage of colleges from abroad are progressively perceived. It is being contended that in addition to the fact that they would increase the offices; they would bring new and better expectations and cause our establishments of advanced education more cutthroat which to have been experiencing stagnation. They could present groundbreaking thoughts obviously content and strategies. They would likewise animate examination.

The arrangement of advanced education assumes a significant part in the improvement of a country taking into account its forward linkage with the corporate world, just as with the general public on the loose. Aside from essential and optional training, advanced education is the main instrument for improvement and change. Advanced education has the incomparable job of getting ready future pioneers for various circles of life: social, monetary, political, social, and logical and innovative. With steady advancement and globalisation of advanced education, the difficulties before the advanced education framework are enormous. All concerned residents of the nation need to understand that it is just a vigorous, imaginative and more brilliant higher instructive framework can help in changing India to enter in to the class of created countries.

Now-a-days, the general interest for advanced education, particularly expertly related courses, is expanding. There are various purposes behind this: evolving socioeconomics, the expanded number of auxiliary school graduates, and the development to long lasting learning, and the development of the information economy. While request is developing, notwithstanding, the limit of the public area to fulfill this need is insufficient. Simultaneously, numerous progressions are happening on the schooling conveyance side: advancements in data and correspondence advances are giving other option and virtual approaches to convey advanced education. New kinds of suppliers are arising, like worldwide organisations, revenue driven foundations, corporate colleges, and IT furthermore, media organisations. Public and private suppliers have started conveying training across public lines to satisfy the expanding the need in different nations moreover. Elective kinds of cross-line programme conveyance, for example, branch grounds and establishment and twinning plans, are being created.

In India however there has been an exceptionally lethargic speed of development of colleges, there has been an unbalanced development in the quantity of foundations, associated to the current colleges. The allies of private drives in advanced education contend that the foundation of private colleges should be worked with to fulfill the need and yet important measures must be taken to manage something similar to guarantee required norms of schooling.

Challenges of higher education

- The street ahead for India is straightforwardly connected to production of value Advanced Education Establishments amazingly to address the difficulty of the information center point, which India is quick becoming.
- India's requirements to have a proactive interest based arrangement towards private advanced education including unfamiliar organisations/colleges burning of setting up of grounds in India or going into joint-adventures. India could offer expense concessions/monetary impetuses for setting up grounds.
- The issue of raising the charges upwards to meet the expense of training is basic in case we are to keep up with and support the nature of instruction. Helped foundations as private establishments are now utilising a higher charge structure. In a cutthroat setting there is no motivation behind why the charges ought not meet a sensible extent of the expense of schooling. A figure of 20 percent of repeating cost is viewed as sensible in the worldwide scale, albeit in certain nations (like South Korea) it could go up to 40 percent.
- The requirement for financing advanced education for understudies, particularly those coming from low pay families needs exceptional consideration. Like the US, we may likewise develop an assurance framework, where understudies coming from low pay families are qualified for an understudy loan without parental security or assurance, so there is no separation because of the monetary foundation of the understudy. Endowment of the loan cost for understudies ought to be founded on his or his family pay.
- Open Colleges should be urged to offer quality projects at the lower cost. This turns into the most practical method of giving advanced education, including specialised and professional instruction.
- In perspective on the growing job of WTO, advanced education would before long turn into a thing under it. We ought to urge unfamiliar colleges to come to India to set up free tasks or work together with existing Indian Organisations, schools/ establishments.
- Universities and Schools ought to be needed to rebuild and change educational plans basically once in three years.

- Introduction obviously credit framework where degrees are conceded based on finishing an essential number of credits from various courses which give understudy decisions.
- Introduction of exploration projects in undergraduate and postgraduate courses to improve advancement and business among Colleges and understudies.
- Re-association and combination of different resources, especially in sociologies, around bury disciplinary and multi-disciplinary courses can likewise help in quality improvement in educating, exploration and consultancy.
- Transparent acknowledge just as decision based credit framework and which could advance versatility of the students ought to be advanced quickly in advanced education framework.
- Attracting and boosting top tier staff to lead research, embracing different models to foster examination capacities in foundations in India, advancing joint efforts among global establishments, industry, and exploration habitats for creating great essential and applied examination be allowed an opportunity.
- Promoting individual based subsidizing, giving serious admittance to public examination awards, empowering corporate and graduated class financing and connecting public financing to institutional execution.
- The issue of access has stayed an extraordinary challenger for that load of strategy producers, organisers and implementers notwithstanding the legislators, administrative bodies, subject specialists and academicians. In India, rising populace asset crunch, education rate, topographical imperatives, accumulated with social, social and conventional connection ups have made the issue a more prominent test than whatever else.
- Access to assets through grants ought to be given to empower understudies to seek after their picked fields of study.
- Rural, metropolitan and sex incongruities should be remembered by strategy producers in arranging and carrying out the advanced education framework.

Conclusion

The ladies interest in advanced education is expanding in practically all states. The ladies enrolment in advanced education is likewise expanding. The pace of increment is delayed in practically every one of the territories of India. The enrolment is subject to ladies instructors.

The assumption is still to accomplish. Subsequently, foundation of higher instructive establishments for ladies particularly in country regions are as yet in deficiency and ladies enrolment is still low as thought about men enrolment. The discipline-wise examination may likewise be finished. At long last, in the twenty first century as advanced education is vital for the social, financial, and political improvement of India, it must be given first concern to contend with different nations. Indian colleges produce the best cycle directors, who additionally show profound social, social and environmental affectability, and they can be the synergistic pioneers and capable residents. Indeed, the Indian alumni of today isn't just a fantastic human asset yet additionally an excellent person.

References

1. All India Study on Advanced education, MHRD, Govt. of India: www.aishe.gov.in
2. Census of India. Temporary Tables, Paper 2, Office of the Enlistment center General and Registration Commission, India, New Delhi 2011.
3. Desai, A.S. Ladies in advanced education and public turn of events, College News, AIU, 1999 Vol. 39, No. 9.
4. Dukkipati, Uttara. Advanced education in India : supporting long haul development, South Asia screen, 2010, 141, 01.
5. Educational Insights initially 2014, MHRD, Administration of India.
6. Everitt, Brian. Bunch examination. Chichester, West Sussex, U.K: Wiley 2011.
7. Ghara, T.K. Arrangement of the Provinces of India dependent on advanced education improvement markers, Diary of Exploration and Strategy in Training, 2016, Vol. 6, No. 6, pp. 65-70.
8. Ghara, T.K. Positioning of the Provinces of India dependent on advanced education improvement markers, The Global Diary of Humanities and Social Examinations, 2016, Vol. 4, No. 6, pp. 1-5.
9. Global Instruction Observing Report. The Training for All Advancement Record 2015.
10. Gupta, Deepti and Gupta, Navneet. Advanced education in India: Design, Insights and Difficulties, 2012, Vol. 3, No. 2, pp. 17-24.
11. Gupta, N.L. Women's schooling through ages, Ideas Publications Co., New Delhi.
12. Kumar, J. furthermore, Sangeeta 2013. Status of ladies schooling in India, Educationia Confab, 2003, Vol. 2, No. 4, pp. 162-176.
13. MHRD Report on advanced education in India-2009-2010.
14. Nath, S. Advanced education and Ladies support in India, Diary of Business. Executives and Sociologies Exploration, 2014, Vol. 3, No. 2, pp. 43-47.
15. Raju, S. Sexual orientation differentials in admittance to advanced education in India - issues related to development, comprehensiveness, quality and money, College Awards Commission, New Delhi, 2008.
16. Rao, R.K. Ladies and Schooling, Kalpaz Publications, Delhi 2001.

35

Local Education System Different Languages - Different Subjects

Dr Nandavaram Mridula

Introduction

Education ranks first among many factors that determine the superiority of a nation. It is a written or unwritten education that has been handed down and shows the human intelligence. Education is the only thing that drives a man after family. The stronger this education is, the more human life will be enriched.

1. School Education: In order for higher education to be strong, the foundations must first be strong.

As India is a major industrial country, our education system should be designed with this background in mind. 'Education' should not be designed in such a way as to destroy our roots.

- Be an uneducated user
- The cleverness of Jadivina Sadasadviveka is the best
- Jaduvaga valayunu people
- Father of Jadivumu in Jadivincheda Naryu (Bhagavatam Saptama Skandham 130)

Hiranyakashipu himself said the greatness of education. He said that the ultimate quality of that study is Sadasadviveka Chatura. He went to the Aryans and asked them to read.

2. Role of Government: Education and Medicine - these two should always be in the hands of the Government. If you want to send it to someone else, it should go to the hands of people who have a sense of service and not to those who have business ideology. There are two ways to choose.

2.1 Normal Schools

2.2 Gurukula Schools

2.1 Normal Schools: Upto fifth standard students have to go to school every day from home. Then family bonds and kinships are taught.

2.2 Gurukula Schools: Gurukula education should be provided from sixth standard onwards. Then the students will receive world knowledge and subject knowledge completely.

3. Level of Teaching: We can distinguish the students into certain groups on the basis of their age and maturity.

3.1 Anganwadi: Children below 5 years

3.2 1st to 3rd class

3.3 From 4th to 5th class

3.4 From 6th to 7th class

3.5 From 8th to 10th class

3.6 From 11th to 12th class

3.7 Degree Education

3.1 Anganwadi: Anganwadi centers are run by the government till children reach five years of age. Lower middle class families are using them. These can be further strengthened and food distribution centers can be taught in the local language i.e. Telugu, songs, poems, English, Hindi words and numbers.

3.2 From 1st to 3rd class: Short lessons in Telugu English Hindi languages should be prepared in one book (various subjects General Social Mathematics).

3.3 From 4th to 5th class: Teaching of literature, grammar, general, social and mathematics of the respective languages should be done in Telugu English Hindi languages.

3.4 From 6th to 7th class: Besides literature, grammar, other sciences in Telugu, English Hindi languages, other local language - Urdu should be introduced.

3.5 Class 8 to 10: Southern language (Kannada/Tamil/Malayalam) should be introduced by teaching same syllabus as taught in class above. Language skills and the culture they provide should be imparted to the students by providing them little by little without cramming the material at the school level.

3.6 Class 11 to 12: Our government tries to integrate intermediate education into school education so we can recognize class 11-12 as higher school. If the textbooks in these classes are designed as school level textbooks, it can be assumed that the students will have a complete understanding of the subjects of the respective languages.

3.7 Degree Education: Language requirements also change with changing times. We have to hold on to the universality of language and adapt to change. When a degree level student completes his studies and expresses himself in the society, he is mainly recognised through language. Reason why interview plays prominent role in job placement.

A student who enters degree education and completes it should face anything in the society. Should be able to fully understand society and family. Hence a degree is the minimum education for all higher level appointments, groups, civils, etc. Therefore, by this stage the student should have a complete understanding of all the subjects. We should design our curriculum accordingly.

3.7.1 Syllabus: It would be good if the syllabus is prepared at this stage as followed in intermediate education.

3.7.1.1 First Year:

- Telugu Literature - Grammar/Economics/Biology
- English Literature - Grammar/Political Science/Mathematics
- Hindi Literature - Grammar/History/Chemistry
- Southern Language - Kannada - Vernacular - Urdu - Ancient Language - Sanskrit.
- Curriculum and grammar should be designed according to the needs and level of students in these three languages.

3.7.1.2 Second year: Syllabus should be designed as above. The curriculum should be taught in the second year as well as in the first year.

3.7.1.3 Third year:- Foreign languages such as Russian, French, Spanish, Arabic can also be introduced keeping in mind the desire of the students.

Apart from education policy formulation there are some other important aspects.

(i) Time Limit

The government is thinking of moving degree education from three years to four years which is something to think about further. Young people in developing countries like India need to complete their studies quickly and get certificates. Intermediate two years, PG two years and degree, four years may not suit the youth of our country. Since 2015,

UG is being offered on semester basis. Being a major agricultural country, our students are able to complete their studies only in year-wise system. Apart from education policy formulation there are some other important aspects.

(ii) Test Procedure

Question paper making is as important as syllabus making. As per UGC norms a degree student has to secure 20 marks through internals and 80 marks through question paper. But the herd marks may be of better quality due to the three-hour system. This policy should be reviewed.

(iii) Question Paper

Creativity in students should be tested through investigative focus. Grammar should be given equal importance.

(iv) Evaluation Procedure

Evaluation should be done with a thorough consideration of scientific aspects while taking linguistic errors seriously.

(v) Teaching Staff

There should be adequate teaching staff to do full justice to the syllabus. There should be a clear division of labour. We studied the calculations of these four elements 'Time - Work - People - Speed' as children. We have to apply them here.

Results

1. From school level to degree, if textbooks are designed on the basis of 'different languages - different subjects', there will be no difference between Telugu medium and English medium.
2. A person's knowledge of several languages gives him confidence. Life skills increase and literary creation increases.
3. Cultural life flourishes.
4. P.G. One can easily understand the medium of English in universities when going to the level. Can read many books.
5. The student is well equipped in all aspects (study, job).
6. All the employees will be ready to work anywhere if there is same educational system in all the state (nation) irrespective of whether they are urban or rural students.

If this system is introduced experimentally in one or two areas and further improvements are made, we will be the ones who have paved the original paths for golden Telangana and even India.

References

1. Umamaheswara Rao, Garapati. 2017. Language crisis in Telugu states. Telugujati Publication - Vijayawada - Andhra Pradesh.
2. Krishnarao, Satthiraja. First Edition 1954, Second Edition 2009, Telugu - Methodology. Good book - Hyderabad.
3. Chandrasekhar, P. (Sampa) 2006. Telugu Language Structure, Style. Distance Education Center P.S.T.V.- Hyderabad. 4. Problems of Teaching Telugu - Solutions.
5. Narasinga Reddy, V.C. (Sampa) March 2006. Issue: I Volume: I 'Bhasha' International Journal of Telugu Linguistics - Forum of Telugu Linguists, Hyderabad.
6. Potana, Bammera. Potana Bhagavatam 2006. Ramakrishna Math - Hyderabad. Chekuri Rama Rao Language Construction Essays Om Sri Devi Hyderabad Vagari First Edition 1963, Second Edition 201, Hots and Letters Hyderabad.

36

Innovation in Higher Education System in India

Dr I. Sandhya Jyotsna

Abstract

Higher education in India is suffering from less competition and appropriate culture and as a result, quality researches are not done. Indian higher education has very rich history, but present does not seem to be effective. Quantitative growth is very good, but qualitative aspect seems to be missing. To work on this issue, Yashpal Committee has done good research and has shown problems and recommendations for uplifting the standard of higher education. This article is focusing on the track of barriers of higher education and its recommendations. It is a well acknowledged fact that Research plays an important role in the economic growth of a country. Research refers to a creative work which is undertaken to in a systematic manner so as to increase one's stock of knowledge. In the context of education, it would refer to solving educational problems in a scientific and systematic way. The research scene in India is a chequered one, while the prestigious institutions and institutions of national importance are excelling in research, the mediocre and poor ones are lacking in the same. The Indian Government has taken a number of steps to promote research. The significance of research arises from its promotion of creative thinking; finding solutions to impending problems in a methodical, scientific and well-determined way; promoting further studies in the area of interest and keeping abreast with the latest developments in the selected field of study. Indian system of education is characterised by a number of constraints and research is one of the main ones. Carrying out Research in India has a number of challenges such as absence of intellectual stimulation, emphasis on rote learning, lack of scientific theory and base, inadequate data, lack of scientific knowledge, and training in Research Methodology. In the globalised world it is imperative to have knowledge driven growth powered by innovation. A number of steps could be implemented to foster research such as industry-academia collaboration, development of vocational skills, provision of more funds and inclusion of research as a criterion for faculty promotion. India has a well-acclaimed Brain Power and promotion Research will only help India move up the global intellectual ladder.

Keywords: Education Research; Industry-Academia Collaboration; Research Bodies.

Introduction

Research plays an important role in the economic development of any country. In fact, research and development form the basis of future competitiveness of an economy. Unfortunately, research in India is showing a downward trend. In this Paper an attempt has been made to discuss the concept of research, examine the importance of research, briefly touch on the research scene in India, look into the challenges and attempt to predict the future.

Objectives of the Study

The study is based on the following objectives:

1. To understand the meaning of research particularly research in education.
2. To get preliminary information on the research scene in India, and
3. To discuss the challenges facing research and throw light on what augurs for the future.

Concept of Research

Research refers to creative work which is undertaken systematically, in order to increase the stock of knowledge of individuals, culture and society and further utilise this stock to devise new applications. In the broad sense, it covers gathering of any data, information and facts for the advancement of knowledge.

Innovation can be considered as the key player of economic growth and subsequent improvement in the quality of living. In this century, there is no doubt about the fact that India has the capability of spearheading global innovation, but the big question that emerges is will Indian higher education support this potential? The entire issue warrants a careful discussion.

Research in education refers to solving educational problems in a systematic and scientific manner and also to understand, explain and predict human behaviour in a more organised way.

Research in India

Education is a prime mover of the society. In order to favourably utilise our demographic potential, the quality of education together with access and equity gathers significance. India has the third largest system of higher education. The overall scenario is that, quality does not match the global standards and there is increased scope and urgency for improving the quality of our country's educational institutions.

The research scenario in India portrays a chequered picture. While some leading world class institutions like the IITs and the IIMs are achieving what was well planned in their objectives others portray a dismal picture in terms of quality and quantity of research.

The first Prime Minister of independent India, Shri Jawaharlal Nehru, believed in the importance of science and education which would facilitate a path of innovations, which in turn would help in the process of development.

Generally India has evolved a large number of high quality research institutions which would provide valuable advice to the policy makers. The institutional framework for research and development can be divided into two broad categories: defence and civilian.

The five apex bodies which are responsible for research and development are:

(a) Indian Council of Medical Research; It is the apex body for the formulation, coordination and promotion of bio medical research.

(b) Indian Council of Agricultural Research; an autonomous body which coordinates guides and manages research and education in agriculture including horticulture, fisheries and animal sciences.

(c) Indian Council for Social Science Research; It was established in 1969 by the Government of India to promote research in social sciences.

(d) Council of Scientific and Industrial Research; It was established in 1942 as an autonomous body and India's largest Research and Development organisation. Its activities include various fields like aero - space engineering, structural engineering, life sciences, environment etc.

(e) Tata Institute of Fundamental Research. It is a Research institution in Mumbai dedicated to basic research in Mathematics and sciences.

India attracts more Research and Development facilities from the US multinationals in the Fortune 500 than any other nation. This could be primarily attributed to the large number of science and engineering PhDs available in the country.

The government wants to increase the spending on Research and Development under the twelfth five year plan (2012-2017) from 0.9 percent to two percent. However, when a comparison is made with other countries India presents a poor picture. In our country there are 119 researchers per million population as against 5287 in Japan and 4484 in United States. She has a little over 6000 Doctorates in Science as compared to 9000 in China and 25,000 in United States.

Most of the Indian colleges and universities lack high end research facilities. The number of PhDs produced every year is very low.

The Government of India has taken several steps to promote the Research and Development sector in India, as mentioned in the Union Budget of 2014-15. Two additional Research Institutes of excellence were set up in Assam and Jharkhand with an initial sum of Rupees 100 crores. In addition the government plans to establish a national level research and referral institute for higher dental studies.

The following are a few examples of recent investments:

1. French tyre manufacturer Michelin is planning to set up an R&D sector in India. This facility was set up in Gurgaon, which will be first of its kind in developing country;
2. Sandwik announced the proposal for the setting up of a world class facility at Chakan which is part of the Maharashtra Industrial Development Corporation Park near Pune;
3. Valvoline Cummins Ltd (VCL), a joint venture between Ashland Inc. and Cummins India Ltd has announced the opening of new labs for Research and Development and Product Development along with a training facility at Lexington, Kentucky, USA.

Importance of Research

Let us discuss the significance of Research:

One, our knowledge is limited and a number of problems need to be solved in different fields of study. Very often we identify a vacuum in our knowledge and try to address it by asking related questions. Research through systematic study makes available a variety of methods which help in finding solutions.

Two, research is regarded as an objective, methodical, well-determined scientific method of investigation. Through research a stock of the current scenario can be taken and this will guide the organisations in their decision taking of the future.

Three, we carry out our mundane daily tasks on the basis of our common sense. However, this may not be the correct approach. We will have to find out what is the best under the current situations and research serves this task the best.

Four, another angle of research is that it helps to gather information. The findings can be recorded and then analyzed to judge the validity of the information.

Five, Research is a systematic investigator into and study of materials and sources. It helps to pursue your interests, learn something new, hone your problem solving skills and come out with results that can contribute to enhancement of knowledge.

In this world of Information and Communication Technology lack of infrastructure and poor quality of digital content are grounds for concern. For making a healthy ICT environment, digitized PhD thesis, e-journals, research journals, e-books etc have to be developed.

It is vital that educational institutions establish a Research Consultancy culture involving faculty, students, professionals and industry to work on a few technologies and facilitate discovery.

Research should be the core area instrumental for inter-face between the academic and corporate world. It must provide a theoretical framework that enables reassessment and refinement of current practices and thinking.

It empowers the faculty with in depth knowledge and instills a sense of curiosity among them. In addition it improves the consultancy capabilities of the faculty.

Challenges for Research in India

The Indian system of higher education has been facing a number of challenges. It requires major investments so as to make human resources productive, by coupling the older general disciplines of humanities, social sciences, natural sciences and commerce, with their applications in the new economy and having adequate field base experience to enhance knowledge with skills and develop appropriate attitudes.

There are several basic problems facing Indian higher education at present. They include inadequate infrastructural facilities; faculty crunch;

low enrolment ratio; over-crowded classrooms; widespread geographical income, gender and ethnic imbalances etc.

India has a low base of researchers and the academic sector contributes less than 14 percent of the total number of researchers. The immediate need in this context would be, to encourage industry-academia collaborations, promote collaborations between the universities and the public authorities as also between the government and Research and Development laboratories and also increase the number and quality of doctoral students.

The Indian education system promotes rote learning and students only use prescribed materials. This trend continues even when pursuing higher education. The examinations are more a test of memory power rather than creativity. When the stage comes to pursue further studies and present research papers, they portray a dismal picture hampering the research process associated with higher education.

As the students are deprived of intellectual stimulation fostered by research, they fall short of invaluable knowledge and skills which are not only important in their careers but also in other areas of life. Even the number of students pursuing research is limited by want of time, and support. The result being them ending up intimidated, confused and frustrated.

One of the main impediments is lack of scientific theory. Many of the researchers are incapable of carrying out sound empirical work; data is often inadequate and even when available not availed of; in addition the problem of bureaucratic inertia is always plaguing the system.

Often there is lack of scientific knowledge and training in Research Methodology. Many of our researchers and guides are not competent enough to carry out sound empirical work.

The following factors can be said to be encouraging good research:

1. A conducive academic environment of the institutions/universities;
2. A well-stocked library and Reference section covering books, e-books, journals, online library etc;
3. Provision of adequate infrastructural facility
4. Existence of Research laboratories having the latest equipments; Availability of adequate finance for purchase of funds;
5. Combining teaching and research related activity in the work profile of the Professors;
6. Instilling a feeling of pride and purposefulness among teachers that their major task is to transformation of the economy.

Future of Research in India

One of the great economists and Nobel Prize laureate, Milton Friedman (Consultant to Ministry of Finance –Government of India -1955), said, "The great untapped resource of technical and scientific knowledge available to India for the taking is the economic equivalent of the untapped commitment available to the US 150 years back".

In the increasingly competitive global economy, it is necessary to have knowledge driven growth powered by innovations. The key to continued success for India is building up of a higher education system which is superior in quality and which encourages research.

Very often, it is the industry which is the beneficiary of several research efforts and therefore interactions between industry and research establishments is important.

In the current age where issues of research are often of global nature active interaction with international institutions of repute must be encouraged.

Vocational skills should be emphasized. Vocational training will play a crucial role preparing the workforce to be productively used to propel the growth process of the economy. There are emerging interest in linking skills and higher education sector.

While creating an enabling environment, note should be made of reducing the teaching hours, greater financial support and providing access to better infrastructure. Awarding of fellowships and encouraging industry collaborations will promote research.

Research can be promoted by following certain guidelines such as inclusion of research as a criterion for faculty for the purpose of promotion, (a system laid down by UGC and is currently been followed by affiliated colleges and universities); institution of awards for distinguished researchers with substantial financial incentives; generation of greater funding; improvement of infrastructure; and possible reduction of teaching hours so that more time can be devoted to research. India has all the potential of being a research hub given her long tradition of teaching and renowned Brain Power. The impediments have to tackled so as to easy the path to economic prosperity.

Conclusion

Research as we have seen plays an important role in the economic development of a country, more so in case of a developing country like India. We face a number of constraints, in the form of ill-stocked libraries, absence of well-equipped laboratories, lack of adequate finance, government intervention etc. In view of the fact that we possess a universally acknowledged Brain Power, the need of the hour is for innovations and inventions. India prides itself in producing Nobel Laureates of Indian origin. The innate talents of our researchers have to be nurtured and fostered to make a mark in the international arena. All this calls for greater financial support, right policy mix together with working on finding solutions to the impairing problems plaguing the Indian society, if we have to be seen as a major player in the global world.

References

1. Chakrabarti, Alok (2007): "The Higher Education and Research in India: an Overview", Sitra Reports, Helsinki.
2. Chania, Payal, (2012): "Importance of Research", THE HINDU, July, 4.
3. Dr. Mathew, PM: "Research in India needs a major boost" – India Education Review.
4. "Education in India" – Wikipedia the free encyclopedia
5. Everitt, Richard (2014): "Understanding India: The future of higher education and opportunities for international cooperation", British Council, February.
6. "Higher Education in India: Vision 2030, FICCI, Higher Education Summit, 2013.
7. Saxena, Vandana, Kulshetra, Sanjay, and Khan Bali (2010): "Higher and Research in India", International Journal of Research and Technology, Volume 1 (1), June.
8. Singh, JD: "Higher Education in India – Issues, Challenges and Suggestions".
9. "The future of Indian higher education and its impact on Research and innovation", A Report for the UK – India Education Research Initiative, (UKRIER).
10. Varghese, Mariamma, A, (2014): "Indian higher education at a crossroad", DNA, September, 23.
11. India, G.O. (2915, November). Government of India, Ministry of Human Reousrce.... Retrieved from www.education.nic.in/
12. Ponmelil, V. A. (2015, November 6). History of history of Higher Education in India. Retrieved from education.newkerala.com/ Indian Education.

37

The Dalits of India: Higher Education and Development

Dr Enapa Upender Rao

Abstract

Modern education has brought the changes in the social and economic life of the Scheduled Caste community in India. But, all the casted included under the category of Scheduled Caste and women of Scheduled Caste category are not incorporated in the mainstream of higher education. Thus, present study is about the Scheduled Caste and higher education. It mainly studies higher education scenario among Scheduled Caste, constitutional provisions for the educational development of Scheduled Caste and factors influencing higher education status among Scheduled Caste. The castes included under Scheduled Caste category are characterised by extreme social, educational and economic backwardness occurred due to traditional practice of untouchability. Hence certain provisions for the educational and economic development of scheduled castes were incorporated in the Constitution of India which is discussed in the present paper. The data about literacy and higher education enrolment among Scheduled Caste students in India is showing positive trend but the increase in Gross Enrolment Ratio is gradual. As well as it can be reflected that enrolment in the higher education is lower compare to primary and secondary level of education. The factor influencing higher education includes adverse economic condition, family background, discrimination in higher education, Language, government provisions, or facility, reservation policy, privatisation, gender disparities, syllabus/curriculum etc. which discussed in detail in the present paper.

Keywords: *Scheduled Caste, Higher Education, Constitutional Provisions, Gross Enrolment Ratio.*

Introduction

Introduction Scheduled Castes and Scheduled Tribes have been identified as the two most backward groups of Indian Society. They include all such castes, races or tribes, which have been declared as scheduled castes and scheduled tribes by the Constitution of India under the provisions of Article 341 and 342 of the Constitution of India. Scheduled Castes generally represent those communities, which have suffered from the stigma of untouchability in one form or the other. Scheduled Tribes are generally those who have been living in seclusion in hills and forests, more or less untouched by modern civilisation and development. Scheduled Castes constitute about 15 percent of the total population of the country while Scheduled Tribes constitute about 7.5 percent of the total Indian Population. Thus, together, these groups constitute a little more than one-fifth of the total population of the country.

This is true for almost every institution in India. On a daily basis, students from SC, ST, and OBC communities face discrimination in these educational places on various levels. The caste and class hegemony in the educational, political, social, and economical spaces by the upper-caste is prominent across the country. Even after controlling most of the spaces and resources of the country, this Supreme Court statement about reservation is quite funny and ironical. From an undergraduate student in Delhi University to a Masters student at IIT Gandhinagar, my experience has taught me that these educational spaces are casteist and elitist, and are controlled by upper castes. These places are more casteist than my village in Bihar.

SC, ST, OBC data from Educational Institutions

Even 12 years after the implementation of OBC reservation for faculty members, there is not a single professor from the community in most of the 40 central universities in India. According to data presented by Education Minister Ramesh Pokhriyal Nishank in the Rajya Sabha, in Indian Institute of Science (IISc) Bengaluru, only 2.1 percent candidates admitted to the PhD programmes were from the ST category, 9 percent were from SC and 8 percent from OBC categories from 2016-2020. And it was the same for integrated PhD programmes: 9 percent of the total admitted candidates were from SC category, 1.2 percent from ST and 5 percent from OBC categories.

In the 17 Indian Institutes of Information Technology (IIITs), 1.7 percent of total PhD candidates were from ST category, 9 percent from SC and 27.4 percent from OBC. These trends are similar or even worse in other institutes like NITs and IISERs. Even after getting admission, it is challenging for students from the reserved category to continue the course. If you see the dropout trends from these premium educational institutions, the majority of the students will be from SC/ST/ OBC categories.

In 2019, Ramesh Pokhriyal Nishank, in a written reply to the Parliament, said that 48 percent of students dropping out of the IITs and over 62.6 percent from IIMs are from the SC, ST and OBC categories. If we look at faculty data in these institutions from reserved categories, the representation is minuscule. According to data by the education ministry, presented in 2019 in Lok Sabha, out of 6,043 faculty members at the 23 IITs, 149 were SCs and 21 were STs — they made up less than 3 percent of the total number of faculty members.

Most of the IITs do not have a single professor from the SC/ST community

The educational system is captured by the upper caste in such a way that it is very difficult for people from reserved categories to invade and make their space. Editors and series editors of reputed journals and big publishing houses, professors, vice-chancellors, director, deans, non-teaching staff — the gatekeepers of the caste system are everywhere to stop the growth of SCs, STs and OBCs.

The Gross Enrolment Ratio (GER) of SC and ST students at the undergraduate level, which stands at 23 percent and 17.2 percent respectively, is unsatisfactory — both numbers being short of the national average of 26.3 percent. These undergraduates are aiming to cross the seas to develop their skills and be part of new ideas, research and innovation. If every deserving child gets the desired support, imagine how much talent and energy will be added to the engine of India's new growth story. This cannot happen through people's charity. It is the duty of the State.

Conclusion

The exclusionary policies in these educational spaces lead the reserved category students to drop out of the educational institutes. The discrimination is so systemic and institutionalised that it is tough for students from reserved categories to survive and continue their academic passion. For instance, if look at subaltern studies, most of the academicians who have made a niche for themselves are upper caste. If we analyse these things through the lens of Edward W. Said's seminal book Orientalism, we can understand more about the discourse relating to upper caste vs the other caste in India, just like the debate of elite vs non-elite and occidental's vs orients.

References

1. Chatterjee, S. K., (2008). 'The Scheduled Castes In India', Gyan Publishing House, New Delhi, pp. 514-523.
2. Chouhan, P.(2013). A study on literacy and education attainment of Scheduled Castes population in Maldah district of West Bengal, India, Journal of Geography and Regional Planning, Vol. 6(1).
3. Education, Volume, pp. 589-594, Oxforf: Elsevier.
4. George, S. andNaseem D.(2010). Hostel Schemes for Dalit Students : How Inclusive and Incentive for Higher Education, Indian Institute of Dalit Studies, working Paper, Volume IV.
5. J. B. G. Tilak. How free is 'free' primary education in India, Economic Political Weekly, February 10,1996. 10 Chouhan, P.(2013), A study on literacy and education attainment of Scheduled Castes population in Maldah district of West Bengal.
6. Kakade S., (2012). 'Amazing Development of Scheduled Castes in Maharashtra', Indian Journal of Economic and Political weekly.
7. Nambissan and S. Srinivasa Rao (Eds.). Sociology of Education in India: Changing Contours and emerging concerns.
8. Nambissan and S. Srinivasa Rao (Eds.). Sociology of Education in India: Changing Contours and emerging concerns.
9. Oxford Univ. Bhatty, K, Educational deprivation in India: A survey of field investigations, Economic amd Political weekly, 1998. Oxford University Press.
10. Position Paper of National Focus Group on Problems of Scheduled Caste and Scheduled Tribe Children by NCERT, New Delhi, 2010.
11. Students of Cuttack Municipality Corporation, Orissa , Journal of Social Science, 10(3), pp. 215-222, 2005.
12. Thorat, S., Senapati, C., (2007). 'Reservation in Employment, Education and Legislature - Status and Emerging Issues'.
13. Wankhede, G. (2013). Caste and Social Discrimination: Nature, forms and consequences in Education, in Geeta.
14. Wankhede, G., (2010). Caste and Education in India, in Peterson-Baker-McGraw (Ed.)International Encyclopedia of Education.
15. Weisskopf, T., Impact of Reservation on admissions to higher education in India, Economic Political weekly, Sep. 25.
16. West Bengal, India, Journal of geography and Regional Planning, Vol. 6(1), pp. 19-30.
17. Acharya T. and Behera D., Factors influencing the educational achievements of the scheduled caste and General caste.
18. Working paper series, Vol. II, Number 05, Indian Institute of Dalit Studies, New Delhi, pp. 4-5.

38

Higher Education Challenges in the Twenty first Century

Dr M. Krishna Kumar

Abstract

The model presented in this paper sets forth a view of the relevance of higher education in the twenty first century that begins from the changes that are taking place in the production of knowledge. The organisation of this model is designed to draw attention to the fact that for the most part universities are organised according to the structures of disciplinary Social science, and that these structures are being altered by social forces. The major change has been the emergence of a distributed knowledge production system within which knowledge is characterised by new attributes. The main change as far as universities are concerned is that knowledge production and dissemination (research and teaching) are no longer self-contained quasi-monopolistic activities carried out in relative institutional isolation. The real challenge for universities will be the training of knowledge workers. The research practices of universities and those of other knowledge producers are drawing closer. Knowledge is less likely to be produced where it will be needed, and universities must make use of intellectual resources they do not own fully so that they can interact effectively with the distributed knowledge production system. Universities of the 21st century will develop more and different kinds of links with surrounding society.

Keywords: Educational Change, Futures, UGC, GER, Higher Education Models, Relevance Education, Social Influences.

Introduction

As higher education systems grow and diversify, society is increasingly concerned about the quality of programmes, public assessments and international rankings of higher education institutions. However, these comparisons tend to overemphasise research, using research performance as a yardstick of institutional value. If these processes fail to address the quality of teaching, it is in part because measuring teaching quality is challenging.[1]

India's higher education is managed by the University Grants Commission (UGC) and the various councils. The UGC, set up under UGC Act 1956, has been empowered to promote and coordinate university education in India and also approve grants to them. The UGC is responsible for coordination, determination, and maintenance of standards and release of grants to universities and research organisations. Various professional councils are responsible for recognition of courses, promotion of professional institutions and provision of grants to undergraduate programmes. In the last six decades, the higher education sector in India has witnessed exponential growth, both in terms of the number of institutions and the rate of enrolment. Nalanda University is one of the world's oldest universities established in India and created history in the higher education system. Since then, India has a strong tradition of higher education. Secular education with an emphasis on scientific inquiry had come to India only with the British. In fact, the first college imparting western education in India was set up in semaphore in Bengal in 1818. The social reform movement of the eighteenth century also accelerated the process of setting up modern universities and colleges. In 1857, the three universities in Calcutta, Bombay and Madras were set up, with 27 colleges affiliated to them. Subsequently more universities and colleges were set up. In 1947 there were 19 universities in India. There has been a rapid rate of increase and in the following years, precisely, by March 2022, On the basis of management, the universities are classified as: exist in 28 states of India as well as three of the union territories: Chandigarh, Delhi and Pondicherry. The state with the most universities is Rajasthan with 74 universities. Gujarat and Uttar Pradesh have the most state universities, 28 each. Rajasthan has by far the most private universities, five in numbers. Uttar Pradesh has five central universities and Delhi has five Central Universities, the largest number of all the states and territories, Central universities 54, State University 443, Deemed University 126, and Private University 403 all universities state central private and deemed 1026 and 46,240 Colleges were constituted in India[2]. India's higher education system is the world's third largest in terms of students, next to China and the United States. Unlike China, however, India has the advantage of English being the primary language of higher education and research. India educates approximately 11 percent of its youth in higher education as compared to 20 percent in China[3]. The main governing body at the tertiary level is the UGC (University Grants Commission) in India, which enforces its standards, advises the government, and helps coordinate between the centre and the state. Universities and its constituent colleges are the main institutes of higher education in India. Gross Enrolment Ratio (GER) in Higher education in India is 27.1, which is calculated for 18-23 years of age group. GER for male population is 26.9 and for female, it is 27.3. For Scheduled Castes, it is 23.4 and for Scheduled Tribes, it is 18.0 as compared to the national GER of 27[4].

The model presented in this paper presents a view of the relevance of higher education in the twenty first century that begins from the changes that are taking place in the production of Knowledge. The aim is to draw attention to the fact that for the most part universities are organised according to the structures of disciplinary science and that these structures are changing. The major change is the emergence of a distributed knowledge production system within this system knowledge is characterised by a set of attributes that we have labelled. The main change, as far as universities are concerned, is that knowledge production and Dissemination — research and teaching — are no longer self-contained activities, carried out in relative institutional isolation. They now involve interaction with a variety of other knowledge producers. In this situation, connections will increasingly involve the use of the potentialities of the new information and communication technologies.The research practices of universities and industry, as well as other knowledge producers, are drawing closer together. All are now, in effect, actors in the knowledge business. The fact of globalisation means that for each actor, the bulk of the knowledge to which access is required will have been produced elsewhere. Over 90 percent of the knowledge produced globally is not produced where its use is required.

The challenge is how to get knowledge that may have been produced anywhere in the world to the place where it can be used effectively in a particular problem-solving context.

Universities have been far more adept at producing knowledge than at drawing creatively (re-configuring) knowledge that is being produced in the distributed knowledge production system. It remains an open question at this time whether they can make the necessary institutional adjustments to become as competent in the latter as they have been in the former. This requires the creation of a cadre of knowledge workers—people who are expert at configuring knowledge relevant to a wide range of contexts. This new corps of workers is described in the text as problem identifiers, problem solvers, and problem brokers. The shift from knowledge production to knowledge configuration is a challenge that is particularly acute for the universities of the developing world.

In order to operate efficiently, universities will need to be much reduced in size, and they will have to learn to make use of intellectual resources that they don't fully control. This is the only way that they will be able to interact effectively with the distributed knowledge production system and with the progressive differentiation of supply and demand for specialised knowledge. Universities in the future will comprise a small core of faculty and much larger periphery of experts of various kinds that are linked to universities in diverse ways. Universities will become a new type of "holding institution" in the field of knowledge production. Perhaps their role will be limited to accrediting teaching done primarily by others while, in research, playing their part by orchestrating problem-solving teams to work on fundamental issues.

Both students and staff realise that their personal success lies in being able to find a niche in the emerging knowledge society. The problem is that in neither teaching nor research do the universities have this turf to themselves. And here lies a threat to the conventional way of doing things. Or is it, perhaps, an opportunity?

During the past twenty years, a new paradigm of the function of higher education in society has gradually emerged. Gone, it seems, is the high-mindedness of a von Humboldt or a Newman' with its pursuit of knowledge for its own sake. In their places has been put a view of higher education in which universities are meant to serve society, primarily by supporting the economy and promoting the quality of life of its citizens. While it is true that universities still retain their role as the "conscience of society," the critical function of universities has been displaced in favour of a more pragmatic role in terms of the provision of qualified manpower and the production of knowledge. These changes are not notional. Rather, they are intended to have direct practical impact on the behaviour and functioning of higher education institutions. The new paradigm is bringing in its train a new culture of accountability as is evidenced by the spread of managerialism and an ethos of value for money throughout higher education systems internationally.

Some Basic Assumptions

The first assumption of this paper is that the new economically-oriented paradigm is not going to be replaced and that the trend towards increasing accountability will not be reversed. In all countries, developed or developing, the culture of accountability is going to become more and more firmly established. Not only will higher education in the twenty first century have to become relevant, but also that relevance will be judged primarily in terms of outputs, the contribution that higher education makes to national economic performance and, through that, to the enhancement of the quality of life. Though arguments of varying weight and coherence that point out the limitations of this pragmatic approach may be expected to come from all sides, it is further assumed, here, that no other rationale or justification will carry equivalent weight. Relevance is going to become something that will need to be demonstrated, not just once but on an ongoing basis. Economic imperatives will sweep all before it and "if the universities do not adapt, they will be by-passed.[5]

In a dynamic environment, of course, change is not a once for all event. Rather, it is a series of more or less continuous adaptations to changes in the environment. Though these adaptations may be local and vary considerably in magnitude, change will be continuous and each innovation will be judged in terms of its "contribution" to overall economic performance. Over time, then, it is to be expected that "relevance" in general will be translated into a nest of performance objectives related to teaching quality and research performance, among others. Each will make its contribution to, and be shaped by, the "culture of accountability" that is already evident internationally across so much of the institutional scene.

In this paper, we will consider the implications for change in higher education systems that derive from shifts in certain demand and supply factors. To set the stage for considering these changes, the paper begins by discussing the attributes of a new mode of knowledge production. This will provide a framework for examining, first, the history of the massification of higher education and, second, the nature of competitiveness in a globalising economy. The key empirical changes to examine, here, are diversification of higher education institutions in terms of mission statements, operating procedures, and clients.

The Emergence of a New Mode of Knowledge Production

It is worth recalling at the outset that it is only recently that universities have organised themselves to conduct research. Although individual research activities can be found in universities going back to the Nineteenth Century and even earlier, it is really only since the end of World War II that research — particularly basic research — was taken up by universities and became one of their core values. Throughout the Twentieth Century, universities have systematically developed structures that allowed them to add the function of generating new knowledge to their previous ones of preserving knowledge and transmitting it.

Some Attributes of Knowledge Production. In the previous paragraphs, the characteristics were presented in outline form. Five attributes were identified:

1. Knowledge produced in the context of application
2. Transdisciplinarity
3. Heterogeneity and organisational diversity
4. Enhanced social accountability
5. More broadly based system of quality control.

1. Knowledge Produced in the Context of Application

The relevant contrast here is between problem-solving which is carried out following the codes of practice relevant to a particular discipline and problem-solving which is organised around a particular application. In the former, the context is defined in relation to the cognitive and social norms that govern basic research or academic science. Latterly, this has tended to imply knowledge production carried out in the absence of some practical goal. In Mode 2, by contrast, knowledge results from a broader range of considerations. Such knowledge is intended to be useful to someone whether in industry or government, or society more generally. This imperative is present from the beginning. Knowledge thus produced is always produced under an aspect of continuous negotiation, i.e., it will not be produced unless and until the interests of the various actors are included.[6]

2. Transdisciplinary

Mode 2 does more than assemble a diverse range of specialists to work in teams on problems in a complex applications oriented environment. To qualify as a specific form of knowledge production it is essential that inquiry be guided by discernible consensus as to appropriate cognitive and social practice. In Mode 2, the consensus is conditioned by the context of application and evolves with it.The determinants of a potential solution involve the integration of different skills in a framework of action, but the consensus may be only temporary depending on how well it conforms to the requirements set by the specific context of application. In Mode 2 the shape of the final solution will normally be beyond that of any single contributing discipline. It will be transdisciplinary.

3. Heterogeneity and Organisational Diversity

Mode 2 knowledge production is heterogeneous in terms of the skills and experience people bring to it. The composition of a problem-solving team changes over time as requirements evolve. This is not planned or coordinated by any central body. As with Mode 1, challenging problems emerge, if not randomly, then in a way which makes their anticipation very difficult.

4. Social Accountability and Reflexivity

In recent years, growing public concern about issues to do with the environment, health, communications, privacy, procreation, and so forth, have had the effect of stimulating the expansion of knowledge production. Growing awareness about the variety of ways in which advances in science and technology can affect the public interest has increased the numbers of groups who wish to influence the outcome of the research process.[7]

5. Quality Control

Criteria to assess the quality of the work and of the teams which carry out research in Mode 2 differ from those of more traditional, disciplinary science. Quality in Mode is determined essentially through the peer review judgments about the contributions made by individuals. Control is maintained by careful selection of those judged competent to act as peers, which is in part determined by their previous contributions to their discipline. In this way, the peer review process is one in which quality and control mutually re-enforce one another.[8]

The Changing "Dynamics of Relevance" for Higher Education

Who will be the students in the twenty first century? Who will be the main "consumers" of higher education, and what are they likely to demand? How will labour markets and employment relations be organised (e.g., the growth of independent contractors), and how will these trends affect individual decisions as to what to study and for how long? What are likely to be the most significant trends in the global economy? How are these likely to affect supply and demand for university graduates (and post-graduate degree holders), and what shape is this demand likely to take? Also, what will be the relationship between the tertiary sector and the private sector? Are tertiary institutions likely to become more frequent corporate partners in training and research, or will their institutional independence remain largely uncompromised? To what extent will learning be incorporated into the workplace as an accepted part of one's job responsibility, i.e. the growing integration of work and learning?[9]

Massification of Education and Research: Customers for Higher Education

The development of mass higher education in modern industrial societies after World War exhibited a rapid growth of enrolments, both in absolute numbers and in the proportion of the traditional age cohort. This was preceded or accompanied by a very large increase in the numbers of young people, first from middle and then from lower middle and working class origins, who were enabled or encouraged to stay on in secondary school beyond school leaving age to the age of transfer. Almost everywhere this required a reform of secondary education, and the creation of a comprehensive secondary school in place of or alongside the traditional elite secondary schools.[10]

Patterns of Massification in Higher Education

A profound transformation of knowledge production inside and outside of universities is currently underway, one which both depends on and contributes to the progressive massification of higher education. In this section we will identify major elements of that transformation with a view to highlighting how they are likely to affect knowledge production not only in the sciences and technology, but also in the social sciences and the humanities. Ten shifts have accompanied demassification of higher education as it has taken place in most industrialised countries.

Collegiality, Managerialism and the Fragmentation of Knowledge

Knowledge can no longer be regarded as discrete and coherent, its production defined by clear rules and governed by settled routines. Instead, it has become a mixture of theory and practice, abstraction and aggregation, ideas and data. The boundaries between the intellectual world and its environment have become blurred as hybrid science combines cognitive and non-cognitive elements in novel and creative ways. Similar changes have taken place in the socio-economic order, partly as a result of the impact of technology. Large and rigid organisations have been overlaid by new means of communication and production that are both more fragile and less formal. The impact of this post-industrialism has mirrored and reinforced the drift towards confusion in the intellectual world.

In this, the massification of higher education is a key phenomenon. To understand knowledge it is necessary to understand the institutions in which it is produced. The most important of these institutions remains the university or more accurately, the extended university. But the traditional university engaged primarily in the formation of academic and professional elites and in pure research is now only a small part of the spreading higher education and research systems possessed by most advanced countries.[11]

Globalisation and International Competitiveness

Competitiveness and globalisation involve a double contingency. The first concerns the emergence of a new international division of intellectual labour as a consequence of the fact that, now, many more countries and firms have acquired the capacity to use research and scientific knowledge produced elsewhere. Science has always been the most international of activities. Despite this feature, the actual ability to engage in research is unevenly distributed throughout the world. As with production, scientific research undergoes constant shifts in international competitiveness, with new countries entering and old dominance patterns breaking up — see for example, the growing pre-eminence of India in software design and engineering. There is clearly a relationship between excellence in science, especially basic research, and international competitiveness in production, but the relationship is not linear or direct.

Multidisciplinary and Transdisciplinary

So far, the two factors we have discussed above, the multiplication of knowledge missions by universities and the shift amongst scientists themselves towards the understanding of complex systems, have been primary forces in the explosion of multidisciplinary educational provision. Practically, universities could do little else, being, as they were, home to the disciplines. It was natural that as scientists tried to grapple with complex problems, they constructed curricula which reflected the need for a multidisciplinary perspective. In the past decades, university courses have been hybridized into "something and something", or "something with something." So there emerged, physics and mathematics, biology and economics, and mechanical engineering with French. Each of these curricular developments were meant to meet one of the universities knowledge missions, often by targeting a particular audience or age group. Often, too, an interdisciplinary perspective was intended to provide a particular context for learning a discipline.

Conclusion

In twenty first century educational leader and teacher play positive role and create such environment which will able to cope with issue and challenges, where student will learn by doing. The education system will meet the current demands of students and globalised world, education will be valuable for all students to succeed in both college and career. The presence of India in the global map has a reasonable visibility; however, the country is in the transit state to meet the target and expectations of everyone. The recent government initiatives are welcomed but to be geared at accelerated rate in implementation. There has been a significant and consistent worldwide reform in higher education. India's ability to emerge as a globally competitive country will substantially depend on its knowledge human capital. The presence of vast challenges insists to carefully choose the proven strategies that lead to real and lasting results for success pathway. The study of rapid change in global requirements, issues and opportunities of higher education in India would help us to take necessary steps to face modern, competitive economy. This shall ensure a strong hold of Indians in the global market and make our country to be a developed nation in a short span of time. The challenge is how to get knowledge that may have been produced anywhere in the world to the place where it can be brought to bear effectively in a particular problem-solving context. This requires the creation of a cadre of knowledge workers—people who are expert at configuring knowledge to a wide range of applications. In order to operate efficiently, universities will be much reduced in size, and they will learn to make use of intellectual resources that they don't own fully. This is the only way that they will be able to interact effectively with the distributed knowledge production system.

References

1. Cambrosio, A. et al "Expertise as a network: a case study of the controversies over environmental release of genetically engineered organisms".
2. Chandler, A. D. Scale and Scope: The Dynamics of Industrial Capitalism. Cambridge, MA. Harvard University Press (1990).
3. Galbraith, J. K., the New Industrial State. London: Penguin (1969).
4. "India's per-capita income rises 6.8 percent to Rs 11,254 a month in FY20", Business Today, Jan 2020.
5. Indians are spending enormously on education even with few jobs in sight", Business Insider, Nov 2019.
6. Jandhyala B. G. Tilak. (Ed). (2013). Higher Education in India: In Search of Equality, Quality and Quantity, Publisher: Orient Black Swan Hyderabad.
7. Matkin, G. W. Technology Transfer and the University. London: Macmillan (1990).
8. National Higher Education Policy 2020.
9. National Knowledge Commission Report 2009.
10. NPE 1968: National Policy of Education 1968.

11. Schofield, A. (ed.). Benchmarking in Higher Education: An International Review. London: Commonwealth Higher Education Management Service.
12. Williams, B. The Direct and Indirect Role of Higher Education in Industrial Innovation.
13. www.aicte.in
14. www.epw.org.in
15. www.globaleducation. edna.edu.au
16. www.indiaeducaton.info
17. www.ugc.ac.in

Footnotes

1. Henard, Fabrice, Report, Learning our Lesson: Review of Quality teaching in Higher Education, 2008.
2. https://en.wikipedia.org/wiki/List_of_universities_in_India
3. https://www.educationstalwarts.com/issues-and-challenges-in-higher-education-in-india
4. aishe 2020-20, 21 - Ministry of Education.
5. Chandler, A. D. Scale and Scope: The Dynamics of In dustrial Capitalism. Cambridge.
6. Jandhyala, B. G. Tilak. (Ed). (2013). Higher Education in India: In Search of Equality, Quality and Quantity Publisher, Orient Black Swan Hyderabad.
7. Ibid.
8. Williams, B. The Direct and Indirect Role of Higher Education in Industrial Innovation.
9. UNESCO (2008). Education and the Search for a Sustainable Future, Policy Dialogue 1: ESD and Development Policy, (http://unesdoc.unesco.org/images/0017/001791/179121e.pdf)
10. Ibid.
11. www.epw.org.in

39

Effectiveness of Entrepreneurship Education Programs in the Global Entrepreneurial Culture

V. Radhika

Abstract

Over the past two decades, the number of entrepreneurship education programmes (EEP) has skyrocketed. To confirm the efficacy of EEPs and their presence in the modern world, a systematic review has not yet been done. The primary goal of this work is to offer a systematic synthesis of EEP, investigating its qualities and efficacy. targeting the creation of entrepreneurial skills and company plans. However, both basic and secondary school provide more focus on entrepreneurship skills. The research demonstrated the success of the majority of these initiatives in encouraging entrepreneurial abilities at all educational levels. As a result, there was no evidence of a rise in the intention to launch a business, which is determined by predisposition, namely sociocultural and familial factors. This programme should be established preferably in the early school years, as that is when predispositions for the development of entrepreneurial abilities and intentions are created, according to this systematic review of the EEP. The global geography of the EEP, which shows that countries have made a long educational journey with strategic options from the standpoint of educational policies defending entrepreneurship among younger generations, is evidence that this condition exists.

Keywords: Entrepreneurial Programs; Pedagogical Interventions; Educational Interventions; Entrepreneurship Education; Entrepreneurial Culture; Effectiveness; Globalization.

1. Introduction

A field for promoting and growing societies, entrepreneurship education (EE) is a catalyst for economic growth, social cohesion, organisational success, and personal fulfilment. Because of this, the number of entrepreneurship education programmes (EEP) has skyrocketed over the past 20 years across all continents. This educational phenomenon began at Harvard Business School, when Myles Mace taught the first entrepreneurship course, Management of New Enterprises, in 1947. A year later, the Research Centre in Entrepreneurial History was established as a research centre in this area. However, programmes started to emerge at numerous American universities, and in 1967 Stanford University and New York University hosted the first MBA programmes on entrepreneurship. Babson College conferred the first degree in this field the following year, in 1968.

Given its importance in finding solutions to new issues, this phenomenon has been growing globally. If the formation and management of businesses were once the main focus, it has since expanded to include entrepreneurial skills, attitudes, and behaviors. In order to reach students from all higher education programmes and educational levels who need to develop these abilities, education toward entrepreneurship started to adopt a methodology. In order to prepare and enable people to face professional challenges, create their own jobs, and develop innovative and worthwhile solutions to a variety of emerging social and economic problems, including the environment, poverty, social exclusion, and sustainability, entrepreneurial programmes have been developed and implemented on all continents.

Additionally, entrepreneurship education took on the goal of supporting an entrepreneurial culture with the necessary skills. With this goal in mind, there has been an increase in interest in educational actions taken in the form of intervention programmes, which are deliberate and methodical actions born out of the identification of a population's needs, targeted at particular goals, based on theoretical models, and suggesting activities and pedagogical resources for their execution and evaluation. As a result, research on these interventions has been conducted on all continents, with the most diverse recipients, including students in higher education, primary and

secondary education, as well as the most diverse contexts outside of the classroom, including municipal, agricultural, and retirement. These references demonstrate the current global expansion of educational initiatives promoting entrepreneurship.

The EEP programme in secondary schools in Hong Kong is a prime example, as presented by Cheung, who came to the conclusions that workshops (46%), competitions, case studies, and mentoring are the most popular teaching methods and that 48% of programmes have activities spread over one or more school years. However, traditional teaching techniques are also used in 75% of the institutions. Accordingly, as has been shown in the research, the targeted objectives, competencies, relationship to the socioeconomic situation, programme facilitator's profile, and activities undertaken are what lead to the positive outcomes obtained through the EEP. When designing, three dimensions should be considered, according to Jardim. According to Jardim there are three dimensions to be taken into account when designing an intervention program: the identity of the program (name of the program, characterization of the recipients and their socioeducational context, objectives, content, skills, and theoretical foundation), pedagogical options (activities, resources, number of sessions, total duration, and facilitators), and evaluation (research design, sample definition, assessment tools, results, and implications for subsequent interventions).

One of the constituent elements of the EEP is entrepreneurial skills (ES), which enable students to face the challenges of the current labor market, such as the sense of initiative, problem-solving, innovation, creativity, and teamwork. For this reason, several approaches and models of ES have emerged. These skills have been progressively included in school curricula, and interventions have been carried out to promote them at all ages. Thus, it is possible to disseminate an entrepreneurial culture for all such that the economy and the market include not only those who were born in a family and socio-economic context favorable to entrepreneurship, but also those who, through learning and training, acquire the skills, competences, values, emotions, and tools of this culture. The development of the elements of entrepreneurial culture requires creating an educational environment favorable to the creation of value propositions, unique socio professional projects, useful products, and innovative services.

This teaching–learning process implies the use of a set of specific pedagogical strategies. They can be educational games, biographies of entrepreneurs, group dynamics, or business models and can be in digital or printed format, virtual or in-person, individual or in a group. As an example, we can observe some of these teaching–learning processes in Europe and around the world Moreover, there is a wide variety of procedures and resources representing evidence of the diversity of proposals according to economic, cultural, and social contexts.

Considering this diversity of approaches, a model composed of twelve strategies distributed over four objective domains was presented: tools to develop ideas, which are intended to be original, practical, and profitable; tools for the validation and dissemination of projects; tools to communicate effectively and quickly with customers; and tools to provide sustainability to organizations. Thus, there was a clear need to design and implement EEP, aiming at promoting entrepreneurial skills, to disseminate an entrepreneurial culture in current society that requires creativity and innovation from all professionals in solving emerging problems. Moreover, multiple studies on entrepreneurship education have been carried out. However, regarding EEP, a review that describes and evaluates its effectiveness has not yet been carried out. For this reason, a systematic review approach was used to comprehensively review the available EEPs and explore their effectiveness in promoting ES. This study includes a summary of the methodologies used in the review, a description of the available EEPs, and a general discussion of the main findings, limitations, and implications for the practice.

Critical Appraisal

The included studies were critically assessed by the review team. The assessment was carried out using the Joanna Briggs Institute (JBI) Statistics Assessment and Review Instruments critical appraisal checklists [57–59] for quasi-experimental studies, case reports, case–control studies, and qualitative studies. Only articles in which more than 50% of the JBI criteria were met were included in the review, following the procedure by Bártolo et al. It should also be noted that the disagreements between the review team members in the evaluations were resolved by discussion.

Results of Interventions

The results achieved by the programs are varied, revealing the diversity of objectives, teaching methods, target groups, and contexts. The quasi-experimental studies, mixed-method study design, and pre-post study revealed consistent statistical results on the interventions' gains. There were global improvements between pre- and post-intervention. The qualitative designs the case studies, and pilot studies also showed, through the data obtained in the interviews and focus groups, that there were improvements in the participants in terms of the acquisition of ES, which demonstrates that the evaluation of entrepreneurial skills training must be carried out not only through statistical analysis but also with content analysis and the triangulation of these types of analyses. Gains can be grouped into three major thematic groups.

These skills are understood as the knowledge, attitudes, and skills that enable someone to be successful in the development of original and valuable projects, products, or services, having as a starting point the needs of a target population and as a result the fulfillment of functional, social, or emotional goals.

In turn, the second thematic group is associated with business management (38%) Business management refers more to the capabilities to maximize the potential of an organization so that the people and resources involved are effective in meeting the expectations of customers and employees. Finally, the third group is related to social entrepreneurship (10%). Social entrepreneurship refers to the set of actions and processes carried out by citizens who create products, services, technologies, or entities with the primary objective of helping people.

At the heart of its operation are community participation and the social responsibility model, motivated by the common good, social gain, and good living conditions. It should be noted that some of these studies deal with more than one thematic area.

The Discovering Entrepreneurship program (DE) brought results regarding motivation, ES, and the creation of new companies. In this sense, it motivated students to be more expansive, to have greater clarity on the value of contributing to the community, to take risks, to focus themselves on the satisfaction of their achievements, for rebellion, to have self-control, high tolerance to ambiguity and novelty, independence, and autonomy, but with a focus on people and the search for challenges. In turn, the developed ES were social skills, leadership in networking, coaching and mentoring, identifying opportunities, creativity, and creative problem-solving. Finally, in terms of creating new companies, there were gains in establishing contacts through networking, risk-taking, and interpersonal skills The Leader Practice program (LP) revealed gains in self-leadership and the role of leader; in addition, students achieved gains in understanding the fact that leaders can delegate tasks and responsibilities and recognized the need for continuous improvement in communication with employees and with their family members; in turn, the Lean Agriculture program (LA) proved to be effective in discovering ways of working smoothly, establishing work routines and following previously established procedures, and managing time in a correct way.

The Project Entreprendre program (PE) proved to be useful in achieving results in the following areas: teamwork, business plan development, interactivity in project development, demand for continuous improvement, self-confidence, empowerment, attention to credibility, and seeking a balance between the formal and the informal. Most studies have shown positive results from the interventions. However, it is worth highlighting a case in which the programs used in primary and middle education did not fully reach the objectives initially defined; this fact is justified by the authors with the possibility that they did not correctly elaborate what was intended to be achieved explicitly with this entrepreneurship education action and/or the fact that the design of the evaluation strategies was not the most appropriate.

Discussion

Regarding the effectiveness of the EEP, this systematic review provided an overview of the current literature, analyzing 29 programs, from 24 countries. Overall, programs dedicated to primary school students showed a positive effect above all on entrepreneurial skills, highlighting the enhancement of individual skills, such as creativity, self-confidence, power of argument, and construction of social skills in relationships and interpersonal and groups settings. In addition, there were gains in the motivation to work on public causes such as sustainability and social innovation; improvements were found in respect for the environment, cooperation, and communication of ideas. Moreover, teachers at this level of education also revealed self-confidence, initiative, innovation, creativity, mindfulness, empathy, self-motivation, and participation in society after the intervention program. These results are consistent with those presented by other studies that indicate gains when these skills are developed in childhood and adolescence. On the other hand, studies related to secondary education revealed that at these ages, in addition to fundamental entrepreneurial skills, it is already possible to deepen some more specific skills, such as business skills, reflection on the probability of founding a startup, perception of the benefits of starting a business, and the awareness of the consequences of choosing to pursue an original professional career. This is in line with studies that refer to the contents to be deepened with secondary school students and the strategies used in its promotion. In turn, in higher education and programs aimed at adult professionals the programs focused on more advanced entrepreneurship concepts, namely networking, target market definition, market research, concept prototyping, financial markets, and intellectual property.

Also significant are the effects on awareness of the difficulties and obstacles to following an entrepreneurial career. Thus, at this level, the programs emphasize those skills related to management, economics, finance, and marketing, highlighting the reference to those that enable them to take advantage of business opportunities, develop business models, prepare marketing plans, to use social networks properly, to deal with the risk inherent to the business activity, and to solve problems and conflicts. This growth in the specification of skills developed over the progressive levels of education is in line with several experts in the area, who point out as essential a progressive and complementary teaching–learning process, which alludes to the fact that it is a time-consuming process. More specifically, the results obtained from this review suggested that approaches focused on ES had a significant effect on the promotion of a certain type of culture, as is clearly shown in the U Kids initial teacher training program, which aims to establish entrepreneurship, especially social entrepreneurship, as an element of teaching in primary schools. Thus, they are more beneficial to participants who would have more difficulty accessing the resources and skills of the programs. For this reason, the dissemination of this culture among all students becomes very significant in the logic of an inclusive education that promotes social ascension.

Considering this contextual complexity, most of the reviewed programs were developed based on the definition of a unique identity, pedagogy, and evaluation but always aiming to educate for the development of a culture where the capacity to create value is predominant. Among the identified entrepreneurial skills are the spirit of initiative, innovation, problem-solving, global leadership, teamwork and networking, digital and communication skills, the use and creation of business models, and marketing and e-commerce. We concluded that the effectiveness of the EEP is mainly due to the quality of the design of the programs themselves, proven, for example, by their pedagogical approach, such as teaching methods, excellence of the facilitator, and activities carried out; by the predispositions of the participants—that is, if they started working on entrepreneurial skills since childhood, it becomes much more natural to be an entrepreneur; and by their integration or not in entrepreneurial ecosystems, verifying that whoever was born and lived in an entrepreneurial family or regional ecosystem more easily takes chances to innovate.

Thus, the promotion of an entrepreneurial culture is the consequence of combining these elements, mobilizing individuals and societies for a continuous creation in this global world. For all these reasons, it is necessary to take advantage of the opportunities and face the current challenges, namely those related to the integration of EE in all levels of education, but giving priority to those aimed at younger generations, as well as seeking to improve the quality of scientific production in this field.

Despite the results obtained, this review is not exempt from limitations. First, the characteristics of the studies included vary widely, for example, in study design, the focus of the intervention, number of sessions, sample size, and main outcomes. For this reason, meta-analyses and statistical comparisons were not possible. Second, by restricting the literature search to include only articles published in scientific journals in the past two decades, publications such as conference papers and dissertations may have been lost.

Finally, although the methodological rigor of the studies has been assessed, it is important to note that this only indicates the overall quality of each study, including details of the program, but not specifically how information and strategies were addressed in the intervention. Further research with rigorous designs is still needed to achieve stronger evidence about the effectiveness of the EEP. Furthermore, we suggest carrying out comparative studies of entrepreneurial pedagogy, in order to assess the effectiveness of the different methods of teaching entrepreneurship used by the different facilitators.

Conclusions

This study demonstrated that there has been a steady increase in EEP, and the vast majority of these programs are aimed at students in higher education, a few in secondary education, and even fewer in basic and pre-school education. In addition, it has been shown that most studies are more conceptual than empirical, thus neglecting cognitive and behavioral results.

When their effectiveness was assessed empirically, the EEP revealed a moderate effect in activating entrepreneurial intent and a more notable effect on the development of ES. It was also found that, more than the EEP, it is the personal predispositions and family, economic, and cultural contexts that most influence the option for the development of entrepreneurial projects. ESs were targeted at all levels of education and in all studies; however, greater attention was paid to these competencies in basic and secondary education. Moreover, the results of the studies show the effectiveness of these programs in promoting self-efficacy, an entrepreneurial attitude, resilience, risk-taking, and openness to novelty. In turn, there is no increase in the intention to create the business itself, since this intention is determined by predisposition, namely socio-cultural and family aspects. The challenges that entrepreneurial leaders have in the current context are also noted, clearly marked by technologies and remote work, by the social complexity and unpredictability of work, and by the need to reconcile health and economy, entrepreneurship and citizenship. Moreover, one of the privileged strategies in this area is the educator himself. The educator's active, inspiring, and differentiating presence in the most diverse promotional contexts of entrepreneurship will allow entrepreneurial culture values. They should be skilled in using these and other useful tools to promote an entrepreneurial mindset. Thus, this systematic review of the EEP points to the need for this type of programs to be applied preferentially since the early school years, since it is at that time that the predispositions for the development of entrepreneurial skills and intentions are created. This condition is corroborated by the EEP's global geography, which demonstrates that, where there is currently an entrepreneurial culture, countries have had a long educational journey, with strategic options from the point of view of educational policies that defend entrepreneurship among the younger generations. Our data also suggested that the promotion of an entrepreneurial culture takes place based on an interdisciplinary approach so that school curricula transversally integrate behaviors such as innovation, initiative, teamwork, and the creation of socio-professional projects based on business models. Finally, this study also demonstrates the urgency of the entrepreneurial sciences, such as management, economics, and pedagogy, to promote a global entrepreneurial culture with the dissemination, through international educational networks, of programs on entrepreneurial skills. These skills will globally enable the transfer of knowledge to society, as they help solve some problems, such as unemployment and poverty, the environment and sustainability, health, and quality of life.

References

1. Pittaway, L.; Aissaoui, R.; Ferrier, M.; Mass, P. University spaces for entrepreneurship: A process model. Int. J. Entrep. Behav. Res. 2019, 26, 911–936.
2. Jardim, J.; Franco, J.E. (Eds.) Empreendipédia—Dicionário de Educação para o Empreendedorismo; Gradiva: Lisboa, Portugal, 2019.
3. Ahmed, T.; Chandran, V.G.R.; Klobas, J.E.; Liñán, F.; Kokkalis, P. Entrepreneurship education programmes: Howlearning, inspiration and resources affect intentions for new venture creation in a developing economy. Int. J. Manag. Educ. 2020, 18, 100327.
4. Jardim, J. Regiões Empreendedoras: Descrição e avaliação dos contextos, determinantes e políticas favoráveis à sua evolução. Rev. Divulg Científica AICA 2020, 12, 197–212.
5. Porfírio, J.A.; Carrilho, T.; Felício, J.A.; Jardim, J. Leadership characteristics and digital transformation. J. Bus. Res. 2021, 124, 610–619.
6. Byun, C.-G.; Sung, C.; Park, J.; Choi, D. A Study on the Effectiveness of Entrepreneurship Education Programs in Higher Education Institutions: A Case Study of Korean Graduate Programs. J. Open Innov. Technol. Mark. Complex. 2018, 4, 26.
7. Carree, M.; Della Malva, A.; Santarelli, E.; Carree, M.; Malva, A.D.; Santarelli, E. The contribution of universities to growth: Empirical evidence for Italy. J. Technol. Transf. 2011, 39, 393–414.
8. Hernández-Sánchez, B.R.; Sánchez-García, J.C.; Mayens, A.W. Impact of Entrepreneurial Education Programs on Total Entrepreneurial Activity: The Case of Spain. Adm. Sci. 2019, 9, 25.
9. Cheung, C.K. Entrepreneurship education in Hong Kong's secondary curriculum: Possibilities and limitations. Educ. Train. 2008, 50, 500–515.
10. Abdelkarim, A. Toward Establishing Entrepreneurship Education and Training Programmes in a Multinational Arab University. J. Educ. Train. Stud. 2018, 7, 1. 8–342.

40

NEP-2020: Restructuring Institutions and Quality of Education

Dr. K. Aruna Bai

Abstract

Training is essential for accomplishing complete human potential, growing an equitable and simply society, and promoting country wide improvement. imparting standard get entry to quality education is the important thing to economic boom, social justice and exceptional, scientific advancement, country wide integration and cultural protection; and for India's endured ascent, progress, and management on the worldwide degree. India will have the best youth populace within the global over the next decade, and our potential to offer instructional possibilities to them will shape the destiny of our country. the arena is undergoing rapid adjustments within the expertise panorama. With the upward push of big information, system mastering, and artificial intelligence, many unskilled jobs international can be taken over by machines, while the want for skilled labour, in particular regarding mathematics, laptop technological know-how and facts technology, alongside multi-disciplinary capabilities throughout the sciences, social sciences and arts, might be in rapidly growing call for. With climate trade and fast depletion of natural assets, there may be a giant shift in how we meet the sector's energy, water, and sanitation needs, once more ensuing in the want for brand spanking new skilled labour, particularly in biology, chemistry, physics, and climate science. There may be a growing call for humanities and artwork, as India movements in the direction of turning into evolved united states and many of the three largest economies in the global.

Keywords: Policy in Higher Education, GER multi-disciplinary, HEIs, NEP 2020.

Introduction

Higher Education in India is up for an overhaul with the National Education Policy 2020 bringing in multi-dimensional changes – right from the regulatory framework to curriculum structure and research environment. First and foremost, the announcement of the much-awaited National Education Policy (NEP) has cleared the path for setting up a single regulatory body for country's higher education. The regulatory body, that is to be named the Higher Education Commission of India (HECI), will function as the single authority for all public and private educational institutions (except those involved in medical and law education). In addition to this, a National Research Foundation will be created to oversee all research activities to be carried out by the various academic institutions in the country. The NEP 2020 has aimed at almost doubling the Gross Enrolment Ratio (GER) in higher education to 50 per cent by the year 2035, as compared to the current GER of 26.3%. It also has provision for greater autonomy to the academic institutions offering quality higher education.

Policy is one of the most potent instruments of bringing out social transformation and change and achieving desirable goals and targets. Higher education has been in the policy gaze since the very beginning of the post Independent India's drive for planned development. The first Commission on education set up in the post-Independent India was on higher education (Radhakrishnan Commission, 1948) which advocated for the expansion of higher education and recommended for the establishment of national regulatory bodies such as the University Grant Commission (UGC) and other bodies to regulate growth of higher education in the country. With a very low and slow start, after passing through over 70 years of planned educational development and implementation of two national education policies (1968 and 1986), the higher education in India has reached the massified stage to be the second largest higher education system in the world after China, with 37.4 million students, and 1.4 million teachers spread over more than forty thousand higher education institutions (MHRD, 2019). The third National Education Policy–2020 presents a fresh and forward looking vision for rejuvenating the Indian higher education system. The main purpose of this Unit is to provide an introductory exposure to the teachers about the National Education Policy-2020 in terms of the context, concepts, policy goals, implementation issues and challenges, and future prospects.

Learning Outcomes

After going through this unit, the higher education teachers would be able to: Explain the key concepts and context of the National Education Policy–2020. Describe the foundational principles and goals of the new National Education Policy in relation to higher education.

Identify current issues and challenges with regard to NEP implementation. Plan for the future prospects of higher education in the country.

The Context of NEP in Higher Education

The NEP–2020 has emerged to address the problems currently faced by the higher education system in India as identified in the policy document. The growth of higher education in the country therefore has been slow, inadequate, and disparate. Despite massive increase in enrolment in higher education in recent decades, the current gross enrolment ratio is still less than the desired level and way behind the developed countries. The unplanned growth of higher education has led to different kinds of disparities, such as regional, social, gender, economic, etc. In terms of regional disparities, the concentration of higher education institutions and associated students' enrolment is higher in certain regions (such as southern and western regions) than in other regions (such as the north, the east and the north-east), and further higher in the urban areas than rural areas. In terms of social group disparities, the disadvantaged groups still remain far behind general categories. Moreover, in terms of gender disparities, although enrolment gaps in higher education are closing fast, there is biasness in terms of choice of courses, as girls are less represented in Engineering and other professional courses than the boys.

Major problems faced by the Indian higher education system Inadequate and uneven growth of higher education. A severely fragmented higher educational ecosystem. Less emphasis on the development of cognitive skills and learning outcomes. A rigid separation of disciplines, with early specialization and streaming of students into narrow areas of study. Limited access particularly in socio-economically disadvantaged areas, with few HEIs that teach in local languages. Limited teacher and institutional autonomy. Inadequate mechanisms for merit-based career management and progression of faculty and situational leaders.

Lesser emphasis on research at most universities and colleges, and lack of competitive peer- reviewed research funding across disciplines. Sub-optimal governance and leadership of HEIs. An ineffective regulatory system. Large affiliating universities resulting in low standards of undergraduate education. The higher education system in India is highly fragmented in terms of levels, institutions and disciplines, creating artificial rigid silos among different forms of knowledge. It is divided into undergraduate colleges, and universities. Most of the universities are affiliating universities having a large number of undergraduate colleges. The large number of affiliating universities and at the same time multiple regulatory bodies are affecting the standard of the undergraduate education. Moreover, the rigid disciplinary boundaries with early specialization create problems for the students in terms of career growth and opportunities. In the HEIs, less emphasis is given on the development of cognitive skills and learning outcomes of the students.

The growth of higher education also witnessed the influx of private institutions offering technical and professional programmes leading to 'disciplinary distortions' (Annandakrishnan, 2010). The private share in the number of HEIs and enrolments has increased substantially. The reckless growth of self-financing private colleges has resulted in number of institutions with poor infrastructure, less qualified faculty, providing poor quality of higher education. Managing quality and equity in a market driven system is a major challenge in the development of higher education in the country (Varghese, 2021).

Furthermore, the HEIs suffer from poor quality of teaching–learning, producing a large number of unemployable graduates in the country. The incidence of unemployment is higher among the higher education graduates. The academic activities in the universities are mainly dominated by undergraduate teaching. The share of post-graduate teaching and research degrees in higher education is very limited. In the higher education system, less emphasis has been given to the research in most of the universities. At the same time, lack of competitive peer-reviewed research funding across disciplines has affected the overall quality of higher education and in particular research in HEIs. The Indian universities not appearing in the top positions in the world university ranking is a matter of serious concern. The mechanism and regulatory framework of quality assurance followed in higher education is quite weak and ineffective. Not only a limited number of HEIs (universities and colleges) are getting accredited, majority of the HEIs have not gone through the accreditation process.

There is limited freedom and autonomy in the higher education system at the institutional and the faculty levels. There is lack of effective mechanism of merit-based career management and progression of faculty and institutional leaders in the higher education institutions. A need has been felt introduce a new governance structure and regulatory framework in the system

Vision, Foundational Principles, and Policy Goals

Foundational Principles

NPE-2020 envisions a complete overhaul and re-energizing of the higher education system to overcome the challenges and deliver high-quality higher education, with equity and inclusion. The vision of the policy is in synch with Goal 4 of the UN Sustainable Development Goal (SDG4) which seeks 'to ensure inclusive and equitable quality education and promote lifelong learning opportunities for all' and based on the Foundational Principles guiding the education system and individuals involved. Based on the vision, the new policy has enunciated a set of Foundational Principles to guide educational system and institutions.

National Education Policy-2020: Foundational Principles Recognizing, identifying, and fostering the unique capabilities of each student. Flexibility to the learners in choosing their learning trajectories and programmes, and their own paths in life according to their talents and interests. No hard separations between arts and sciences, between curricular and extra-curricular activities, between vocational and academic streams, etc. Multidisciplinary and a holistic education across the sciences, social sciences, arts, humanities, and sports for a multidisciplinary world. Emphasis on conceptual understanding rather than rote learning and learning-for-exams. Creativity and critical thinking to encourage logical decision-making and innovation; Ethics and human & Constitutional values. Promoting multilingualism and the power of language in teaching and learning. Life skills such as communication, cooperation, teamwork, and resilience. Focus on regular formative assessment for learning. Extensive use of technology in teaching and learning, removing language barriers, increasing access for Divyang students. Respect for diversity and respect for the local context. Full equity and inclusion as the cornerstone of all educational decisions. Synergy in curriculum across all levels of education from early childhood care and education to school education to higher education.

A 'light but tight regulatory framework to ensure integrity, transparency, and resource efficiency of the educational system – through autonomy, good governance and empowerment. Outstanding research as a requisite for outstanding education and development. Continuous review of progress based on sustained research. A rootedness and pride in India, and its rich, diverse, ancient and modern culture and knowledge systems and traditions. Education is a public service; access to quality education must be considered a basic right. Substantial investment on public education system as well as the encouragement and facilitation of true philanthropic private and community participation. Policy Goals The NEP–2020's vision and foundational principles include the following key changes to the current system as the policy goals:

Moving towards a more multidisciplinary undergraduate education

Drawing from the ancient tradition of holistic and multidisciplinary learning, the NEP-2020 aims at carrying out major structural reforms in higher education by transforming higher education institutions into large multidisciplinary universities colleges and knowledge hubs. Multidisciplinary means integration of disciplines to develop better understanding and insight into the phenomena or problem (Bhushan, 2021). It is to be noted 'multidisciplinary education', based on liberal education, is an academic and pedagogical approach to develop multiple capacities in the students by integrating formal and informal learning opportunities in teaching, research and community engagements and promoting interdisciplinary perspective in academic practice (NIEPA, 2020, p.114; Kasturirangan, 2021). Being multidisciplinary, the institutions will restructure the pedagogy permitting the scope for choices of subjects to students, and it is also expected that affiliated colleges will gradually phase out giving ways to multidisciplinary universities and colleges by 2035. By 2040, all higher education institutions shall aim to become multidisciplinary institutions and shall aim to have larger student enrolments preferably in thousand, for optimal use of the infrastructure and resources. The overall higher education sector will be integrated into one higher education system, including professional and vocational education. It is expected that at least 50% of the learners through both school and higher education shall have exposure to vocational education. Moreover, the policy also recommends to build a world class multidiscipli-nary HEIs called Multidisciplinary Educational Research University (MERU).

Revamping curriculum, pedagogy, assessment, and student support

Based on the holistic and multidisciplinary approach to education, the NEP proposes to revamp curriculum, pedagogy, assessment and support to the students for the overall improvement in the learning environment. In place of the current practice of teacher focused teaching, student focused teaching and learning method will be enforced. The new policy recommends to establish an Academic Bank of Credit at the national level to provide flexibility in acquiring degrees and multiple entry-exit option at all levels of education. Several digital platforms have been proposed to encourage online learning. The evaluation and assessment model suggested under the new policy is also going to change from End semester examination system to continuous assessment system. All the HEIs will give due emphasis on knowledge, skills and values.

Autonomy and freedom

Following the principles of self-governance, the NEP-2020 envisions university as an autonomous structure with an empowered structure of governance at the institutional level. The idea of institutional autonomy within the framework of graded autonomy is one of the governance reforms recommended under the new policy. The policy proposes an empowered structure of Board of Governors for each higher education institution. The

HEIs will have the freedom and autonomy to move gradually from one category to another, based on their plans, actions, and effectiveness. The graded autonomy will also be given to non-public universities. This autonomy will be based on their accreditation, participation in research innovation and quality education delivery. Within the institutions, the faculty will have freedom to design their own curricular and pedagogical approaches within the approved framework, including textbook and reading material selections, assignments and assessments. The teachers will be choosing pedagogy to teach effectively in their classrooms. They will be recognized for the innovative approaches to teaching that improve learning outcomes in their classrooms.[1]

Medium of instruction and languages

The medium of instruction and language is a critical issue in higher education and requires a careful examination (Jayaram, 1993). NEP-2020 advocates the use of Indian languages, art and culture at all levels of education, including higher education. The policy makes it explicit that proficiency in Indian languages will be included as part of qualification parameters for employment opportunities. The universities dedicated to languages will become multidisciplinary, and where relevant may also offer dual degrees in education and a language to develop language teachers in that language. The policy also advises the HEIs to use mother tongue or home language as the medium of instruction and offer bilingual programmes in higher education to increase access and GER. For each of the 22 languages listed under the Eighth Schedule of the Constitution, separate 'Academies' will be established to promote the languages. For making available high quality materials in Indian languages, the policy has proposed establishing an Indian Institute of Translation and Interpretation (IITI). It is expected that the HEIs will use mother tongue/regional/local languages to help students grasp the concepts better. As far as the use of Sanskrit language in higher education is concerned, the policy makes it explicit that Sanskrit will be mainstreamed in schools and higher education institutions.

Issues and Challenges Access-related Issues and Challenges in Higher Education

Higher education in India is currently at the stage of massification in terms of enrolment with GER pegged at 26.3%. The NEP-2020 aims at increasing the GER in higher education to 50% by 2035 (NEP 2020, Section 10.06). The target will also include enrolments through online mode and students covered under vocational and other streams. The universalization goals and targets need to be seen in terms of areas and groups, as the states and groups within a state are at different levels of educational attainment. It is expected that universalization of school education will provide scope for maximising enrolment in higher education. The focus will be on covering the underserved areas and groups.

Equity and Inclusion related Challenges in Higher Education

The Policy envisions ensuring equitable access to quality education to all students, with a special emphasis on SEDGs. The policy takes cognizance of certain facets of exclusion which include issues such as, lack of knowledge of higher education opportunities, economic opportunity cost of pursuing higher education, financial constraints, admission processes, geographical and language barriers, poor employability potential of the higher education graduates among the SEDGs, and lack of appropriate student support mechanisms.

In these regards, a multi-pronged strategy needs to be adopted by both the government and the HEIs to address the equity and inclusion related problems. Some of the measures, for instance, may include the initiatives such as:

(a) Earmarking suitable government funds to meet targets for the education of SEDGs,

(b) Establishing more high-quality HEIs in aspirational districts and Special Education Zones containing larger numbers of SEDGs,

(c) Developing high-quality HEIs that teach in local/Indian languages or bilingually,

(d) Mitigating opportunity costs and fees for pursuing higher education,

(e) Making admissions processes and curriculum more inclusive,

(f) Making HEI buildings and classrooms disabled-friendly,

(g) Developing bridge course materials for students from disadvantaged educational backgrounds,

(h) Providing socio-emotional and academic support and mentoring for all such students,

(i) Ensuring sensitization of faculty, counsellor, and students on gender-identity issue, and enforcing all no-discrimination and anti-harassment rules.

Quality-related Issues and Challenges

Ensuring quality in a highly diversified system of higher education is a major challenge. On quality parameters, most of the higher education institutions (HEIs) fall much behind the HEIs in development countries. The case of Indian universities not appearing on top positions in the world university rankings is a matter of serious concern. Although accreditation as quality assurance measure has been in implementation for a number of years, the process has not been very effective. As far as the External Quality Assurance within the country is concerned only around one third of the universities and one fifth of the colleges have been accredited in the past 25 years of NAAC (Varghese, 2021). Moreover, Internal Quality Assurance (IQA) established in universities are not fully functional.

Governance-related Issues and Challenges

Reforming the governance of higher education is one of the important transformative agenda of the NEP-2020. The policy envisions the governance reforms as prerequisite for achieving the policy goals and targets (NIEPA, 2020). The policy proposal of setting up the Higher Education Commission of India (HECI) with four verticals (for regulation, accreditation, funding and academic standard) is radical in nature with far reaching. The agenda comprises restructuring of governance of the higher education at the national, sub-national and institution levels. There is a need of harmonizing the HEIs with the state and the national level structures and processes. The common feature of all world-class institutions globally including India has indeed been the existence of strong self-governance and outstanding merit-based appointments of institutional leaders. It is expected that new governance structure and leadership will bring in a culture of excellence and innovation in higher education institutions in the country.

Financing-related Challenges of Higher Education

The financing of expanding higher education is a major challenge, as it falls short of the goals and targets. With decline in public funding, the task has become difficult. Some of the higher education proposals under the NEP having financial implication include activities such as, a) investment in teacher education and continuing professional development of teachers; b) revamping of colleges and universities to foster excellence; c) cultivating research; d) use of technology and online education. The policy commits to raise the public expenditure on education to the recommended level of 6% of GDP as envisaged by the 1968 policy.

Future Prospects of Higher Education in India

The NEP-2020, launched after over three decades since the last NEP (1986), will guide development of higher education in the country for a very long period of time. The NEP-2020 envisages universalizing higher education, facilitating institutional restructuring and consolidation based on multi-disciplinary approach and following flexible pathways of learning, making use of the technological developments and introducing new regulatory and governance structures. The major focus is on improving learning outcomes and achieving quality with equity.

Further Expansion to Universalize Higher education

With 2040 as the deadline to fulfil the policy goals and targets, the NEP aims that all higher education institutions (HEIs) shall be doubling the GER of HEI from the current level of 26.3 % GER to 50%. The proximity to universalization of higher education is linked with the universalization of school education with students completing the full cycle of education from the foundation stage to the higher education stage. As the states and social groups are at different stages of their participation, the states and the groups will be having their own trajectories of achieving the policy goals. Despite the transition rate from secondary to higher education level being high, unless school education is sufficiently expanded in the educationally less developed states and groups, the national goal of universalization of higher education may not be realized.

Institutional Restructuring and Consolidation – Towards Holistic and Multidisciplinary Education with Multi Entry and Exit.

The NEP-2020 proposes to follow 'holistic and multidisciplinary education' and to transform existing institutions into multi-disciplinary institutions with due emphasis on teaching and research - Research University, Teaching University, and Multidisciplinary Autonomous Colleges. The policy also recommends to develop world class Multidisciplinary Education and Research University (MERU) and to put an end to the system of affiliated colleges over a period of next 15 years. The flexible pathways to learning in higher education will have flexibility of curricular choice as an important element of the restructuring of pedagogy. Besides being multi-disciplinary, a higher education institution under the NEP is also supposed to have a minimum of 3000 student enrolment. As large number of HEIs are small size located in rural areas, having single discipline and running under private management, it may not be easy to consolidate colleges under the same management.

Quality Enhancement through New Accreditation System and Research

Quality in higher education is a major concern as reflected in the national and international rankings. The NEP-2020 emphasizes on enhancing the quality of higher education system. The quality assurance efforts also have not succeeded to accredit a majority of institutions. The new policy suggests setting up of a meta-accreditation agency called the National Accreditation Council (NAC) with a set of accreditors at the lower levels to create an ecosystem of accreditation. It is expected that these decentralized efforts of expanding accreditation facilities will increase the number of institutions accredited in the coming years.

New Governance of Higher Education

The new policy has proposed transforming the governance system in higher education by setting up a single regulator as Higher Education Commission of India (HECI) with four verticals: National Higher Education Regulatory Council (NHERC) for regulation, national Accreditation Council (NAC) for accreditation, Higher Education Grants Council (HEGC) for funding and General Education Council (GEC) for academic standard. The idea of creating a single regulator with four verticals has been termed as 'light but tight' as it incorporates checks-and-balances in the educational governance system avoiding concentrations of power. All the professional bodies, except medical and law stream of education will be under the HECI. The private and public sector institutions of higher education will have the same set of regulations. Through a suitable system of graded accreditation and graded autonomy, and in a phased manner over a period of 15 years, all HEIs in India will aim to become independent self-governing institutions pursuing innovation and excellence.

It is envisaged that all HEIs will be incentivized, supported, and mentored during this process, and shall aim to become autonomous and have such an empowered BoG by 2035. The BoG shall be responsible and accountable to the stakeholders through transparent self- disclosures of all relevant records. It will be responsible for meeting all regulatory guidelines mandated by HECI through the National Higher Education Regulatory Council (NHERC).

Internationalization in Education

The NEP-2020 call for creating avenues for having larger number of international students studying in India and providing opportunities to students interested in studying abroad, will go a long way toward towards internationalization in education and putting India on the world education landscape. The policy points out that high performing Indian universities will be encouraged to set up campuses in other countries, and similar, selected universities, e.g., those figuring among the top 100 universities in the world ranking will be facilitated to operate in India. A legislative framework facilitating such entry will be put in place, and such universities will be given special dispensation regarding regulatory, governance, and content norms on par with other autonomous institutions of India.

Conclusion

Thus, NEP-2020 is quite comprehensive and radical and is aimed to revamp and rejuvenate the Indian higher education system and to place it high on the world education landscape. Based on the high sounding foundational principles, the policy is quite comprehensive in terms of the policy goals of universalizing quality higher education, restructuring and consolidating HEIs to become multidisciplinary, equipping the educated with 21st century knowledge and skills, having well rounded personality and well prepared to cope with the fast changing world. The policy calls for radical transformation in the curriculum and pedagogic structure in the multi-disciplinary framework, providing optimal learning environment and support to the students, ensuring equity and inclusion, granting freedom and autonomy to the faculty and institutions, assuring quality of the highest order, giving boost to academic research and transforming the regulatory and governance structure of the higher education in the country.

References

Ministry of Human Resource Development (MHRD 2019). All India Survey of Higher Education. Department of Higher Education, Government of India, New Delhi.

Government of India (2020). National Education Policy 2020. https://www.mhrd.gov.in/sites/upload_files/mhrd/files/NEP_Final_English _0.pdf, MHRD, New Delhi.

Jayaram, N. (1993). Language Question in Higher Education: Trends and Issues.

Higher Education, Vol. 26, 93-114.

Kasturirangan, K. (2021). Liberal Education – A 21st Century Initiative. Fifteenth Foundation Day Lecture, NIEPA, New Delhi, 11th August, available on http://niepa.ac.in/download/Foundation%20day/15th%20NIEPA%20Foun dation%20Day%20Lecture.pdf.

NIEPA (2020). NEP 2020: Implementation Strategies. NIEPA, New Delhi, available on http://niepa.ac.in/Download/NEP%202020%20Implementation%20Strateg y_W.pdf.

Varghese, N. V. (2021). Directions of Change in Higher Education : From Massification to Universalization. In Chattopadhyay, Saumen, Simon Marginson and N.V. Varghese (Eds.) Changing Higher Education in India. London, Bloomsbury Academic, 23-46.

Notes

1. https://www.researchgate.net/publication/353452302_NEP_2020_An_Effort_Towards_Transforming_India%27s_Education_Landscape.

41

Multidisciplinary focus of NEP 2020 - Transforming India

Dr. M. Vigneshwar Reddy

Abstract

By 2030, one large multidisciplinary college in every district - this was a headline that one could not miss when the National Education Policy 2020 was announced. The headline encapsulates the bold reforms that will be implemented in the Indian higher education system. The study focus on making education multidisciplinary is a significant step that will benefit the students, and one that will have far-reaching effects. The Government of India has done a tremendous job in creating an enabling ecosystem for offering multidisciplinary education to flourish and making a difference to students, who in turn will make an impact on the future of our country. The flexibility to choose subjects from sciences and humanities with the ability will also learn fine arts and sports which offers the students a wide range of subjects to choose without the restrictions they were faced earlier. With creative combi-nation of subjects, cutting edge curriculum, flexible options, and multiple entry and exit options during the undergraduate course, students can explore their areas of interest and also choose careers of their choice. In addition, this kind of approach will foster intellectual curiosity, a critical thought process, self-reflection, leadership and teamwork skills, a sense of commitment, professionalism and a heightened sensitivity to one's socio-cultural environment. The introduction of multidisciplinary approaches in the field of humanities, the students would be empowered, augmenting the potentiality of human resources and this paves the way for accelerating the process of social, economic and environmental development and sustainability.

Keywords: approaches, interdisciplinary, multidisciplinary, societal needs, strategies.

Introduction

This profound concept from the Rigveda illustrates the recognition of limitless learning in the Vedic Period. India has a rich tradition of the multidisciplinary approach since ages, as exemplified by the ancient institutions such as Nalanda and Takshashila. These higher learning centres of ancient India were known for teaching every branch of knowledge, such as singing, painting, chemistry, mathematics; vocational fields such as carpentry, clothes-making; professional fields such as medicine and engineering; and soft skills such as communication, discussion and debate. Over the centuries the broader learning opportunities got narrowed and gradually in recent years the focus moved to specialization in particular subjects resulting in the growth of single-stream institutions. The National Education Policy 2020 (NEP 2020), suggests several policy directions for offering multidisciplinary education.

'Holistic and Multidisciplinary Education' is the central recommendation of the National Education Policy-2020. It is said to be the architecture of 21st century knowledge economy with a focus on problem solving approach. At the first sight, it may appear to be a simple proposition. A deeper analysis shows that multidisciplinary education as a concept and process is more complex than it looks. The purpose of this unit is to discuss the multidisciplinary education at an introductory level and motivate teachers to probe further and pave the way for multidisciplinary teaching and research in higher education institutions. Another recommendation of NEP-2020 is the introduction of multiple entry-exit in Indian higher education institutions through a flexible and innovative curricular structure with a view to allow learners to get certification at yearly interval and possibly create the scope for joining job market. The system will reduce the drop out and increase the internal efficiency of higher education, besides creating the possibility of life long education. This unit also examines the concept of multiple entry-exit and throws up some issues and challenges associated with it.

The National Education Policy 2020 proposes a "Holistic and Multidisciplinary Education". It refers to ancient education in India which provides for comprehensive understanding of all fields of knowledge from social sciences, physical sciences, life sciences, humanities, vocational and professional education. NEP-2020 claims that all branches of knowledge are considered 'arts', which modern education signifies it in terms of 'liberal arts'. There is a call to return to holistic and multidisciplinary education in the above sense. The rationale to a holistic and multidisciplinary education is given in terms of increasing the creativity, critical thinking, problem solving abilities and developing capacities of human beings – intellectual, aesthetic, social, physical, emotional, and moral.

NEP-2020 in Section 11 refers to holistic education, multidisciplinary education and liberal education synonymously. Holistic is multidisciplinary, and multidisciplinary is holistic, and furthermore holistic and multi-disciplinary is liberal education. Moreover, two different times in history, ancient and modern (21st century), are compared without making distinction of the qualitative differences of two time periods in the evolution of knowledge. This raises few questions: (a) In what way knowledge is arts? (b) How knowledge of all arts lead to holistic education? (c) What does it mean to return to ancient education? (d) Does policy advocate the end to disciplinary basis of specialized knowledge which is still preferred in universities worldwide? (e) Whether policy advocates the move to less theory orientation or more practical orientation or a mix of both. The interpretations of various terms vary in the academic circles and need to be debated to have a clear grasp of holistic, multidisciplinary and liberal, and interconnections between them. For the sake of clarity, notwithstanding the differences in the academic community. The three terms which are very crucial connected with NEP-2020 are of the following

Holistic Education

Holistic education refers to the development of physical, emotional and cognitive capacities. It refers to all round development of personality. It is a more philosophical notion. Normatively speaking, it means what ought to be the conception of good life. Education is valuable in intrinsic terms. However, it also has an instrumental value to realize the good life. In a democratic country, holistic education refers to the citizenship values. It refers to tolerance, secular values, and inclusion as an important value. The purpose of all education, whether disciplinary or multi-disciplinary, is holistic education. Hence, holistic does not necessarily mean multi-disciplinary.

Liberal Education

Liberal education is scientific pursuit of knowledge. It develops questioning and critical thinking of knowledge as we all know that knowledge advances when, in the course of progress, the existing knowledge is questioned and, in the process, an alternative hypothesis is presented and examined. New knowledge is established with the questioning of old knowledge. Liberal education does offer the choice to students to follow the pursuit of knowledge through the choice of a particular discipline. However, students may be offered the opportunity to explore before the choice of a particular discipline is made final by them. For example, an undergraduate liberal education in US allows to explore in early semesters to choose any subjects of choice before a specialized discipline is selected.

In this connection in Indian higher education the student will opt core and electives as a major or minor. How does liberal education help achieve holistic education? In my opinion, it is by creating the power of reason that an individual can decide what is good life that he/she values. It means that liberal education may achieve holistic education in particular ways for each and every individual. There cannot be a yardstick of holistic that can be imposed from above. If the criterion of liberal education is reason, then it may happen in both forms of education – disciplinary as well as multi-disciplinary.

Multidisciplinary Education:

The conjointment of various disciplines is multidisciplinary education. The term is used in generic sense to denote that knowledge streams from various disciplines can sometimes give better insight to understand social, economic and natural phenomenon. The interaction of various disciplines can happen in various ways – simple and complex. The understanding of such interaction is essential to understand the variable ways of knowledge construction. At the turn of the 20th century, the basic disciplines were limited to, say, Physics, Chemistry, Biology, Mathematics, Economics, Sociology, Political Science, Geography, Psychology, Language and Philosophy. Later, various applied branches of knowledge were introduced, such as Engineering, Law, Medicine, etc. Gradually, multidisciplinary was introduced in teaching even basic disciplines. For example, the teaching of Economics to an undergraduate also required teaching of Mathematics and Statistics. With the conjointment of Economics with Mathematics and Statistics, Economics flourished as it allowed Economics to grow as empirical science and allowed modelling in estimation and forecasting with greater precision. Mathematics and Statistics were of instrumental purpose to develop Economics.

Multidisciplinary, Interdisciplinary and Transdisciplinary Education

Multidisciplinary

Multidisciplinary education is the conjointment of disciplines without any integration or synthesis of knowledge from various disciplines. Two or three disciplines come together with ideas and methods from respective disciplines which could be useful to understand a problem under consideration. For example, Economics and Statistics are useful as they help to apply economic theory forempirical testing for which statistical tools are useful. No new knowledge is created. To take another example, students of Management are taught Economics as well as Statistics. Management of a firm is concerned with profit maximization principle derived from

Economics, and Statistics helps in market survey research. In this example, Economics and Statistics have instrumental role in Management. The syllabus of Management is an example of multidisciplinary education. The Department of Management hires subject experts of Economics and Statistics in the department or hires from outside the department to teach. Multiple examples can be constructed by the subject experts of different departments. Multidisciplinary in this simple form exists in various departments in teaching.

Interdisciplinary

The meaning of the word interdisciplinary is also the conjointment of disciplines. However, integration or synthesis of knowledge from respective disciplines takes place in order to generate new knowledge which can help to solve problem of a society – the problem which cannot be solved from a disciplinary or multidisciplinary basis of knowledge. Few examples will clarify the concept of interdisciplinary education. Take for instance Development Studies as the area of study taught in many universities. Development Studies is interdisciplinary, co-constituted through disciplines such as Law, Anthropology, Sociology, Gender, Economics, Political Science and International Relations, Geography, Critical Historical Studies, Environmental Humanities, Indigenous Studies, and Decolonial and Postcolonial studies as well as some of the technical and natural sciences. However, the combination of these disciplines adds to the methodological and theoretical rigour of Development Studies. Another example is Women's Studies. This area of knowledge requires the understanding of women' lives from different disciplines like Sociology, Anthropology, Economics, History and Philosophy. Conjointment as well as integration of knowledge from different disciplines can effectively address the problem of women. Policy Studies is an interdisciplinary field of study that integrates knowledge from disciplines such as Economics, Political Science, Public Administration, Sociology and Philosophy. It is a matter of deeper analysis in the field of interdisciplinary education as to how the knowledge from different disciplines develop over a period of time and a synthesis of knowledge develops to understand interdisciplinary field. The process through which interdisciplinary knowledge occurs is a subject matter that subject teachers themselves can explore and update the kmowledge.

Transdisciplinary

Transdisciplinary education is extreme interdisciplinary where synthesis of knowledge sub-ordinates individual disciplines. For example, post modernism takes ideas from History, Economics, Sociology, and Philosophy, and is used to explain many social phenomena of identity, voice, control, hierarchy, power where disciplinary identity is fused. Most appropriately NEP-2020 has a strong message to develop an inter-disciplinary education architecture in Indian universities. Hence, it would be appropriate to understand ways of invoking interdisciplinary through curriculum restructuring.

Practicing Interdisciplinary Education

As noted above, multidisciplinary education is conjointment of many disciplines and when interdisciplinary is added, the conjointment adds to the synthesis of knowledge, and generation of a new knowledge which cannot be seen from the lens of a particular discipline. In substantive terms, synthesis of knowledge from two or more disciplines gives us a new light to the problem and solution. Disciplines are after all artificial boundaries in relation to a complex problem which are inherently interdependent. Dropout of poor girls in rural area is a complex problem that needs lens from Economics, Sociology, Geography, Psychology as well as from Women' Studies and Social Work perspective. Therefore, the question is: how can universities equip themselves to understand such a complex problem? Some of the following approaches may be useful.

(i) Choice of a research project: The research project should be chosen around an important problem that cuts across different disciplines. Problems of global warming, pollution, ethnic conflict, area research, neurosciences, natural disaster, migration etc. are areas of interdisciplinary approach.

(ii) Building collaboration: The lead department which is planning a research project around a complex problem should identify the team members and collaborate with them in discussing the problem and developing research proposal. The research team should work closely in conceptualizing proposal, defending it before funding agency and finally work in a team during entire period of research.

(iii) Joint research: Joint research should be a process of close interaction of ideas during which each member experiences the idea and method applied across the group members of different disciplines. The joint research develops an entirely new perspective and participative culture for all group members that goes beyond the boundary of a discipline.

(iv) Joint teaching: Collaborative research experience should then be built into a teaching programme of a university. The curriculum restructuring should be done in which complex problem could be introduced and joint teaching of a course can be initiated. Joint teaching can provide an opportunity among teachers of different disciplines to reflect back on understanding a problem from new interdisciplinary perspective.

(v) Joint review of teaching: At the end of a course, joint review with teachers and students is an excellent opportunity to extend research and teaching in interdisciplinary areas.

(vi) Joint publication: The joint experience of research and teaching provides ample opportunity for a group of teachers to publish papers. After many interactions with group research and teaching interdisciplinary may be intensified by the faculty.

Needless to say, the above schematic design is neither unique nor necessary to follow. There may be various ways of doing them. In fact, joint teaching may begin first, and joint research and publication may follow thereafter. Interdisciplinary can be initiated even with the joint publication. A culture of collaboration in higher education is the pre-requisite of new environment of interdisciplinary education. It is equally important to note that developing interdisciplinary architecture is not a short run phenomenon. It may take long years to integrate interdisciplinary education in universities. There are many challenges of higher education, namely, shortage of teachers, research funding, infrastructure, etc. Hence, curriculum restructuring to promote interdisciplinary education requires support of universities on various counts, chiefly, higher degree of autonomy, less bureaucratic hassle and funding support without which interdisciplinary education shall remain a dream only.

Academic Bank of Credit

In a gazette notification issued by government of India on 28th July 2021, a regulation on Academic Bank of Credit was issued by UGC. (UGC, 2021a) Section 3 of the regulation notes that "Academic Bank of Credits, shall be a national-level facility to promote flexibility of curriculum framework and interdisciplinary or multidisciplinary academic mobility of students across Higher Education Institutions in the country with appropriate credit transfer mechanism created through these regulations and shall facilitate students to choose their own learning path to attain a Degree or Diploma or Post Graduate diploma or academic qualification, working on the principle of multiple entry-multiple exit as well as any-time, any-where, and any-level learning." (UGC, 2021a, p.10) Regulation on Academic Bank of Credit specifies the objectives, organizational structure, functions, eligibility criteria for approval of Higher Education Institutions to register with Academic Bank of Credits.

National Credit Transfer

The Government of India constituted a committee on a Framework of National Credit Transfer between higher education institutions in January 2021. The framework of National Credit Transfer would enable student mobility between institutions at different exit points.

Implementation of Multiple Entry-Exit: Issues and Challenges

As noted above, there are guidelines on Multiple Entry-Exit, regulation on Academic Bank of Credits and attempts at creating a framework for National Credit Transfer. However, an institution head and teachers of higher education should note some of the issues and challenges in the implementation of multiple entry-exit system.

Conclusion

The study focusses on the distinction between the holistic, liberal and multidisciplinary education. Holistic education is a normative idea. It concerns with education that allows higher capabilities of student: higher opportunities to live a life that he chooses. The aim of liberal education is to develop the capacity of mind to reason. Multidisciplinary education is the conjointment of disciplines and interdisciplinary allows a synthesis of knowledge emerging from the conjointment of disciplines with a view to solve the problems of society. Teachers of higher education should be encouraged to have joint research, teaching and publication to promote interdisciplinary. The paper discusses the guidelines of multiple entry-exit, regulation on ABCs that opens the possibilities for multiple entry-exit. However, there are challenges of a single pathway through which curricular restructuring is suggested. The ungraduated curricular restructuring should not be reduced to vocationalization of education sacrificing the speciali-zation. New roles are being carved out with the changing times and in an era of exponential change and development, an undiscovered future awaits young India. Even recruits are on the lookout for hiring multidisciplinary talent. Narrow training is giving way to transferrable and dynamic skills. Through a multidisciplinary approach, a student gains an arsenal of skills problem-solving, critical thinking, time-management, self-management, communication and writing, analysis and research methodologies, team work, and much more that are easily transferable across work environments. Youngsters can now find very interesting careers in new and emerging fields as a result of a vibrant multidisciplinary background. It gives them the exposure, education and experience to branch out into different directions and expands their avenues.

References

1. Dual Degree Program in Bachelor of Technology (B. Tech) and Master of Business Administration (MBA) – IIT Jammu & IIM Jammu.
2. Gaff, Jerry G. (1971). Cluster Colleges and their Problems, The Journal of General Education (Penn State University Press), Vol. 23 (1), April, pp. 21-28.
3. Govt of J&K (2018). Cluster University Act, Government of Jammu and Kashmir, Srinagar/Jammu.
4. Bhushan, Sudhanshu (2021). Multidisciplinary Approach in Higher Education. Ed Tech https://www.cemca.org/ckfinder/userfiles/files/EdTech-Notes-Multi-disciplinary-Approach-in-Higher-Education.pdf
5. Klein, J. T. (1990). Interdisciplinarity: History, Theory, and Practice. Detroit, MI: Wayne State University Press.
6. UGC. (2021).Guidelines for Multiple Entry and Exit in Academic Programmes offered in Higher Education Institutions. Available on https://www.education.gov.in/sites/upload_files/mhrd/files/upload_document/ab c_doc.pdf
7. UGC. (2021a).Establishment and Operation of Academic Bank of Credits in Higher Education Regulation, 2021. Available on https://www.ugc.ac.in/ugc_notices.aspx?id=NDIxMw.

Index

Y